By the River Chebar

By the River Chebar

Historical, Literary, and Theological Studies in the Book of Ezekiel

DANIEL I. BLOCK

CASCADE Books • Eugene, Oregon

BY THE RIVER CHEBAR
Historical, Literary, and Theological Studies in the Book of Ezekiel

Copyright © 2013 Daniel I. Block. All rights reserved. Except for brief quotations in critical publications or reviews, no part of this book may be reproduced in any manner without prior written permission from the publisher. Write: Permissions, Wipf and Stock Publishers, 199 W. 8th Ave., Suite 3, Eugene, OR 97401.

Cascade Books
An Imprint of Wipf and Stock Publishers
199 W. 8th Ave., Suite 3
Eugene, OR 97401

www.wipfandstock.com

ISBN 13: 978-1-62032-999-3

Cataloguing-in-Publication data:

Block, Daniel I.

By the river Chebar : historical, literary, and theological studies in the book of Ezekiel / Daniel I. Block.

xx + 316 pp. ; 23 cm. Includes bibliographical references and indexes.

ISBN 13: 978-1-62032-999-3

1. Bible. O.T. Ezekiel—Criticism, interpretation, etc. 2. Bible. O.T. Ezekiel—Theology. 3. I. Title.

BS1545.52 B57 2013

Manufactured in the U.S.A.

Contents

List of Illustrations vii

Preface ix

Acknowledgements xiii

List of Credits xvii

List of Abbreviations xviii

1. Preaching Ezekiel   1
2. The Theology of Ezekiel   25
3. The God Ezekiel Wants Us to Meet   44
4. Divine Abandonment: Ezekiel's Adaptation of an Ancient Near Eastern Motif   73

   Excursus A: The Prophetic Speech of Marduk   100

5. Chasing a Phantom: The Search for the Historical Marduk   108
6. The Prophet of the Spirit: The Use of רוּחַ in the Book of Ezekiel   141
7. Beyond the Grave: Ezekiel's Vision of Death and Afterlife   169
8. Text and Emotion: A Study in the "Corruptions" in Ezekiel's Inaugural Vision (Ezekiel 1:4–28)   199

   Excursus B: Ezekiel 1:6, 8–10, 15–21, and 10:9–22 in Parallel   223

9. Ezekiel's Boiling Cauldron: A Form-Critical Solution to Ezekiel 24:1–14   227

   Appendix: In Praise of Moshe: A Tribute to Moshe Greenberg   253

Contents

Bibliography 259
Index of Modern Authors 283
Index of Ancient Authors 289
Index of Selected Subjects 290
Index of Scripture References 294

Illustrations

Figures

1. The Structure of the Book of Ezekiel   6
2. The Structure of Ezekiel's Oracles against the Nations   7
3. The Place of 28:24–26 in Ezekiel's Oracles against the Nations   7
4. Ezekiel's Dated Oracles in Historical Context   8
5. A House of Pride: The Foundations of Israel's Security   11
6. The Relationship between Ezekiel's Judgment and Salvation Oracles   12
7. The Israelite Covenantal Triangle   14
8. The Message and Method of Ezekiel   18
9. The Structure of Ezekiel 16:1–14   20
10. Marduk, the Serpent-Dragon of Babylon   109
11. The Fluctuating Fortunes of a Divine Phantom   139
12. The Usage of רוּחַ in Ezekiel   146
13. Ezekiel's Three Tiers of Existence   178

Tables

1. A Comparison of Ancient Near Eastern Accounts of Divine Abandonment   90
2. The Forms and Distribution of רוּחַ in Ezekiel   143
3. The Semantic Range of רוּחַ in Ezekiel   144

Preface

MY FASCINATION WITH EZEKIEL began in 1978, when it dawned on me that Ezekiel was the only prophet to fulfill his ministry entirely in a foreign land. I began to ask how his environment might have colored his ministry and the book that preserves his work. I discovered that links and influences are everywhere: in his geographic references, the *akkadianisms* and *aramaisms* in his vocabulary, his iconographic images, and his conceptual framework. This is just one of many reasons why the book is both so fascinating and such a riddle. As Christian interpreters of the Hebrew Bible we must always ask at least three questions: (1) What does the text say [the text-critical question]? (2) What did the text mean to the original audience [the hermeneutical question]? (3) What does the text mean to me [the theological and practical question]? However, there is a fourth that is especially important when reading Ezekiel: (4) Why does the text say it like that [the generic and cultural question]? Without reference to the world in which Ezekiel lived many features in the book remain enigmatic and unclear, if not confusing and meaningless.

At first the riddle of Ezekiel was a personal and private matter. A telephone call from R. K. Harrison in Toronto in 1982 changed all that. When he asked if I would be interested in producing a commentary on this book for the New International Commentary on the Old Testament series (Eerdmans), I thought foolishly that it might take me four or five years. Little did I realize what a challenge and delight this project would be. After living with this prophetic priest for fifteen years I sometimes felt like I knew the man personally; at other times he left me totally bewildered by his utterances, if not angry over his portrayal of God.

All that is known of Ezekiel derives from his book. He was a son of Buzi (1:3), taken captive to Babylon in 597 BCE, along with King Jehoiachin and 10,000 others, including political and military leaders and skilled craftsmen (2 Kgs 24:14–16). As noted above, Ezekiel was the only

Preface

Israelite prophet to carry out his ministry entirely outside Israel's homeland. He received his call five years after he was deported to Babylon by Nebuchadnezzar in 597 BCE. This tragedy, foreseen by the Prophet Isaiah more than one hundred years earlier (2 Kgs 20:16-18), represented the culmination of a series of historical events. After the horrendous apostasies of Manasseh, the godly king Josiah (640-609 BCE) attempted sweeping religious reforms (2 Kgs 23:1-25), but it was too little and too late. The doom of the nation had already been determined. According to the Hebrew historians, Josiah's successors were all wicked. His son, Jehoahaz, ruled only three years before the Egyptians deposed him and replaced him with his brother Jehoiakim (609-598 BCE). Babylon replaced Egypt as the dominant political force in the ancient Near East after the battle of Carchemish in 605 BCE. Under Nebuchadnezzar the Babylonian army marched as far south as Jerusalem, claiming Judah as his vassal. At this time Daniel and his three friends were taken to Babylon apparently as hostages, but from the divine perspective in order that they might prepare the way for the arrival of masses of Judeans in 597. Because Jehoiakim rebelled against Babylon in that same year, Nebuchadnezzar removed him from the throne and replaced him with his son Jehoiachin, but he too resisted the Babylonians, and Nebuchadnezzar deported him and all the upper classes (including Ezekiel) to Babylon and put his uncle Zedekiah on the throne. Remarkably, Zedekiah also resisted Nebuchadnezzar's authority. Finally, in 587 BCE Nebuchadnezzar's armies besieged Jerusalem, and the city fell in 586 BCE.

Ezekiel lived in his own house near the River Chebar, an irrigation canal that channeled the Euphrates River into surrounding arid areas. He was married and ministered from his own home (3:24; 8:1; 33:30-33). His wife died suddenly (24:18), but he was not allowed to mourn his loss. But we know Ezekiel primarily as a prophet who received oracles from God and passed them on to the people (cf. 2:5; 33:33). However, his obvious priestly interests give good reason to interpret him primarily as a priest who also functioned as a prophet. YHWH's call to him came in his thirteenth year (1:1), the age priests normally were inducted into office (Num 4:30). In Jerusalem, he would have inherited the priestly office and prepared for it by traditional means. However, in exile the call came dramatically and directly from God. In a vision he was called into divine service and ushered into the presence of God. In autobiographical notes Ezekiel described his reactions to events with priestly sensitivities, especially to issues involving cleanness and uncleanness (4:14). Some of the actions God assigned to him were appropriate only for a priest: "bearing the iniquity" of the people (4:4–6) and not mourning the death of his wife (24:15–27; cf. Lev 21:4–5). This is especially true of temple visions in which YHWH himself took Ezekiel into the temple and guided him throughout the building (chs. 8–11; 40–43). In both visions Ezekiel's legitimate presence in the temple is contrasted with the illegitimate presence of others (8:7–18; 44:1–14). In his preaching and teaching Ezekiel fulfilled the role of a priest charged with the responsibility of teaching the Torah in Israel (Lev 10:11; Deut 33:10a). Ezekiel delivered oracles received from God, permeated by Mosaic theology and forms. Priestly ministry is associated with sacrifices and other tabernacle/temple rituals (cf. Deut 33:10b). But removed from Jerusalem, Ezekiel could not carry out temple duties. The primary priestly function left was teaching. Ezekiel presents a model of the priest as teacher of the Torah.

This is not to deny him prophetic status or prophetic functions. Normally priests engaged in prophetic ministry through the Urim and Thummim (Num 27:21). However, denied official priestly vestments, Ezekiel could not use these objects. As a prophetic priest he received messages directly and verbally from God. Like his contemporary Jeremiah, Ezekiel initially resisted God's call. This accounts for the nature of the opening vision, the intent of which was to overwhelm him and break his resistance (1:1–28a); for YHWH's warning to him not to be rebellious (2:8); for Ezekiel's deep emotional disturbance at his call (3:15); for the harshness of YHWH's warning not to fail as a watchman (3:16–21); and for the severe restrictions of his call (3:22–27). Once he accepted the call, he proclaimed God's messages fearlessly. Because he displayed many bizarre actions, some have characterized Ezekiel as neurotic, paranoid, psychotic, or schizophrenic. However, his unusual behavior derives from his utter obedience to God. Ezekiel was gripped by the Spirit of God, had a profoundly theological perspective on contemporary historical events, and exhibited an unflinching determination to deliver the messages just as God gave them.

The present volume reflects my longstanding interest in Ezekiel, the man and his book. This collection is arranged as follows: a general essay on preaching the message of Ezekiel; a synthetic essay on the theology of the book; a series on more specific theological topics, and two literary studies focused on specific texts that frame the first half of the book (chs. 1 and 24). Additional essays dealing mostly with the second half of the book are available in the companion volume, *Beyond the River Chebar: Studies in Kingship and Eschatology in Ezekiel*.

Acknowledgments

FOR MORE THAN TWENTY-FIVE years now I have been immersed in the study of the book of Ezekiel. My findings regarding this enigmatic prophet have been publicized in my two-volume commentary on the book (NICOT, Eerdmans), and in the more than two dozen studies I have presented at professional meetings or published in separate journals and monographs. With the encouragement of Robin Parry and the administrators of Wipf and Stock Publishing, we have collected eighteen of these papers and prepared them for publication in two volumes. Although I am responsible for these essays, both volumes are the fruit of a community of friends and scholars who have inspired, nurtured, pushed, and corrected me.

Of course, in acknowledging those who have aided and inspired me along the way pride of place must go to the prophet himself, as well as to those who collected, organized, and edited the prophetic priest's work to produce the biblical book of Ezekiel. The adventure represented by this volume (and its sequel) began more than a quarter century ago, when my eyes were opened to the rich resources from the ancient Near East that could be used to interpret the oracles from the River Chebar. Because the essays in this volume were produced over a span of twenty-five years the quality may be uneven, and the references in earlier essays dated. Our commitment to publishers to reproduce these essays virtually as they were originally published (with allowance for correction of known errors and stylistic consistency), we have generally not updated the bibliography. My work, *The Gods of the Nations*, represents a notable exception. All references are to the most recent reprinting of the second edition (Wipf & Stock, 2013). However, I should note that apart from the Appendix, the pagination of the 2000 Baker/Apollos is retained.

Throughout my pilgrimage the voice of Ezekiel has been ringing in my ears, but there have been many who have aided him by supporting me in my research on this remarkable book. I am especially indebted to colleagues and friends from the Ezekiel Section of the Society of Biblical Literature, who have accompanied me on this quest. We often disagree in our methods and our conclusions, but these have not prevented us from carrying on our conversations with respect and civility. My own work on Ezekiel has been especially influenced and framed by two scholarly giants from the Jewish world. No one has inspired me more nor had a greater affect on my work than Moshe Greenberg, the author of countless articles on issues related to Ezekiel and two magnificent volumes on the book in the Anchor Bible series.[1] Although Professor Greenberg would undoubtedly disagree with many of my conclusions, after decades of atomizing approaches to biblical interpretation his appeal for a "holistic interpretation" was both refreshing and encouraging.[2] The other significant influence has been Jacob Milgrom. Given the "priestly" nature of Ezekiel's ministry and the "priestly" character of much of his book, Milgrom's massive commentaries on Leviticus proved invaluable for interpreting this book. Most recently, it was a special joy to learn that he also found my work useful as he sought to complete Greenberg's project.[3] Between these two Ezekiel scholars I have had the pleasure of getting to know many others, including those whose essays and commentaries on the book have greatly enhanced my understanding and challenged me to think more deeply on interpretive cruces: Leslie Allen, Iain M. Duguid, Christopher J. H. Wright, Katheryn Pfisterer Darr, Margaret S. Odell, Steven Shawn Tuell, and Paul Joyce.

I also acknowledge the influence of students who have walked with me as I have walked with Ezekiel. In addition to undergraduates and graduate students in this country and in Canada, I have had the inestimable privilege of sharing my discoveries from the book in international educational settings in Moscow, Copenhagen, Athens, Singapore, Hong Kong, and Medellin, Colombia. Not only have students' interest all over

---

1. Moshe Greenberg, *Ezekiel 1–20: A New Translation with Introduction and Commentary* (Anchor Bible 22; New York: Doubleday, 1983); and Greenberg, *Ezekiel 21–37: A New Translation with Introduction and Commentary* (Anchor Bible 22A; New York: Doubleday, 1997). I expressed my indebtedness to Professor Greenberg in a short paper, "In Praise of Moshe: A Tribute to Moshe Greenberg," at a memorial session in his honor at the annual meeting of the Society of Biblical Literature in Atlanta, GA, 2010.

2. See further Appendix B, In Praise of Moshe: A Tribute to Moshe Greenberg, below, 251–56.

3. See Jacob Milgrom and Daniel Block in conversation, *Ezekiel's Hope: A Commentary on Ezekiel* (Eugene, OR: Wipf & Stock, 2012), 38–48.

Acknowledgments

the world inspired me, but in each context they have offered keen insights to which my North American eyes are blinded.

I must acknowledge the specific help of faculty colleagues and student assistants who have read and encouraged me along the way. Some of these are acknowledged in footnotes to the essays included here. Many assistants have performed mundane tasks for me, scouring databases and libraries for secondary materials that might aid in our interpretation, or proofreading drafts for factual errors and stylistic infelicities. Specifically, for this project I must acknowledge the assistance of Jordan Brown, who had the difficult task of retrieving all the essays in this volume and creating editable documents, and Carmen Imes, who provided invaluable counsel in planning this volume, proofreading and editing, and assembling the bibliography. I am grateful to my wife Ellen and Austin Surls for their assistance in the tedious task of indexing this volume. I am also grateful for the editorial assistance provided by the editors at Wipf and Stock, without whose work this project would never have seen the light of day.

Since most of the essays in this volume have been published elsewhere, I must express my deep gratitude to editors of journals and publishers of books for their grace and willingness to let us reprint what they had made available earlier. In keeping with our promise, we have acknowledged the original place of publication on a separate page below, as well as at the beginning of each reprinted article. The versions presented here retain the essence of each original publication. Naturally, to produce a coherent volume and to follow the stylistic standards of Cascade Books we have had to modify these essays stylistically—some more than others. Where needed, we have corrected errors of substance or form in the original, and in a few minor details my mind has changed. But readers should find no dissonance between the present forms of these essays and the original publications. Special thanks are due to Robin Parry and Christian Amondson, for their enthusiasm for this project and the efficiency with which they have handled all the business and editorial matters. From the first overture from Robin prior to the annual meeting of the Society of Biblical Literature in Atlanta, they have encouraged us and offered all the help we needed to produce it to their specifications. I am also deeply grateful to Patrick Harrison in editing these essays and preparing them for publication.

I am grateful to the administrators and my faculty colleagues at Wheaton College, for the unwavering institutional support and encouragement they offer, not only by creating a wonderful teaching environment,

Acknowledgments

but also for providing the resources for our research. I am deeply grateful to Bud and Betty Knoedler, who have given so generously to underwrite my professorial chair. It is a special grace to know them not only as supporters of Wheaton College, but also as personal friends. Ellen and I are grateful for their daily prayers on our behalf. I eagerly also acknowledge Ellen, to whom I dedicated the first volume of my NICOT commentary (Eerdmans). She is indeed מַחְמַד עֵינַי, "the delight of my eyes,"[4] who has stood by me as a gracious friend and counselor for more than four decades. Without her love and wisdom, the work represented here would either never have been finished, or it would have taken a different turn.

Finally, we must give praise to God. Unlike others who serve gods of wood and stone, that have eyes but don't see, ears but don't hear, and mouths but don't speak, we have a God who speaks. In ancient times he spoke through the mouths of his servants the prophets, including Ezekiel, but he has spoken more recently and even more clearly in the person of Jesus Christ his Son (Heb 1:1–2). Although many have difficulty finding divine grace in the book of Ezekiel, the God Ezekiel serves is embodied in Jesus Christ, full of grace and truth (John 1:16–17). To him be all the praise and glory.

---

4. See Ezek 24:16.

Credits

I HEREBY GRATEFULLY ACKNOWLEDGE permission to republish articles that have appeared elsewhere:

Chapter 1: "Preaching Ezekiel" was originally published as *"He Began with Moses...": Preaching the Old Testament Today*, edited by G. J. R. Kent and P. J. Kissling (Nottingham: InterVarsity, 2010), 157-78, and in *Reclaiming the Old Testament for Christian Preaching*, edited by G. J. R. Kent and P. J. Kissling (Downers Grove, IL: InterVarsity, 2010), 157-78.

Chapter 2: "The Theology of Ezekiel" was originally published as "Ezekiel, Theology of," in the *New International Dictionary of Old Testament Theology and Exegesis*, edited by Willem VanGemeren (Grand Rapids: Zondervan, 1997) 4.615-28.

Chapter 4: "Divine Abandonment: Ezekiel's Adaptation of an Ancient Near Eastern Motif" was originally published in *Perspectives on Ezekiel: Theology and Anthropology*, edited by Margaret S. Odell and John T. Strong (SBL Symposium Series 9; Atlanta: Scholars, 2000), 15-42.

Chapter 5: "Chasing a Phantom: The Search for the Historical Marduk" was originally published in *Archaeology in the Biblical World* 2 (1992) 20-43.

Chapter 6: "The Prophet of the Spirit: The Use of רוּחַ in the Book of Ezekiel" was originally published in *The Journal of the Evangelical Theological Society* 32 (1988) 27-50.

Chapter 7: "Beyond the Grave: Ezekiel's Vision of Death and Afterlife" was originally published in *Bulletin for Biblical Research* 2 (1992) 113-41.

Chapter 8: "Text and Emotion: A Study in the 'Corruptions' in Ezekiel's Inaugural Vision (Ezekiel 1:4-28)" was originally published in *Catholic Biblical Quarterly* 50 (1988) 1-25.

Chapter 9: "Ezekiel's Boiling Cauldron: A Form Critical Solution to Ezekiel 24:1-14" was originally published in *Vetus Testamentum* 41 (1991) 12-37.

Abbreviations

AbB	F. R. Kraus, *Altbabylonische Briefe in Umschrift und Übersetzung.* Leiden: Brill, 1964.
ABPh	A. Ungnad, *Altbabylonische Briefe aus dem Museum zu Philadelphia.* Stuttgart: F. Enke, 1920.
AHW	*Akkadisches Handwörterbuch*, edited by W. von Soden, 3 vols. Wiesbaden: Harrassowitz, 1965–81.
ANET	J. B. Pritchard, editor, *The Ancient Near East in Pictures Relating to the Old Testament*, 3rd ed. Princeton: Princeton University Press, 1954.
ARAB	D. D. Luckenbill, *Ancient Records of Assyria and Babylonia*, 2 vols. New York: Greenwood, 1968 (reprint of 1927 edition).
BBSt	L. W. King, *Babylonian Boundary Stones and the Memorial Tablets in the British Museum.* London: 1912.
BCE	Before the Common Era, traditionally referred to as B.C.
BDB	F. Brown, S. R. Driver, and C. A. Briggs, *A Hebrew Lexicon of the Old Testament.* Oxford: Clarendon, 1907.
BHS	*Biblia Hebraica Stuttgartensia.*
CAD	A. L. Oppenheim, et al., editors. *The Assyrian Dictionary of the Oriental Institute of the University of Chicago.* Chicago: The Oriental Institute, 1956–.
CBS	Tablets in the collections of the University Museum of the University of Pennsylvania, Philadelphia.
CE	Common Era, traditionally referred to as A.D.

Abbreviations

CH	R. F. Harper, *The Code of Hammurabi, King of Babylon*. Chicago: University of Chicago Press, 1904.
COS	*The Context of Scripture.* Vol. 1: *Canonical Compositions from the Biblical World*, edited by William H. Hallo and Lawson K. Younger Jr. Leiden: Brill, 1997.
CT	Cuneiform Texts from Babylonian Tablets in the British Museum. London: 1896–.
DISO	C.-F. Jean and J. Hoftijzer. *Dictionnaire des inscriptions sémitique de l'ouest.* Leiden: Brill, 1965.
ESV	*English Standard Version.*
GKC	*Gesenius' Hebrew Grammar*, 28th ed. edited by E. Kautsch and translated by A. E. Cowley. Oxford: Clarendon, 1910.
KAI	H. Donner and W. Röllig, *Kanaanäische und Aramäische Inscriften*, 3 vols. Wiesbaden: Harrassowitz, 1962.
KAR	E. Ebeling, *Keilschrifttexte aus Assur religiösen Inhalts.* Berlin: 1919, 1923.
KB	L. Koehler and Walter Baumgartner. *Lexicon in Veteris Testamenti Libros.* Leiden: Brill, 1953.
KTU	M. Dietrich, O. Loretz, and J. Sanmartin, *Keilalphabetische Texte aus Ugarit*, vol. 1. Kevalaer: Butzon & Bercker; Neukirchen-Vlyun: Neukirchener, 1976.
LIH	L. W. King, *The Letters and Inscriptions of Hammurabi.* London: Luzac, 1898–1900.
LXX	The Septuagint (more precisely the Greek Old Testament).
MT	Masoretic Text
NASB	New American Standard Bible
NEB	New English Bible
NIV	New International Version
NJB	New Jerusalem Bible
NJPSV	New Jewish Publication Society Version (*Tanakh*)

Abbreviations

NRSV	*New Revised Standard Version*
NT	New Testament
OT	Old Testament
RSV	*Revised Standard Version*
SBL	Society of Biblical Literature
TCL	Textes Cunéiformes. Musée du Louvre. Paris.
UT	Cyrus H. Gordon, *Ugaritic Textbook*, Analecta Orientalia 38. Rome: Pontifical Biblical Institute, 1965; supplement, 1967.

1

Preaching Ezekiel[1]

THE PROBLEM WITH PREACHING EZEKIEL

MY ASSIGNMENT IN THIS chapter is both enviable and unenviable. It is enviable because when we preach from Ezekiel we preach from one of the most fascinating books in the entire canon. It is unenviable because textbooks on preaching from the Old Testament—whether by homileticians or OT scholars—offer no help in preaching Ezekiel. They abound with references to Genesis, Joshua, the Psalms, Isaiah, Amos, and Hosea, but they rarely mention Ezekiel. Could it be that Christians have heeded the counsel of Jewish rabbis who forbade Jews under thirty from reading the beginning and ending of the book? If so, we have extended the prohibition to the whole book, perhaps assuming that there would always be people under thirty in our congregations.

It has not always been this way. Origen (CE 185–254) composed at least fourteen homilies on Ezekiel, which were translated into Latin by Jerome. Gregory the Great (CE 540–604) preached twenty-two homilies on Ezekiel 1–3 and 40 between 595 and 594, expressing delight in clarifying obscure texts. By his time the interpretation of the four living creatures

---

1. This essay was originally published in *"He Began with Moses . . .," Preaching the Old Testament Today*, edited by G. J. R. Kent and P. J. Kissling, (Nottingham, UK: InterVarsity, 2010), 157–78; and in *Reclaiming the Old Testament for Christian Preaching*, edited by G. J. R. Kent and P. J. Kissling (Downers Grove, IL: InterVarsity, 2010), 157–78. An earlier version was presented to the Tyndale Fellowship in Cambridge, UK, in July, 2009.

in the opening vision as the four evangelists was well established, but he proposed that the four creatures represent all preachers of the word. From the medieval period, Andrew of St. Victor's overriding concern in reading Ezekiel's vision was not only to recapture the picture so he could draw it like he drew the temple, but also to know what it meant for the people for whom Ezekiel recorded it. Of the Reformers, Calvin's expositions of Ezekiel are significant because they represent his last written work. Racked by pain, his emaciated body gave out at the end of chapter 20. Nevertheless, his commentary reflects the vigor of his mind and his high view of all Scripture.[2] Modern American evangelical interest in the book tends to revolve around Ezekiel's eschatological vision, particularly the participation of Gog and Magog in the final battles, and the role of the temple and its cult in the millennium. In my native dispensationalist world, Ezekiel was mentioned exclusively in the contexts of prophecy ("end time") conferences, which now seem to have been quite oblivious to the exilic prophet's lofty theology or the practical nature of his message.

So the daunting task before us is to rehabilitate this prophet and to rediscover the vitality of the book that bears his name. This challenge is much greater today than it was, say, forty years ago. Because of (rightful) increasing sensitivity to issues of gender in recent decades, many are repulsed by the image of God presented in the book, especially in chapters 16 and 23.[3] If in the past Christians *would not* read or preach the book of Ezekiel because they were perplexed by the prophet's visions or the forms of his oracles, today some *cannot* preach it because the book and the God portrayed in it seem irredeemably problematic. According to some interpreters he is devoid of any grace at all. How can pastors today declare its message with authority, vitality, and clarity? I propose to answer the question with a series of propositions that together might yield a strategy for thinking about preaching Ezekiel.

Four Propositions for Preaching from Ezekiel

Proposition 1: In order to preach from Ezekiel with authority and clarity, we need to understand the prophet—his character (ethos), passion (pathos), and argumentation (logos).

All we know about Ezekiel we learn from the book that bears his name. Ezekiel's own name ("May God strengthen/toughen") may express the

2. Calvin, *Commentaries on Ezekiel*, 2 vols.
3. For further detail see the essay below, "The God Ezekiel Wants Us to Meet."

optimism of his parents at the time he was born, although it also provides a commentary on his life. The third-person commentary on the superscription (1:3) identifies Ezekiel as the son of Buzi. He was called into priestly ministry in his thirtieth year, on 31 July 593 BCE, which means his birth in 623 BCE coincided with the mid-point of Josiah's reign (640–609 BC), shortly before the rediscovery of the Torah in the temple (2 Kgs 22:3). Despite Josiah's efforts at reform, his untimely death in 609 BCE dashed the prospects for a comprehensive political and spiritual renaissance to the ground. Within the next eleven years three kings would succeed him. Everyone would be judged by the Deuteronomist as "doing evil in the sight of YHWH," for revitalizing the old apostate ways of Manasseh. In the meantime, the land of Judah, which had been a vassal of Egypt, fell under the control of Nebuchadnezzar. Fed up with Jehoiachin's treasonous behavior, finally, in 597 BCE, Nebuchadnezzar's armies marched into Jerusalem and seized direct control. Nebuchadnezzar deported the royal family and thousands of the nation's foremost citizens (2 Kgs 24:15–16)—including Ezekiel.

Ezekiel's professional office is specified in 1:3. Although some interpret "the priest" as a reference to Buzi, the epithet actually applies to Ezekiel himself. This is critical for understanding the prophet's role. It is true that chapters 1–3 describe Ezekiel's call to prophetic ministry, and he obviously functioned as a prophet. However, the timing of the opening vision and call in his thirtieth year (1:1), when priests were inducted into office (Num 4:50), and the pervasively priestly stamp in the book, suggests that we should view Ezekiel as a prophetic priest, rather than as a priestly prophet.[4] This book portrays Ezekiel serving the exiles, who had no access to temple and altar service, as pastor and prophetic priest. Although he appears to have resisted the call at first,[5] Ezekiel served YHWH and his people faithfully for more than two decades (cf. 29:17).

Apart from his professional role, we know Ezekiel for his eccentric behavior. While prophets were known often to act and speak erratically for rhetorical purposes, in Ezekiel we find a unique concentration of bizarre features: muteness, lying bound and naked, digging holes in the walls of houses, emotional paralysis in the face of his wife's death, images of strange creatures, hearing voices and the sounds of water, his withdrawal

---

4. Ezekiel's priestly background is reflected in his thorough familiarity with the temple layout, his access to the temple (chs. 8–11; 40–46), his understanding of orthodox and pagan cult forms, his mastery of the spiritual heritage of Israel, specifically levitical/priestly issues, and his concern for a rebuilt temple.

5. See Block, *Ezekiel 1–24*, 11–12.

symptoms, fascination with feces (4:12–15)[6] and blood,[7] pornographic imagery, an imaginative understanding of Israel's past, etc. Some attribute these features to a pathology arising from early abuse and an Oedipus complex, but this misconstrues the profundity of his message and the sensitivity of his personality. His prophetic experiences, symbolic actions, and oracular pronouncements derived from encounters with God that affected his entire being. What other prophets spoke of, Ezekiel suffered. As one totally possessed by the spirit of YHWH, called, equipped, and gripped by the hand of God, Ezekiel was a מוֹפֵת, "a sign, a portent" (12:6, 11; 24:24, 27), carrying in his body the oracles he proclaimed and redefining the adage, "The medium was the message." To preach Ezekiel faithfully, we will need to understand the man.

Proposition 2: In order to preach from Ezekiel with authority and clarity, we need to understand his audience.

The purpose of prophetic preaching is to transform the audience's thinking about historical and theological realities, particularly their own spiritual condition, and to bring about change in disposition and action. In Ezekiel's case we identify two audiences: the hypothetical audience and the real rhetorical audience. Many of Ezekiel's oracles are formally addressed to outsiders, hypothetical target audiences often introduced with the hostile orientation formula, "set your face toward," and a stronger variant, "fix your face toward" (4:3). These idioms reflect the common gesture of turning towards the person one is addressing. Although the oracles following the formula tend to be cast in the second person of direct address, it is unlikely that the purported addressee ever heard or read the pronouncements.[8] Ezekiel's (and God's) real audience is his fellow exiles; it is *their* minds and actions he seeks to change. But we never see him preaching in public or to the exiles as a whole. For the first eight years of his ministry he is locked up in his house (3:22–27), which means that if people want to hear him they must come to him. And they do. On three occasions we read of the people's representatives, the elders, sitting before him waiting for a word from YHWH (8:1; 14:1; 20:1–3), although 33:30–33 suggests that ordinary people would come to his house for entertainment as well.

---

6. Also his reference to idols as גִּלּוּלִים, "dung pellets."
7. The word דָּם, "blood, bloodshed," occurs fifty-five times.
8. See especially the oracles against foreign nations (25:2; 28:21; 29:2; 38:2) and insentient entities (6:2; 21:1–4[20:45–48]; 35:2).

Preaching Ezekiel

The book paints a picture of a hardened audience, characterized as "a rebellious house" (2:5–8; 3:9, 26–27; 12:2–4, 9, 25; 24:3) with obstinate face (2:4), stubborn heart/mind (2:4), stubborn of forehead (3:7, 8), obstinate of heart/mind (3:7), and resistant to messages from God (3:5–11). Indeed, YHWH tells Ezekiel that if he intended him to see fruit for his labors, he would send him to a foreign nation where people would listen to him. The book offers no hint of any softening during Ezekiel's life, nor any indication that the fulfillment of Ezekiel's announcements of judgment on Jerusalem (33:21–22) had any effect on the audience. Their hardness plays a significant role in determining the content and shape of his proclamation.

The people's rebellious actions, particularly idolatry (14:1–11), provide the most obvious sign of their hardened condition. But their disposition towards YHWH was actually ambivalent. On the one hand, they were embittered and cynical towards him for having betrayed them and letting Nebuchadnezzar's armies enter Jerusalem and drag them off into exile. On the other hand, they continued to bank on YHWH's covenant commitments to them. Until the news came that Jerusalem had fallen, they staked their security on YHWH's eternal covenant promises—his grant of the land of Canaan to Abraham and his descendants as an eternal possession; his irrevocable covenant with Israel at Sinai; his promise to David and his descendants of eternal title to the throne of Israel; and his election of Jerusalem/Zion as his eternal residence. But their sense of security in YHWH was delusional: they forgot that enjoyment of covenant blessings is contingent upon grateful and wholehearted obedience to the covenant Lord. Until 586 BCE, Ezekiel's rhetorical aim was to destroy this false sense of security by demolishing the pillars on which it was based. However, once the city had fallen his goal was to rebuild the structure, for these were in fact eternal promises.

Proposition 3: In order to preach from Ezekiel with authority and clarity, we need to understand the nature and structure of the book.

The book displays several features that set it apart from other prophetic books. First, if we can get past the first chapter, we discover this book to be the most intentionally structured of prophetic books. It consists of forty-eight chapters, divided evenly into two major sections, oracles of woe for Judah and Jerusalem (chs. 1–24) and oracles of weal for Judah and Jerusalem (chs. 25–48; see Fig. 1).

Figure 1: The Structure of the Book of Ezekiel

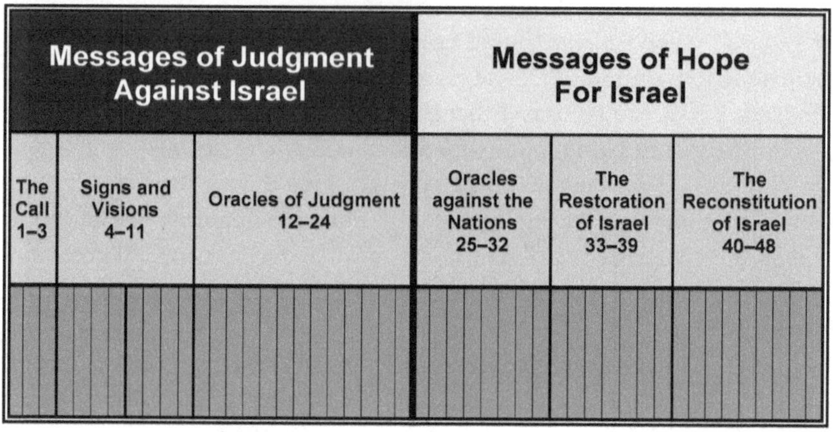

Messages of Judgment Against Israel			Messages of Hope For Israel		
The Call 1–3	Signs and Visions 4–11	Oracles of Judgment 12–24	Oracles against the Nations 25–32	The Restoration of Israel 33–39	The Reconstitution of Israel 40–48

Within these sections there is further evidence of deliberate planning. The form and structure of the collection of oracles against foreign nations are obviously governed by the number seven. Seven nations/states are addressed: Ammon (25:1–7), Moab (25:8–11), Edom (25:12–14), Philistia (25:15–17), Tyre (26:1–28:19), Sidon (28:20–23), and Egypt (29:1—32:32). Seven mini-oracles are incorporated into the first half,[9] and seven oracles against Egypt are preserved in 29:1—32:32, signaled by the sevenfold occurrence of the word event formula (29:1, 17; 30:1, 20; 31:1; 32:1, 17). And seven date notices break up the oracles (26:1; 29:1, 17; 30:20; 31:1; 32:1, 17). But there is more. On the basis of the Hebrew verse division, these indirect oracles of hope divide into two virtually equal parts: oracles of judgment against the six (25:1; 28:23) and oracles of judgment against Egypt (29:1—32:32), both made up of ninety-seven verses. But the significance of these oracles against the nations is highlighted by 28:24–26, placed at the precise mid-point and functioning as a fulcrum on which the surrounding oracles balance (see Fig. 2).

Moshe Greenberg noticed some time ago that individual oracles are often deliberately "halved." This feature is most striking in the oracle against Gog, which consists of two panels consisting of 38:1–23 (365 words) and 39:1–29 (357 words). Although the word event formula in 38:1 serves as a general heading for both chapters, the intentionality of this division is confirmed by a remarkable correspondence between the respective introductions to each part (38:2–4a; 39:1–2a) (see Fig. 3). These

---

9. Egypt is dropped, but compensated for by doubling the oracle(s) against Ammon (25:1–5 and 6–7).

structural features suggest the book is the product of deliberate design, reflecting a concern for precision that many believe characterized priestly scribes.

Figure 2: The Structure of Ezekiel's Oracles against the Nations

7 Mini Oracles							7 Oracles against Egypt						
A	B	C	D	E	F	G	A	B	C	D	E	F	G
A. Ammon A			25:1–2				A.			29:1–16			
B. Ammon B			25:6–7				B.			29:17–21			
C. Moab			25:8–11				C.			30:1–19			
D. Edom			25:12–14				D.			30:20–26			
E. Philistia			25:15–17				E.			31:1–18			
F. Tyre			26:1—28:19				F.			32:1–16			
G. Sidon			28:20–23				G.			32:17–32			

Figure 3: The Place of 28:24–26 in Ezekiel's Oracles against the Nations

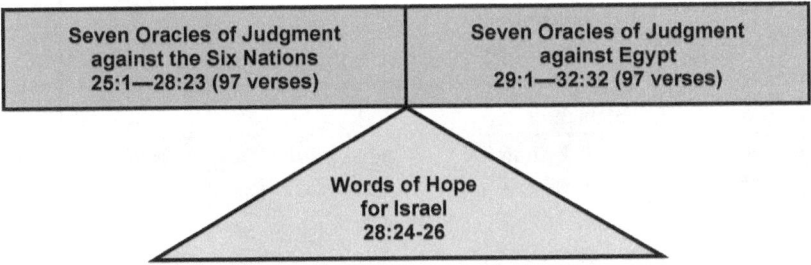

The second distinctive feature of the book—for which preachers should be grateful—is its clear demarcation of literary units. These are usually signaled by the word event formula, "The word of YHWH happened to me, saying, . . ." variations of which occur fifty times in the book. This formula perceives the divine word as an almost objective, concrete reality that emanates from YHWH and confronts the prophet. The boundaries between oracles are seldom blurred.

Figure 4: Ezekiel's Dated Oracles in Historical Context

Year BCE	Biblical Text	Historical Event	Ezekiel's Experience	Cited Date# Yr/mo/day	Modern Equivalent
640	2 Kings 22:1	Accession of Josiah			
627	Ezekiel 1:1		Birth of Ezekiel (623?)		
626		Nabopolassar wins Babylon			
614		Ashur falls to the Medes			
612		Nineveh falls			
609	2 Kings 23:29–30	Death of Josiah at Megiddo; Accession of Jehoahaz			
609/8		Accession of Jehoiakim			
605		Battle of Carchemish: Accession of Nebuchadnezzar in Babylon			
604	Daniel 1:1	Daniel and friends are taken to Babylon			
597	2 Kings 24:10–17	Accession of Jehoiachin; Exile of Jehoiachin, Ezekiel, and nobility Accession of Zedekiah			
593	1:1—3:21	Anti-Babylonian vassals meet in Jerusalem (Jer 27:1–3) Hananiah's prophesies imminent return of exiles (Jer 28:1–4);	Ezekiel is called to prophetic ministry	5.4.5	July 31
	3:22–27	Zedekiah visits Babylon (Jer 51:59)	Ezekiel is inducted into the prophetic ministry; Ezekiel's mouth is closed	One week later	August 7
592	8:1	Unknown	First temple vision	6.6.5	September 18

Year BCE	Biblical Text	Historical Event	Ezekiel's Experience	Cited Date# Yr/mo/day	Modern Equivalent
591	20:1	End of Hananiah's two-year prophecy (Jer 28:1–4)	Elders visit Ezekiel oracle of Israel's abominations	7.5.10	August 14
587	24:1	Siege of Jerusalem begins	Ezekiel records the day	9[10].10.10	January 5
	29:1	Pharaoh Hophra attempts to relieve the pressure on Jerusalem	Ezekiel's wife dies (?) Oracle of Egypt's Doom	10.10.12	January 7
586	30:20	See previous note.	Oracle of Egypt's doom	11.1.7	April 29
	31:1	See previous note.	Oracle of Egypt's doom	11.3.1	June 21
585	33:21	Fugitive announces to Ezekiel, "The city has fallen!" Ezekiel's mouth is opened		12.10.5	January 8
	26:1	Nebuchadnezzar begins thirteen year siege of Tyre	Oracle of Tyre's doom	12.11.1*	February 3
	32:1	Unknown	Oracle of Egypt's doom	12.12.1	March 3
	32:17	Unknown	Oracle of Egypt's doom	12.12.15	March 18
573	40:1	Babylonian New Years Festival	The second temple vision	25.1.10	April 28
571	29:17	Nebuchadnezzar's siege of Tyre ends	Oracle of Egypt's doom	27.1.1	April 26
562		Death of Nebuchadnezzar			
539	Ezra 1:1–4	Cyrus issues decree authorizing the exiles to return to Jerusalem			

Based on Jehoiachin's Exile.

A third distinctive feature of the book is the care with which many of the oracles are dated.[10] Apart from 1:1, which is enigmatic and general, and 3:16, which is linked to 1:2–3, fourteen oracles are introduced by date notices that tend to be variations of the stereotypical pattern found in 8:1, "It happened in the sixth year in the sixth [month] on the [day] of the

10. Ezekiel's precision is observable elsewhere only in Zechariah (1:7; 7:1; cf. 1:1) and Haggai (1:1, 15a, 15b; 2:10, 20), undoubtedly under his influence.

month" (1:2–3; 20:1; 24:1; 26:1; 29:1; 29:17; 30:20; 31:1; 32:1; 32:17; 33:21; 40:1). Although a special clustering is evident in the collection of oracles against Egypt (29:1—32:32), these date notices are distributed throughout the book, providing a clear chronological and historical framework for Ezekiel's ministry (see Fig. 4).

This interest in chronological precision seems to reflect his awareness of the significance of the events of which he is a part. Israel's history as the nation has known it has come to an end; God must start over again.[11] But the date notices also have an authenticating function. As he edits his oracles, Ezekiel marks the evidence, documenting the fact that YHWH had given his word long in advance of the events, and even though no one had paid attention, his word had been fulfilled (12:25, 28; 17:24; 22:14; 36:36; 37:14). These notes invite readers of every age to acknowledge the veracity and power of the divine word, and to recognize in Ezekiel a true prophet of YHWH (2:5; 12:26–28; 33:33).

Fourth, unlike any other prophetic books, the consistently autobiographical first-person cast of Ezekiel's oracles creates the impression of private memoirs, perhaps his *memorabile*. The I-form is abandoned in favor of the third person only in 1:2–3.[12] Although the oracles are presented in autobiographical narrative style, rarely does the prophet actually admit the reader into his mind. He records his reaction only six times, venting revulsion at what he sees or acknowledging the incomprehensibility of YHWH's actions (4:14; 9:8; 11:13; 21:5[20:49]; 24:20; 37:3). In spite of the autobiographic form, one wonders if the real Ezekiel is ever exposed. What we see is a man totally under the control of the spirit of YHWH; only what God says and does matters.

Proposition 4: In order to preach from Ezekiel with authority and clarity, we need to understand the message that Ezekiel proclaims.

Ezekiel's proclamations represent direct responses to the people's theological delusions. Economically and socially, the Judean exiles flourished in Babylon. Probably thanks to the intervention of Daniel, they were settled as a community in favorable circumstances at Tel Abib near the river Kebar (Ezek 1:1; 3:15), where they were able to maintain their own ethnic

---

11. The only date notice in the salvation oracles (40:1) designates the new beginning as רֹאשׁ הַשָּׁנָה (*rōš haššānâ*), "the head of the year." Cf. Exod 12:1.

12. Other prophets rarely use the first person autobiographical form. But see Amos 7:1–8; 8:1–12; 9:1–4; Hos 3; Isa 6; Jeremiah (1:4, 11, 13; 2:1; etc.) and Zechariah (4:8; 6:9) use the word event formula in the first person.

Preaching Ezekiel

identity and social cohesion. Although the exiles from Judah were humiliated by their deportation, in exile they flourished, so that when Cyrus issued his decree in 539 BCE permitting the Judeans to return to Jerusalem, many apparently preferred not to go.[13]

The crises to which Ezekiel responded were not social or economic, but theological. The first half of the book consists of oracles of judgment deliberately aimed at demolishing the pillars on which the exiles' security rested. The theological system may be represented graphically as in Figure 5.

Figure 5: A House of Pride: The Foundations of Israel's Security

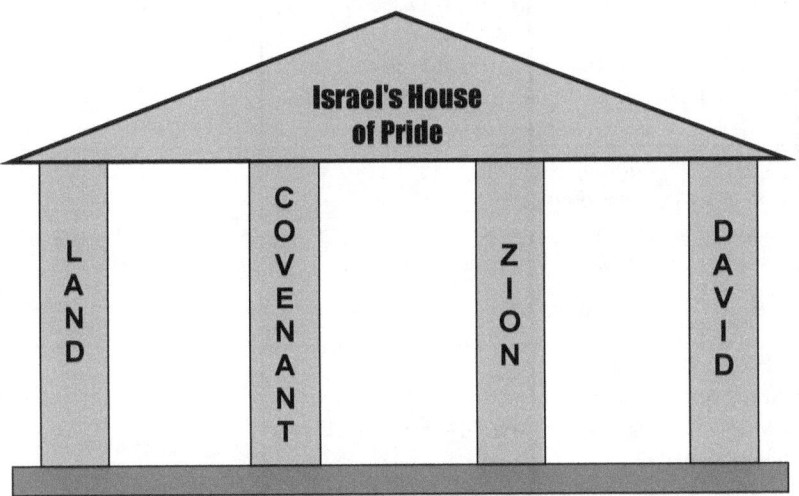

Most of the pronouncements address one or more of the four pillars on which their security rested. However, once the city had fallen, Ezekiel's tactic changed. Thereafter he systematically reconstructed the covenantal pillars, demonstrating that YHWH's promises were indeed eternal. The judgment could not be the last word. On the relationship between specific oracles and the promises, see Figure 6.

---

13. Ezra 2 tallies more than 42,000 returners, but the majority must have remained behind.

Figure 6: The Relationship between Ezekiel's Judgment and Salvation Oracles

The Pillar of Orthodox Theology	The Demolition Pronouncements	The Reconstruction Pronouncements
YHWH, the divine patron of Israel, has entered into an eternal covenant with his people.	3:16–21; 5:4, 16–17; 6:11–14; 14:1–23; 15:1–8; 16:1–60; 18:1–32; 20:1–44; 23:1–49; 33:1–20; 33:23–29	34:1–31; 36:16–32, 37–38; 37:1–14; 37:15–21; 37:25–28; 39:21–29
YHWH, the divine patron of Israel, has given the nation the land of Canaan as their eternal territorial possession.	4:1–3; 4:9–17; 5:5–15; 6:1–7, 11–14; 7:1–27; 11:1–21; 12:17–20; 14:12–23; 15:1–8; 16:1–63; 21:6–22[1–17]; 21:23–32[18–27]; 22:1–31; 23:1–49; 24:1–15	34:25–29; 35:1—36:16; 36:33–36; 38:1—39:20; 47:1—48:7, 23–29
YHWH, the divine patron of Israel, has chosen Jerusalem as his eternal residence, from which he exercises sovereignty over his people.	7:20–24; 8:1—10:22; 11:22–25; 24:16–27	37:26–27; 40:1—46:24; 48:8–22, 30–35
YHWH, the divine patron of Israel, has promised the Davidic house eternal title to and occupancy of the throne of Israel.	12:1–16; 17:1–24; 19:1–14; 21:30–32[25–27]	34:23–24; 37:22–25

While Ezekiel's preaching was firmly grounded in the Scriptures and the traditions of Israel, the goal of his preaching was to change the people's thinking about YHWH and their disposition towards themselves. The universalism of Isaiah stands in sharpest contrast to the parochialism of Ezekiel. From beginning to end, the God who confronts the reader in this book is the God of Israel, not only passionate about his relationship with his people, but willing to stake his reputation on their fate or fortune. He does indeed sit on his throne in the heavens as cosmic king, and his rule extends to the furthest corners of the earth (1:1–28), but his chosen residence is in Jerusalem,[14] in the land of Canaan/Israel (chs. 40–48),

---

14. Compare the departure of YHWH from the temple in Jerusalem as described in chapters 8–11 with his return to the temple in chapters 40–43.

among his own people (48:35). Even in the exercise of his sovereignty over the nations, his agenda is focused on Israel. To Ezekiel, Nebuchadnezzar's place in history is determined by his role as wielder of the divine sword directed at Judah and Jerusalem (21:5-37[1-32]), and as protector of the remnant, so that when the holocaust is over a population (11:14-21) and a scion of David (17:3-4, 22-24) will have survived. While the oracles against the nations (chs. 25-32) reflect YHWH's universal sovereignty, the rise and fall of foreign powers have historical significance primarily as these events affect the fate of YHWH's people (28:24-26). Gog and his hordes, the archetypical enemies of Israel gathered from the four corners of the earth (chs. 38-39), are puppets brought in by YHWH himself to prove his enduring commitment to his people. By eliminating them he magnifies himself (38:23), makes himself known (38:23) and sets his glory (39:21) among the nations. He is indeed concerned that the whole world recognizes his person and his presence in their affairs, but his agenda is always focused on Israel. Ezekiel's vision of restored Israel has room for non-Israelites, but only as they are integrated into Israelite society and culture (47:21-23).

Space constraints preclude discussion of other theological themes,[15] but we may summarize some of these. First, although Ezekiel avoids the expression "Holy One of Israel," the opening vision and the visions of the temple (chs. 8-11, 40-46) declare his transcendent holiness and cosmic sovereignty. Second, YHWH is the gracious covenant-making and covenant-keeping God of Israel (cf. ch. 16). Indeed, both judgment and restoration oracles are based on past covenantal warnings (Lev 26; Deut 28) and commitments. Third, more than any other prophet, Ezekiel is a prophet of the Spirit. But he not only spoke of the power of the Spirit, he also embodied the Spirit's power in his own person. Finally, despite the morbid tone of much of Ezekiel's preaching, God is on the side of life, not death. Not only does Ezekiel have a remarkably extensive vocabulary of death, the God who speaks through him has at his disposal a wide range of death-dealing agents—famine, wild animals, pestilence, bloodshed, sword, fire—but through his breath/Spirit he brings to life those who have languished under the curse (37:1-14).

If Ezekiel's God is glorious in his transcendence and immanence, his vision of his own people is realistic and sober. His people prided themselves on descent from Abraham and banked on the permanence of the

---

15. For fuller discussion, see Block, *Ezekiel 1-24*, 46-60; "Ezekiel: Theology of," 615-28, reprinted below as "The Theology of Ezekiel."

triangular covenantal relationships involving YHWH, his people, and his land (see Fig. 7).

Figure 7: The Israelite Covenantal Triangle

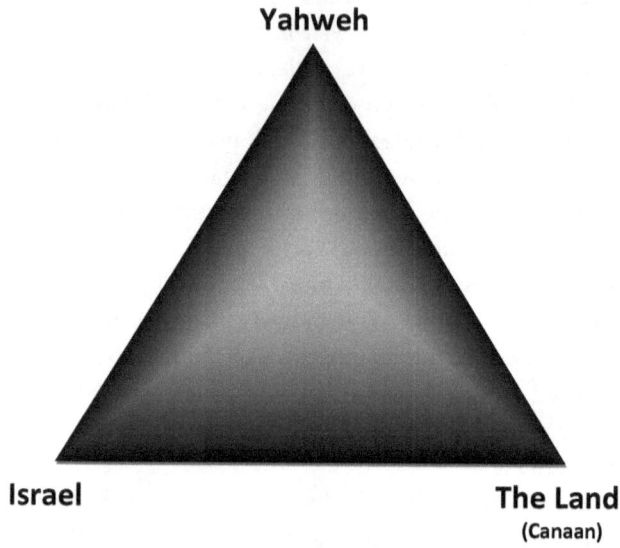

But Ezekiel paints a picture of persistent rebellion, from the beginning of the nation's history to the present. In his revisionist histories (chs. 16, 20, 23) he recalls the abominations of the past. But his view of the people's present is no better. Although his countrymen complain about being punished for sins committed by their predecessors, Ezekiel responds that every generation stands before the divine Judge on its own merits/demerits; no innocent person is punished for the sins of the fathers (18:1–32). But however wicked God's people have been, and however horrendous the judgment—based upon the covenant curses (Lev 26:14–39 and Deut 4:25–28; 28:15–68; 29:14–29)—also certain is Ezekiel's vision of restoration-based on the covenant promises (Lev 26:40–46; Deut 4:30–31; 30:1–10). Indeed, Ezekiel envisions a future when the covenantal triangle that is demolished by the judgment will be completely restored, and the pillars of Israel's security will be restored. YHWH himself will guarantee the nation's peace and security, with the agency of the David shepherd he installs over his people (34:23–24; 37:24–28). But the restoration presupposes a fundamental transformation of the people themselves, as YHWH removes their heart of stone and replaces it with a heart of flesh, responsive to his will and resulting in unreserved obedience (36:22–32).

Preaching Ezekiel

Proposition 5: In order to preach from Ezekiel with authority and clarity, we need to understand Ezekiel's rhetorical and homiletical strategy.

Rhetoric involves communicative strategies employed to break down resistance to the message in the audience and to render the message more persuasive. According to classical definitions, rhetoric involved five elements,[16] each of which is relevant for understanding Ezekiel.

1. Invention—the discovery of relevant materials. Ezekiel received his speeches directly from God by divine inspiration, although consistently in response to the circumstances facing the prophet. I noted earlier that Ezekiel's preaching was firmly grounded in the Scriptures and the traditions of Israel. This is most evident in the links between his pronouncements of judgment and the covenant curses of Leviticus 26 (and to a lesser extent Deuteronomy 28), and his vision of Israel's restoration in 34:25–30 and the covenant blessings in Leviticus 26:4–13. But sometimes Ezekiel's pronouncements go against the grain of Israel's tradition, as in his identification of Jerusalem's/Israel's ancestry in the Amorites and Hittites of Canaan (16:3) rather than Abraham from Ur of the Chaldees, his characterization of YHWH's ordinances (חֻקִּים) as "not good" and his laws (מִשְׁפָּטִים) as not yielding life (20:25), and his introduction of Nebuchadnezzar as the royal figure to whom Genesis 49:10 alludes. But here and elsewhere Ezekiel functions primarily as a rhetorician rather than as a dogmatic theologian or interpreter governed by modern rules of grammatical historical exegesis.

2. Arrangement—the organization of the material into sound structural form. Like the proclamations of other prophets, Ezekiel's pronouncements were crafted according to well-known rhetorical conventions. Based on form-critical considerations alone, this book incorporates a great variety of rhetorical forms: vision reports, dramatic sign acts, disputation speeches, parables, and riddles, etc. This variety is evident in both the judgment oracles and the restoration pronouncements.

3. Style—the appropriate manner for the matter communicated and the occasion. Ezekiel's daring style is widely recognized. In chapter 16 alone we find shocking imagery,[17] rare vocabulary, obscure forms

---

16. Cuddon, *Dictionary of Literary Terms*, 794.

17. In chapter 16, flailing about in blood, engaging in harlotry with male images, slaughtering children as food, spreading the legs for every passer-by, pouring out "your juice," Egypt's swollen member, a bloody victim of wrath and jealousy, hacking in pieces with swords, paying clients to receive her sexual favors.

and usages, anomalous grammatical forms. YHWH had warned the prophet at the outset that he will be dealing with a hardened audience, so he pulls no punches in trying to break down that resistance. The abhorrence with which he views the syncretistic ways of his country folk is reflected in the strong sexual and fecal language (e.g., chs. 6, 16, 23), which translators tend to soften to accommodate the sensitivities of modern bearers. In fact, no other prophet presses the margins of literary propriety as severely as Ezekiel.

4. Memory—guidance on how to remember speeches. While the forms Ezekiel used in the rhetorical situation are striking, his penchant for the number "seven" (as in the oracles against the nations, chs. 25–32) and the "halving" of texts into panels of roughly equal length will have made his utterances more memorable.

5. Delivery—the technique employed in actually making the speech. For all YHWH's commands to speak and to act, on only four occasions does he report his rhetorical actions (11:13; 11:25; 24:18–19; 37:7, 10). Ezekiel 12:7 represents the fullest report of actual prophetic performance: "And I did as I was commanded. I brought out my baggage by day, as baggage for exile, and in the evening I dug through the wall with my own hands. I brought out my baggage at dusk, carrying it on my shoulder in their sight" (*ESV*). YHWH's instructions concerning the sign act involving two sticks (37:16–23) anticipate the people asking for clarification, and then prescribe Ezekiel's answer, but all this is contained within the speech. The text does not say he performed the act, let alone interpreted it. Ezekiel 21:5 [20:49] and 33:30–33 suggest that the audience's response varied between annoyance with and being entertained by Ezekiel's performances.

Proposition 6: In order to preach from Ezekiel with authority and clarity, we need to plan carefully.

If a person devoted a sermon to each literary unit in Ezekiel, preaching through the book would take two years. While some congregations would tolerate this strategy for the Gospel of Mark or Paul's epistle to the Romans, none would have the patience for this kind of series on Ezekiel. How then should we proceed?

First, a series on Ezekiel must recognize the pervasive ignorance of Christians with reference to the OT as a whole and this book in particular. People will not recognize the immediate relevance of such a series and they will need a lot of practical guidance along the way. In reality, once we get beyond the first chapter, the book of Ezekiel is no more difficult than Isaiah or Jeremiah or Hosea. But with sound pedagogical wisdom we must move from the known to the unknown. Unless congregations already have great confidence in their pastors, no series on Ezekiel should last longer than twenty-five or thirty weeks. But there should be enough theological and literary variety in this book to sustain interest this long. Through our preaching we should inspire hearers to dare to read obscure texts, and provide guidance in reading those texts.

Second, the selection of texts for a sermon series on Ezekiel should be based on several complementary principles.

6. Include texts with which people are moderately familiar: the opening vision and call (1–3), the sermon on sour grapes (18), the good shepherd text (34), the heart transplant text (36:22–32), the resuscitation of the dry bones text (37:1–14).

7. Include texts from every part of the book—not simply the "good news" texts of chapters 34, 36, and 37.

8. Include texts representing a variety of literary and rhetorical forms. Having selected representative texts from a variety of forms, by explaining typical structures and vocabulary we may encourage the congregation to transfer this information to similar texts and interpret them on their own. (For a classification of texts according to form, see Fig. 8.)

Figure 8: The Message and Method of Ezekiel

(Texts may appear in more than one category)

Type of Text	Prophecy of Judgment	Prophecy of Restoration
Ezekiel: Call and Commission of the Prophetic Priest	1:1–28a; 1:28b—3:15	
Ezekiel: Watchman	3:16–21; 6:1–14; 7:1–27; 33:1–9	
Ezekiel: True Prophet	12:21–28; 13:1–23; 14:1–11; 22:23–31; 33:21–22	
Ezekiel: Message Incarnate	3:22–27; 24:15–27; 33:21–22; 33:30–33	
Ezekiel: Visionary	8:1—10:22; 11:22–25; 37:1–14	37:1–14; 40:1—48:35; 43:1–14
Ezekiel: Dramatist	4:1—5:17; 12:1–20; 21:23–32[18–27]	37:15–28
Ezekiel: Spinner of Parables, Metaphors and Riddles	17:1–24; 19:1–14; 21:1—22[20:45—21:17]; 22:17–22; 27:1–36; 29:1–21	34:1–31; 36:16–38
Ezekiel: Debater	11:1–13; 11:14–21; 12:21–25; 12:26–28; 18:1–32; 24:1–14; 31:10–20; 31:23–33	33:10–20; 33:23–29
Ezekiel: Prosecutor	14:12—15:8; 16:1–63; 20:1–44; 22:1–16; 23:1–49	
Ezekiel: Judge of the Nations	25:1–17; 26:1–21; 27:1–36; 28:1–10; 28:11–19; 28:20–23; 29:1–16; 29:17–21; 30:20–26; 31:1–18; 32:1–16; 31:1–18; 35:1–15	30:1–19; 32:17–32
Ezekiel: Messenger of Woe	13:1–16; 13:17–23; 34:1–10	
Ezekiel: Lamenter	19:1–14; 26:1–21; 27:1–36; 28:11–19; 30:1–19; 32:1–16; 32:17–32	

Type of Text	Prophecy of Judgment	Prophecy of Restoration
Ezekiel: Miscellaneous Forms	12:17–20; 25:1–7; 25:8–9; 25:12–14; 25:15–17; 28:1–10; 28:20–23; 29:20–26	36:1–15
Ezekiel: Herald of Good News	6:8–10; 11:14–21; 16:60–63; 28:24–26	34:1–31; 35:1—36:15; 36:16–38; 37:1–14
Ezekiel: Literary Cartoonist	38:1—39:29	38:1—39:29
Ezekiel: A New Moses		40:1—48:35

9. Include judgment and restoration texts that deal with each of the four pillars on which the Israelites based their security (see Fig. 6 above).
10. Be sure that every sermon offers grace to the congregation. Not all texts in the book include notes of grace, but they all assume Israel's past experience of grace and/or anticipate a future work of grace.

Third, prepare the people well for the series and for individual sermons. Invite them during the week to read aloud repeatedly the text to be considered the following Sunday, and introduce them to related texts. Provide helpful notes, explanations, and diagrams in church publications.

Fourth, carefully analyze the specific passage selected as the basis for the sermon. This may begin by exploring the genre of the passage and the degree to which it fits idealized genres. Often the distinctive message is discovered in recognizing the deviations from the norm. It will also be helpful to examine inductively the vocabulary and discourse structure of the passage before moving to homiletical considerations, to ensure that the text speaks its message, rather than the message we impose on it (see Fig. 9).

By the River Chebar

Figure 9: The Structure of Ezekiel 16:1–14

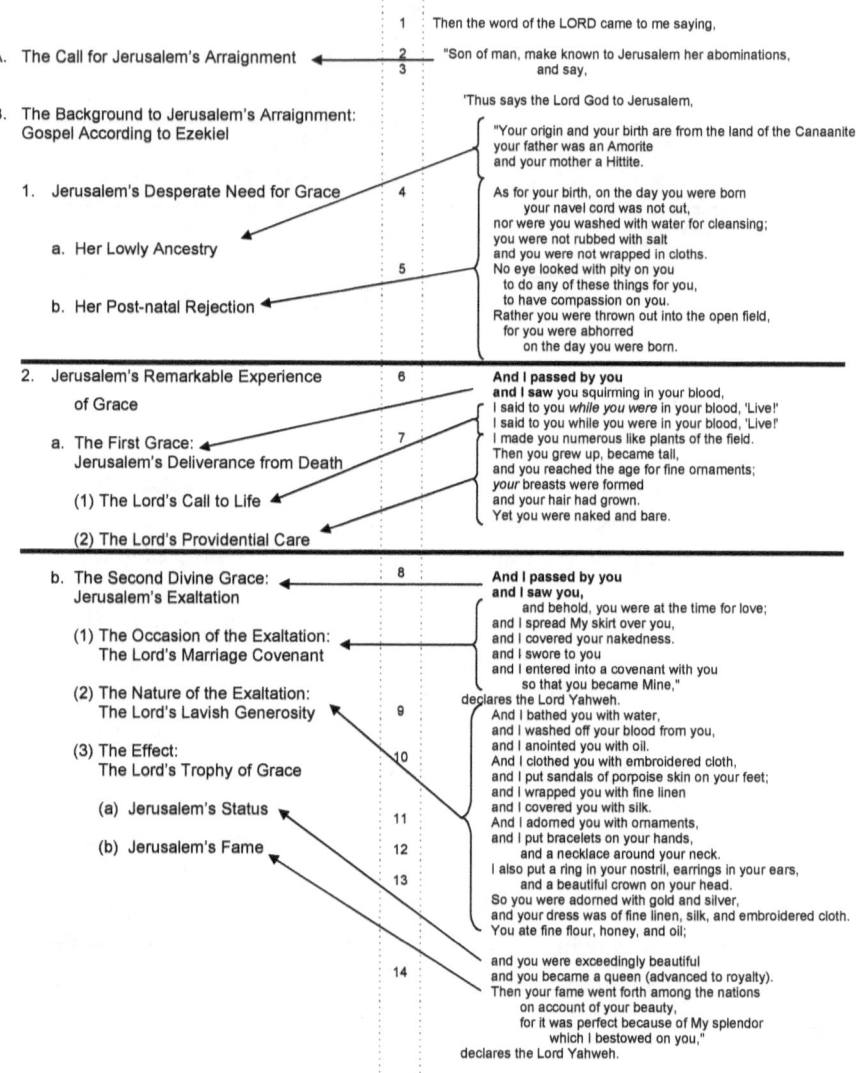

Fifth, in the delivery let the people hear the voice of God by reading entire literary units, not just selected verses, and then develop the theology of the passage. Remind the people often that sermon texts have come to them complete, and then read expositorily, with clarity, appropriate emotion and emphasis, so that in the reading the people hear the voice of God.

Sixth, make appropriate application. Recognize that Ezekiel was not preaching evangelistically to the world, trying to win outsiders to Yahwism;

he was preaching to his own people, those who claimed to be the people of God. Herein lies the relevance of his message for our time. Israel was called to be a light to the nations, to embody righteousness and declare by her well-being the glory and the grace of her Redeemer and covenant Lord. In so doing she was to play a paradigmatic role, representing to all nations and peoples the treasure of divine grace and responding with righteous living. Israel was called to bear his name with honor. The message of this prophetic priest was addressed to people who had besmirched the reputation of God, first by their unrighteous living, and second by being in exile. Underlying Ezekiel's preaching is a profound theology that is continuous with the theology of the OT as a whole and the NT as well. Our task as preachers is to establish that theology and translate it into forms that are understandable and relevant in our context. We may do this by asking of each text what it tells us about:

11. God.
12. The world and society in general.
13. The human condition, the nature of sin, the destiny of humankind.
14. The way God relates to his creation in general and human beings in particular.
15. An appropriate ethical and spiritual response to God's work of grace in our lives.

A Test Case—Ezekiel 16:1–14: "The Gospel according to Ezekiel"

How does this strategy work in specific cases? For an example I have selected Ezekiel 16:1–14. This is the opening section of the longest single literary unit in the book. At around 850 words, this chapter alone is longer than half the Minor Prophets (Obadiah, Jonah, Nahum, Habakkuk, Zephaniah, Haggai) and only slightly shorter than Malachi. Within the constraints that govern most pastoral preaching, it is too difficult treat the entire chapter in one sermon, especially if one would read the entire text. Minimally one should treat this text in two or three sessions. The first would involve a dramatic and expository reading of the entire text, concluding with some synthetic comments on the overall theme: "Trampling under Foot the Grace of God." The second might focus on verses 1–14, which presents one of the most profound portrayals of the boundless and undeserved love of God in all of Scripture. With this strategy we will confront the congregation with many of the big questions of Scripture: the nature of grace, the innate human condition and our propensity to ingratitude and rebellion, the cause and nature of divine fury, and ultimately the triumph of grace. Beyond these normal theological questions, Ezekiel 16 poses unique hermeneutical, sociological, and ethical challenges: What are the boundaries of appropriate rhetoric? What does this text say about gender relations? What are we to make of its portrayal of God? These questions are not easily answered,[18] but texts like this demonstrate that spiritual and theological realities cannot be reduced to formulas, and God himself will not be domesticated.

Genetically and structurally, as one of four *rib* oracles in the book, Ezekiel 16 has a strong legal flavor, as the following broad outline illustrates:

A. The Call for Jerusalem's Arraignment (vv. 1–3a)
B. The Indictment of Jerusalem (vv. 3b–34)
　1. Jerusalem's Lowly Origins (vv. 3b–5)
　2. Jerusalem's Exaltation (vv. 6–14)
　3. Jerusalem's Shamelessness: Her Response to Grace (vv. 15–34)
　　a. Her Religious Promiscuity (vv. 15–22)
　　b. Her Political Promiscuity (vv. 23–34)
C. The Sentencing of Jerusalem (vv. 35–43)
　1. A Summary of the Charges (vv. 35–36)
　2. YHWH's Response (vv. 37–42)
　3. A Concluding Summary (v. 43)
D. The Analysis of Jerusalem's Problem (vv. 44–52)
　1. The Indicting Proverb (v. 44)
　2. Jerusalem's Family Portrait (vv. 45–46)
　3. Jerusalem's Shameful Personality (vv. 47–52)
E. The Double Ray of Hope for Jerusalem (vv. 53–63)
　1. The Bad Good News: The Qualification for Grace (vv. 53–58)
　2. The Good Good News: The Triumph of Grace (vv. 59–63)

Our text represents the first half of Jerusalem's indictment in which Ezekiel describes her conduct against the backdrop of divine grace extended to an utterly hopeless city. Jerusalem's roots are in the general human

---

18. For a brief consideration of factors to consider in dealing with the troubling aspects of texts like Ezekiel 16, see Block, *Ezekiel 1–24*, 467–70.

population, represented by her Amorite father and Hittite mother. As a child rejected by mother and father, her doom was certain. But YHWH came by just in time, rescued her from certain death at the jaws of jackals and beaks of vultures, and caused her to flourish and grow up—that is, survive as a common human being. But then she became vulnerable to human predators, and just in time YHWH passed by again. With obvious allusions to Sinai, he married her, entering into covenant relationship with her, lavishing on her all his resources and elevating her to the status of his queen.

Although Ezekiel 16 is framed by good news (vv. 1–14 and 60–63), three-fourths of the chapter is taken up with relentless accusation and disturbing pronouncements of the divine response. Not many congregations will endure such proportions in our preaching. I was invited once to preach a four-part series on this text—that was the request. I broke it down into its four constituent parts and delivered four messages with all the enthusiasm I could muster.

- A. The Impassioned Love of God (vv. 1–14)
- B. The Spurned Love of God (vv. 15–34)
- C. The Tough Love of God (vv. 35–43)
- D. The Triumphant Love of God (vv. 44–63)

By the time I had finished the third sermon, some had had enough of this brutal image of judgment and did not return for the gospel with which the passage ends.

Like the dry bones in chapter 37, in this text Jerusalem functions paradigmatically. At the literal level this text concerns the fate and fortune of Israel, but at another level the way God deals with his chosen people mirrors the way he deals with humanity. In recounting the OT version of the gospel, Ezekiel has announced all the elements of the gospel that Christians proclaim.

1. God's perspective on the history of his people—including the church universal and local congregations—probably looks quite different from the idealized histories we write. This chapter is not written to the world out there; it is written to those who claim to be God's people. It forces us to ask, "If God were writing our story, what would it look like?" Have we, like Israel, trampled underfoot his grace, and used all that he has lavished on us for selfish purposes and wicked ends?

2. Like Jerusalem, apart from the intervention of divine grace, all humanity is morally destitute and doomed (Rom 3:23; Eph 2:1–3).

3. Apart from common grace, the sentence of physical death hangs over all humanity.[19]
4. Survival does not mean our problems are solved. It is possible to live physically, but still to lack spiritual life, which is possible only through covenant relationship with God.
5. God's grace is the only hope for a lost humanity. By nature destitute, this is the only solution for the human condition.
6. Covenant relationship with God is the highest privilege imaginable.
7. As the objects of God's saving and covenant grace, we have been blessed with every spiritual blessing in Christ Jesus (Eph 1:14).
8. As the undeserving recipients of God's grace, we are called to joyful and faithful living, as trophies of his grace proclaiming the excellencies of him who has called us out of darkness into his marvelous light (Deut 26:19; 1 Pet 2:9–10).

Proposition 7: In order to preach from Ezekiel with authority and clarity for the church, we need to link his message with that of the New Testament responsibly.

There is no need to resort to allegorical methods of interpretation to recognize the Christian gospel in Ezekiel 16. Jerusalem/Judah/Israel does indeed function paradigmatically for all humanity in its lost condition and the church in particular as the object of divine grace. However, we need to remind our people that YHWH, the God who rescued Israel from her hopeless condition (in Egypt), is incarnate in Jesus the Christ, who saves us from our sin and through whom God the Father lavishes his blessings on us.

Conclusion

It is high time that the church rediscovered the book of Ezekiel and claimed its message as her own. We too have grown complacent, mouthing profound creedal statements and for our security banking on the promises of God, when in reality we have abandoned him for all kinds of competing idolatries. For this reason the book is as relevant today as it ever was. May the Lord rekindle in our hearts the passion for God and his people exhibited by Ezekiel, and may he open our eyes to the covenantal faithlessness we demonstrate every day.

19. YHWH's first call to Jerusalem to "Live" holds off the sentence of the fall.

2

The Theology of Ezekiel[1]

OLD TESTAMENT CONTEXT

EZEKIEL MINISTERED IN A turbulent World. Internationally the major players on the ancient Near East stage were switching roles and smaller nations were disappearing from the scene altogether. Within his lifetime he witnessed the demise of the neo-Assyrian empire and the rise of the Babylonians. Indeed, he felt the impact of the latter's power personally when, in 597 BCE, he was carried off into exile to Babylon, along with King Jehoiachin and many of the upper class from Jerusalem (Ezek 1:1–3; cf. 2 Kgs 24:8–17). During his tenure as a prophet, Judaeans were located in three principal areas: Judah, Egypt, and Babylon. According to the Bible, the Babylonians deported virtually the entire population of Judah following the earlier attack (597 BCE) and the devastations of 588–586 BCE; only some of the "poorest people of the land" (מִדַּלּוֹת הָאָרֶץ) were left behind to tend the vineyards and olive groves (Jer 52:16). Of the few that were left, many fled to Egypt in the wake of the assassination of Gedaliah, the governor installed by the Babylonians (2 Kgs 25:25–26; Jer 41:1–2). Among these were Ezekiel's fellow prophet Jeremiah and his scribe Baruch. In general, the people that remained in Jerusalem suffered from severe depression expressed in economic poverty, political lethargy, and spiritual numbness. A new class (relatively) soon emerged, but they had

---

1. This essay was originally published as "Ezekiel, Theology of," 4.615–628.

no understanding of their rich religious heritage and no sensitivity or pity for their deported compatriots (Ezek 11:14–16).

Ezekiel's primary audience was the community of Jews in Babylon. Many questions concerning the exilic social scene remain, but certain pieces may be pieced together. First, although Jehoiachin lasted on the throne of David only three months, after the initial humiliation of deportation he seems to have fared relatively well in Babylon (2 Kgs 25:27–30; *ANET*, 308). Ezekiel consistently insults the current throne-holder, Zedekiah, by dating his oracles after the time of the deportation rather than by the date of Zedekiah's accession (Ezek 1:2; 33:21; 40:1; cf. 8:1; 20:1). Ezekiel ministered to his fellow exiles at Tel Abib, by the Chebar River (3:15). Although humiliated by the experience of deportation, the exiles do not appear to have suffered economic hardship. Daniel 1 indicates that some Judaeans quickly distinguished themselves and rose to the top in the Babylonian court. Documents of the Murashu Archive from the last half of the fifth century BCE suggest Jews quickly got involved in mercantile and banking enterprises. Within a couple of generations the Murashu family at least must have become wealthy. According to Jer 29:5–7 some exiles engaged in agriculture. In fact, the Jews in Babylon flourished so well that when Cyrus issued his decree in 539 BCE permitting the Judaeans to return to Jerusalem, many apparently preferred not to go.

Although Judaean exiles may have integrated quickly into the Babylonian economy, in general they managed to remain a distinct ethnic and social community. This sense of ethnic cohesiveness was promoted and/or reflected in the careful keeping of family records (Ezra 2; Neh 1) and it continued communication with Jerusalem, especially before the fall of the city (Jer 29). In contrast with the Egyptian scene, we have no record of a temple for YHWH in Babylon. Nevertheless, it appears that externally at least, Israelite religious institutions like circumcision and the Sabbath were maintained (cf. Isa 56:2–4; 58:13; Ezek 44–46). But from the prophecies of Ezekiel we learn that the underlying spiritual condition was much different. The people seen to have brought all their apostatizing baggage with them, including their tendencies toward idolatry and all kinds of social evils (Ezek 18).

In truth, the exiles suffered from an intense condition of theological shock. Even though the prophets justifiably denounced the people of Judah for their idolatrous and socially criminal ways, throughout the Babylonian crisis the people had maintained confidence in YHWH's obligation to rescue them. In keeping with standard ancient Near East perspectives,

The Theology of Ezekiel

this sense of security was based upon the conviction of an inseparable bond involving the national patron deity (YHWH), the territory (land of Canaan), and the people (nation of Israel). More specifically, Israelite confidence in YHWH was founded upon an official orthodoxy, resting on four immutable propositions, four pillars of divine promise: the irrevocability of YHWH's covenant with Israel (Sinai), YHWH's ownership of the land of Canaan, YHWH's eternal covenant with David, and YHWH's residence in Jerusalem, the place he chose for his name to dwell there. The nearer the forces of Nebuchadnezzar came, the more the people clung to the promises of God.

But Jerusalem fell, the Davidic house was cut off, the temple was razed, and the nation was exiled from the land. The spiritual fallout was more difficult to deal with than the physical. Nebuchadnezzar's victory left the Judaeans emotionally devastated, raising many questions about YHWH—questions of divine impotence, betrayal, and abandonment. To all appearances, Marduk, the god of Babylon, had prevailed. Ezekiel faced an audience that was disillusioned, cynical, bitter, and angry. The house of rebellion (בֵּית מְרִי) had collapsed, with no one to rescue them. This was the crisis the prophet was sent to address.

The present book of Ezekiel, which represents a collection of messages he received from and delivered on behalf of God, is a testimony to the faithfulness of the prophet and the rhetorical force of his delivery. But it is also a testimony to a theology desperately needed by his people in the sixth century BCE, one that needs to be recovered in our time as well.

Literary Structure

Part One: Messages of Doom and Gloom for Judah/Israel (1:1—23:27)

I. The Call to the Prophetic Ministry (1:1—3:27)
   A. The Superscription (1:1-13)
   B. Ezekiel's Inaugural Vision (1:14-28a)
   C. The Commissioning of Ezekiel (1:28b—3:11)
   D. The Preparation of Ezekiel (3:12-15)
   E. YHWH's Induction Speech for Ezekiel: Four Case Studies (3:16-21)
   F. The Initiation of the Prophet (3:22-27)

By the River Chebar

   II. Signs and Visions of Woe for Israel/Judah (4:1—11:25)
      A. Dramatizing the Fall of Jerusalem (4:1—5:17)
      B. Proclaiming Judgment against the Mountains of Israel (6:1-14)
      C. Sounding the Alarm for the Land of Israel (7:1-27)
      D. Envisioning the Profaning of the Temple (8:1—11:25)
   III. A Collection of Judgment Oracles against Israel (12:1—24:27)
      A. Signs of the Times (12:1-20)
      B. Prophecy—True and False (12:21—14:11)
      C. The High Price of Treachery (14:12—15:8)
      D. The Adulterous Wife: Trampling Under Foot the Grace of God (16:1-63)
      E. Messages of Sin and Retribution (17:1—22:31)
         1. The Eagle and the Vine: A Fable (17:1-24)
         2. Disputing the Justice of God (18:1-32)
         3. A Lament for the Davidic Dynasty (19:1-14)
         4. Rewriting Sacred History (20:1-44)
         5. The Avenging Sword of YHWH (21:1-37[20:45—21:32])
         6. Woe to the Bloody City! (22:1-31)
      F. O Oholah! Oholibah! (23:1-49)
      G. The Boiling Cauldron (24:1-14)
      H. The End of an Era (24:15-27)

PART TWO: MESSAGES OF HOPE AND RESTORATION FOR JUDAH/ISRAEL (25:1—48:35)

   I. Negative Messages of Hope: The Oracles against Foreign Nations (25:1—32:32)
      A. Oracles of Judgment Concerning the Six Nations (25:1—28:23)
         1. Short Oracles against Israel's Neighbors (25:1-17)
         2. Ezekiel's Oracles against Tyre (26:1—28:19)
      A. YHWH's Agenda for the Nations (28:20-26)
      B. Oracles of Judgment Concerning Egypt (29:1—32:32)
   II. The End of an Era (33:1-20)
      A. The Final Summons (33:1-20)
      B. The Final Word (33:21-22)

The Theology of Ezekiel

   C. The Final Disputation: Staking Our Claims (33:23-39)
   D. The Final Vindication (33:30-33)
III. Positive Messages of Hope for Israel: The Gospel according to Ezekiel (34:1—48:35)
   A. Proclaiming the Good News: "Stand by and see the salvation of YHWH!" (34:1—39:29)
      1. The Salvation of YHWH's Flock (34:1-31)
      2. The Restoration of YHWH's Land (35:1—36:15)
      3. The Restoration of YHWH's Honor (36:16-38)
      4. The Resurrection of YHWH's People (37:1-14)
      5. The Renewal of YHWH's Covenant with Israel (37:15-28)
      6. The Guarantee of YHWH's Protection over Israel (38:1—39:29)
         a. Preamble (38:1)
         b. The Defeat of Gog (39:1-29)
         c. Interpretive Conclusion (38:23)
         d. The Disposal of Gog (39:1-29)
         e. Interpretive Conclusion (39:21-29)
   B. Envisioning the Good News: "Stand by and see the return of YHWH!" (40:1—48:35)
      1. The New Temple (40:1—43:11)
         a. Preamble to the Temple Vision (40:1-4)
         b. The Design of Sacred Space (40:5—42:20)
         c. The Return of YHWH of His Temple (43:1-9)
         d. Epilogue to the Temple Tour (43:10-11)
      2. The New Torah (43:12—46:24)
      3. The New Land (47:1—48:29)
      4. The New City (48:30-35)

Theological Emphases

A discussion of Ezekiel's message may be conveniently grouped under three heads: (1) Ezekiel's vision of God; (2) Ezekiel's vision of the people of God; (3) Ezekiel's vision of the Messiah.

1. Ezekiel's Vision of God.

(a) The parochialism of Ezekiel stands in sharp contrast to the universalism and cosmic intent of Isaiah. In no other prophet do the wonder and grandeur of God receive such eloquent and sublime expression as in Isaiah,[2] where YHWH, the Holy One of Israel, is not only the one and only God; he is the omniscient Creator, the omnipotent Sustainer, the omniscient Director, and omniscient Judge of the universe. From beginning to end, however, the God who confronts the reader in Ezekiel is first and foremost the God of *Israel*, not only passionate about his relationship with his people but willing to stake his reputation on their fate or fortune. He does indeed sit as cosmic king on his throne in the heavens, and through his heavenly chariot his rule extends to the farthest corners of the earth (Ezek 1:1-28); but his chosen residence is in Jerusalem (compare the departure of YHWH from the Jerusalem temple as described in chs. 8-11 with his return to the temple in chs. 40-43), in the land of Canaan/Israel (chs. 40-48), among his own people (48:35).

Even in the exercise of his sovereignty over the nations, YHWH's agenda is focused on Israel. As far as Ezekiel is concerned, Nebuchadnezzar's place in history is determined by his role as wielder of the divine sword directed at Judah and Jerusalem (Ezek 21:5-37[1-32]). The oracles against the nations (chs. 25-32) leave no doubt about YHWH's sovereignty over all, but the rise and fall of foreign powers have historical significance primarily to the extent that these events touch the fate of YHWH's people (28:24-26). Gog and his hordes, the archetypical enemies of Israel gathered from the four corners of the earth (chs. 38-39), are puppets brought in by the divine hand to prove YHWH's enduring commitment to the safety of his people. By eliminating them he magnifies himself (הִתְגַּדֵּל; 38:23), manifests his holiness (הִתְקַדֵּשׁ; 38:23), makes himself known (נוֹדַע; 38:23), and sets his glory (נָתַן כְּבוֹדוֹ; 39:21) among the nations. He is indeed concerned that the entire world recognizes his person and his presence in their affairs, but his agenda is always focused on Israel. Ezekiel's vision of restored Israel has room for non-Israelites, but their incorporation into the new order in 47:21-23 assumes adaptation to and integration into what is clearly Israelite society and culture.

(b) Although Ezekiel does not use the title "Holy One of Israel" (קְדוֹשׁ יִשְׂרָאֵל) common in Isaiah (Isa 1:4; 5:19; etc.),[3] the attribute of divine holiness

---

2. Cf. Oswalt, *Isaiah 1-39*, 132-36.
3. See ibid., 33.

The Theology of Ezekiel

is prominent in his mind. From the form and radiance of the inaugural vision—especially the throne of YHWH separated from the supporting cherubimic creatures by an awesome crystal-like platform (רָקִיעַ; Ezek 1:22-26)—to the concentric gradations of holiness built into the design of the temple in the final vision (chs. 40–43), everything about YHWH's character and actions proclaims "Holy! Holy! Holy!" His disposition toward his people in particular is driven by passion for the reputation of his holy name. He must visit them with his judgment because their idolatry and other abominable actions have defiled (טמא/חלל) his temple (5:11; 8:5–18; 23:38–39), his land (36:16–18), his people (20:7, 31, 43), his Sabbaths (20:13, 21, 24), and his name (שֵׁם קָדְשׁוֹ; 20:39). Because of his passion for his holy name he has not utterly destroyed his people in the past (20:9, 14, 22, 44), and for this reason he must restore his people to himself and to his land in the future (20:44; 36:20–32).

A wicked Israel behaving like Sodom and Gomorrah defiles the reputation of God. But so does his nation in exile and his ruins. Overlooking the human causation, the international observers to this calamity conclude that YHWH either is unable to care for his people or has willfully abandoned them. In either case, his sacred name has been defiled. Accordingly, after the judgment, when YHWH deals with Israel's enemies, regathers his people, restores them to their hereditary homeland, and revitalizes them by the infusion of his Spirit, he acts not in accordance with what they deserve, but in defense of his holy name, that he might be sanctioned through his people among the nations (Ezek 28:22; 25; 36:16–32; 38:16, 23; 39:7, 27).

(c) YHWH is the gracious covenant-making and covenant-keeping God of Israel. The covenantal basis for his relationship with the nation is evident not only in the prophet's designation of Israel as עַמִּי, "my people" (more than 25x), but also in numerous citations of and allusions to the covenant formula, "I will be your God and you will be my people" (e.g., Ezek 11:20; 14:11; 34:24, 30–31; 36:28; 37:23). Explicit references to the covenant (בְּרִית) itself occur seventeen times in the book, though six of these in chapter 17 apply more narrowly to Nebuchadnezzar's covenant with Zedekiah (17:13, 14, 15, 16, 18), also referred to as YHWH's covenant (v. 19). Because his contemporaries treated YHWH's covenant promises to Israel as unconditional guarantees of security, the prophet spends chapters 1–24 seeking to debunk this illusory conviction. Apart from faith in the covenant Lord and obedience to the terms of the covenant, there is no safety either from human enemies or from YHWH himself. Israel "is a rebellious family (בֵּית מְרִי), whose wickedness exceeds the abominable practices of the heathen nations (5:5–7; 16:44–53). Because the nation has rejected his covenant standards (מִשְׁפָּטִים) and ordinances (חֻקּוֹת), YHWH will impose on them the covenant curses spelled out in Leviticus 26 and Deuteronomy 28. The people's rebellion has become so intense that no screaming for help will move him to pity (8:18; 9:10; 24:14).

However, the furious outpouring of the covenant curses that Ezekiel predicts in his judgment oracles should not blind the reader to the prophet's fundamentally positive disposition toward the covenant. In the extended allegory of Ezekiel 16, YHWH is presented as a gracious and compassionate God, who not only rescues Jerusalem (a metonymic reference to Israel), an abandoned infant, from certain death, but when she has grown he rescues her a second time, marries her, and, with unrestrained expressions of love, elevates her to the status of queen (16:1–14). All that Israel has and is she owes to his generosity. According to Ezekiel, YHWH's present and imminent judgment of the nation should not be interpreted as abandonment of the covenant, but as strict adherence to its small print. Israel has brought on herself its curses by trampling underfoot the covenant grace of YHWH (16:15–43). But YHWH will not and cannot abandon his fundamental commitment to his people. Ezekiel's prophecies of hope and restoration are based on the eternality of the covenant (note בְּרִית עוֹלָם, "eternal covenant," in 16:60 and 37:26) and YHWH's undying passion for the well-being of his people (see 34:25–31 on the בְּרִית שָׁלוֹם, "covenant of peace," that he makes with Israel).

(d) Closely related to the foregoing, according to one specific form of the divine self-introductory formula, אֲנִי יְהוָה דִּבַּרְתִּי וְעָשִׂיתִי, "I am YHWH, I have spoken, and I will do it" (Ezek 17:24; 22:14; 24:14; 36:36; 37:14); YHWH is by definition a God who acts. Ezekiel offers no sublime poetry on the attributes of God or lofty lectures on his personality. As in the events associated with Israel's original exodus from Egypt (Exod 1–15), knowledge of his person and character is gained primarily by observing his performance. Indeed this collection of prophecies leaves the impression that when YHWH acts in judgment against his people, it is not primarily in order to punish them, but in order that they and the world might know him. The same is true of his restorative actions on behalf of Israel (cf. the recognition formula, וְיָדְעוּ כִּי־אֲנִי יְהוָה, "Then they will know that I am YHWH," distributed throughout the book). His primary goal in bringing down foreign powers is not to destroy the enemies of Israel but to manifest his greatness, glory, and holiness (e.g., the oracles against Gog and his

The Theology of Ezekiel

hordes [Ezek 38:23; 39:21–23]). Similarly, his aim in restoring Israel is to demonstrate his holiness (36:16–32).

(e) More than any other prophet, Ezekiel is a prophet of the Spirit.[4] Exploiting the word spirit/wind/breath, to its full, he presents the Spirit of YHWH as the signature of divine presence in many different contexts: (i) as agency of conveyance (Ezekiel is picked up and transported by the Spirit [Ezek 3:12, 14; 8:3; 11:24; 37:1; 43:5; cf. the more physical idiom, "The hand of the Lord YHWH came/fell upon me," associated with the movement of the prophet in 8:1; 37:1; 40:1]); (ii) as agency of animation (the "living creatures" bearing the divine throne, 1:19, 21; 1:28—2:2; 3:23–24; 10:17; deceased Israel, 36:26–27; 37:1–14; cf. Jesus' comments to Nicodemus in John 3:1–8); (iii) as agency of prophetic inspiration (Ezek 11:24, cf. 2:2; 3:24; ch. 13; cf. 2 Pet 1:21); (iv) as the sign of divine ownership (39:29). Ezekiel, however, not only spoke of the power of the Spirit; he also embodied the Spirit's power in his own person.

(f) As a corollary, despite the morbid tone of much of Ezekiel's preaching, God is on the side of life, not death. Not only does Ezekiel have a remarkably extensive vocabulary of death,[5] but the God who speaks through him also has at his disposal a wide range of death-dealing agents: famine, wild animals, pestilence, bloodshed, sword, fire (Ezek 5:17; 6:11; 7:15; 12:16; 14:21; 28:23; 39:6). Sometimes he executes the sentence of death himself: He wields the sword in his own hand, cuts off people, destroys, causes to perish, consumes in his fury, causes people to fall, and sends them down to the Pit.[6] This mortuary tone obviously derives from the judgmental nature of many of the prophecies. However, the pervasiveness of the motif does not mean that YHWH delights in death. On the contrary, the people have brought this fate on themselves by rejecting the One who had called them to life (16:6), thus bringing upon themselves the curses about which they had been forewarned. YHWH's fundamental disposition is in the interest of life, even for the rebellious among the exiles, if only they would repent of their sin and turn to him (18:30–32). This is his desire for all humankind.

---

4. See my full discussion in "The Prophet of the Spirit," 27–49; reproduced below, 140–67.

5. See Block, "Beyond the Grave," 15–16; reproduced below, 168–97.

6. Ibid., 17–19; reproduced below, 168–97.

2. Ezekiel's Vision of the People of God.

With his narrowly parochial view, Ezekiel links the identity of the "people of God" inextricably with the nation of Israel, which consists primarily of the descendants of the eponymous ancestor Jacob/Israel, as reflected in his frequent references to בֵּית יִשְׂרָאֵל "household/family of Israel," and his occasional בְּנֵי יִשְׂרָאֵל, "sons of Israel." Although the nation had divided into two kingdoms in the tenth century and ten of the twelve tribes had been swallowed up in the neo-Assyrian empire in the eighth century, like the rest of the prophets, Ezekiel uses the designation, "Israel," for all who are left of that nation, currently represented primarily by the rump state of Judah and the exilic community in Babylon.

(a) Ezekiel's perception of Israel's past. Despite his assumption that Israel's ethnic origins are to be traced to the patriarchs—Abraham, Isaac, and Jacob—Ezekiel pays little attention to the nation's pre-Egyptian history. The patriarchs are named only four times in the book: Abraham only once (Ezek 33:24), Isaac never, and Jacob only three times (28:25; 37:25; 39:25). In 39:25 Jacob functions simply as a correlative of Israel; in each of the other texts the names are associated with YHWH's promise and deliverance of the land of Canaan to the Israelites. When Ezekiel mentions the "fathers" (אָבוֹת) he refers more generally to the ancestors of the present generation (2:3; 18:2; 20:27; 31:25). Ezekiel offers two surveys of Israel's history, both in the context of lengthy legal proceedings initiated by YHWH against the nation. Both accounts are radically revisionistic, reconstructing the nation's past from God's perspective, rather than from the idealistic view of the prophet's contemporaries.

In chapter 16 Ezekiel's historical survey is cast in the form of an extended allegory. The first fifteen verses highlight the role of YHWH in Israel's history, which begins in the land of Canaan. Jerusalem (functioning metonymically for the nation) was a helpless infant, abandoned by her parents and left to die until YHWH came by and rescued her, calling her. When she had grown up and matured as a woman, YHWH came upon her a second time and married her. Not only did he enter into a covenant relationship with her, but he also lavished his affection on her with unrestrained generosity, elevating her to the status of queen. The point is clear: All that Israel is and has is attributable to the grace of God.

In chapter 20 Ezekiel divides Israel's history into seven eras, each of which is characterized by YHWH's gracious actions on the nation's behalf and Israel's rejection of his covenant. From Ezekiel's perspective the past is represented by the first three phases. In the first phase (vv. 5–9) Ezekiel traces the origins of the nation to Egypt, where YHWH chose (בָּחַר) Israel, made himself known (נוֹדַעְתִּי), committed himself on oath (וָאֶשָּׂא יָדִי לָהֶם, "I raised my hand to them") to be the nation's God, and promised on oath to take them out of Egypt and bring them to the most glorious of all lands [Canaan], which he had personally "spied out" (תּוּר) for them. In response to these gracious acts he quite reasonably demanded that they abandon their abominable behavior and give up their Egyptian gods. However, they refused on both counts, inciting his fury. Nevertheless, for the sake of his holy name, YHWH restrained himself and in a gracious act of deliverance from Egypt he revealed himself to the nations.

In the second phase (Ezek 20:10–17) YHWH brought Israel into the desert, where he revealed to them his specific will, promising them life in return for obedience, and gave them the Sabbath as a sign of his covenantal commitment. However, they profaned his name by rejecting the covenant, so YHWH refused to bring them to the Promised Land. Even so, his concern for his holy name prevented him from destroying them in the desert. Instead, in phase three (vv. 18–26), he chose to begin again with the next generation, to whom he revealed new ordinances intended to yield life for them. Again they refused, inciting his wrath. However, acting again for the sake of his reputation, instead of destroying the nation he determined to scatter them among the nations and replace their life-giving laws with decrees that would lead to death. Acting again for the sake of his name, in the fourth phase (vv. 27–29) YHWH finally brought Israel to the land he had promised them. But they still rejected his grace, breaking faith (מַעַל) with YHWH by means of all kinds of idolatrous abominations. This picture of Israel's response to YHWH in the land is consistent with YHWH's description of the nation as a house in revolt from the beginning in his first commissioning speech for the prophet (2:3), with the prophet's first series of sign acts, according to which Israel has been committing iniquitous acts for 390 years.[7]

In sum, YHWH's relationship with Israel began as a sheer act of grace. By grace he chose them to be his people. By grace he established his covenant with them. By grace he revealed to them his Torah. By grace he gave them the land of Canaan as their possession. Although the maintenance of this deity-nation-land relationship was clearly motivated by YHWH's concern for his sacred name, Ezekiel offers little information on YHWH's original motivation for the election of Israel. In contrast to Isaiah's vision

---

7. For this interpretation of 4:5, see Block, *Ezekiel 1–24*, 175–79.

of a "light to the nations" (Isa 42:6; 49:6; 51:4; 60:1, 3), Ezekiel's narrowly parochial perspective is reflected in Ezek 5:5, according to which YHWH has set her "in the center of the nations, with countries all around her." The reference is not to a cosmic center, but to Jerusalem's position in the context of her neighbors (contra a common interpretation of טַבּוּר הָאָרֶץ, "the navel of the earth" in 38:12). Under the gaze of the surrounding nations, Israel's charge was to honor the name of YHWH by accepting his divine lordship and by faithfully adhering to his covenant, a response that would be rewarded with divine blessing and protection. Through the prosperity and well-being of the people of God, the positive reputation of the divine patron would be acknowledged among the nations. Conversely, when they rebelled against God and the blessings of covenant relationship were withheld and replaced with the covenant curses, the name of YHWH was defiled.

Herein one may recognize several enduring principles regarding the relationship between God and his people. First, God's people are rendered such by the sovereign choice and gracious redemption of God. The call to be his people is not based upon prior qualifications or merit; it is often contrary to natural human disposition. Second, God's gracious call to covenant relationship must be responded to with grateful, unreserved devotion to the covenant Lord and unrestrained obedience to his will. The people of God are characterized by a disciplined life of holiness and loyal worship, not to earn the favor of God (which would be legalism), but as an expression of gratitude and praise for favor already received. Third, God stakes his reputation among the nations on the health and well-being of his people. While we must take care not to translate God's promise of material well-being to Israel into promises of health, happiness, and success for the contemporary Christian, it remains a truism that God's reputation in society is determined by the health of the church and the extent to which she achieves the spiritual goals he has set for her.

(b) Ezekiel's perception of Israel's present. Despite their claims to the contrary (Ezek 18:1–2), in Ezekiel's estimation, Israel is a household in revolt (בֵּית מְרִי, 2:3; 5:6, etc.). Like their ancestors, the nation has compromised her status as the people of YHWH by worshiping other gods (6:1–14; 8:5–17; 16:15–22; 20:30–31, etc.), patterning her conduct after the customs of the pagans (their wickedness exceeds that of the pagans, 5:6–7; 16:44–52), and relying on foreign powers for satisfaction and security (16:23–29; 23:5–21). All the while they are claiming a right to divine protection, based upon the immutable promises of God. Nevertheless,

Ezekiel is uncompromising in his exposure of the nation's hypocrisy. The covenant promises of blessing are not unconditional guarantees of favor; security and well-being are contingent upon accepting YHWH's exclusive claims to their allegiance and uncompromisingly obeying his will. Since they have failed in both areas, the present generation stands under the threat of the covenant curses. In fact, the fate of Judah and Jerusalem has been irrevocably sealed. YHWH has summoned his agent of destruction, Nebuchadnezzar, and delivered his sword into his hand. His own abandonment of the temple and the attendant fall of the city are only a matter of time. The special claims of the people to the favor of YHWH, particularly of those who still reside in Jerusalem, are empty in the absence of true devotion to him.

At the same time, YHWH has not abandoned his promises or his people absolutely. Ironically, the future lies with the exiles, those who have been removed from the land and deprived of access to the temple. Like the ark at the time of the great deluge (Gen 6–9), the region around the Chebar River holds the key to Israel's continued existence. Like the period of the flood, the time of exile represents an incubation period, from which will emerge a new community. But individual exiles may not deduce from this that they have an automatic right to participation in the new work of God. Like their countrymen in Jerusalem, they also stand under divine condemnation, inasmuch as they have not altered their conduct since their deportation (Ezek 14:1–11). The same sentence of death that hung over their fathers and that hangs over their kinsfolk back home, hangs over them, unless they repent of their ways and redirect their devotion to YHWH (18:1–32). Participation in the future hope depends on their spiritual transformation.

From these observations the reader may draw some theological conclusions regarding the relationship between God and his people. First, the Christian has no right to claim the promises of God if that claim is not matched by exclusive devotion to him and faithful obedience to his will. God is absolved of all obligation to those who turn to any other god, refuse to take seriously all his ethical and moral demands, or rely on any other power for their security. We have no right to sing "Every promise in the book is mine" while claiming "every privilege and ethical choice is mine." Second, the enjoyment of divine favor does not depend on direct physical access to YHWH's house or his land. It depends, rather, on the worship of God in spirit and truth (cf. John 4:23–24) and on grateful adherence to his moral and ethical demands.

(c) Ezekiel's perception of Israel's future. In view of the hopeful words expressed at the end of the covenant curses in Lev 26:40-46 and in Deut 30:1-20,[8] it is not surprising that in Ezekiel's surveys of Israel's history he is able to look beyond the imminent and/or present judgment to a new day when the nation will be restored to YHWH and will prosper in the land of Canaan. According to his seven-part scheme in Ezekiel 20, the present (fifth) period of exile (vv. 30-31) will be followed by a sixth, in which the people find themselves in the "desert of the nations," where YHWH purges them of their sins and brings them "into the bond of the covenant" (וְהֵבֵאתִי אֶתְכֶם בְּמָסֹרֶת הַבְּרִית, vv. 32-38). But this *ante-eventum* turn history of the nation climaxes in a seventh era, when the fortunes of the nation are fully restored. While the prophet has sketched out the main features of this new day in several earlier oracles (cf. similar hopeful pronouncements in earlier judgment oracles: 6:8-10; 11:16-20; 16:60-63), following the fall of Jerusalem in 586 BCE the theme of the nation's restoration will play a major part in his preaching (see chs. 34-48). Although many additional details are offered, Ezekiel paints a picture of Israel in which all the wrongs of the past are redressed and the nation finally lives up to the potential promised in YHWH's original covenant. As noted earlier, in the process the very pillars on which the nation had falsely based their earlier security (but which Ezekiel had systematically demolished in the judgment oracles) are restored. As it turns out, YHWH's promises are eternal: (i) Israel is his covenant people forever; (ii) the land of Canaan has been given to them as their territorial homeland forever; (iii) YHWH will dwell in the midst of his people forever; (iv) YHWH's commitment to his servant David endures forever. He will not go back on his word. After all, as he himself declares, אֲנִי יְהוָה דִּבַּרְתִּי וְעָשִׂיתִי, "I am YHWH; I have spoken; I will perform."

The main features of YHWH's future activity on Israel's behalf are readily recognized: (i) In a new exodus, YHWH will gather the scattered people out of the countries to which they had been scattered (Ezek 11:16-17a; 20:41; 34:11-13a, 16; 36:24a; 37:21a); (ii) YHWH will bring them back to their hereditary homeland, which has been cleansed of its defilement (11:17b-18; 20:42; 34:13b-15; 36:24b; 37:21b); (iii) YHWH will revitalize his people spiritually, renewing his covenant with them, giving them a new heart, and infusing them with his Spirit, so that they may walk in his ways (11:19-20; 16:62; 34:30-31; 36:25-28; 37:23-24; (iv) YHWH will restore the dynasty of his servant David as an agent of well-being

---

8. On which see McConville, *Grace in the End*, 134-39.

and symbol of unity for the nation (34:23-24; 37:22-25); (v) YHWH will bless Israel with unprecedented prosperity and guarantee the security of the nation in their own land (34:25-29; 36:29-30; 37:26; 38:1—39:29); (vi) YHWH will establish his permanent residence in their midst and reorder the worship of the nation (37:26b-28; 40:1—48:35).

Conservative scholars differ widely on the implications of Ezekiel's restoration pronouncements for the future of Israel and the church. On the one hand, in the light of the redefinition of the kingdom of God in spiritual and supranational terms in the New Testament, amillennialists tend to view these and other Old Testament predictions concerning Israel to be subsumed in the blessings extended to and inherited by the church. Accordingly, Ezekiel offers a picture of the new spiritual Israel, gathered from all the nations, transformed by the work of God's Spirit, and enjoying spiritual blessings of well-being and peace under the reign of Christ, the Messiah.[9] On the other hand, millenarian conceptions of the future rely heavily on Ezekiel. According to this view the present age will end with the return of Christ, who will rule over a regathered Israel and a redeemed earth. During this period Satan will be bound and the world will enjoy 1,000 years of unprecedented peace. Ezekiel provides much of the evidence for the pronounced Jewish tone of the millennium and the sequence of eschatological events recognized especially by dispensationalist premillenarians.[10]

The view taken here is that, while the New Testament recognizes fresh significances in its reading of Old Testament texts (the church is heir to the spiritual promises of God to Israel), Ezekiel's own understanding of his oracles must be determinative in our interpretation.[11] If one could ask Ezekiel whether or not he expected a literal regathering of his people, their return to the land of Israel, their spiritual rejuvenation, and the restoration of a Davidide on the throne, one would expect an unequivocally affirmative answer. After all, YHWH has given his word, and he will not renege on his eternal promises to Abraham, Moses, and David. However, although Ezekiel's restoration oracles predict literal events, not all of his descriptions portray the events literally.[12] In fact, from Ezekiel 34 to 48 his prophecies of hope become increasingly abstract and ideational. It is

---

9. Cf. the survey of this approach by Hoekema, "Amillennialism," 155-87.

10. Cf. L. E. Cooper, *Ezekiel*, 45-52.

11. Cf. W. W. Klein, Blomberg, and Hubbard, *Introduction to Biblical Interpretation*, 144.

12. Cf. ibid., 369.

not difficult to envision the regathering and revitalization of the nation as described in chapters 34 and 36:16-38, and the main elements should be taken seriously (similarly 37:15-28). However, 37:1-14 is cast as a vision, with the dry bones functioning symbolically for Israel; the Gog-Magog oracle (chs. 38-39) reads like a literary cartoon, with many unreal and bizarre features; the final temple vision is quite ideological with many idealistic and fantastic elements that are difficult to reconcile with geographical and cultural realities. While Ezekiel undoubtedly envisages a real return of Israel to the land of Palestine, the appointment of a Davidic Messiah, and a protracted period of peace and prosperity for the nation, his vision remains narrowly nationalistic. Apart from YHWH's guarantee of protection, even from universal conspiracies against Israel (chs. 38-39), Ezekiel has little to say about the cosmic implications of the new order. Since he does not offer a clear chronology of latter-day occurrences, one is cautioned against using the details in his descriptions to construct a sequential calendar of eschatological events.

3. Ezekiel's Vision of the Messiah.

Although more than one-fourth of Ezekiel's prophecies look forward to Israel's glorious tomorrow, overt references to the Messiah in the book are remarkably few. Apart from the vague allusions in the topmost crown of the cedar, identified as a יֹנֶקֶת, "sprig, shoot," in Ezek 17:22, and the horn (קֶרֶן) in 29:21, explicit statements only occur in two contexts, 34:22-23 and 37:22-25 (see our fuller discussion in "Bringing Back David"[13]). Only by inference can the נָשִׂיא ("prince") of chapters 40-48 be identified as a Davidide, and his role is described in other than royal terms. It is evident from 34:22-23 and 37:22-25 that Ezekiel's messianic hope involves the inverse of his pronouncements of judgment on the house of David in the first half of the book. But Ezekiel's messianic vision is at home in the ideological and cultural milieu of ancient Mesopotamia. In several ancient texts, following accounts of divine abandonment and judgment of a land, the divine appointment of a human king represents a fundamental element, if not the climax, of the normalization of the relationship between a deity and his land/people.[14] Accordingly, Ezekiel's anticipation of a new (messianic) king over his own people would have been understood by ancient Israelite and alike.

13. Reprinted in Block, *Beyond the River Chebar*, 72-91.
14. For texts and discussion, see Block, *Gods of the Nations*, 134-48.

Whereas the messianic visions of other prophets tended to be inclusivistic, incorporating peoples and lands beyond Israel, Ezekiel's Messiah is a *national* ruler, whose principal features are reflected in the titles and role designations he bears. As David he is heir to the eternal dynastic promises made by YHWH to Israel's greatest king through the prophet Samuel (2 Sam 7; cf. Isa 8:23—9:6[9:1–7]; 11:1–5; Jer 23:5–6; Amos 9:11; Hos 3:5; Mic 5:1–4[2–5]). As עַבְדִּי, "my servant," he enjoys a special relationship with YHWH. In this fundamentally religious role, he derives his authority by divine appointment rather than personal acumen or democratic election. As נָשִׂיא, "prince, chieftain," he stands at the head of his people, not as a tyrannical ruler, but as one who has been called from their ranks to represent them. As מֶלֶךְ, "king," he is a royal figure, symbolizing the nation's new unity. All other pretenders to the throne have been dismissed so that Israel may be "one nation" (גּוֹי אֶחָד) under "one king" (מֶלֶךְ אֶחָד) occupying the land of Israel. As רֹעֶה אֶחָד, "one shepherd," he will seek the welfare of the flock, protecting and nurturing them after the pattern of YHWH himself (ch. 34), and in fulfillment of the ancient Mosaic charter for kingship (Deut 17:14–20). In all these roles, Ezekiel's Messiah symbolizes the realities of the new age. Remarkably, he plays no part in the restoration of the nation. He neither gathers the people nor leads them back to their homeland. Furthermore, unlike other prophets, Ezekiel makes no mention of the Messiah as an agent of peace (Isa 9:5–6[6–7]; 11:6–9; Jer 23:6; Mic 5:5; Zech 9:9–10) or righteousness (Isa 9:5–6[6–7]; 11:2–5; Jer 23:5–6).[15] These he attributes to the direct activity of God. But the Messiah's personal presence symbolizes the reign of YHWH in the glorious new age.

The נָשִׂיא ("prince, chieftain") in Ezekiel's concluding vision (chs. 40–48) is an enigmatic figure (for the privileges and responsibilities of the נָשִׂיא in Ezekiel's new order, see 44:3; 45:7–8; 45:21—46:12; 48:21). He is clearly an exalted figure, far more important than the "princes" of the pre-monarchic period. However, not only is the vision account silent on the Davidic connection; Zion/Jerusalem seems to be out of the picture as well. Indeed the prince and his land are deliberately separated from the city bearing the name יְהוָה שָׁמָּה, "YHWH is there" (48:35), and from the temple, YHWH's true residence. Furthermore, not only is the נָשִׂיא's authority tied to the land of Israel (as opposed to a cosmic rule), his rights are severely restricted. YHWH may authorize him to eat before him in the

---

15. On the relationship of Ezekiel's Messiah with other biblical portraits see Moenikes, "Messianismus," 289–306.

eastern gate, but as a mortal he must enter by another way; that entrance is reserved for YHWH. Most problematic of all, the realism of the description of the prince contrasts sharply with the gloriously idealistic portrayal of the Messiah in 34:23-24 and 37:21-25. Not only must offerings be presented on his behalf, but also specific ordinances warn him not to exploit and abuse his subjects as Israel's kings had done in the past (46:18).

It seems that one of the keys to interpreting the significance of the נָשִׂיא in Ezekiel 40-48 is to recognize the shift in genre between the earlier restoration oracles (ch. 34 is a genuine salvation oracle, 37:15-28 an interpreted sign-act) and the idealistic final vision. Whereas the former are closely tied to history, anticipating a wholesale reversal of the events surrounding the fall of Jerusalem in 586 BCE, the latter is contrived, ideational, and symbolic, and many of its features are unimaginable.[16] Contrary to common popular opinion, the description of the temple is not presented as a blueprint for some future building to be constructed with human hands. This vision picks up the theme of divine presence announced in 37:26-27 and describes the spiritual reality in concrete terms, employing the familiar cultural idioms of temple, altar, sacrifices, נָשִׂיא, and land. In presenting this theological constitution for the new Israel, YHWH announces the righting of all old wrongs and the establishment of permanent, healthy deity-national-land relationships. Ezekiel's final vision presents a lofty ideal: Where God is, there is Zion. Where God is, there is also order and the fulfillment of all his promises.

Furthermore, the primary concern in this vision is not political but cultic. The central issue is not the return of David but the presence of YHWH. Accordingly, the role is facilitative, not regally symbolic. Unlike past kings, who perverted the worship of YHWH for selfish ends and/or sponsored the worship of other gods, this נָשִׂיא's charge is to promote the worship of YHWH in spirit and in truth. In this vision (and only here), with its radically theocentric portrayal of Israel's future, the נָשִׂיא emerges as a religious functionary, serving the holy community of faith, which itself is focused on the worship of the God who dwells in their midst. The נָשִׂיא is not responsible for the administration of the cult. Not only does he not participate actively in the ritual; neither does he build the temple, design the worship, or appoint the priests; these prerogatives belong to YHWH. This agrees with the image of the נָשִׂיא in 34:23-24, who is installed as under-shepherd by YHWH only after the latter has personally rescued

---

16. Cf. the introductory comments to chapters 40-48 in Block, *Ezekiel 25-48*, 494-506.

Israel.[17] In this ideological presentation the נָשִׂיא functions as YHWH's appointed lay patron and sponsor of the cult, whose activity ensures the continuance of between deity and subjects. The God of Israel has fulfilled his covenant promises, regathering the people and restoring them to their/his land. More important, he has recalled the people to himself and established his residence in their midst. Now let them celebrate, and let the נָשִׂיא lead the way!

---

17. Cf. Duguid, *Ezekiel and the Leaders*, 50–55.

3

The God Ezekiel Wants Us to Meet[1]

Introduction: Contemporary Images of the God of Whom Ezekiel Speaks

THE GOD OF WHOM Ezekiel speaks has come under serious fire in recent times. While some marginalize this deity by speaking of him as a creation of Ezekiel's mind, others find the God of Ezekiel (whether the prophet himself or the book that bears his name) to be a narcissistic, self-absorbed, ruthless, and graceless deity. Such characterizations come from a wide range of commentators. For many interpreters Ezekiel contributes significantly to the Scripture's portrayal of YHWH as an abusive husband, who wounds, heals, and wounds again; he is the humiliator of the oppressed woman. If the Scriptures offer any good news it is that he is not consistently abusive; sometimes he is loving and merciful.[2] David Halperin

---

1. This paper was originally presented at the Annual Meeting of the Society of Biblical Literature in San Francisco in November, 2012. I am grateful to Jason Gile, Austin Surls, and Jordan Brown for their assistance in preparing this paper, and for the helpful counsel of my friend Elmer Martens for helpful suggestions for its improvement. However, any infelicities in argumentation and conclusions are my own responsibility.

2. Thus Blumenthal, *Facing the Abusing God*, 240–48. For variations of this perspective, see Weems, *Battered Love*, esp. 58–64 and 96–104; Carroll, "Desire Under the Terebinths," 275–307; van Dijk-Hemmes, "Metaphorization of Woman," 167–76; Exum, "Prophetic Pornography," 101–28, esp. 114; Dempsey, "The 'Whore' of Ezekiel 16," 57–78; Shield, "Multiple Exposures," 5–18; Dempsey, "An Abusive God?," 129–51; L. Day, "Rhetoric and Domestic Violence," 205–30; L. Day, "The Bitch Had It Coming to Her," 231–54; Yee, "Two Sisters in Ezekiel," 111–34; Mandolfo, *Daughter Zion*,

views Ezekiel's God as "a monster of cruelty and hypocrisy," whose restoration of Israel is driven by "his thirst for self-aggrandizement, his obsessive fear that no one is going to know who he is."[3]

Baruch Schwartz resists Halperin's psychiatric and psychological speculation concerning the origins of Ezekiel's perception of God. However, his portrayal of it is equally negative. Building on an earlier essay by Moshe Greenberg,[4] Schwartz focuses on the restoration oracles and visions, but he finds God in Ezekiel to be completely devoid of covenant faithfulness or love.[5] YHWH promises unilateral action to restore the nation in spite, to cause Israel "to feel the eternal remorse that the exile failed to bring about."[6] The prophet never speaks of Israel's restoration "as an act of mercy, compassion, forgiveness, deliverance, redemption, kindness, joy, faithfulness to the covenant, reconciliation, or consolation."[7] Rather, the restoration of Israel's fortunes will be "the act of a raging God of zealous justice (קִנְאָה) who acts out of self-interest and a consuming concern for his reputation."[8] Instead of inviting them to rejoice over their newfound prosperity, "Israel's restoration will be carried out in order to shame her in the eyes of all nations and to render her eternally speechless, her self-esteem gone forever (16:52–63). In Ezekiel *Israel is never forgiven;* rather she remains perpetually ashamed" (italics his).[9]

Although Lena-Sofia Tiemeyer claims to "read the text *with* . . . rather than against the grain,"[10] to her Ezekiel was an accomplice in YHWH's cruel and vindictive judgments:

54, 50. For helpful responses to these approaches, see Patton, "Should Our Sister Be Treated Like a Whore?," 221–38; Kim, "Yhwh as Jealous Husband," 127–47.

3. See Halperin, *Seeking Ezekiel*, 170–71. Halperin allows that YHWH may sometimes act with kindness, but Ezekiel's God is a hateful deity. Ezekiel's portrayal betrays a deep hatred of God, reflecting his own psychological wounds as a result of abuse by his father and mother when he was a child. Ibid., 208 *et passim*.

4. Greenberg, "Anthropopathism in Ezekiel," 1–10.

5. See Schwartz, "Ezekiel's Dim View," 43–67; and even more emphatically in "The Ultimate Aim of Israel's Restoration," 305–19.

6. Schwartz, "Ezekiel's Dim View," 49.

7. Ibid., 55.

8. Ibid., 65.

9. Ibid., 64. Cf. 16:61–63; 20:42–43; 36:31–32. Elsewhere he concludes: "YHWH condemns his people to nothing less than a paralyzing, unrelieved condition of self-hatred" ("The Ultimate Aim of Israel's Restoration," 307).

10. Tiemeyer, "To Read—Or Not to Read," 482 (italics hers).

Throughout all this, Ezekiel never challenges God's sanctity, morality and power, and he always attempts to justify God's actions by accusing the people of wrongdoings in order to protect God, his righteousness and his justice. In a sense Ezekiel strives to describe Judah's crime in such a way as to make it fit God's punishment.[11]

She admits there is grace in Ezekiel (ch. 36). However, this is not reconciling grace, but a part of Israel's punishment, an act of ritual expiation intended to evoke in Israel eternal remorse (16:61–63). "In fact, Israel's restoration is entirely loveless. As there is no love, there is very little in terms of *forgiveness, consolation* or *comfort* in Ezekiel. In the rare cases where these words are used, the intention is sarcasm" (italics hers).[12] Tiemeyer admits the Supreme Being may and can execute judgment over his creation any way he wants, but questions whether it is right for a compassionate God to do so. Claiming Abraham (Gen 18:23–33), Moses (Exod 32:10–14), and Amos (7:1–9) as precedents, she argues we must challenge Ezekiel's imagery and resist his picture of God's punishment and Jerusalem's sin.[13]

Finally, I note the paper presented to this Society in 2009 by Louis Stulman, "Speaking on Behalf of the Losers: Reading Ezekiel as Disaster/Survival Literature."[14] Stulman reads the book of Ezekiel as trauma literature, the response of a community of losers to the trauma of defeat, destruction, and forced exile.[15] We should not underestimate the eco-

---

11. Ibid., 483.

12. Ibid., 484. For example, in 14:22 Israel will "relax, breathe easier" (נחם, *niphal*; Tiemeyer, "be comforted") when they realize they got the punishment they deserved. In 5:13 YHWH will be appeased (נחם, *hithpael*; Tiemeyer, "be consoled") when he has vented his anger fully. וְהִנֶּחָמְתִּי, with assimilated ת, is a hapax *hithpael* form. The expression signifies "to breathe easier," an effect achieved by dealing fully with an evil situation. In 16:42, which contains a similar heaping up of expressions for divine anger, הִתְנַחֵם is replaced by שָׁקַט, "to be at ease, to be calm." On the verb, see Scharbert, *Der Schmerz im Alten Testament*, 62–65.

13. Tiemeyer, "To Read—Or Not to Read," 486. Tiemeyer also cites Amos 8:1–3, but it is difficult to see how this text relates to the issue at hand.

14. The major part of the essay is published in Stulman and Kim, *You are My People*, 145–81.

15. With Stulman's interpretation of Ezekiel as trauma literature, compare those of Smith-Christopher, "Listening to Cries from Babylon," 75–104; Evans, "Ezekiel's Recognition Formulae," 216–59; Garber, "Trauma, History, and Survival," 2005; more briefly in "I Went in Bitterness," a paper presented to the Society of Biblical Literature in Washington, DC, 2006.

nomic, psychological, and social dimensions of the exiles' degradation and humiliation. However, in a conceptual environment that assumes that earthly events reflect heavenly realities, and that these heavenly realities determine human well-being, the spiritual dimensions of the trauma become more acute than the other dimensions. Stulman is right in drawing our attention to the traumatized state of the exiles, but in her review of the paper to this society last year Katheryn Pfisterer Darr cautioned against transferring this trauma to Israel's God. If YHWH, the sovereign Lord of history, becomes a vulnerable victim, a divine refugee in the midst of the dispirited Judaean refugees, how could he offer hope for the despairing people? Does God really become a construct of the human imagination seared by the traumatic experience of exile?[16]

These discussions leave the impression that the book of Ezekiel is totally devoid of divine grace. But not all interpreters are so negative. Paul Joyce writes,

> Both the righteousness that would not avert disaster and the sin that does not prevent deliverance highlight that all depends on God's continuity of providential activity. "Grace" is absolutely characteristic of Ezekiel; though the word ḥēn, "grace," is not used, the concept is central. And far from being an anachronistic imposition of New Testament ideas, it is Christianity that is the borrower here.[17]

Following a lengthy excursus on shame and self-loathing, Jacqueline E. Lapsley concludes her discussion of Ezekiel 36:26–32 with the following comment:

> In sum, for Ezekiel shame is not an inherent part of human identity, a "given" of the human condition, but something bestowed from an external source. But the inversion of conventional thinking about shame goes even further: the very capacity to experience shame constitutes a salvific act by Yahweh—it is a gift from God. This disgrace-shame is a gift from God because it strips the people of their delusions about themselves, their old self disintegrates, paving the way for the people's identity

---

16. In response to Garber ("I Went in Bitterness," 20 in my version of the manuscript), who writes, "The trauma theory reading asks the questions: why would one testify to one's traumatic history in a way that constructs such a vengeful and savage deity. In this reading, the deity becomes a reflection of the trauma itself. The destructive forces of the traumatic event become aligned with the destructive characteristics of the deity."

17. Joyce, *Ezekiel*, 27.

to be shaped in a new way by the self-knowledge that results from the experience of shame. And this new identity, in which people see themselves as "they really are," i.e., as Yahweh sees them, will ultimately lead to the restoration of their relationship with Yahweh.[18]

While acknowledging negative features of the restoration, especially in Ezekiel's pre-fall oracles, Tova Ganzel identifies optimistic verses in the post-fall oracles,[19] and argues that these statements are integral to the book. Responding especially to Schwartz' dim view that the restoration of Israel is part of Israel's punishment, she acknowledges that later restoration prophecies "convey the themes of atonement, return, compassion, and deliverance."[20]

Building on these observations, I shall argue that elements of "grace" and "hope" are not even limited to restoration texts that offer hope for the future, but the notion underlies the *entire* book. I shall also argue that Ezekiel's message can only be understood against the backdrop of the history of YHWH's (com)passion for his people and Israel's response thereto. I shall explore this notion in three parts: (1) the problem of Ezekiel's vocabulary; (2) the nature of divine self-introduction in Ezekiel; and (3) Ezekiel's portrayal of Israel's story.

Ezekiel's "Graceless" Vocabulary

There is no denying Ezekiel's emphasis on the YHWH's fury. His vocabulary of divine wrath includes variations of expressions like "the fire of my wrath" (אֵשׁ עֶבְרָתִי),[21] "I will pour out my wrath" (אֶשְׁפּוֹךְ חֲמָתִי),[22] "to spend my wrath" (כַּלָּה חֲמָתִי כָלָה),[23] "to spend my anger" (כָלָה אַפִּי כָלָה),[24] and "to

---

18. Lapsley, *Can These Bones Live?*, 145; the paragraph is repeated almost verbatim in "Shame and Self-Knowledge," 159.

19. Ezek 11:14–21; 16:59–63; 20:33–34. Ganzel, "Description of the Restoration," 197–211.

20. Ganzel, "Description of the Restoration," 199–200.

21. Ezek 21:36; 22:21, 31; 38:19; cf. "the fire of my passion" (אֵשׁ קִנְאָתִי) in 36:5.

22. Ezek 7:8; 9:8; 14:19; 20:8, 13, 21, 33, 34; 30:15; 36:18; cf. "to pour out my indignation" (זַעְמִי), 21:36[31]; 22:31. The word זַעַם also occurs in 22:24.

23. Ezek 5:13; 6:12; 13:15. The word "wrath" (חֵמָה) is used of divine wrath elsewhere in Ezek 5:13, 15; 8:18; 13:13; 16:38, 42; 19:12; 21:22[17]; 22:20; 23:25; 24:8, 13; 25:14, 17; 36:6; 38:18.

24. Ezek 5:13; 7:8; 20:8, 21.

send my anger" (וְשִׁלַּחְתִּי אַפִּי).²⁵ In most instances Israel is the object of YHWH's fury, a disposition reinforced by expressions like "my eye will not pity" (לֹא־תָחוֹס עֵינִי)²⁶ and "I will not spare" (לֹא אֶחְמוֹל).²⁷ If this were the only image of God Ezekiel offered, or if we interpret the book in isolation from Israel's history and her spiritual traditions, it is a dim picture indeed. But there is more to Ezekiel's portrait of God.

Many have observed that Ezekiel lacks the basic vocabulary of grace or even divine sympathy for Israel.²⁸ The roots חסד and חן/חנן are missing altogether;²⁹ the root אהב is only used of Israel's "lovers, paramours";³⁰ רחם, "to show compassion, tenderness,"³¹ occurs only once (39:25), but even this occurrence is often deemed suspicious.³² Accordingly, even Greenberg characterized YHWH's restoration of Israel in Ezekiel as "loveless and necessary."³³ However, this reasoning suffers from the fallacy of the negative proof³⁴ (i.e., that absence of evidence is evidence of absence). The approach assumes that the presence or absence of a concept depends upon the presence or absence of technical vocabulary for the notion.³⁵ By

---

25. Ezek 7:3. The word אַף, "anger," occurs elsewhere in 5:15; 13:13; 22:20; 25:14; 35:11; 38:18; 43:8.

26. Ezek 5:11; 7:4, 9; 8:18; 9:5 (command to executioners not to show pity), 10; 24:14. In 20:17 YHWH actually expressed pity on Israel in the desert.

27. Ezek 5:11; 7:4, 9; 8:18; 9:5 (command to executioners not to spare), 10. The only time YHWH says he "spares" (i.e., has concern for) the object is his own name (36:21).

28. Greenberg, "Anthropopathism in Ezekiel," 9. Schwartz writes ("The Ultimate Aim of Israel's Restoration," 305), "Nowhere in his prophetic teaching is YHWH thought to do anything out of love, longing, compassion, or grace; indeed the entire vocabulary pertaining to these concepts is missing from Ezekiel." On Ezekiel's vocabulary, see Zimmerli, *Ezekiel 1*, 21–24.

29. However, this argument is weakened by the relative paucity of occurrences of the latter in the prophets: חן occurs only once each in Jeremiah and Nahum, and three times in Zechariah, but never in Isaiah or the rest of the prophets; חנן occurs only five times in Isaiah, and once each in Hosea, Amos, and Malachi.

30. Ezek 16:33, 36, 37; 23:5, 9, 22.

31. As translated by Milgrom in *Ezekiel's Hope*, 29; cf. 33.

32. See Zimmerli, *Ezekiel 2*, 319–21. Tooman (*Gog of Magog*, esp. pp. 271–74) has recently argued that the entire Gog oracle (chs. 38–39) is non-Ezekielian, deriving from the Hellenistic period. For a response, see my review of this volume in *Biblica*, forthcoming. For discussion of the issues involving 39:21–29, see Block, "Gog and the Pouring out of the Spirit," 257–61.

33. "Anthropopathism in Ezekiel," 9.

34. For discussion of the fallacy, see Fisher, *Historians' Fallacies*, 47–49.

35. Compare the recent study by Butterworth, Reeve, Reynolds, and Lloyd, "Numerical Thought," 13, 179–13, 184, who established that thoughts are indeed

this reasoning we could argue that Ezekiel knows nothing of Zion theology, because the expressions "Zion" (צִיּוֹן), "YHWH Ṣĕbāôt" (יהוה צְבָאוֹת), and "to sit [enthroned]" (יָשַׁב) never occur in the book.[36] Moreover, not only does Ezekiel apply expressions for divine fury in Israel's interests to their enemies (25:14; 30:15; 35:11; 38:18–19), but he also applies to his people traditional expressions reflecting YHWH's close relationship with Israel: עַמִּי, "my people";[37] צֹאנִי, "my flock";[38] עַבְדִּי, "my servant";[39] in addition to variations of the traditional covenant formula, "They/you shall be my people and I will be their/your God" (11:20; 14:11; 34:24, 31; 36:28; 37:23, 27).

THE EVIDENCE OF THE SELF-IDENTIFICATION FORMULA

Through a series of essays published by Walther Zimmerli in the 1950s Ezekiel scholars have come to recognize the significance of the self-identification formula (אֲנִי יְהוָה, "I am YHWH") for the message of this book.[40] This formula occurs more than seventy times in Ezekiel, most often within some form of the recognition formula, וְיָדְעוּ כִּי־אֲנִי יְהוָה, "And they will know that I am YHWH." Contra Zimmerli, who argued for its origins in a northern prophetic tradition, John Evans has recently demonstrated that Ezekiel's use of the formula is rooted in the exodus tradition and exhibits a radical revision of its usage in the Exodus texts.[41] Whereas in the book of Exodus these formulas were always associated with YHWH's great acts of salvation on Israel's behalf, in Ezekiel they are usually associated with acts of judgment against Israel—one of the features that gives this book its severe tone. In Ezekiel Israel and the nations will know that YHWH is YHWH when he has spent his fury on Israel (5:13).[42] The image painted

---

possible even without the words to express them.

36. Last year John T. Strong ("The God that Ezekiel Inherited") reminded us that this is obviously not the case.

37. Evenly distributed between oracles of judgment and restoration; Ezek 13:9, 10, 18, 19, 21, 23; 14:8, 9; 21:17[12]; 25:14; 33:31; 34:30; 36:12; 37:12, 13; 38:14, 16; 39:7; 44:23; 45:8, 9; 46:18.

38. Ezek 34:6, 8, 10, 11, 12, 15, 17, 19, 22, 31.

39. Used of Jacob, the ancestor of the Israelites (28:25; 37:25), but also of David (34:23, 24; 37:24, 25), and the prophets (38:17).

40. Zimmerli, "Ich bin Jahwe," 179–209; Zimmerli, *Erkenntnis Gottes*; Zimmerli, "Das Wort des göttlichen Selbsterweises," 154–64.

41. Evans, "Ezekiel's Recognition Formulae."

42. That is, when he has poured out his wrath on them (22:22), set his face against

by adaptations of the recognition formula is indeed the opposite of that represented by its use in the Exodus narratives.

However, we should not be so preoccupied with this transformation that we overlook the positive use of these formulas. Like Pharaoh and the Egyptians in the earlier context, Israel and the nations will know that YHWH is YHWH when he acts against the nations for the benefit of Israel. In 17:24 Ezekiel declares in principle how YHWH reverses the fates of the nations: "All the trees of the field shall know that I am YHWH; I bring low the high tree, and make high the low tree; I dry up the green tree, and make the dry tree flourish. I am YHWH; I have spoken, and I will do it." YHWH applies many of the actions against Israel associated with the recognition and self-identification formulas to their neighbors,[43] promising to intervene against the nations and bring down the high tree for the benefit of Israel. But YHWH also exalts the low. Although Ezekiel never associates these formulas with salvific actions on behalf of the nations,[44] he often associates them with promises of Israel's rehabilitation and restoration as the covenant people of YHWH.[45] A cursory

---

them (15:7), executed "this disaster" on them (6:10), stretched out his hand against them (6:14), made the land desolate (6:14; 12:20; 33:29), punished them according to their ways (7:4, 9, 27), executed judgment against Israel (11:10), scattered the population among the nations (12:15; 17:21), sent them into exile among the nations (39:28), permitted (only) a few to escape (12:16), acted against the false prophets (13:9, 21, 23), cut off idolaters (14:8), destroyed the city and their illusions (13:14), had Israel bear the penalty for their idolatry (23:49), and had the city and sanctuary destroyed (24:24, 27).

43. Specifically, he will make Rabbah a pastureland for camels and flocks (25:5); stretch out his hand against the Ammonites, hand them over to the nations as plunder, cut them off from the peoples, and destroy them (25:7); execute judgments against Moab (25:11), Israel's other neighbors (28:26), Sidon (28:22), Egypt (30:19), and Gog and his allies (39:21–22); direct his vengeance and wrath against Edom (25:14) and the Philistines (25:17); have the "daughters" of Tyre killed (26:6); level Tyre (26:14); send pestilence, blood, and the sword against Sidon (28:23); capture and abandon Pharaoh to scavenging beasts and birds (29:5); bring the sword on Egypt, cut off its living things, and leave the land desolate (29:9; 32:15); lay Edom to waste (35:4, 9, 15); neutralize the influence of Egypt (29:16); burn Egypt and destroy her allies (30:8); put the sword in Nebuchadnezzar's hand to wield against Egypt (30:25); scatter the Egyptians among the nations (30:26); and send fire on Gog and his allies (39:6).

44. So also Evans, "Ezekiel's Recognition Formulae," 269–85, who concludes, "The idea of the nations' salvation as a part of Yahweh's plan is neither propounded nor contradicted; it is simply absent in Ezekiel. The recognition formulae spoken to the nations lend no support to those like Reventlow, who wish to interpret Ezekiel as prophesying the conversion of the nations to trust and worship Yahweh as their own God."

45. He will rescue (הִצִּיל) the Israelites from the power of false prophets (13:21),

examination of the self-identification and recognition formulas in Ezekiel reveals that hopeful utterances associated with them both match the declarations of judgment in terms of number, and reverse the disasters that YHWH pronounces upon Israel. Only through selective reading can we dismiss the formulaic evidence for grace in the book of Ezekiel.

God's Grace in Israel's Experience

I turn now to an exploration of Ezekiel's presentation of Israel's story. I shall do so in three parts: God's grace in Israel's past, their present, and their future.

God's Grace in Israel's Past

In Ezekiel YHWH recounts Israel's past history in three primary texts, chapters 16, 20, and 23. These texts are linked by three features: (1) a common genre, all being cast as judgment speeches (ריב) involving YHWH as plaintiff and judge and Israel as the defendant; (2) a common charge to Ezekiel to arraign Israel and present the divine case against her by declaring all her abominations (16:1-2; 20:2-4; 23:36); (3) an imaginative and rhetorically powerful retelling of Israel's story—a story that looks quite different from the way Israelites were used to hearing it.

Ezekiel 16

Many in Ezekiel's audience will have found the prophet's opening volley shocking: "Your roots are in Canaan; your father was an Amorite and your mother was a Hittite" (v. 3). This contradicts the nation's tradition, which affirms Jerusalem's/Israel's origins in Mesopotamia and Egypt and highlights her distinction from the Canaanites. Strictly speaking, the city's

---

establish his covenant with them (16:62), bring them back to the land of Israel (20:42), cease to deal with them according to their corrupt ways (20:44), execute judgments on their neighbors who treated them with contempt (28:26), cause a horn to sprout for Israel (29:21), liberate (הִצִּיל) them from those who enslaved them (34:27), be with them and renew the covenant (34:29-30), multiply the populations of humans and living creatures (36:11, 38), do more good to them than ever (36:11), rebuild the ruined places and replant the desolate landscape (36:36), bring Israel back to life (37:6, 13, 14), put his spirit within them (37:14), place them in their own land (37:14), sanctify them (37:28), establish his sanctuary in their midst permanently (37:28), and leave none of the exiles among the nations (39:28).

roots were Jebusite, rather than Amorite or Hittite,[46] but Ezekiel is not giving a lecture on ethnography, that is, Israel's physical DNA. Rather, he is speaking about the spiritual DNA of the current population of Jerusalem. Even so, in verses 4–14 he continues as if he is telling a real story about real people, making two principle points.

First, apart from YHWH's intervention, Jerusalem would have survived neither her infancy (vv. 4–6) nor her adolescence (vv. 7–8). At her birth, in the nick of time YHWH came by and rescued her from certain death. The fact that "no one showed pity on her" (לֹא־חָסָה עָלַיִךְ עַיִן) by caring for her or by showing compassion (לְחֻמְלָה עָלַיִךְ, v. 5), as parents normally do with a newborn, suggests that YHWH's double declaration, "Live!" was indeed an act of compassion. Having done nothing to commend herself to YHWH, it was also an act of grace—by definition.

Second, YHWH demonstrated unrestrained love by entering into covenant relationship with Jerusalem/Israel (vv. 9–14). Discovering her naked a second time and ready for love (דֹּדִים), he rescued her from potential danger by marrying her. He spread his skirt over her as a gesture of both tenderness and protection, whose true significance is clarified in the following statements: "I swore [my troth] to you and entered into covenant relationship with you . . . and you became mine" (16:8). The first two clauses highlight YHWH's initiative and the third the effect. Jerusalem's status as the delight of YHWH's eyes and the object of his deep affection[47] is evident from the unrestrained benefits he lavished on her (vv. 9–14). Indeed he elevated this destitute foundling to the status of royalty (מְלוּכָה). While the word אָהֵב/אֲהַב is absent from this text, if we are correct in understanding this expression as "covenant commitment demonstrated in actions in the interests of the other person," then surely the concept of love (אָהֵב) is present.[48] Hereafter the story concerns how she responded to this love.

---

46. Since the Jebusites are regularly mentioned along with Hittites and Amorite in lists of the pre-conquest peoples of Canaan (Gen 10:15–16; 15:20–21; Exod 3:8; Num 13:29; Deut 7:1; 1 Kgs 9:20; etc.), Ezekiel may be using these expressions loosely.

47. Cf. 24:21, where the temple is characterized as מַחְמַד עֵינֵיכֶם וּמַחְמַל נַפְשְׁכֶם, "the desire of your eyes and the object of your personal delight," which adapts YHWH's characterization of Ezekiel's relationship with his wife (v. 16).

48. On the meaning of אָהֵב/אֲהַב, see Malamat, "You Shall Love Your Neighbor as Yourself," 111–15; for a more popular treatment, see Malamat, "'Love Your Neighbor as Yourself': What It Really Means," 50–51. These discussions are carried further by Susan Ackerman, "The Personal is Political," 437–58.

By the River Chebar

Ezekiel 20

While the issue is essentially the same as in chapter 16, Ezekiel's rhetorical strategy in chapter 20 is quite different. Following the preamble (vv. 1-4), he traces Israel's history of rebellion. Although he divides that history into seven distinct phases,[49] our concern is the first three phases, which represent Israel's distant past. The bulk of each phase consists of condemnation and outbursts of divine fury, but the context is set by rehearsing YHWH's previous acts of grace.[50] Alluding to significant elements of Israel's tradition, in Phase I (vv. 5-9) YHWH recalls that while they were in Egypt (1) he chose Israel for a special relationship with himself;[51] (2) he bound himself by oath to Israel;[52] (3) he revealed himself as covenant partner;[53] (4) he promised on oath to take them out of Egypt;[54] (5) he announced on

---

49. Israel's rebellion in the distant past (Phases I–III): (1) Israel in Egypt (vv. 5-9); (2) Israel in the desert—the first generation (vv. 10-17); (3) Israel in the desert—the second generation (vv. 18-26); Israel's rebellion in the recent past (Phases IV-V): (4) Israel in the land (vv. 27-29); (5) Israel in exile (vv. 30-31); Israel's future transformation (Phases VI-VII): (6) Israel in the desert of the peoples (vv. 32-38); Israel on YHWH's Holy Mountain (vv. 39-44).

50. In the telling the story exhibits a remarkable progression: Phase I devotes forty-two of ninety-four words to describing YHWH's initiative in this story; in Phase II the proportion drops to thirty of 104 words; and in Phase III, the longest of these three sections, the prophet dispenses with describing YHWH's initiative, except to warn the Israelites not to follow their ancestors' laws, but that he is their God, and they need to observe his laws.

51. The Deuteronomic term בָּחַר, "to choose," occurs only here in the book. On the word, see Weinfeld, *Deuteronomy and the Deuteronomic School*, 327.

52. Ezekiel refers to the metonymic gesture of "raising my hand" repeatedly (vv. 15, 23, 28, 42, 36:7; 44:12; 47:14). It occurs elsewhere only in Exod 6:8; Num 14:30; Deut 32:40; Neh 9:15.

53. The form of the expression וָאִוָּדַע לָהֶם, usually rendered "I made myself known to them," recalls YHWH's statement to Moses in Exod 6:3, "My name, YHWH, I had not made known (נוֹדַעְתִּי לָהֶם)." The statement is embedded in a divine speech (Exod 6:2-8) that is framed by "I am YHWH," echoes of which can be heard not only in the covenant formula in the following line, but throughout the chapter (cf. Ezek 20:7, 12, 19, 20, 26).

54. Apparently alluding to Exod 6:8, where נָשָׂאתִי אֶת־יָדִי is associated with YHWH's promise to bring the Israelites to the land that he had sworn to give to the patriarchs. Variations of לְהוֹצִיאָם מֵאֶרֶץ מִצְרַיִם, "to take them out of the land of Egypt," recur in verses 9, 10, 14, 22. The phrase is traditional, being found repeatedly in the Pentateuch, and deuteronomistic writings. Cf. also Ps 105:37, 43; 136:11; 2 Chr 7:22; Dan 9:15. Even Abraham's departure from Chaldaean Ur is described in these terms (Gen 15:7). Apart from Ezekiel, of the writing prophets only Jeremiah uses the phrase (Jer 7:22; 11:4; 31:32; 32:21; 34:13).

oath that he had spied out for them a homeland of their own, spontaneously productive[55] and superlative in beauty.[56] Whereas tradition locates some of these events at Sinai, he has them happening in Egypt. Even so, allusions to elements of Israel's sacred tradition are obvious; Ezekiel is well aware of YHWH's past grace to his people.

Though dealt with more briefly, the beginning of Phase II (vv. 10–11) reinforces this conclusion. Having kept his promise and brought Israel out of Egypt, YHWH brought them to the desert (alluding to Sinai), where he revealed his will in the form of ordinances (חֻקּוֹת) and judgments (מִשְׁפָּטִים) in order to promote life for his people. As gracious gifts there he granted them the Sabbaths, which provided occasions to celebrate his redemption and reminders that he had sanctified them.[57] According to Deuteronomy 4:6–8 the nations considered their possession of these ordinances a mark of Israel's supreme privilege. Reminiscent of our text, the miniature creedal statement of Deuteronomy 6:21–25 highlights YHWH's significant gracious actions at the nation's founding: the rescue from the slavery of Egypt, the gift of land, and the revelation of the terms of the covenant, which were revealed to promote fear of YHWH, for Israel's good, to maintain life (v. 24), and for their righteousness (צְדָקָה, v. 25). If the remainder of Ezekiel 20 emphasizes YHWH's fury against Israel, it is because of their response to these favors.

---

55. The idiom, זָבַת חָלָב וּדְבַשׁ, a land "flowing with milk and honey," is traditional. See Exod 3:8, 17; 13:5; 33:3; Lev 20:24; Num 13:27; 14:8; 16:13, 14; Deut 6:3; 11:9; 26:9, 15; 27:3; 31:20; Josh 5:6; Jer 11:5; 32:22.

56. צְבִי הִיא לְכָל־הָאֲרָצוֹת, "It is beautiful to all the lands," occurs only here (v. 6) and in v. 15.

57. While the gender of חֻקּוֹת in this standardized pair changes (cf. חֻקִּים, v. 25), these expressions serve as shorthand for the entire Sinai revelation (plus addenda delivered on the way to the Promised Land). In verse 25 the shift to the masculine gender of חֻקִּים and the absence of the first person suffix on חֻקִּים and מִשְׁפָּטִים signal a shift in referent. Whereas חֻקּוֹתַי and מִשְׁפָּטַי (e.g., v. 19) stereotypically represent the Sinai revelation, חֻקִּים and מִשְׁפָּטִים function generically and non-technically for the divine response/determination in the face of Israel's rebellion. In contrast to the Sinai revelation, which was for Israel's good and for their life (Deut 6:19), this decree guaranteed their punishment and death like the scroll that Ezekiel swallowed, inscribed with laments, mourning, and woe (Ezek 2:10). For similar interpretation and fuller discussion, see Friebel, "Decrees of Yahweh," 21–36.

By the River Chebar

Ezekiel 23

Chapter 23 scarcely alludes to YHWH's earlier grace to Israel. The prophet comes the closest in 23:4, where he declares that Oholah and Oholibah became YHWH's and they bore him sons and daughters. The remainder of this lengthy oracle describes Israel's response to YHWH and his punitive reaction. If this chapter contained all Ezekiel knows about Israel's past, we could justifiably say his God was loveless and graceless. However, this chapter assumes both the earlier accounts and Jerusalem's awareness of the nation's spiritual traditions.

Scholarly distress with these chapters, especially chapters 16 and 23, arises not from the central issue (Israel's infidelity to her covenant Lord), but from the way they handle biblical metaphors, particularly YHWH's supposedly unwarrantedly brutal and abusive treatment of Jerusalem (16:27–43; Oholibah in 23:22–35) and Samaria (Oholibah in 23:9–10). Focusing on the *vehicle* of the metaphor (Jerusalem as wife and YHWH as husband in chapter 16; Samaria and Jerusalem as sisters in chapter 23), rather than the *tenor* (Israel's conduct within the ancient socio-historical context), YHWH's primary role as offended suzerain and judge is minimized. Inserting another metaphor, Israel has trampled underfoot YHWH's past grace by (ab)using for lustful purposes the benefits he lavished on her and going after other gods/political alliances. Preoccupation with the imagery inhibits wrestling adequately with the central issue.[58]

God's Grace in Israel's Present

Although the search for divine grace in Israel's past yields some positive results, explicit declarations of grace in the present are scarce. With its ominous warnings of a dire future,[59] and the sign act involving a scroll fully taken up with laments (קִנִים), mourning (הֶגֶה), and woe (הִי), the opening vision sets the tone for the first twenty-four chapters. Donna Petter helpfully suggests that the key to the book is found in Ezekiel's adaptation of the Sumerian city lament genre.[60] She observes many of the nine

---

58. For helpful critiques of feminist preoccupation with sexual dimensions of the texts, see Patton, "Should Our Sister Be Treated Like a Whore?" 221–38; Kim, "Yhwh as Jealous Husband;" and more briefly, Gile, review of *Sexual and Marital Metaphors*.

59. On the portentous nature of Ezekiel's opening vision, see Petter, *Ezekiel and Mesopotamian City Laments*, 106–9.

60. The prophet's geographical location in the outskirts of the sacred Mesopotamian city of Nippur, within sight of the ziggurat and temple of Enlil (the *Ekur*), and

features that characterize these laments in Ezekiel: (1) subject and mood; (2) structure and poetic techniques; (3) the motif of divine abandonment; (4) divine responsibility for the destruction; (5) the deity's involvement of secondary agents; (6) descriptions of the devastation; (7) the involvement of a weeping goddess; (8) lamentation; (9) the restoration of the city and the return of the deities. Symbolizing the certainty of Judah's doom, the scroll the prophet swallows plays a critical role in the book: Jerusalem's demise can be neither averted nor amended. Analogous to the role of goddesses in Mesopotamian laments, all the prophet can do is mourn the city's fall. However, Ezekiel does not describe Judah's crime in such a way that it fits God's punishment,[61] but the reverse; he goes to great lengths to show that God's punishment fits the nation's crimes.[62]

Where then is the grace in the present? It is in the exile itself. And here we need to rethink how we view the exile. To be sure, this was an aspect of the divine punishment, predicted in the curses of Leviticus 26:33–39 and Deuteronomy 28:64–68, complete with descriptions of the symptoms of post-traumatic stress. While Ezekiel offers ample evidence of the deportees' stress, he also invites us to view the exile positively.

The Hair in the Hem (5:3)

To symbolize the fate of the population of Jerusalem, within the first complex of sign-acts, Ezekiel cuts all the hair off his head, including his beard, and divides it into three equal piles. One-third he burns (representing victims of the razing of Jerusalem), one third he chops up with his sword (representing victims slaughtered by enemy soldiers), and one third he scatters to the wind (representing those who will flee but are pursued and killed). In a puzzling move he isolates a few hairs and tucks them away in the hem of his garment. However, from these he takes some and throws them into the fire. Although the prophet offers no interpretation of these

---

the fact that the destruction of this city [among others] is specifically lamented in the Nippur Lament, reinforce her thesis. For the lament, see Kramer, "Lamentation over the Destruction of Nippur," 1–26. An electronic version of the lament is available at http://etcsl.orinst.ox.ac.uk/cgi-bin/etcsl.cgi?text=t.2.2.4#.

61. Contra Tiemeyer, "To Read—Or Not to Read," 483.

62. Note the repeated phrase, "according to your ways/abominations": 7:3, 8, 9; 18:30; 24:14; 33:20. The only exception occurs in 20:44, where YHWH declares that in the future (after the judgment) he will not deal with Judah according to the judgment her corrupt ways demand.

actions, setting aside certain hairs and tucking them in his hem, suggests a providential grace.

The Prediction of a Remnant (6:8–10)

Ezekiel speaks explicitly of a surviving remnant in 6:8–10, declaring that some will escape death by the sword (פְּלִיטֵי חֶרֶב) of enemy armies and be scattered abroad. Although he does not present them as fugitives who got away, but as captives dragged away by the enemy, he notes the divine hand in their fate: "I will spare some" (וְהוֹתַרְתִּי). He does not declare the grounds for YHWH leaving survivors either as a group or as individuals, but the effects are clear: in exile they will remember YHWH and realize the grief they have caused him with their harlotrous infidelity. Having pursued their dung pellets (גִּלּוּלֵיהֶם), they will loathe themselves (קוֹט, *niphal*), be ashamed of the evils (הָרָעוֹת) and abominations (תּוֹעֵבֹת) they have committed, and recognize that YHWH was fully justified in inflicting this disaster (הָרָעָה הַזֹּאת) on them. Since YHWH's sparing of this remnant is obviously unmerited, the action falls within the semantic field of grace.

The Future Lies with the Exiles (11:14–21)

Defying logic and the theology on which the people of Judah had based their security, in 11:16–21 the prophet declares that Israel's future lies with the exiles, not with those who remain back home. Responding to the claim of the people in Jerusalem, that their continued presence in Jerusalem was a mark of divine favor, while the exiles' expulsion from the land was obviously a sign of YHWH's rejection (v. 15), Ezekiel declares that in the present YHWH has become a sanctuary for his people in small measure (מִקְדָּשׁ מְעַט). Whatever the meaning of this enigmatic phrase, it clearly expresses favor, contrasting the divine estimation of the exiles' status with that of the people back home—YHWH will offer the latter no such sanctuary.[63]

While the following declaration of the exiles' hopeful future (vv. 17–21) adds depth and texture to the significance of this statement, seeing

---

63. Although the first phase of Ezekiel's ministry was essentially negative, his call to priestly service to the exiles signaled YHWH's presence among them. Contra Odell ("You are What You Eat," 229), who interprets chapters 1–5 as "an account of a prolonged initiation in which Ezekiel relinquishes certain elements of his identity as a priest to take on the role of prophet." On Ezekiel's priestly role, see Mein, "Ezekiel as a Priest," 199–213; Betts, *Ezekiel the Priest*.

this utterance in the context of the preceding disputation speech reveals an even stronger force. The prophet's own speech was precipitated by the arrogant claims of the leaders of the people: "It [this city] is the pot and we are the flesh." The common cooking pot (סִיר) provided prophets with a versatile teaching aid.[64] Like the quotation itself, the present image is ambiguous. As a cooking pot containing choice cuts of meat simmering over the fire to be served at a banquet, the meat represents the newly emergent leaders, in contrast to their victims who are but offal.[65] But since pots were used for many additional purposes, the leaders probably view this as a storage vessel, perhaps a crock with a lid to protect meat from insects or marauding animals. By this interpretation *la nouvelle noblesse* represented by אֲנַחְנוּ, "we," are not contrasting themselves with the ordinary citizens whom they exploit, but with those who had been carried off into exile.[66] The new rulers are invulnerable within the city walls, as opposed to those in exile (cf. 11:15) who obviously no longer enjoy the protection of God.

Undoubtedly Nebuchadnezzar's deportation of these elements of the population caused the exiles great distress, but in so doing he served as an agent of divine grace, removing them from the conflagration that is about to overwhelm Jerusalem. Just as Egypt had provided Jacob's clan refuge from a famine and a home where they could survive and grow into a nation in an earlier time (Gen 41–47), so Babylon provided refuge from the violence of the invading hordes, but especially from the fury of YHWH. In the short run, the exile represented divine punishment for persistent rebellion (1 Kgs 24:1–17; and the prophet's audience is still in a rebellious state); however, in the long run, this would turn out to be a providential favor. While Jerusalem went down in flames, YHWH would be with the exiles.

---

64. Ezekiel himself will pick up the image in another disputation speech in 24:3–6, and give it a new and sinister twist. For Micah the pot served as a figure of cannibalistic oppression (Mic 3:3); for Jeremiah it symbolized judgment and disaster (Jer 1:13).

65. Ezek 24:3–6 transforms the image of a cauldron over the fire from a symbol of privilege to a symbol of judgment.

66. According to 2 Kgs 24:14–15, Nebuchadnezzar deported the entire upper crust of Judahite society: all the officials (כָּל־הַשָּׂרִים) and all the mighty men of valor (כָּל־גִּבּוֹרֵי הַחַיִל), all the craftsmen and the smiths (כָּל־הֶחָרָשׁ וְהַמַּסְגֵּר), King Jehoiachin, his mother and wives, his officials (סָרִיסָיו), the chief men of the land (אוּלֵי הָאָרֶץ), all the men of valor (כָּל־אַנְשֵׁי הַחַיִל), the craftsmen and the metal workers (הֶחָרָשׁ וְהַמַּסְגֵּר), and all the warriors (הַכֹּל גִּבּוֹרִים עֹשֵׂי מִלְחָמָה), leaving behind only the poorest of the land (דַּלַּת עַם־הָאָרֶץ).

By the River Chebar

The Preservation of the Tender Sprig (17:3–4, 22)

Ezekiel's riddle of the eagle and the cedar sprig in chapter 17 reinforces this positive interpretation of the exile.[67] Whereas chapter 11 involved the exiles as a group, 17:3–4 and 22 in particular involve a single figure, portrayed initially as a young twig at the top of a cedar tree. Plucked off by a magnificent eagle, the twig was brought to "a land of merchants" (אֶרֶץ כְּנַעַן) and set in "a city of traders" (עִיר רֹכְלִים). If the cedar represents the Davidic dynasty, the freshness of the sprig (יְנִיקוֹתָיו) suggests either a youthful king or one whose tenure was cut off before his reign could be established.[68] Theoretically these qualifications could apply either to Jehoahaz, the twenty-three-year-old son of Josiah, who reigned only three months before he was taken away to Egypt (2 Kgs 23:31–34), or to Jehoiachin, the eighteen-year-old-son of Jehoiakim, who also reigned only three months before he was taken to Babylon (2 Kgs 24:8–16). Since Ezekiel identifies the magnificent eagle with the king of Babylon and expressly declares in his interpretation of the riddle of the vine that he came to Jerusalem and took its king (and the princes) back to Babylon (Ezek 17:12), the sprig obviously refers to Jehoiachin.

But what are we to make of the "land of merchants" (אֶרֶץ כְּנַעַן) to which it was taken and "the city of traders" (עִיר רֹכְלִים) in which it was set? While one's first impulse is to associate these expressions with Israel's native land,[69] since the prophet had previously glossed אֶרֶץ כְּנַעַן with כַּשְׂדִּים, "Chaldeans," that is, "Babylonia" (16:29), the prophet's referent in אֶרֶץ כְּנַעַן

---

67. For a detailed discussion of this matter, see Block, "The Tender Cedar Sprig," 173–202. This essay will be reproduced in volume 2.

68. Compare the characterization of the sprig as רַךְ, "tender," in verse 22 with Proverbs 4:3–4, "When I was a son with my father, tender (רַךְ), and my mother's favorite, he taught me and said to me, 'Let your heart hold fast my words; keep my commands, and live.'"

69. To which אֶרֶץ כְּנַעַן always refers outside this book (Gen 17:8; 45:25; Exod 6:4; 16:35; Lev 14:34; 18:3; 25:38; Num 13:2, 17; 32:32; 33:51; 34:2; Deut 32:49; Josh 5:12; 22:11, 32; 24:3; 1 Chr 16:18; Ps 105:11), and which from earliest times was associated with cities (Num 13:19, 28; Deut 1:22; 6:10; 20:16; etc.). Situated between the anchors of the Fertile Crescent, with Egypt in the south and Aramaeans, Hittites, Assyrians, and Babylonians to the north and East, occupants of the land of Canaan played an important mercantile role. The mercantile significance of כְּנַעַן is most obvious in Hos 12:8 and Zeph 1:11, but the gentilic כְּנַעֲנִי means "traders" in Prov 31:24; Is 23:8; Zech 14:21. On רֹכֵל, meaning "traders, vendors," see 1 Kgs 10:15; Ezek 27:3, 13, 15, 17, 20, 22, 23, 24; Nah 3:16; Song 3:6; Neh 3:31, 32; 13:20. Ezekiel capitalizes on this role for his metaphorical portrayal of Tyre as a merchant ship in Ezekiel 27.

The God Ezekiel Wants Us to Meet

and עִיר רֹכְלִים is clear.[70] Situated on the Euphrates, Babylon played a significant mercantile role in ancient Mesopotamia. However, for Jehoiachin and Ezekiel's immediate audience Babylon was the land of exile. But what does he mean by "land of merchants" and "city of traders"? Since cities generally involved sites surrounded by defensive walls for the protection of the residents, presumably the sprig was brought there to protect it, as merchants protect their goods in warehouses within the walls of the city.[71] In any case, Ezekiel paints both the bird and his actions in positive strokes, quite unlike the second eagle (Egypt) and the vine (Zedekiah) in 17:7–21. In contrast to 2 Kgs 24:9 and 2 Chr 36:9,[72] rather than suggesting a negative reason for the twig's removal from the cedar and his deportation to Babylon, the references to "the land of merchants" and the "city of traders" open the door for a beneficent rather than punitive purpose.[73]

The coda of verses 22–24 reinforces this interpretation of the eagle's actions. Many delete these verses as a post-exilic insertion,[74] but without it the earlier riddle (vv. 3–4) remains unexplained. Like the explanation of the vine (vv. 11–21), the coda declares that the hand of YHWH is behind the actions of the magnificent eagle. Ultimately he is the one who plucks a shoot from the top of the cedar, and sets it in a secure place, until the time is right to retrieve a fresh twig from its top and plant it on a high and lofty mountain. Whereas earlier the riddle (vv. 3–4) had focused on the great eagle, who plucked off the fresh twig of the cedar and brought it to Babylon,[75] now Ezekiel portrays YHWH as the primary mover in the revival of the sprig. Disregarding secondary agents, the coda highlights YHWH's role. YHWH declares emphatically, . . . וְלָקַחְתִּי אָנִי . . . וְנָתַתִּי . . . אֶקְטֹף וְשָׁתַלְתִּי אָנִי . . . אֶשְׁתֳּלֶנּוּ, "I myself will take . . . and I will set . . . I will pluck . . . and I myself will plant . . . I will plant it" (vv. 22–23a), suggesting

70. Ezekiel uses כַּשְׂדִּים as a toponym in 11:24 and 23:16, and as a gentilic ("Chaldeans") in 1:3; 12:13; 23:14, 15.

71. Verses 5–6 reinforce this positive image of the place of exile; the eagle plants the sprig in fertile soil with access to abundant water.

72. Both texts declare that Jehoiachin "committed the evil in the eyes of YHWH." Jeremiah shared this dim view of Jehoiachin (Jer 22:24–30). If our identification of the first branch of 19:10–13 with Jehoiachin is correct, Ezekiel does not whitewash Jehoiachin, but implicates him in the characteristic hubris of the Davidic house.

73. 2 Kgs 25:27–30 indicates Nebuchadnezzar's successor, Evil-Merodach, also had a favorable view of Jehoiachin.

74. For a defense of its inclusion see Block, *Ezekiel 1–24*, 549–50.

75. The use of the verb הֵבִיא, "to bring," rather than הוֹלִיךְ, "to take" (2 Kgs 24:15) describes the event from the Babylonian viewpoint (where Ezekiel and the exiles are found).

that ultimately he was responsible for the removal of the sprig from the cedar in verses 3–4 as well. YHWH's action in setting (נָתַן) the sprig refers to the divine hand behind the eagle's action in bringing the sprig to the land of merchants and depositing it (שִׂים) in the city of traders (v. 4) for safekeeping.[76] However, shifting from the present to the future, Ezekiel introduces a new element, a tender sprig (רַךְ), which YHWH will pluck off and plant on the high mountain of Israel (vv. 22b–23). But this represents a future development.

The riddle of chapter 17 reinforces Ezekiel's image of Nebuchadnezzar as more than a divine agent of judgment on Israel. He was simultaneously an agent of preservation. While YHWH's fury raged at home, he provided refuge for the exiles and rescued the Davidic house by bringing Jehoiachin to Babylon. In a truly remarkable twist, the coda of 17:22–24 declares that by removing Jehoiachin from the throne and taking him to Babylon before he destroyed Jerusalem, Nebuchadnezzar (and YHWH) set the stage for Ezekiel's final restoration oracles.[77]

God's Grace in Israel's Future

While Tova Ganzel's exploration of Ezekiel's restoration texts demonstrates the distinctive features of each and argues for their integrity, in the process she alerts us to many positive features, especially in prophecies that date after the fall of Jerusalem. In chapter 34 she finds a "gentler" tone, involving the image of "a shepherd tenderly caring for his flock." Here God's words are intended to encourage his people.[78] She characterizes the tone of other texts as "conciliatory,"[79] "optimistic," "hopeful," "offering a promise of restoration and compassion to a people ravaged by exile and despair."[80] She takes seriously YHWH's self-characterization in 39:25 as "merciful" (וְרִחַמְתִּי). Space constraints force me to limit my comments to a summary

---

76. The verbs שִׂים in verse 4 and נָתַן in verse 22 function as virtual synonyms for שָׁתַל, "to transplant." Cf. the actions with respect to the vine (vv. 7, 8) and the sprig at the end (vv. 22, 23), as well as in 19:13.

77. According to 34:23–24 and 37:21–28, in the future, after YHWH brings remnants of all the tribes back to their ancestral homeland and reestablishes justice among the people, he will install the ideal David as shepherd, prince, and king over his people.

78. Ganzel, "The Description of the Restoration," 206.

79. Ibid., 208.

80. Ibid., 209.

of my own perspective and brief consideration of the relationship between YHWH's concern for his name and Israel's self-loathing.

Although Ezekiel 6:8–10 falls short of predicting a future restoration of the deity-nation-land triangle, this text could be added to Ganzel's list of pre-fall oracles under consideration. Not only does it refer to a remnant that YHWH will preserve, but in predicting their response to their fate scattered among the nations, it also plants thematic seeds that will be developed later. Verse 9 is remarkable for its references to the inner workings of both divine and human minds. In the first instance, the cryptic expression, אֲשֶׁר נִשְׁבַּרְתִּי אֶת־לִבָּם הַזּוֹנֶה, "how broken[hearted] I have been over their promiscuous heart," reminds modern readers that YHWH's response to Israel's infidelity is neither loveless nor heartless. This statement helps us understand the divine passion reflected in the word קִנְאָה. Often translated as "jealous," the English word is associated with envy and covetousness, or exaggerated and illegitimate possessiveness over what one already owns.[81] In psychiatric terms, jealousy amounts to "vindictiveness born of sexual frustration."[82] While both perspectives perceive "jealousy" as a negative quality, I doubt Ezekiel would have accepted either. Instead of treating קִנְאָה cynically, one should hear in the word God's legitimate passion for one whom he loves. Elsewhere the word speaks of the passion aroused when a wholesome relationship is threatened by interference from a third party, particularly in a marriage relationship when another "lover" enters the picture.[83] Since marriage is a common metaphor for understanding YHWH's covenant with Israel, the characterization of his response to infidelity with קִנְאָה is logical and natural. Indeed, קִנְאָה is not

---

81. The Hebrew word may indeed be used of envy (Gen 26:14; Ezek 31:9). While in popular usage the English words are often used interchangeably, Ben-Ze'ev correctly defines the difference. *Envy* is: "The emotional attitude of wishing to have what someone else has and which is important for the subject's self-definition." *Jealousy* is: "The emotional attitude of wishing not to lose something (typically a favorable human relationship), which is important for the subject's self-definition, to someone else," ("Envy and Jealousy," 489–90; cf. Ben-Ze'ev, *Subtlety of Emotions*, 282–83). For further discussion, see also Kim, "YHWH as Jealous Husband," 129–14. On God's jealousy, see 130–39.

82. Halperin, *Seeking Ezekiel*, 121.

83. Prov 6:32–35. The תּוֹרַת הַקְּנָאֹת, "instruction of passions," in Num 5:12–31 regulates how men may respond when they are suspicious of such interference. Milgrom (*Numbers*, 303, n. 42) notes that in Arabic and Syriac *qn'* means "to become intensely red," a reference to the effects of anger on one's facial complexion. Cf. also Greenberg, *Ezekiel 1–20*, 115.

merely an attribute of God; it is a virtual epithet.[84] Having demonstrated his commitment to Israel by redeeming them from bondage, YHWH rightfully expects grateful and exclusive loyalty in return. The intensity of his wrath toward threats to this relationship reflects the depth of his love. Unlike the gods of the nations around Israel, the God of Israel tolerates no rivals. This love is fueled, not by an exploitative need to dominate, but by ardor for the well-being of the object.[85]

Since the word קִנְאָה is naturally at home in marital contexts,[86] we should not be surprised by Ezekiel's use of the term.[87] According to 6:9, when the remnant is scattered among the nations, they will understand YHWH's brokenness over their response to his affections, described here as , "their whoring heart that has turned away from me, and their eyes that whored after their dung pellets." And when they understand the heart of God, they will loathe themselves (קוֹט, *niphal*), for the evils and abominations they have committed.

But what does this mean? Ezekiel presents the semantic field of humiliation and shame with four words that fall generally on a continuum ranging from shame felt because of a loss of status—in relation to an observing world outside—to shame that is entirely personal, arising from one's own observance of one's conduct and status:

| חֶרְפָּה[88] | נִכְלָם[89] | בּוֹשׁ[90] | קוֹט[91] |

⟵─────────────────────────────⟶

---

84. Cf. the self-introduction formula in Exod 20:5 and Deut 5:9: אָנֹכִי יְהוָה אֱלֹהֶיךָ אֵל קַנָּא, "I am YHWH your God, El Qanna' [Impassioned God]." Cf. also Exod 34:14; Deut 4:24. In Deut 6:15, Josh 24:19, and Nah 1:2, קַנָּא/קַנּוֹא functions attributively in reference to God.

85. Song 8:6–7 expresses the security the object of legitimate passion feels.

86. With the exception of Nah 1:2, the phrase אֵל קַנָּא always occurs in contexts dealing with idolatry.

87. This expression occurs ten times in this book: of God toward humans: 5:13; 8:3, 5; 16:38, 42; 23:25; 36:5, 6; 38:19; of humans against enemies: 35:11. The denominative verb occurs in 8:3; 31:9 and 39:25.

88. Meaning "reproach, disgrace, slander, scorn." The word occurs in 5:14, 15; 16:57; 21:33[28]; 22:4; 36:15, 30.

89. Meaning "to feel humiliated, shamed, ignominy." The word occurs in 16:27, 54, 61; 36:32; 43:10, 11.

90. Meaning "to be ashamed." The word occurs in 16:52, 63; 32:30; 36:32.

91. In *niphal* meaning "to be ashamed, be disgusted with oneself." The word occurs in 6:9; 20:43; 36:31.

The God Ezekiel Wants Us to Meet

The distinctions among these expressions are not absolute, and their semantic fields exhibit considerable overlapping, but the image visualizes the interrelatedness of the expressions. At the left end of the spectrum people feel shame because of what outsiders think of them; they are shamed by the scorn and insults of others.[92] The shame represented on the far right is private, arising from their own realization that they have made an error of judgment, committed a wrong action, spoken inappropriately, or exhibited a fundamentally flawed disposition.[93] Lapsley correctly concludes that texts like Ezekiel 6:9, 20:43, and 36:31 involve private shame. In 6:9, when the remnant in exile wakes up and realizes that in the nation's punishment they have received from YHWH exactly what they deserved, they will ask themselves, "What is wrong with us that we have turned away from YHWH, the God of our fathers, our divine Redeemer, and gracious covenant Lord, and have whored after dung pellets? We have become like the gods we worship."[94] Whereas 6:9 says nothing of restoration, in 20:43 and 36:31, the disposition expressed by קוט (*niphal*) arises after YHWH has reconstituted the deity-nation-land covenantal relationships. According to the former, having brought his people to his holy mountain all will serve him, and he will accept them and their offerings. The latter text describes the scenario in even greater detail. After YHWH has brought the people back and transformed them from the inside out, and they flourish in the land, they will ask themselves, "What is wrong with us that we have abandoned this God and committed all these evils?" and "How could YHWH do this for us [the restoration] after the way we have responded to him?"[95]

---

92. For the most recent discussion of these expressions specifically, and the notion of shame-honor in Ezekiel, see D. Y. Wu, "Honour, Shame and Guilt in the book of Ezekiel." In critiquing interpretations that highlight the contrast between honor-shame based societies Wu offers a very convincing and nuanced view of the function of shame in Ezekiel.

93. Many have studied the motifs of honor and shame in Ezekiel in recent years. See especially Odell, "An Exploratory Study of Shame and Dependence," 217–33; Odell, "The Inversion of Shame and Forgiveness," 101–12; Lapsley, "Shame and Self-Knowledge," 143–73; Lapsley, *Can These Bones Live?*, 130–58. For the most thorough and most recent study, see Wu, "Honour, Shame and Guilt in the Book of Ezekiel."

94. See Beale, *We Become What We Worship*.

95. I see the significance of Israel's post-restoration shame quite differently than Schwartz, "The Ultimate Aim of Israel's Restoration," 307–13. Milgrom (*Ezekiel's Hope*, 114–15.) observes that when the people observe the prefect proportions of the temple and the details of its structure they will be ashamed (כָּלַם, *niphal*) of their prior deeds—that led to the exile, and their remorse will qualify them to measure the sacred spaces of the sanctuary.

Ezekiel casts the answer to this question in two forms. First, he responds negatively: the people may take no credit for the restoration. Ezekiel 36:22–32 is framed by לֹא לְמַעַנְכֶם אֲנִי עֹשֶׂה בֵּית יִשְׂרָאֵל, "It is not on your account that I am acting, O house of Israel" (vv. 22, 32). On the surface this statement is ambiguous, meaning either, "It is not in your interests or for your advantage that I am acting," or "It is not because of any merit on your part that I will act." The context points to the latter as the appropriate reading.[96] When YHWH poured out his fury on them, he executed judgment in precise accord with their defiling behavior and their abominable idolatry (vv. 17–19). But his new disposition is not motivated by a change of heart or conduct in his people.[97] In 20:44 YHWH announced the suspension of the principle of just deserts: "You shall know that I am YHWH, when I deal with you for my name's sake, not according to your evil ways (כְּדַרְכֵיכֶם הָרָעִים), or corrupt deeds (כַּעֲלִילוֹתֵיכֶם הַנִּשְׁחָתוֹת), O house of Israel."

Cast positively, Ezekiel declares that when YHWH restores Israel he acts for the sake of his name (לְמַעַן שְׁמִי, 20:44), that is, his holy name (לְשֵׁם־קָדְשִׁי, 36:21, 22; cf. 39:25; 43:7, 8), and to sanctify his great name (וְקִדַּשְׁתִּי אֶת־שְׁמִי הַגָּדוֹל, 36:23) that has been profaned (מְחֻלָּל, 36:23) among the nations.[98] Is this the response of a pathetic deity, "an outraged and exasperated lover,"[99] who cannot tolerate the bad publicity the Israelites have caused him, who is obligated to restore Israel to compensate for his "colossal error" in venting his rage on them,[100] and who "must resurrect his own people for his thoroughly egocentric reasons" because he is a king without subjects[101] to "soothe his injured majesty."[102] All this "he will do for his own sake, not for them."[103] In Schwartz' view, "YHWH has no

---

96. In Moses' first address in Deuteronomy he uses the positive construction to cast blame on his people for YHWH's refusal to let him enter the land: וַיִּתְעַבֵּר יְהוָה בִּי לְמַעַנְכֶם, "YHWH was angry with me because of you" (Deut 3:26). גַּם־בִּי הִתְאַנַּף יְהוָה בִּגְלַלְכֶם (4:21); גַּם־בִּי עַל־דִּבְרֵיכֶם (1:37); Cf. וַיהוָה הִתְאַנַּף.

97. Against Rom-Shiloni ("Ezekiel as the Voice of the Exiles," 1–45), I agree with Schwartz ("The Ultimate Aim of Israel's Restoration," 309, n. 11), that Ezekiel's view of the exiles was no more favorable than his view of those who remained in the homeland.

98. For a helpful study of this notion, see Milgrom, "The Desecration of YHWH's Name," 69-81.

99. Thus Lemke, "Life in the Present," 176.

100. Cf. Schwartz, "Ezekiel's Dim View," 57.

101. Ibid., 58–59.

102. Ibid., 60.

103. Ibid., 61.

The God Ezekiel Wants Us to Meet

choice but to let his people dwell in their land secure and prosperous, but on no condition will he let them enjoy it—nor will he."[104] He adds,

> Ezekiel predicts, YHWH is bound and determined to embark on a most ungracious project of forced rehabilitation, in order to correct the failures of history once and for all and ultimately to derive the satisfaction for which he has striven for so long. For his people, this is anything but a relief.[105]

Is this really what it means to act for his name's sake? Is Ezekiel's God really that small?

As is the case with any text, ancient or modern, interpreters of the Scriptures are faced with two dangers. First, we may strain the text to make it say what we want it to say. I am probably often guilty of this hermeneutical crime—perhaps even in this essay. Some may view the tint in the lenses of my glasses so rosy that everything has a positive hue. In my own work on Ezekiel I have tried hard to let the text have its own voice, taking seriously the dark side of Ezekiel's personality, of his view of his people, and of his view of his God. We dare not excuse or soften the tone of outbursts like, "When my anger will be spent, and I will have vented my fury against them, then I will be appeased. And when I have spent all my fury against them, they will know that I am YHWH, I have spoken out of my passion" (5:13). But does this mean we are left with a deity who delights in wrath and is heartless toward his people? The second potential problem is the opposite: the lenses in our glasses may be so dark that we cannot see any rays of light even when they shine directly in our faces. The default interpretation of ambiguous texts is negative and texts others interpret positively are forced into this negative paradigm. This seems to be what happens when divine actions "for the sake of my name," are treated as pathologically egotistical and narcissistic. But can we not read the expression more positively?

Ezekiel was not the first to hang YHWH's reputation on the fate or fortune of his people. Faced with YHWH's threat to destroy his people first at Sinai and then at Kadesh-barnea, Moses' appealed to YHWH's reputation as motivation for a positive divine response:

> Why should the Egyptians say, "It was with evil intent that he brought them out to kill them in the mountains, and to consume them from the face of the earth"? Turn from your fierce wrath; change your mind and do not bring disaster on your people. (Exod 32:12, *NRSV*)

104. Ibid., 63.
105. Ibid., 67.

> Then the Egyptians will hear of it, for in your might you brought up this people from among them, and they will tell the inhabitants of this land. They have heard that you, O LORD, are in the midst of this people; for you, O LORD, are seen face to face, and your cloud stands over them and you go in front of them, in a pillar of cloud by day and in a pillar of fire by night. Now if you kill this people all at one time, then the nations who have heard about you will say, "It is because the LORD was not able to bring this people into the land he swore to give them that he has slaughtered them in the wilderness." (Num 14:13–16, *NRSV*)

In the wake of Israel's defeat at Ai Joshua picked up this theme:

> The Canaanites and all the inhabitants of the land will hear of it, and surround us, and cut off our name from the earth. Then what will you do for your great name? (Josh 7:9, *NRSV*)

If Israel's calamities reflected negatively on the name of YHWH, then her prosperity would send out a positive image of their God. As noted above, this notion is explicit in the plague and exodus narratives, one of whose goals was to declare to Israel, Egypt, and the world who YHWH is (Exod 7:5; 14:4, 8). The agenda recurs at least four times in the Deuteronomistic history.[106] It also underlies several statements in Deuteronomy, most notably 26:18–19 and 28:8–12:

> Today the LORD has obtained your agreement: to be his treasured people, as he promised you, and to keep his commandments; for him to set you high above all nations that he has made, in praise and in fame and in honor; and for you to be a people holy to the LORD your God, as he promised. (Deut 26:18–19, *NRSV*)

> The LORD will command the blessing upon you in your barns, and in all that you undertake; he will bless you in the land that the LORD your God is giving you. The LORD will establish you as his holy people, as he has sworn to you, if you keep the commandments of the LORD your God and walk in his ways. All the peoples of the earth shall see that you are called by the name of the LORD, and they shall be afraid of you. The LORD will make you abound in prosperity, in the fruit of your womb, in the fruit of your livestock, and in the fruit of your ground in the land that the LORD swore to your ancestors to give you. (28:8–11, *NRSV*)

---

106. Note the revelatory goals of crossing the Jordan (Josh 4:21–24), David's defeat of Goliath (1 Sam 17:46), the construction of the temple (1 Kgs 8:60), and YHWH's deliverance of Israel from the Assyrians (2 Kgs 19:14–19).

This notion plays a prominent role in Ezekiel. No fewer than twenty-six occurrences of the recognition formula speak of the nations knowing YHWH.[107] Apparently alluding to Moses' intercessory arguments in Exodus 32:12 and Numbers 14:13–16, in Ezekiel's review of Israel's history in chapter 20, the first three phases climax with YHWH withdrawing his resolve to destroy his people to prevent the profanation of his name in the sight of the nations (vv. 9, 14, 22). Had he destroyed them, not recognizing the human causation the nations might have drawn faulty conclusions concerning YHWH: He was either impotent and unable to sustain his people, or fickle and faithless, failing to keep his word. They would not recognize either Israel's rebellion as just cause for YHWH's punishment or YHWH's fidelity to the covenant in carrying out consequences explicitly predicted for persistent rejection of him (Lev 26:14–39; Deut 28:15–68).[108] In 20:39 profaning the divine name takes a different turn. Since Israel was stamped with YHWH's name (cf. Exod 20:7; Deut 5:11; 28:10), their conduct always reflected on his character.[109] If they claim to be his people but go after their own idols, they reduce him to the status of the other gods (who tolerated the veneration of other divinities) and violate his demand for exclusive devotion. The restoration will end this spiritual ambivalence and the consequent profanation of YHWH's holy name.

The scenario described in Ezekiel 36:16–21 reinforces the significance of the message on the scroll that Ezekiel had swallowed at the beginning (2:8—3:3) and the exceptional nature of the events surrounding the fall of Jerusalem in 586 BCE. Whereas in the past, concern for his name had caused YHWH to shrink back from imposing on his people the imprecations built into the covenant (ch. 20), by the time of Ezekiel's call (indeed by the time of Josiah, 2 Kgs 22:14–17), Israel's cup of iniquity was overflowing and her doom had been decreed. The time had come for YHWH to vent his fury. However, since the nations were blind to the righteousness of YHWH's actions, the scattered remnant caused questions to be raised concerning his identity and character. Was he really unable to care for them? Had his covenants with Abraham, Israel, and David, and his election of Zion as the place for his name really been retracted? For the

---

107. The nations in general: 36:23, 36; 37:28; 38:23; 39:7; cf. the modifications of the formula in 38:16 and 39:23. Specific nations: Bene Ammon (25:5, 7); Moab (25:11); Philistia (25:17); Tyre (26:6); Sidon (28:22, 23); Egypt (29:6, 9, 16; 30:8, 19, 25, 26; 32:15); Edom/Seir (35:4, 9, 12, 15); Gog of Magog (39:6). For discussion, see Evans, "Ezekiel's Recognition Formulae," 148–50.

108. Cf. the clear recognition of this in Daniel's prayer, Dan 9:4–19.

109. On which, see further Block, "Bearing the Name of the LORD," 61–72; Block, "No Other Gods" 237–71.

sake of his name, YHWH had to act: He is YHWH; he has spoken; he will act (in accord with his word). He had kept his word in destroying Israel; now he must keep it in restoring them (cf. Lev 26:40–45; Deut 4:30–31; 30:1–10).

The judgment of Israel had declared to the nations one side of YHWH's great and holy name; persistent infidelity must and would be punished. However, this was only one side of his character, as evidenced by YHWH's own self-definition in Exodus 34:6–7:

יְהוָה יְהוָה אֵל רַחוּם וְחַנּוּן	YHWH, YHWH, a God compassionate and gracious,
אֶרֶךְ אַפַּיִם וְרַב־חֶסֶד וֶאֱמֶת	slow to anger, and abounding in steadfast love and faithfulness,
נֹצֵר חֶסֶד לָאֲלָפִים	who keeps steadfast love for a thousand generations,
נֹשֵׂא עָוֹן וָפֶשַׁע וְחַטָּאָה	who forgives iniquity and transgression and sin,
וְנַקֵּה לֹא יְנַקֶּה	yet by no means clears the guilty,
פֹּקֵד עֲוֹן אָבוֹת עַל־בָּנִים	but visits the iniquity of parents upon children
וְעַל־בְּנֵי בָנִים	and the children's children,
עַל־שִׁלֵּשִׁים וְעַל־רִבֵּעִים	to the third and the fourth generation.

Although we hear echoes of this creedal-like statement throughout the Hebrew Bible,[110] we find few in Ezekiel,[111] presumably because Israel's

---

110. E.g., Num 14:18; Joel 2:13; Jonah 4:2; Mic 7:18–20; Pss 51:3(1); 86:5, 15; 103:8[7]; 108:5(4); 145:8; Neh 9:17.

111. The roots חנן, and חסד never occur; רחם is found only in 39:25. אף in the sense of "anger" is a key word in the book, occurring thirteen times (5:13, 15; 7:3, 8; 13:13; 20:8, 21; 22:20; 25:14; 35:11; 38:18; 43:8), but never with אֶרֶךְ meaning "slow to anger"; on the contrary, in the first twenty-four chapters YHWH's patience with Israel has run out. נָשָׂא + designations for sin occur in Ezekiel, but the meaning of the idiom shifts from "to forgive" (iniquity, rebellion, and sin in Exod 34:7) to "to bear, to suffer for" (with עָוֹן, 4:4–6; 14:10; 44:10, 12; with חֵטְא, 23:49). נָשָׂא does not occur in Ezekiel with פֶּשַׁע, "transgression, revolt against a higher authority," but this word occurs repeatedly in the book (2:3; 14:11; 18:22, 28, 30, 31; 20:38; 21:29[24]; 33:10, 12; 37:23; 39:24). אֱמֶת, "truth, fidelity," occurs twice (18:8, 9), but it is used of human rather than divine integrity. However, this does not mean the concept is missing. When YHWH declares "I am YHWH; I have spoken; and I will act" (אֲנִי יְהוָה דִּבַּרְתִּי וְעָשִׂיתִי, 17:24; 22:14; 24:14; 36:36; 37:14), or "I am YHWH; I have spoken" (אֲנִי יְהוָה דִּבַּרְתִּי, 5:15, 17; 17:21; 26:14; 30:12; 34:24; 37:14), or simply "I have spoken" (אֲנִי דִבַּרְתִּי, 23:34; 26:5; 28:10; 39:5; cf. 36:5; 39:8), the reference is primarily to the ancient covenant promises, which YHWH must and will keep. Contra Schwartz ("The Ultimate Aim of Israel's Restoration," 305–6), who asserts that Ezekiel does not "expect YHWH to act out of faithfulness to his covenant or promise," and "For Ezekiel, YHWH's remembrance of this covenant is thus not a way of keeping his word but a way of breaking his word—because his people broke theirs (16:59–62)." Even Greenberg, who insists that for Ezekiel the change of human nature was not a gracious act, declared, "The old order had failed, but God was faithful to his covenant and would restore Israel, and restore it permanently" (*Ezekiel 21–37*, 737).

The God Ezekiel Wants Us to Meet

history had reached a critical state and the doom of the city had been irrevocably decreed. However, the Judaeans' exile raised questions concerning the character of YHWH: Where is his compassion? His mercy? His fidelity? His forgiveness? These will all be demonstrated in the restoration, which renewed Israel will recognize entirely as an act of grace and divorced from any merit. Unlike the picture anticipated in Leviticus 26:40–41, Deuteronomy 4:29–31, and 30:1–5, in Ezekiel YHWH does not wait for a positive response from his people. The restoration does indeed proceed on his terms and by his initiative,[112] but it is a gracious divine act from start to finish.

Finally, what about Schwartz' contention that the restoration does not actually have the interests of the Israelites in mind, that for YHWH's people "this is anything but a relief"? Chapter 34 offers a clear answer. Whereas Schwartz interprets God's actions here as arrogating "to himself the care of the sheep,"[113] the portrayal of YHWH is fundamentally pastoral, and his actions involving his people are all in their interest. In contrast to their human rulers, who fleece and abuse the people, YHWH not only claims them as his flock (צֹאנִי),[114] but also performs a series of actions to secure their well-being: he rescues them from the mouths of their captors (vv. 10, 12),[115] searches for them and inspects them (vv. 11–12, 16a), gathers them from the lands where they have been scattered (vv. 13, 16), feeds them on the mountains of Israel in lush pasture (vv. 13b–15a), provides rest for them (v. 15b), tends to the maimed and sick (v. 16a), protects them from "bullies" in their midst (vv. 16b, 17–19, 20–22), provides a human leader who will tend them himself and be their (under-)shepherd (vv. 23–24), commits himself to them to be their God (vv. 24a, 30–31), makes a covenant of peace with them (v. 25a), provides security against outside threats (vv. 25b, 28), makes the countryside around his hill a blessing, thereby guaranteeing fertility of the land (vv. 26–27a, 29), and commits to being personally present among them (v. 30). Only faulty vision prevents us from seeing this as a positive picture.

---

112. See Joyce, "Ezekiel and Moral Transformation," 139–58.

113. Schwartz, "The Ultimate Aim of Israel's Restoration," 312.

114. Ezek 34:6, 8, 10, 11, 12, 15, 17, 19, 22, 31.

115. The verb הִצִּיל is frequently used of YHWH's rescue of Israel from the Egyptians (Exod 3:8; 5:23; 6:6; 18:8, 9, 10; Judg 6:9; 1 Sam 10:18; etc.). The notion of rescuing from the mouth of a captor occurs elsewhere only in 1 Sam 17:35 (David would rescue lambs from the mouths of bears and lions) and Amos 3:12. Ezekiel's statement may have been inspired by the latter: "As the shepherd rescues from the mouth of the lion two legs, or a piece of an ear, so shall the people of Israel who live in Samaria be rescued, with the corner of a couch and part of a bed" (*NRSV*).

By the River Chebar

Conclusion

I return to the question I asked at the outset: "Who is this God Ezekiel wants us to meet?" The answers offered by the book that bears his name are multi-dimensional. On the one hand, he is sovereign over the nations, a sovereignty that will be challenged by neither his people's indiscretions nor the gods and armies of enemy nations. The visions in chapters 1, 8–11, and 41–43 declare that he leaves and returns to Jerusalem by his own free will and in his own time; no foreign king drags him off, and he waits for no one to bring him back. But he is also sovereign over his own people. The scroll the prophet swallows (2:8—3:3) symbolizes his decree to put an end to his city, and to bring in Nebuchadnezzar to punish his people for their covenantal infidelity. This judgment is driven by a fury that will have traumatized the people of Judah and certainly troubles modern readers.

But the God Ezekiel wants us to meet is complex. His fury at human rebellion is balanced by grace. If we define "divine grace" as "the free and unmerited favour of God as manifested in the salvation of sinners and the bestowing of blessings,"[116] that is precisely what we find in this book. This definition is probably more at home in Christian conversation than among our Jewish colleagues, but since the word "grace" is commonly used by scholars in discussions of the God Ezekiel serves, it seems appropriate to use it in this context. We should not be reductionistic when we speak of the motivation underlying YHWH's restoration of Israel as Ezekiel understood it. To be sure, he will do so to vindicate his name, but he will also do so to redeem his people, that is, to effect a new exodus. However, this time he will not only liberate his people from the hands of a foreign oppressor (36:24), but he will also "deliver" (הוֹשִׁיעַ) them from all their "uncleanness" (טֻמְאוֹת, 36:29) and from all their "defections by which they have sinned."[117] The prophet wants his hearers (and readers) to meet this God, who suspends the rule of justice and restores his people despite their undeservedness. This is a working definition of grace.

---

116. *Compact Edition of the Oxford English Dictionary*, 1:326.

117. Reading מכל משובתיכם, literally "from all their turnings," in place of MT's מכל מושבתיהם, "from all their settlements," with support from LXX (ἀνομιῶν) and Sym (ἀσεβειῶν). The masculine form of the latter is attested in 34:13, but this sense seems out of place here. Apparently MT represents a metathetical error involving שׁ and ו. The noun מְשׁוּבָה occurs frequently in Jeremiah (2:19; 3:6, 8, 11, 12, 22; 5:6; 8:5; 14:7), as well as in Hos 11:7; 14:5; Prov 1:32. Ezekiel's usage reflects Jeremianic influence. Even if one prefers MT (*NJPSV*; Greenberg, *Ezekiel 21–37*, 752, 756), the deliverance is from a context involving their own, rather than someone else's sin.

4

Divine Abandonment

Ezekiel's Adaptation of an Ancient Near Eastern Motif[1]

INTRODUCTION

SCHOLARS HAVE LONG RECOGNIZED the centrality of the "travels" of the glory of YHWH in the prophecy of Ezekiel. The prophet himself receives a harbinger of things to come in the opening vision, when the heavenly chariot bearing the divine glory suddenly appears to him by the Chebar Canal in Babylon (1:1–28). As the initial element in a lengthy and complex call narrative, the overwhelming magnificence of the glory of YHWH represents the first in a series of volleys by which YHWH seeks to break down Ezekiel's resistance to the call to prophetic ministry.[2] However, as Ezekiel will discover, the vision also introduces him to one of the fundamental motifs in his prophetic proclamation: the movements of the glory of YHWH. In fact, visions of the divine *kābôd* (כָּבוֹד) will appear twice more in the prophet's ministry. Fourteen months after the inaugural vision Ezekiel observes in visionary form the glory of YHWH move by stages out of the temple and then disappear over the horizon east of Jerusalem

---

1. This essay was originally published in *Perspectives on Ezekiel: Theology and Anthropology*, edited by Margaret S. Odell and John T. Strong, 15–42. SBL Symposium Series 9. Atlanta: Scholars Press, 2000.

2. See my comments in *Ezekiel Chapters 1–24*, 11–12 and, *passim*.

(8:1—11:25).³ Almost two decades later⁴ the vision returns. After being taken on a tour of the temple, Ezekiel sees the *kābôd* of YHWH (כְּבוֹד־יְהוָה) returning from the east, passing through the east gate, and entering the temple.

Ezekiel was not the only prophet to speak of a deity abandoning his subjects or his cult city. In a satirical attack on the impotence of Babylon's gods, Isaiah declares,

> Bel bows down, Nebo stoops,
> their idols are on beasts and cattle;
> these things you carry are loaded
> as burdens on weary beasts.
> They stoop, they bow down together;
> they cannot save the burden,
> but themselves go into captivity. (Isa 46:1–2 *NRSV*)

In Jer 48:7, Ezekiel's contemporary offers a similar description of the patron deity of the Moabites: "Chemosh shall go out into exile, with his priests and his attendants." The fate of Milkom, the divine patron of the Ammonites, is described in identical terms in 49:3.⁵

Nor was Ezekiel the first in Israel to apply the motif of abandonment to YHWH. The general absence of YHWH is assumed in the oft-repeated question, "Where is your/their God?"⁶ But in tracing the history of this motif we may recognize five specific dimensions of YHWH's abandonment contemplated in the Old Testament: (1) YHWH's absence from an individual, devotee or otherwise;⁷ (2) YHWH's absence from his people,

---

3. The inaugural vision is dated the fifth day of the fourth month of the fifth year of Jehoiachin's exile (1:1–2 [=July 31, 593 BCE]); the first temple vision is dated the fifth day of the sixth month of the sixth year of the exile (8:1 [= September 18, 592 BCE]).

4. According to 40:1 the concluding vision occurred on the tenth day of the first month of the twentieth year of the exile (=April 28, 573 BCE).

5. Arguing that מַלְכָּם, "their king," should be repointed מִלְכֹּם, "Milkom," Emil Puech finds a related declaration in Amos 1:15 ("Milkom," 177–25).

6. Micah 7:10; Joel 2:17; Pss 42:4, 11[3, 10]; 79:10; 115:2.

7. This notion is expressed directly with the verbs עָזַב, "to leave, abandon" (2 Chr 12:5; 75:2; Pss 9:11[10]; 22:2[1]; 27:9 [//הִסְתִּיר פָּנָיו//נָטַשׁ]; 37:25, 28; 119:8; cf. Gen 28:15. where YHWH promises Jacob not to abandon him until he returns to the land of Canaan, and Isa 41:17, where YHWH promises not to forsake the afflicted and needy), and נָטַשׁ, "to give one up" (Ps 27:9 [//עָזַב//הִסְתִּיר פָּנָיו]). The sense is different in Ezek 29:5 and 32:4, where YHWH threatens to abandon his adversary Pharaoh in the desert, and in paraphrastic expressions like הִסְתִּיר פָּנָיו, "to hide his face" (Ps 13:2[1]; //שָׁכַח, "to forget"]; 22:25[24]; 27:9; 30:8[7]; 69:18[17]; 88:15[14] //זָנַח, "to reject"; 102:3[2]; 143:7; Job 13:24; 34:29). In Ps 10:11 the psalmist complains that

the nation of Israel;[8] (3) YHWH's absence from the land of Israel;[9] (4) YHWH's absence from Jerusalem/Zion;[10] (5) YHWH's absence from his sanctuary.[11] The present study is not concerned with the first.

The references cited in the preceding notes demonstrate that the possibility of YHWH's absence from his people, land, and sanctuary was widely recognized in the Old Testament. However, it is remarkable that although the covenant curses list a host of disastrous consequences for persistent rebellion against YHWH, neither version hints that this has ever occurred. Leviticus 26 warns that YHWH will set his face against,[12] will act with hostility toward,[13] and will send a host of agents of destruction against Israel; that his soul will loathe them;[14] and that he will expel them from the land. But there is no mention of abandoning them.[15] On the contrary, YHWH affirms that he will not reject (מָאַס) or loathe (גָּעַל) them to destroy them. Similarly Deuteronomy 28, which emphasizes even more strongly YHWH's direct (even if destructive) involvement in the na-

---

YHWH has hidden his face (//הִסְתִּיר פָּנָיו), whereas in 51:11[9] he pleads that he would hides his face from his sins. In Ps 10:1 the psalmist wonders why YHWH "stands far away" (תַּעֲמֹד בְּרָחוֹק) and closes his eyes (תַּעְלִים) to his troubles (cf. Lam 3:56, "you close your ears [תַּעְלֵם אָזְנְךָ]). Cf. also Jer 23:23, which contemplates YHWH's being distant (מֵרָחֹק) from a person. For a full study of the motif in the Old Testament, see Balentine, *The Hidden God*.

8. This notion is expressed similarly with the verbs עָזַב, "to leave, abandon" (Deut 31:6, 17 [//הִסְתִּיר פָּנִים]; Josh 1:5; 1 Kgs 6:13; 8:57 [//נָטַשׁ]; Lam 5:20; Ezra 9:9; Neh 9:28; 2 Chr 24:20; Ps 94:14 [//נָטַשׁ], נָטַשׁ, "to give up" (Judg 6:15; 1 Sam 12:22; 1 Kgs 8:57 [//עָזַב]; 2 Kgs 21:14; Isa 2:6; Jer 7:29 [//מָאַס]; 23:33, 39; Ps 94:14 [//עָזַב]), as well as נוה hiphil, "to leave someone somewhere" (Jer 14:9), and with הִסְתִּיר פָּנִים, "to hide his face" (Deut 31:17–18 [//עָזַב]; 32:20; Ps 44:25[24] [//שָׁכַח]; Isa 8:17; 54:8; 59:2 [//הִבְדִּיל, "to divide, separate"]; 64:6[7]; Ezek 39:23, 24, 29; Mic 3:4. Psalm 104:29 contemplates YHWH's hiding his face from animals, removing their breath [רוּחַ] so they die).

9. Expressed directly with the verb עָזַב, "to leave, abandon." This notion is extremely rare, being explicitly declared only in Ezek 8:12 and 9:9. However, the geographic sense is not far from Jeremiah's mind when he asks in 14:8, "Why are you like a stranger (גֵּר) in the land, or like a traveler (אֹרֵחַ) who has pitched his tent for the night?" Nevertheless, verse 9 reflects the more common emphasis: "Yet you, O YHWH, are in the midst of us, and we are called by your name; do not abandon us!"

10. This notion is also expressed directly with the verb עָזַב, "to leave, abandon," (Isa 49:14 [//שָׁכַח]; 54:7), and paraphrastically with הִסְתִּיר פָּנִים, "to hide his face" (Jer 33:5).

11. This notion is expressed directly with the verbs עָזַב, "to leave, abandon" (Jer 12:7 //נָטַשׁ), and נָטַשׁ, "to give up" (Jer 12:7 [//עָזַב]; Ps 78:60 [his מִשְׁכָּן at Shiloh]).

12. V. 17, וְנָתַתִּי פָנַי בָּכֶם.

13. V. 24, וְהָלַכְתִּי אַף־אֲנִי עִמָּכֶם. Cf. vv. 28, 41.

14. V. 30, וְגָעֲלָה נַפְשִׁי אֶתְכֶם.

15. The verb עָזַב does indeed occur, but only of Israel leaving the land. Cf. v. 43.

tion's fate from the onset of the curses to the people's expulsion to foreign lands, to their return from exile.

Although Ezekiel bases so many of his pronouncements of judgment upon the covenant curses, remarkably it falls to him to develop most fully the motif of YHWH's abandonment of land and people, which does not even appear in those curses. But perhaps this should not be so surprising. The prophet was himself an exile in the land where traditions of divine abandonment were common. Indeed accounts of divinities abandoning their cities and lands span more than two millennia and occur in a variety of literary genres, including narratives that preserve early Israelite traditions about the ark.[16] Whether or not Ezekiel's association of the fall of Jerusalem with YHWH's departure from his temple and his land was inspired by Mesopotamian traditions, an examination of the latter certainly domesticates his portrayal of Judah's last days, particularly his radically theocentric interpretation of the nation's fall. The remainder of this paper will seek to shed light on Ezekiel's prophecies by interpreting them within the religious and literary culture from which they emerged. To achieve this goal we shall compare a dozen ancient Near Eastern literary accounts of divine abandonment, paying particular attention to the causes and effects of divine absence and the prospects for a return of the deity to his land or cult center. We shall conclude by comparing our findings with Ezekiel's portrayal of YHWH's abandonment of the temple in Jerusalem.[17]

ANCIENT NEAR EASTERN ACCOUNTS OF DIVINE ABANDONMENT

As in Israel, ancient Near Easterners in general feared the prospect of divine abandonment, whether from the individual, the clan, or the state. Our concern is with the departure of titular deities from their cities and/or states. The extra-biblical accounts available to us may be divided into three groups: Sumerian accounts, second-millennium BCE Akkadian accounts, and first-millennium Akkadian accounts.[18] We shall deal with each in turn.

---

16. For a discussion of the ark tradition, see Miller and Roberts, *The Hand of the Lord*.

17. This essay expands and modifies my presentation of the issue in chapter 6 of *Gods of the Nations*, 125–61. Compare the work of Bodi, *Ezekiel and the Poem of Erra*, 183–218.

18. To date no Northwest Semitic texts describing the departure of a deity from his/her land or city with such detail has been discovered. The most promising text is

Sumerian Accounts of Divine Abandonment

Time and space constraints preclude a detailed discussion of the Sumerian literature, but we may summarize the perspectives reflected in two types of texts represented by "The Curse of Agade" and the Sumerian lament literature. In the former, Inanna abandons her cult shrine in Agade, apparently at the command of Enlil because of the crimes of Naram-Sin (2254–2218 BCE) in sacking Nippur, and turns on her own subjects. The text is silent on any hope for her return, presumably because of the Nuppurian interests of the author.[19] A century and a half later, Ur and the surrounding Sumerian cities suffered a similar fate as Agade, a tragedy that is commemorated in a series of poetic laments.[20] Sumerian account of gods abandoning their cities most commonly occur in literary texts widely acknowledged as laments, composed "as liturgical accompaniments to the royal rebuilding of destroyed temples, which involved the inevitable razing of their remains—a potential sacrilege against their gods."[21] The common denominator in all these laments is the portrayal of the disastrous effect the departure of the titular deity has on a city. Several laments anticipate the god's return (Sumer and Ur Lament, Uruk Lament, and Nippur Lament), the divine selection of a ruler (Uruk Lament, Nippur Lament), and the return of peace and prosperity (Nippur Lament).

---

the ninth-century BCE stele inscription of Mesha, a Moabite king, commemorating his victory over the Israelites. For English translations of the text, see *ANET*, 320–21, and Gibson, *Hebrew and Moabite Inscriptions*, 1:71–83. Some such event may be implied in the comment, "Omri, King of Israel, had oppressed Moab many days, for Chemosh was angry with his land" (lines 4–5). The statement creates the impression that the deity had been absent during the Omride occupation, but had now returned. In any case, the text provides no hint concerning the cause of Chemosh's anger.

19. The most detailed study of the text is provided by J. S. Cooper, *The Curse of Agade*. For another translation, see Kramer, "Curse of Agade," 646.

20. On "The Nippur Lament," see Kramer, "Lamentations," 89–93; Kramer, "Lamentation," 1–26. For "The Uruk Lament," see Green, "The Uruk Lament," 253–79. For "The Eridu Lament" see Green, "The Eridu Lament," 127–67. For "The Lament over the Destruction of Ur," see Kramer, *Lamentation*; for a more recent translation, see J. Klein, "Lamentation," 535–39. All these laments seem to have been inspired by "The Lamentation over the Destruction of Sumer and Ur." Piotr Michalowski offers the most recent translation and commentary on the text (*Lamentation*, 4–8). For an earlier translation, see Kramer, *ANET*, 611–19.

21. Thus Hallo, *Origins*, 224–25.

By the River Chebar

Akkadian Accounts of Divine Abandonment

In their radical theological interpretation of historical events, Amorites, Babylonians, and Assyrians were all heirs of the Sumerians. Allusions and explicit references to the abandonment of their shrines by titular deities are ubiquitous in the Akkadian texts of these cultures. The texts selected for the following discussion represent a variety of times, contexts, and literary genres.

A Prophetic Letter from Mari

A precursor of more complex texts to follow may be found in the Mari correspondence from the time of Zimri-Lim (eighteenth century BCE), specifically *ARM* X No. 50. This tablet contains a letter of a prominent woman of the court in which she communicates a prophetic dream she had as follows:

> Say to my lord: Thus Addu-duri, your maid-servant. Since the fall of your father's house I have never had such a dream. My earlier omens were like this. In my dream I entered the temple of Belet-ekalim. Belet-ekalim was not there, and the statues standing in front of her were not [there]. When I saw this I began to weep. This was the dream of the first watch of the night. [In another dream] I saw Dada, the priest of Ištar-pišrā standing at the temple door of Belet-ekalim. A hostile voice kept calling out in the following manner: "Come back, Dagan! Come back, Dagan!" This is what it called.[22]

With respect to the issues that concern us in this paper, the text is silent on the causes (divine or human) and effects of Dagan's absence, and says nothing about the prospects for his return.

The Tukulti-Ninurta Epic (Middle Assyrian)

The Tukulti-Ninurta Epic is a lengthy historiographic "victory song" composed to celebrate the victory of Tukulti-Ninurta I of Assyria (1244–1208

---

22. This is an adaptation of the translation provided by Bodi, *Ezekiel and the Poem of Erra*, 207. For other translations, see those of Moran (*ANET*, 631) and Schmökel (*Near Eastern Texts*, 136–37). Schmökel compares the dream account with Ezek 8–11. For the transliterated full text, see Dossin, *Divination en Mésopotamie*, 77–86. Cf. also Friedrich Ellermeier, *Prophetie in Mari*, 64–66.

BCE) over the Kassite king Kaštiliaš IV (1242–1235 BCE).[23] After opening with a laudatory introduction of the protagonist (now largely unintelligible), the text presents the Kassite king and a theological explanation for his defeat. The segment of text of interest to us, I:32'–46', reads as follows:

32' [The gods were angry at] the treachery/ies of the king of the Kassites (committed) by the stand[ard *of Šamaš*.]
33' Against the oath-breaker, Kaštiliaš, the gods of heave[n (and) earth *decided to send* punishment.]
34' They developed wrath against the king, the land, and the peopl[e.]
35' With the forceful/obstinate one, the shepherd over them, they were angry and [ ]
36' The Enlilship of the lord of all the lands became distressed, so that Nippu[r he *cursed/abandoned*,]
37' So that the habitation of Dur-Kurigalzu he *no longer* approaches...[.]
38' Marduk abandoned his august sanctuary, the city. [.]
39' He cursed the city of his love, Kar-[.]
40' Sin left Ur, [his] cult center [.]
41' With Sippar and Larsa, Šamaš *became wroth* [.]
42' Ea [abandoned] Eridu, the house of wisdom. [.]
43' Ištaran became angry w[ith Der.]
44' Anunitu *no longer* approaches Agade [.]
45' The mistress [of] Uruk gave up [*her city*.]
46' The gods were extremely angry and [.][24]

This account differs from the Sumerian laments in several important respects. First, it attributes the departures of the deities to human causes. The king of the Kassites is accused of treachery (*ṣaliptu*, line 32'), breaking his oath with the gods (*etiq mamīti*, line 33'),[25] and being obstinate (*parriku*, line 35'). Second, it highlights the gods' emotional response, with expressions like "wrath" (*rašû*, line 34'), "anger" (*sabsu*, lines 35', 43'), "distress" (*ašāšu*, line 36'), and "extreme anger" (*kamālu*, line 46'). Third, Marduk's abandonment of his sanctuary is associated with a curse (*arāru*) that he invokes on his beloved city (lines 39–40). Fourth, the role of the deities

---

23. The most thorough study of the text is provided by Machinist, "Epic of Tukulti-Ninurta I." See also Machinist, "Literature as Politics," 455–82. For a more recent translation of the text, see Foster, *Before the Muses* 298–317; for further bibliography, see 317; Foster, *From Distant Days*, 178–96.

24. Thus Machinist, "The Epic of Tukulti-Ninurta I," 62–65; cf. Foster, *Before the Muses*, 300–301.

25. Cf. YHWH's accusation against Zedekiah in Ezek 17:19–20.

changes. According to the Sumerian laments the collapse of the Ur III period occurred because the high god had decreed that the kingship that had been granted to Ur be transferred to another state, and the destruction of the rest of the cities of Sumer and Akkad was a part of this decree. The gods of the respective cities tried to intervene on behalf of their shrines, but to no avail. Reluctantly and with great lamentation they abandoned their shrines. In this epic, fury over the crimes of Kaštiliaš has spread to all the gods of Sumer and Akkad. Far from defending their shrines, the gods take the side of the invader and unleash all the forces of destruction upon their respective cities.[26]

The differences in the roles of the titular deities is undoubtedly due to the changes in points of view of the authors of the respective texts.[27] The Sumerian laments were composed by victims of the disaster—poets of Ur and the other cities trying to give a theological explanation for the political and economic collapse of the Ur III civilization. Composed to laud the accomplishments and character of Tukulti-Ninurta I, the epic reflects the perspective of the conquerors. The gods have abandoned their subjects and transferred their support to the invader.

The Marduk Prophecy (Middle Babylonian)

The "Marduk Prophecy," composed with reference to the reign of Nebuchadnezzar I of Babylon (1125–1104 BCE), represents the only extant autobiography by a deity in cuneiform sources.[28] In this purportedly divine speech Marduk reminds his hearers of the three occasions in which he had left his city, traveling successively to Hatti,[29] Assyria, and Elam. These departures appear to correspond to the conquests of Babylon by

---

26. Machinist, "The Epic of Tukulti-Ninurta I," 118–22; see also 349–65 for Machinist's commentary.

27. So also Machinist, "The Epic of Tukulti-Ninurta I," 153–54.

28. So also Borger, "Der Gott Marduk," 21. Borger provides a full transcription, translation, and commentary on the text. For an English translation, see Appendix A, below. For other translations and discussions of the text, see Longman, *Fictional Akkadian Autobiography*, 132–42, 233–35; Longman, *COS*, 480–82; Foster, *Before the Muses*, 388–91; Neujahr, *Predicting the Past in the Ancient Near East:* 27–41. A translation of the text is provided in Excursus A, below, 100–4.

29. The return of the cult statue and reconstruction of Esagila from Hatti is commemorated in an autobiographical account by the Kassite king Agum-Kakrime (mid-fifteenth century BCE). See Foster, *Before the Muses*, 360–64, for translation and bibliography.

Divine Abandonment

Mursili I (1620–1590 BCE), Tukulti-Ninurta I, and Kudur-Naḫḫunte (ca. 1160 BCE). On the human plane, the events in question apparently involve the successive forceful entrances of these enemies into the temple of Marduk, and the dragging off of his statue. The composition itself glorifies the achievements of Nebuchadnezzar in reconstructing the Ekursagila in Babylon and his restoration of Marduk's image to its proper place.

For our purposes, the significance of Marduk's prophetic speech lies in its portrayal of divine involvement in the series of catastrophes that struck Babylon. The spoliations of Marduk's image are presented as journeys undertaken by Marduk of his own volition. In each instance he continued to function as the divine patron of the Babylonians, serving as ambassador in the foreign land, promoting the interests of his city by establishing transportation connections between his place of sojourn and his home city.

The Elamite exile is described most fully. Marduk portrays himself as having ordered the termination of the temple cultus and the expulsion of the gods of the herds and grain. Like the Sumerian laments, this text offers no hints of human causation. Nevertheless, the effects of the departure of the divine patron from his city are catastrophic, and graphically described (II:1–11). A change in the fortunes of the city follows, however, when the disposition of the deity changes. When Marduk had fulfilled his days in exile, he yearned for his city and recalled all the goddesses. The text does not speak specifically of the god's appointment of a new king (Nebuchadnezzar I), but this is implied in the "prophetic" portion (II:19–32). With the predicted arrival of the new ruler a dramatic transformation within the city will occur, and prosperity, peace, and security return.

The Seed of Kingship (Middle Babylonian)

A fragmentary "historiographic" bilingual (Sumerian/Akkadian) text, K 4874, derives from the same general period and deals with the same spoliation of the statue of Marduk by the Elamites.[30] Unlike the "Marduk Prophecy," this text explicitly attributes the anger of the gods to human evil, as the following excerpt demonstrates:

> At that time, in the reign of a previous king, conditions changed.
> Good departed and evil prevailed.

---

30. For transliteration, translation, and commentary of the text, see Lambert, "Enmeduranki and Related Matters," 128–31. Compare the more recent translation by Foster in *Before the Muses*, 376–80, and *From Distant Days*, 797–201.

> The lord became angry and furious;
> He gave the command and the gods of the land abandoned it
> [...]
> The guardians of peace (*ra-bi-[ṣu šul-me]*) became furious,
> and went up to the dome of heaven.
> The spirit of justice stood aside,
> ..., who guards living beings, prostrated the peoples.
> They all became like those who have no god.
> Evil demons filled the land, the namtar-demon [...] ...
> They penetrated the cult centers,
> The land diminished, its fortunes changed.[31]

The text goes on to describe the awesome intensity of Marduk's fury. Unfortunately the end is too mutilated to determine if it originally recounted the return of the divine patron.

The Poem of Erra and Ishum (Neo-Babylonian)

Although the circumstances are extraordinary, the composition of "Erra and Ishum" offers one of the fullest portrayals of divine abandonment of any ancient Near Eastern document.[32] The date of this text is disputed. Since the poem reflects the historical events surrounding the decline of Babylon and refers to the Sutu on several occasions,[33] the Sutu invasion around 1050 BCE provides a firm *terminus a quo*. Since the poem envisions the restoration of Babylonian power, it must have been composed prior to the Assyrians' ascent to supreme political power in Mesopotamia in mid-eighth century BCE.[34]

In stark contrast to the independence of Marduk depicted in the "Marduk Prophecy," this composition portrays the divine patron of

---

31. K 4874, lines 15–22, adapted from Lambert, "Enmeduranki and Related Matters," 130.

32. For the transliterated text, see Cagni, *Das Erra-Epos, Keilschrifttext*; for English translation and commentary, see Cagni, *The Poem of Erra*. See also Foster, *Before the Muses*, 880–911; Foster, *From Distant Days*, 132–63; Dalley, *Myths from Mesopotamia*, 282–315; Dalley, *COS*, 404–16. For a discussion of the portrayal of divine abandonment in this text and its relation to Ezekiel, see Bodi, *Ezekiel and the Poem of Erra*, 191–97.

33. See "Erra and Ishum" IV:54, 69, 133; V:27.

34. Wolfram von Soden proposes a precise date of composition between the end of 765 BCE and the beginning of 763 BCE ("Entemenanki," 255–56). For further discussion and bibliography on the date, see Bodi, *Ezekiel and the Poem of Erra*, 54–56.

Divine Abandonment

Babylon as an apparently weak-willed, if not senile personality.[35] He seems unaware of the state of his domain and powerless before Erra. It is the latter who must ignite Marduk's anger over his people and incite him to abdicate his throne and leave the city to Erra's destructive fury.

"The Poem of Erra and Ishum" deliberately and explicitly presents the rebellion of the inhabitants of Babylon as the catalyst for all these divine schemes. Hear Erra's provocative report in I:120–29:

> All the (other) gods are afraid of battle,
> So that the black-headed people despise (them).
> But I, because they no longer fear my name,
> And since prince Marduk has neglected his word
> and does as he pleases,
> I shall make prince Marduk angry,
> and I shall summon him from his dwelling,
> and I shall overwhelm his people."
> Warrior Erra set his face toward Shuanna,
> city of the king of the gods.
> He entered Esagila, palace of heaven and earth,
> and stood in front of him (Marduk),
> He made his voice heard and spoke to the king of the gods,
> "Why does the finery, your lordship's adornment
> which is full of splendor like the stars of heaven, grow dirty?
> The crown of your lordship which made Ehalanki shine like E-temen-anki—
> its surface is tarnished."[36]

Marduk's initial response is to recall how, many years ago, he had become angry (the cause is not indicated), risen from his seat, and contrived the deluge. His suspension of rule had precipitated the upsetting of the entire natural order and produced total chaos on earth. Even the statue of Marduk was damaged. But Marduk had it repaired in a way that could never be duplicated. In fact, the human and material resources employed in the previous refurbishing have all been sent down to the Apsu. But now the image had been sullied once again. However, the only way to retrieve the needed resources from the Apsu is for Marduk to get them himself. Erra promises to watch over the world order while he is away (I:140–93).

Marduk accedes to Erra's plan. Unfortunately, however, the description of his departure is poorly preserved. But sufficient text remains to link

---

35. Cf. the discussion by Cagni, *The Poem of Erra*, 19, following Landsberger, "Akkadische-Hebräische Wortgleichungen," 198. For a contrary opinion, see Bodi, *Ezekiel and the Poem of Erra*, 793–94.

36. As translated by Dalley, COS, 407.

the ensuing cosmic disturbance predicted by the king of the gods with his abandonment of his throne:

> He rose up from his inaccessible dwelling
> and set his face towards the dwelling of the Anunnaki.
> He entered his . . . and st[ood before them,]
> [Discarded] his radi[ance] and let his rays fall [. . .]
> [Because(?)] he had set his face towards another place
> and no longer [. . .] the earth,
> [The winds(?)] rose up,
> and bright day was turned into darkness.[37]

Tablets II–IV go on to expound in great detail the havoc that Erra and his evil forces wreak on Babylon in Marduk's absence. In Tablet V Erra's fury is finally placated through the mediation of his herald Ishum. He resolves to restore the prosperity of Akkad and to reprovision Babylon and Esagila. Although Erra orders Ishum to restore to their temples all the gods who had fled their shrines (V:31), the absence of any reference to the return of Marduk and the restoration of the city without him are striking.

Esarhaddon's Rebuilding of Babylon (Neo-Assyrian)

The description of the reconstruction of Babylon by Esarhaddon (680–669 BCE) provides the most helpful account for our discussion, not only because it was composed within one century of Ezekiel's ministry, but also because it offers the most complete extra-biblical account of the cycle of divine abandonment and return. The story, preserved in several different versions,[38] must be interpreted against the background of the fall of the city and the demolition of Esagila in 689 BCE by Esarhaddon's predecessor, Sennacherib. Like the "Marduk Prophecy" and "the Poem of Erra and Ishum," Esarhaddon's account is generally interpreted as an "apologia," intended to gain the favor of the Babylonians[39] by emphasizing that this Assyrian ruler had been specially chosen by Marduk, the patron deity of Babylon, to govern his city and to restore its prosperity.

---

37. "Erra and Ishum" II 4:1–10, as translated by Dalley, *COS*, 408.

38. These have been edited, transliterated, and translated by Borger, *Die Inschriften Asarhaddons*, 10–29, episodes 1–41. For a valuable, though older English translation, see Luckenbill, *Ancient Records*, 2.242–47, §§640–51. For a helpful discussion of segments of the text, see Cogan, *Imperialism and Religion*, 12–13. See also Brinkman, "Through a Glass Darkly," 35–42.

39. Cf. Cogan, *Imperialism and Religion*, 72; also Tadmor, "Autobiographical Apology," 36–57.

Divine Abandonment

The Reasons for Marduk's Departure from Babylon

Esarhaddon's account attributes Marduk's abandonment of Babylon to several factors. At the cosmic level, during the reign of the previous king "evil forces" (*idâti lemnêti*^{meš}); appeared in Sumer and Akkad (2 A:18–21). This malaise was reflected at the human level by a series of offenses. Text A speaks of moral crimes like deceit and falsehood; Texts B and G of a "murderous trap" (*naḫ-ba-lu šag-ga-šu*) expressed by the exploitation of the weak and their deliverance into the hands of the mighty, oppression and bribery, thievery, sons publicly cursing their fathers, and insubordination on the part of male and female servants (3 G:4–16; B:2). Equally reprehensible were the cultic misdemeanors. Not only were taboo foods introduced, but the regular offerings were also suspended, and conspiracies plotted (against the cult?). Texts A and D speak of sacrilegious treatment of Esagila, Marduk's shrine. Out of bounds for lay persons, the palace of the god was invaded and its treasures stolen and squandered off to Elam as the price for assistance against Assyria (4 A:28–33). The local divinities also seemed to be involved in the general disintegration as gods and goddesses abandoned their normal functions (3 B:25–27). This degenerate state of affairs in Babylon infuriated Marduk.[40] In response "He plotted evil (*ik-ta-pu-ud lemuttim*), determining to level the land and to bring its population to ruin" (5 A:34–37). An "evil curse" (*ar-rat ma-ru-uš-ti*) was found in his mouth (5 B:10).

The Effects of Marduk's Anger toward Babylon

Marduk's fury had disastrous consequences for Babylon. The evil forces in heaven and earth persisted, the symmetry (*mit-ḫur-tim*) of the cosmos disappeared, the orbits of the stars were altered, all of which signified impending doom for Babylon (6 B:11). On earth the mighty and reliable

---

40. The texts describe his anger in several ways:

> 5 A:34–35 *i-gu-ug-ma* ^{d}*en-lil(-la) ilani*^{meš} ^{d}*Marduk*
> "Marduk "Marduk, the lord of the gods, grew furious."

> 5 B:8 *e-zi-iz lib-ba-šu ka-bat-tuš iṣ-ṣa-ri-iḫ*
> "His heart fumed; his liver raged."

> 5 E1: 11–14 *bêlu rabû(ú)* ^{d}*Marduk i-gu-ug i-ru-um-ma[it]-ti E-sag-gil*
> "The great lord Marduk shook with rage against Esagila."

> 5 E2:4–6 *ù Bâbil*^{ki} *e-zi-is-libba-šu zi-nu-tu it-s ši*
> "and (against) Babylon his heart raged."

85

By the River Chebar

Araḫtu canal overflowed its banks in a flood reminiscent of the great deluge, leveling the city with a mighty torrent. The residences and temples of Babylon, including Esagila, were turned into a wasteland, the resulting swamp providing refuge for innumerable fish and fowl. Simultaneously, all the deities in the city flew to heaven like birds (7 A:38–8 A:47; 7 E:8–9 E:14). As for the people, they were scattered in foreign lands, either fleeing as exiles seeking a place to hide (9 4:46–48; B:18), or as captives destined to a life of slavery (9 D:8–11).

Marduk's Change of Heart Toward Babylon

The turning point in the story occurs in episode 10, which reads as follows:

> Although he had written down (on the tablets of destiny) 70 years as the duration of its desolation, after his heart had been calmed (*lib-ba-šu i-nu-uḫ-ma*) he forthwith inverted the digits and commanded its (Babylon's) rebuilding in the eleventh year.[41]

Esarhaddon's rebuilding of Babylon represents the effect of Marduk's change of disposition toward his own city. The reconstruction transpired in a series of discrete stages. (a) Esarhaddon is appointed "shepherd" of the Assyrians for Marduk's sake, and commissioned to rebuild the city (11 A:9–23; cf. 12 B:21–22a). (b) The astrological signs indicate an alteration in the disposition of the forces (*idât* ^{meš}), as a result of which the angered gods are reconciled to Akkad (12 A:29–40; D:9–14). (c) An omen is given, indicating the imminent return of Marduk to Esagila (14 B:5–8), and Esarhaddon is commissioned to prepare the way by rebuilding his temple (14 A:41–15 A:49). (d) Fearing to begin the reconstruction of Marduk's temple, Esarhaddon pays homage to the god and receives confirmation of his commission (16 A:7–17 A:17). (e) The project is completed with the help of the citizens of the land who had previously been taken captive, but whom Esarhaddon had regathered (episodes 19–31). (f) The cult statues are duly redecorated and the rituals reinstituted (episodes 32–35). (g) The state images that had been removed to other lands are returned (episode

---

[41]. "Essarhaddon Account," 10 A:2–9; B:19–20. This numerical effect may be achieved by transposing the cuneiform symbols for 70 (𒐕𒌋), which yields 11 (𒌋𒐕). See the discussion by Nougayrol, "Textes hépatoscopiques," 65. Cf. Borger, *Die Inschriften Asarhaddons*, 65. Jeremiah's prophecy in 29:10 suggests that a 70 year period of exile as a result of an angered divinity was a well-known motif in the ancient Near East. Cf. Whitley, "The Term Seventy Years Captivity," 60–72; Orr, "Seventy Years of Babylon," 304–6; Ackroyd, "'Seventy Year' Period," 23–27; Borger, "An Additional Remark," 74.

36). (h) The king restores the oppressed citizenry of Babylon to free and secure status, and the transportation routes to other lands are reopened (37 A:16–40).

Interpretation

The departure of Marduk from Babylon is not explicitly mentioned, but it is implied in episode 8, which describes the flight of the gods to heaven, and is required by the reference to the reentry of Marduk into Esagila in episode 14. Of special interest to us is this account's depiction of the correlation between human and divine causation in the city's calamity, the effects of divine abandonment on the city, and Marduk's later return to Babylon. Consistent with the extra-biblical witness elsewhere, Marduk's change of heart is motivated primarily by his concern for a geographic site, and apparently occurs independently of any alteration in the citizens' behavior. The text suggests that Marduk was simply homesick for his city.

The Autobiography of Adad-guppi

Chronologically even nearer Ezekiel's lifetime than the Esarhaddon inscription is the autobiography of Adad-guppi, the 104-year-old mother of Nabonidus, king of Babylon (555–539 BCE).[42] Classified by Longman as fictional royal autobiography,[43] the prayer recalls the destruction of Harran by the Babylonians in 609 BCE, to which the departure of Sin, the city's patron deity correlates. Sin's abandonment of his residence is described in one short statement:

> Whereas in the sixteenth year of Nabopolassar, king of Babylon, Sin, the king of the gods, became angry (*iz-nu-ú*) with his city and his house, and went up to heaven (with the result that) the city and its people were transformed into a ruin.[44]

Again of special interest for us is the motive for Marduk's departure: the anger of the deity toward his people. No human offenses are cited as

---

42. For the primary edition, with Akkadian text, translation, and commentary, see Gadd, "Harran Inscriptions," 35–92. For more recent translation and discussion, see Longman, *Fictional Akkadian Autobiography*, 97–101, 225–28; Longman, COS, 477–78. Cf. also ANET, 560–62.

43. Longman, *Fictional Akkadian Autobiography*, 97–701; Longman, COS, 477–78.

44. Autobiography of Adad-guppi, I:6–9, as translated by Longman, COS, 478.

reason for the departure, though the reference to the temple might suggest some cultic misdemeanor. As expected, the divine abandonment resulted in the destruction of the city. The text goes on to describe the penitential intercession of Adad-guppi, as the result of which Sin's "wrathful heart quieted down" (*ug-ga-ti lib-bi-šú i-nu-uḫ-ma*, I:36–37), and he became reconciled with Eḫulḫul, his divine residence (I:29–39). Expressive of his change of heart, Marduk appointed Nabonidus, Adad-guppi's son, to the kingship of Sumer and Akkad. This king's primary task would be to reconstruct the temple of Sin in Harran, and then to reinstitute his worship in the city (II:1–11).

The Cyrus Cylinder

The final text to be considered here is the well-known inscribed clay cylinder in which Cyrus, the Persian king (557–529 BCE), gloats over his conquest of Babylon without a fight.[45] Although the first part of the text is incompletely preserved, A. Leo Oppenheim's translation makes the general sense sufficiently clear:

> a weakling has been installed as the *enû* of his country; [the correct images of the gods he removed from their thrones, imi]tations he ordered to be placed upon them. A replica of the temple Esagila he has . . . for Ur and the other sacred cities appropriate rituals . . . daily he did blabber [incorrect prayers]. He (furthermore) interrupted in a fiendish way the regular offerings, he did . . . he established within the sacred cities. The worship of Marduk, the king of the gods, he [chang]ed into an abomination, daily he used to do evil against his (i.e. Marduk's) city. . . . He [tormented] its [inhabitants] with corvée-work (lit.: a yoke) without relief he ruined them all.
>
> Upon their complaints the lord of the gods became terribly angry (*ez-zi-iš i-gu-ug-ma*) and [he departed from] their region, (also) the other gods living among them left their mansions, wroth that he had brought (them) into Babylon.

The sins committed by the king, which precipitated Marduk's departure, included both cultic (inappropriate rituals, incorrect prayers, dispensing with the regular sacrifices, general sacrilege against Marduk) and moral

---

45. For the text in transliteration, German translation, and commentary, see Berger, "Der Kyros-Zylinder," 192–234. Cf. the earlier edition by Weissbach, *Keilinschriften*, 2–3. For the text in English, see *ANET*, 315–16.

crimes (oppression of the citizens). Again the divinity's departure resulted in the ruination of the temples and the city, along with the annihilation of the population, as the following lines indicate. A return to good fortune in Babylon occurred only after Marduk's anger had subsided and he had displayed mercy toward the city. This was expressed concretely by calling out Cyrus as the righteous king who should lead Marduk once more in the annual procession.

Summary Observations

To synthesize our findings on the Mesopotamian descriptions of divine abandonment we may tabulate the elements in the accounts that have been relevant to our discussion (see Table 1). While the wrath of Enlil is expressed in the Sumerian laments, the emotions of the titular deities of the cities of Sumer are the opposite of fury. Reflecting the perspective of the victims of conquest, the gods of the respective cities defend and intercede on behalf of their subjects and their shrines. Intent on glorifying Tukulti-Ninurta, the "Epic" highlights him as an agent of divine fury against the Kassites. The positive tone of the Marduk Prophecy is striking, lacking any hint of human causation behind the abandonment, or of divine anger. Marduk departs of his own will, but even in his absence from Babylon he serves the city's interests. The "Seed of Kingship" seems to promise the entire sequence of events involved in accounts of divine abandonments. Unfortunately, it breaks off at a critical point, leaving us to speculate whether Marduk had a change of heart and the city was restored. The Erra Epic goes its own way in presenting Marduk, the divine patron, as a passive figure, leaving the fate of the city in the hands of Erra, the divine agent of disaster. The failure of the text to mention the appointment of a new ruler over Babylon who will institute a new era of peace may be attributed to the fact that the poem focuses on Erra, not the divine patron of Babylon.

In terms of the motifs that concern us, the last three texts are the most complete. Like the Tukulti-Ninurta Epic, each one functions as an apologia for the current ruler. All three contain mythological features and reflect fully the theological perspective on history common throughout the ancient world. However, being more closely tied to history than most of the earlier texts, they also deal more fully with the earthly implications of divine abandonment.

Table 1: A Comparison of Ancient Near Eastern Accounts of Divine Abandonment

Text	Date (BCE)	Genre	Cause: Human Provocation	Motive: Divine Anger	Effect: Disaster	Deity's Altered Disposition	Deity's Return to City	Divine Selection of a Ruler	Final Peace and Prosperity
Curse of Agade	2100	Historiographic Poem	X(?)		X				
Sumer and Ur Lament	1940(?)	Poetic Lament			X[1]		X[2]		
Ur Lament	1940(?)	Poetic Lament			X[1]				
Uruk Lament	1940(?)	Poetic Lament	X[3]		X[1]		X	X[4]	
Eridu Lament	1940(?)	Poetic Lament			X[1]				
Nippur Lament	1940(?)	Poetic Lament		X	X	X	X	X	X
Prophetic Letter from Mari	1700	Dream Report							
Tukulti-Ninurta Epic	1230	Victory Song	X	X	X				
Marduk Prophecy	1110	Divine Autobiography			X	X	X	X	X
Seed of Kingship	1110	Historiographic Poem	X	X	X				
Erra and Ishum	800	Mythic Poetry	X	X	X	X[5]			X[6]
Esarhaddon Account	670	Annalistic Apologia	X	X	X	X	X	X	X

Text	Date (BCE)	Genre	Cause: Human Provocation	Motive: Divine Anger	Effect: Disaster	Deity's Altered Disposition	Deity's Return to City	Divine Selection of a Ruler	Final Peace and Prosperity
Adad-guppi'	540	Royal Autobiography		X	X	X		X	X
Cyrus Cylinder	530	Autobiographical Annal	X	X	X	X	X	X	X
Ezekiel	593–570	Prophetic Vision	X[7]	X[8]	X[9]	X[10]	X[11]	X[12]	X[13]

1. To be precise, in the Sumerian laments the disaster struck prior to the departure of the gods. Their leaving was the result of, rather than the cause of the catastrophe. The latter had been decreed by the supreme deity, Enlil, against whose will the titular gods of the respective cities were powerless to act.
2. Nanna does indeed return to the city with Enlil's permission, meaning the city will be spared, but the residents mourn.
3. The noise of humans.
4. The election of the ruler is not described, but the naming of Ishme-Dagan assumes it.
5. The change of heart is experienced by Erra, the god of such calamities, rather than the patron of the city who has departed.
6. Expressed as a hope by Erra, rather than an accomplished fact.
7. Ezek 8:5–18.
8. Ezek 8:17—9:10.
9. Predicted in 9:5–8 and 10:6, but fully developed in Ezekiel's judgment oracles in chapters 4–24.
10. Never formally mentioned in the visions, but see 11:16–21, a disputation speech inserted in the vision narrative. This prophecy promises the divine presence, in limited measure, to the exiles and their eventual restoration to the homeland. See also 39:25–29, placed immediately prior to the concluding vision.
11. Ezek 43:1–5.
12. Not within the vision accounts, but see 34:23–24 and 37:21–25.
13. Ezek 47:1—48:35; cf. also 34:25–32; etc.

By the River Chebar

Mordechai Cogan has established that underlying the notion of divine abandonment was the ancient Near Eastern politico-military policy of the spoliation of divine images.[46] Since the statue of a god was perceived to be indwelt by the spirit of the divinity,[47] no experience could be more devastating psychologically than to lose the image. Without the god the people were doomed. It is in the light of such notions that Ezekiel's visions of the departure of YHWH from and his eventual return to the temple (8–11; 43:1–5) must be interpreted, a subject to which we now turn.

Ezekiel's Prophecies of Divine Abandonment

Perhaps the full development of the motif of divine abandonment and return fell to Ezekiel, rather than any other Israelite prophet, because he lived in Babylon, where he was surrounded by images of deities and where stories of divine abandonment flourished. Ezekiel was undoubtedly familiar with Babylonian presentations of catastrophes such as Jerusalem experienced. However, although the accounts discussed above follow a certain pattern, especially the later texts, the Israelite prophet could not adopt the Mesopotamian model wholesale. In contrast to the idolatrous cults, in which the deity was thought to indwell the image of him/herself, Yahwism was a spiritual religion. The temple in Jerusalem housed no image of YHWH; his presence was represented by his glory, the *kābôd*, which under normal circumstances rested above the sacred ark of the covenant inside the most holy place.[48] Furthermore, in the mind of orthodox Yahwists of Ezekiel's day, Yahwism was also an exclusive religion. The "YHWH-alone" party,[49] to which he belonged, could not accept that historical events were merely the consequences of capricious and arbitrary decisions of the gods

---

46. Cogan, *Imperialism and Religion*. Note his conclusion on p. 40:

> NA spoliation of divine images was meant to portray the abandonment of the enemy by his own gods in submission to the superior might of Assyria's god, Ashur. Accordingly, foreign gods were not treated as captives nor displayed in Assyrian temples as trophies, but were held, at times not far from their homes, for as long as it took Assyria to secure guarantees of loyalty from the defeated.

See also Kutsko, "Turning Swords into Plowshares," 2–3.

47. See Jacobsen, "The Graven Image," 15–32.
48. Cf. de Vaux, *Ancient Israel*, 297–302.
49. On this exclusivism, see Lang, *Monotheism and the Prophetic Minority*; Lang, "No God but YHWH!," 41–49; Lang, "Zur Entstehung," 135–42.

Divine Abandonment

nor of feuds between members of the heavenly realm. Accordingly, we expect Ezekiel's presentation of the motif to go its own way. But we must not forget that he is dealing with an Israelite audience that has to a large extent bought into the pagan perspectives on historical and spiritual reality. He knows his audience well, and his rhetorical strategy is carefully designed to expose both the heresy and the futility of their beliefs. Accordingly, in Ezekiel's representation of YHWH's departure from his temple in Jerusalem, we may expect features common to other ancient Near Eastern accounts. But he exploits these elements polemically, to expose the bankruptcy of pagan religious notions: YHWH will defeat the gods in their own game.[50]

The interpretation of the details of Ezekiel 8–11 need not detain us here. That YHWH's abandonment of his temple is the central idea is clear, not only from the general drift of the narrative, but also from several explicit statements. The literary complexity of this text is apparent even to a casual reader, but from beginning to end the motif of divine abandonment provides a unifying thread.[51] With glorious irony, explicit declarations of YHWH's departure from Jerusalem come only from the lips of those whose religious ideas have been influenced by neighboring peoples, and whose actions are characterized as abominable (תּוֹעֵבוֹת, 8:9). Twice, in what turns out to be a self-fulfilling prophecy, YHWH's abandonment of the land is declared to be an event that has already transpired:

אֵין יְהוָה רֹאֶה אֹתָנוּ   YHWH does not see us;
עָזַב יְהוָה אֶת־הָאָרֶץ   YHWH has abandoned the land. (8:12)

עָזַב יְהוָה אֶת־הָאָרֶץ   YHWH has abandoned the land;
וְאֵין יְהוָה רֹאֶה   And YHWH does not see. (9:9)

The implications the people draw from YHWH's apparent absence are disturbing. Instead of confessing their sin and pleading for his return, as did the mother of Nabonidus, they use YHWH's absence as a pretext for rationalizing their evil actions (all kinds of cultic offenses in chapter 8, moral and social crimes in chapter 9). The form of Ezekiel's presentation exposes the perversion of the people. Pagans would have assumed that

---

50. Recently Kutsko has argued that YHWH's restoration of his people, who are his image, represents another way in which the Mesopotamian ideology is turned on its head. See his brief treatment in "Turning Swords into Plowshares," 3–7, but especially his detailed study *Between Heaven and Earth*.

51. Cf. Ackroyd, *Exile and Restoration*, 40–41.

the event had been precipitated by their sin and responded to the departure of their god with confession and prayer. But in the minds of Ezekiel's audience, cause and effect have been reversed. To the Babylonians a deity's abandonment of his temple and his city was provoked by the sins of the people; to the people of Judah, the former justified the latter. Having formerly based their security on YHWH's unconditional commitment to them, they now treat his abandonment as betrayal, absolving them of any moral and spiritual obligation to him. The statements made by these residents of Jerusalem are indeed false—YHWH has not yet left—and the implications they draw are quite erroneous. But the prophet utilizes their declarations to announce his own theme in the pericope: YHWH's departure is imminent. Ezekiel's vision elaborates in great detail on the causes and consequences of such perversion. But when placed alongside other ancient accounts of divine abandonment, several additional observations may be made.

First, the repeated references to the evils being committed in Jerusalem emphasize that YHWH's abandonment of the temple is provoked by human action. The offenses described in 8:3–16 are primarily cultic in nature: the introduction of the idol of jealousy into the court of YHWH's temple, the worship of carved images of every sort, the women weeping the Tammuz,[52] and twenty-five men paying homage to the sun. In 8:17 YHWH, through the prophet, accuses the people of social and moral crimes—they have provoked the ire of YHWH[53] by filling the land with violence. This is reiterated in 9:9, which speaks of a land filled with blood and a city filled with perversion (מַטֶּה). These evils are denounced with the sharpest language as abominable (תּוֹעֵבוֹת, 8:6a, 9, 13, 15, 17; 9:4), detestable (שֶׁקֶץ, 8:10), wicked (רָעוֹת, 8:9). It is no wonder that YHWH's passion (קִנְאָה, 8:3, 5) and ire have been provoked (הַכְעִיס, 8:17). Twice YHWH declares his response in terms reminiscent of the extra-biblical accounts:

---

52. Although most translations have them weeping for Tammuz, the article on Tammuz suggests that Tammuz denotes a special genre of lament, rather than the deity himself. Since this scene follows immediately after the elders' assertion that YHWH had abandoned the land, it appears that these women have either equated YHWH with Tammuz or they are expressing their grief at their own deity's departure by adapting a Tammuz ritual. In either case, Ezekiel observes the people in Jerusalem replacing the vital worship of the living God with lamentations for the dead. See further Block, *Ezekiel 1–24*, 294–96.

53. "Sticking the branch to the nose" describes a physical gesture that is not only painful but also extremely insulting. Here the expression is employed idiomatically, referring to the entire complex of crimes portrayed in the foregoing scenes. See further Block, *Ezekiel 1–24*, 297–300.

Divine Abandonment

> Therefore I will deal in wrath (חֵמָה); my eye will not spare, nor will I have pity (חָמָל); and though they cry in my ears with a loud voice, I will not hear them. (8:18)

> As for me, my eye will not spare, nor will I have pity, but I will bring their conduct upon their own heads. (9:10)

Second, YHWH leaves of his own volition. Although the ancient Near Eastern accounts of divine abandonment generally create the impression that the gods voluntarily leave their shrines,[54] I have noted earlier that enemy invasions and the spoliation of divine images lie behind these accounts. In Ezekiel's mind, YHWH's departure does indeed coincide with the destruction of Jerusalem and the temple at the hands of Nebuchadnezzar. However, since the temple contained no image of the deity, such spoliation with respect to YHWH is impossible. On the contrary, Ezekiel highlights YHWH's independence at each stage of his departure. (1) The *kābôd* rises from the cherub over the Ark of the Covenant within the holy of holies and moves over to the threshold of the temple, filling the entire court with its emanating brightness (9:3; 10:4). (2) A magnificent vehicle,[55] with total and absolute freedom of movement, bearing an object resembling a throne appears (10:1–13). (3) The *kābôd* moves from the threshold and rests above the vehicle (10:18). (a) The vehicle, bearing the *kābôd*, rises from the earth and pauses at the entrance of the east gate of the temple (10:19). (5) The *kābôd* departs from the midst of the city and stands over the mountain to the east (11:23). Like the sudden termination of a dream, at this climactic moment the vision breaks off. But the description of the vehicle bearing the throne, with its absolute freedom of movement and limitless maneuverability, sends a clear and unequivocal message: YHWH will not be transported like any other image from his dwelling place by any human monarch.

Third, the vision describes the disastrous effects that would attend the departure of the deity from the city. YHWH would turn upon his subjects, delivering them into the hands of strangers who would execute them with the sword (11:7–11) within the borders of Israel (גְּבוּל יִשְׂרָאֵל), which had, ironically, been viewed as sacrosanct. This description is reminiscent

---

54. But the Sumerian laments portray local deities as subject to the will of Enlil, and Marduk's freedom in the Erra Epic seems more limited than in the Marduk Prophecy.

55. According to 10:15, 20, the prophet recognizes it as the same one he had seen in his inaugural vision (1:4–28).

of extra-biblical texts in which divinities abandon their shrines and then turn on their subjects as if they were the enemy.[56]

Fourth, Ezekiel's vision holds out the prospect of an eventual normalization of relations between YHWH and his people (11:14–21), but with an extraordinary twist. In keeping with common oriental perceptions, those among Ezekiel's compatriots who had not been exiled interpreted their continued presence in Jerusalem as a mark of divine favor. Because the exiles had been expelled from the land, they had obviously been rejected by YHWH. "Go far from YHWH," they declare heartlessly. "This land has been given to us as a possession" (מוֹרָשָׁה, 11:15). But the prophet pulls the rug out from under their feet by announcing that the opposite is in fact the case. Breaking with convention, YHWH promises to follow the exiles and become a sanctuary for them in small measure (מִקְדָּשׁ מְעַט) "in the lands where they have arrived" (11:16). Ironically, the ones who are rejected by the deity are those who remain at home. As a sign (not precondition) of his continued interest in the exiles, YHWH promises to regather them from their scattered locales and return them to the land of Israel. The prophet will undoubtedly have interpreted YHWH's appearance to him in Babylon as a deposit and confirmation of this divine commitment, to be reported to his fellow exiles (cf. 11:25).

Fifth, whereas extra-biblical texts tend to emphasize the deity's change of heart prior to his/her return to the shrine, Ezekiel emphasizes that by a divine act the subjects' hearts will be changed (11:18–11).[57] Instead of having his subjects polish a dirtied image (as in the Erra and Ishum composition), YHWH declares that he will cleanse his subjects of their iniquity and give them a new heart so they will walk in his ways, and he may renew the covenant.[58] Those who insist on going their own way, he will reject.

But this does not mean that Ezekiel will not recognize a change in YHWH's disposition. On the contrary, intensely jealous for his land, in 35:1—36:15 YHWH directs his wrath against those who had tried to capitalize on Israel's misfortune, and comes to the defense of the land where he is at home (35:10) and which he claims as his own (36:5). Previously

---

56. Inanna in the Curse of Agade; the gods of Sumer and Akkad in the Tukulti-Ninurta Epic.

57. Cf. 36:16–32.

58. Kutsko argues that in this presentation Ezekiel assumes that the Israelites function as the image of YHWH ("Turning Swords into Plowshares," 3–4).

Divine Abandonment

YHWH had been against Jerusalem, the capital of the land of Judah,[59] and had threatened to impose all the covenant curses upon her (5:7–17). In the sequel, he had set his face against the *land* of Judah, determined to destroy it completely. But in 36:1–15 YHWH adopts the opposite stance, announcing that he has turned toward Judah.[60] He will restore prosperity to the land and defend it in the face of the insults of the nations.

In 36:16–38 Ezekiel announces the change of YHWH's disposition toward the people of Israel. Whereas previously he had poured out his wrath on them, now he will regather the scattered population, bring them back to their ancestral homeland, cleanse them of their sin, and cause them to walk in new obedience to him. However, the text is emphatic that this will not be done because Israel deserves it. YHWH's actions are driven by a concern for the sanctity of his name (36:19–23, 37–32).

Sixth, the links between Ezekiel's vision of YHWH's departure from the temple in chapters 8–11 and extra-biblical accounts of divine abandonment suggest to the reader that the prophet's story cannot end with YHWH's exit from the land (17:22–23). The pattern of Mesopotamian accounts leads one to expect the appointment of a new king, the institution of peace and prosperity to the people, and the return of YHWH to his temple. Although Ezekiel is silent on these matters in this context, in long-range terms he does not disappoint. Indeed these three elements represent major motifs in his restoration oracles proclaimed after Jerusalem had fallen in 586 BCE (33:21–22). First, in 34:23–24 and 37:22–24 a new ruler is announced. Even though Ezekiel's designation of this person as "shepherd of YHWH's people" derives from the Davidic tradition (2 Sam 7), it echoes similar titles in the extra-biblical texts.[61] However, in keeping with YHWH's eternal promise to David, this person had to be identified as a (new) David. Second, the appointment of the new shepherd signals the beginning of a new utopian period of peace, security, and prosperity (34:25–31; 36:28–38; 37:25–28). Third, Ezekiel envisions the return of YHWH to his shrine (40:1—43:5), an event that is interpreted as follows:

---

59. See 4:1–17. Note the hostile orientation formula, הִנְנִי עָלַיִךְ גַּם־אָנִי, "Behold I myself am against you," in 5:8.

60. The formula, הִנְנִי אֲלֵיכֶם, "Behold, I am for you," followed by וּפָנִיתִי אֲלֵיכֶם, "and, I will turn toward you," in 36:9 deliberately reverses YHWH's disposition.

61. The Nippur Lament (*kirugu* 6, line 174) calls Išme-Dagan Enlil's "beloved shepherd" (Kramer, "The Lamentation over the Destruction of Nippur," 18); the "Esarhaddon Account" (episode 11 A:22) declares that Marduk endowed Esarhaddon with "shepherdship," over Assyria.

> Son of man, this is the location of my throne, and the place of the soles of my feet, where I will reside in the midst of the sons of Israel forever. And the house of Israel will not defile my holy name again.... They have defiled my holy name by their abominations which they have committed. For this reason I have consumed them in my anger. Now let them put away their harlotry and the corpses of kings far from me, and I will reside in their midst forever. (43:7–9)

The sequel notes that the return of YHWH will be accompanied by the reestablishment of the cultic and moral orders (43:10—46:24), the healing of the landscape (47:1–12), and the equitable distribution of the land among the twelve tribes (47:13—48:29). Although not functioning as the shrine of YHWH, nonetheless the central city proclaims the new order in its name: יְהוָה שָׁמָּה, "YHWH is There!"

With promises like this, YHWH's journeys, and with them the fortunes of Israel, have come full circle. Deity, nation, and land exist once more in a state of eternal *shalom*. These latter texts do not represent parts of Ezekiel's original vision of the departure of YHWH from his temple, the primary concern of this paper. But in the light of the Mesopotamian parallels (not to mention the eternal promises of God) they are almost inevitable. They fill out a picture that had been adumbrated earlier, but whose completion could not be secured or even fully envisioned prior to the climactic historical moment, the fall of Jerusalem. Before 586 BCE the sins of the people had called for judgment. Only when the warnings have been fulfilled does the prophet more fully develop his vision of hope for the future.

Conclusion

Recent scholarship has recognized that the interpretation of biblical texts involves a conversation between the written text and the reader. The disposition of the reader plays a vital role in the establishment of the significance of a passage. We must indeed be ever mindful of the assumptions and expectations we bring to the text. However, at the same time we must recognize the danger of imposing modern, and for the most part, alien Western definitions of literary and semantic propriety upon ancient texts. This is particularly true of the book of Ezekiel. This is an ancient Near Eastern literary document and, as such, must be interpreted according to the literary standards and conventions of the world from which it derives. Many of the riddles in the book can be understood only in the light of the cultural and literary contexts from which this written record derives. A comparison of the shape of Ezekiel's message with similar accounts from Mesopotamia has important implications, not only for the unity of the book as a whole, and individual pericopes in particular, but also for the very nature of the prophetic task. And the fact that Ezekiel's later oracles pick up themes begun earlier, but never completed, should caution against drawing the distinctions between the various modes of prophetic utterance too sharply.

We should not be surprised if the content of Ezekiel's vision bears some relationship to Mesopotamian literature. After all, he resides in Babylon and his message is directed primarily to exiles in Babylon. The picture the book paints of the spiritual condition of the Judaeans in Babylon is far from complimentary. They are in revolt against YHWH, their own divine patron (2:3-4; 3:7-8), cynical toward the prophetic messages directed their way (12:17-28), defiled by idolatry (14:1-11), immoral and exploitative in their ethical conduct, in general perpetuating the abominations of the ancestors (20:1-44). Indeed, Ezekiel's audience had been infected by many of the prevailing religious ideas among Israel's neighbors. It is appropriate, therefore, that the account of the vision of impending destruction of their own beloved city should be cast in terms and employ motifs with which they had become fascinated. Even without Israel's own longstanding traditions of YHWH's association with Zion, his portrayal of YHWH leaving Jerusalem would have had a familiar ring.

On the other hand, his vision of YHWH's departure could no more fit the pattern of the religious beliefs of the native Mesopotamians than could the representation of YHWH in his temple. The God of Israel remained sovereign, not only over the fate of his people, but over his own destiny as well. Nebuchadnezzar would not drag him forcibly from his residence. He would leave of his own will, under his own power, and for his own reasons. Furthermore, even after he had left, his primary interest would remain with his covenant people. The land would serve this relationship.

Both Ezekiel and his contemporary Jeremiah attack with great vigor official temple theology, according to which YHWH's commitment to his people and his residence in the temple were treated as firm guarantees of the security of the people. Nevertheless, there is a certain irony in the fact that even as Nebuchadnezzar's battering rams were beating at the walls of the city the very theology that the prophets were challenging was being confirmed. So long as YHWH remained in his temple the city stood. However, once he had left, neither gods nor humans could prevent the mighty Babylonian conqueror from storming in.

EXCURSUS A

The Prophetic Speech of Marduk

A Translation[1]

Column I

1. O Ḫaḫarnum, Ḫayyašum,
2. Anum, Enlil,
3. Nudimm[ud], Ea,
4. Muati, Nabu.

1. The text is admittedly fragmentary. For the *editio princeps*, see Rykle Borger, "Der Gott Marduk und Gott-König Šulgi als Propheten. Zwei prophetische Texte," *Bibliotheca Orientalis* 28 (1971) 3–24. For further bibliography see Block, *Gods of the Nations* (1st ed.), 134 n. 18. This text was included as an appendix to the first (1988) edition of this monograph, but was omitted in the second (2000) edition. When the first edition was published no English translations were available. In the meantime, it has been translated by several scholars: Tremper Longman III, *Fictional Akkadian Autobiography: A Generic and Comparative Study*, 233–35. Winona Lake, IN: Eisenbrauns, 1991; Tremper Longman III in *The Context of Scripture*, vol. 1, *Canonical Compositions from the Biblical World*, edited by William W. Hallo and K. Lawson Younger, 480–81. Leiden: Brill, 1997; Benjamin Foster, *Before the Muses: An Anthology of Akkadian Literature*. 3rd ed. Bethesda, MD: CDL, 2005; Matthew Neujahr, *Predicting the Past in the Ancient Near East: Mantic Historiography in Ancient Mesopotamia, Judah, and the Mediterranean World*, 27–41. Brown Judaic Studies 354. Atlanta: Society of Biblical Literature, 2012. This translation, reproduced in *Gods of the Nations*, ***, is a revised version of my translation in the first edition of this monograph and included here, not because other published versions are defective, but because the text is critical for understanding a particular part of the discussion above, as well as the following essay in this volume, "Chasing a Phantom: The Search for the Historical Marduk." To provide a smooth reading in English in some cases I have rearranged specific lines.

100

The Prophetic Speech of Marduk

5. You great gods, learned in my secrets!
6. After I gird up my loins, I will declare my name.
7. I am Marduk, the Great Lord.
8. the surveyor, walking about on the mountains.
9. I survey, traveling through the lands.[2]
10. Throughout all the lands,
11. from the rising of the sun to the setting of the sun,
12. [. . .] I have walked about.
13. I issued the order, and went out to the land of Ḫatti.
14. I inquired of Ḫatti.
16. In its midst I erected
15. the throne of my divinity (Anum-dignity).
17. During the twenty-four years that I lived there
19. I established in its midst
18. the commerce of the citizens of Babylon.
20. Its (i.e., the land of Ḫatti) [. . .] Its merchandise and its goods (were sent)
21. to (?) Sippar, Nippur,
22. [and Babylo]n.
23. [A king of Babylon(?)] arose
24. and led me in procession [lit. "grasped my hand(?)"].
25. [. . . to] Babylon
26. which [. . .] was in good order,
27. The processional street (?) of Babylon(?) was beautiful.
28. The crown of my divinity (Anum-dignity) [. . .]
29. and the image [. . .]
30. water and winds (?) [. . .]
31. Three days [. . .]
32. The crown of my divinity (Anum-dignity)
33. and the image [. . .]
34. for my body [. . .]
35. I returned home. [With reference to Babylon I declared(?)],
36. "Bring [your tribute]

---

2. Lines 8–9 rendered according to *CAD* Ḫ 159b.

37. O land[s to Babylon!]"
38. [...]
3'. [...] Baltil (Assyria) [...]
4'. [...] The temple of Baltil (Ekur-Baltil) [...]
5'. Its [shrines he polished] like jewels (*zalāqu*-stone).
6'. I bestowed [on him?] luxurious [...]
7'. [...]
8'. [...] year after year [I blessed it].
9'. I marshaled the people of Enlil with him (?).
10'. I provided him with wings like a bird.
11'. I filled all the lands.
12'. I completed (my days); I blessed Assyria.
13'. I handed him [... (the tablet)] of destinies.
14'. I established him.
15'. I returned home. With reference to Babylon I declared,
16'. "Bring your tribute, O lands,
17'. to Babylon!"
18'. I am Marduk, the Great Lord.
19'. I am the Lord of Destinies and Decrees.
20'. Who has undertaken such a journey (like this)?
21'. As I departed (?), so I have returned. I issued the order.
22'. I went to the land of Elam,
23'. and all the gods went (with me). I issued the order myself.
24'. The meal offerings (*nindabê*) of the temples I terminated myself.
25'. Šakkan (the god of cattle) and Nisaba (the goddess of grain) I sent up to heaven.

Column II

1. Siris (the goddess of beer) made the heart of the country sick.
2. The corpses of the people blocked the doorways.
3. Brothers consumed one another.
4. Friends beat each other up with weapons.
5. The nobles (*mārū banî*)

The Prophetic Speech of Marduk

6. stretched out their hands
5. against the poor.
7. The scepter was shortened. Disaster struck the land.
8. Kings (*šarrānū*) reduced the land.
9. Lions blocked the roads.
10. Dogs [went mad] and bit people.
11. None whom they bit recovered; they died.
12. I fulfilled my days; I completed my years.
14. I longed
13. for my city, Babylon,
14. and Ekur-Sagila within.
15. I called all the goddesses.
16. I issued the order, "Bring your tribute,
17. O lands, to Babylon!"
18. [. . .]
19. A king of Babylon will arise.
20. The amazing temple,
21. Ekur-Sagila, he will restore.
23. In Ekur-Sagila he will redraw
22. the plans of heaven and earth.
24. He will increase (?) its height.
25. In my city, Babylon, he will establish
24. exemption from taxes.
26. He will lead me in procession [lit. "grasp my hand"] into my city, Babylon,
27. and bring me into the Ekur-Sagila forever.
28. He will restore the (procession) ship, Matusha.
29. He will plate its rudder with *ṣāriru*-gold.
30. He will [overlay?] its bow with *pašallu*-metal.
32. Sailors who man it,
31. he will bring on board.
33. They will be stationed to the right and to the left.
34. A king (?), who like the star (?) of Ekur-Sagila.
35. [. . .]

By the River Chebar

....

1'. [...]
2'. forever (he will bring in?)
3'. Madaḫḫe[du he will restore].
4'. Its rudder [...]
5'. Its bow [...]
6'. Sailors [...]
7'. in it [...]
8'. Nabu, the son of [...]
9'. enter (?)
10'. and Ekur [...]
11'. forever [...]
12'. This prince [...]
13'. Ekur-E[...]
14'. River of the god [...]
15'. Pure water [...]
16'. Ekur-E [...]
17'. the hand of (the god) Nin [...]

Assur III

1'. [he will] forever (bring him in)
2'. [...]
3'. [...]
4'. [...] he will establish
5'. Ekur-E[...]
6'. his [...] he will grant him.
7'. [The prince] will experience the goodness of god.
8'. [The days/years] of his reign will be long.
10'. He will polish
9'. Ekur-Egišnugal
10'. [to shine] like jewels.
11'. [...] of Ningal,

The Prophetic Speech of Marduk

12′. the temple (?) of Sin,
13′. with its treasures (?) of silver and its properties [...]
14′. and its possessions
15′. at the gate of the god
16′. [...]

Assur IV

1. With Sin [...]
2. of Egišnug[al ...]
3. the entire land [...]
4. This prince will be mighty and without rival.
5. He will rule the city and gather the dispersed.
6. Ekur-Egalmah} and the other shrines
7. he will polish [to sparkle] like jewels. Ningal,
8. Gula, Kurnunītum (?),
11. he will bring back
9. from the city of Ḫariddi itself
10. and [restore] to the temples, the chambers of their delight,
12. This prince will permit the land to [enjoy] his lush crops.
13. His days will be long.
14. [...]
15. [...]
16. [...]
17. [...] cities
18. He will polish the shrines [to sparkle] like jewels.
20. He will bring back (?).
19. all the gods.
21. He will gather the scattered land
22. and consolidate its foundation.
23. The gate of heaven
24. will be opened permanently.
25. [...]

By the River Chebar

ASHUR V, COLUMN III

1'. [...] will be opened
2'. [...]
3'. [...] will receive
4'. [...] he will establish permanently.
5'. Ningirsu will rule.
6'. The rivers will yield fish.
7'. The fields will be full of produce.
8'. The grass of winter will last till summer.
9'. The grass of summer will last till winter.
10'. The harvest of the land will be plentiful. The market will be good.
11'. Evil will be brought to order.
12'. Disturbances will be cleared. Evil will be exposed.
13'. Clouds will be present constantly.
14'. Brother will show mercy to brother.
15'. A son will fear his father like a god.
16'. A mother will [...] her daughter.
17'. A bride will wear a wreath (marry ?). She will honor her husband.
18'. Compassion will endure among people.
19'. A young man's reward (?) [...] will be secure.
20'. That prince will rule all the lands.
21'. Then I and all the gods
22'. will be his friend. He will destroy Elam.
23'. He will demolish its cities.
24'. He will [...] its fortresses.
25'. The great king of Der
26'. he will restore in his dwelling.
27'. He will repair his desolate state.
28'. [...] his misfortune. He will grasp his hand,
30'. and let him move permanently
29'. to Der and Ekur-Dimgalkalamma.

Column IV

1'. [...]
2'. [...]
3'. 40 liters [...]
4'. 40 liters [...]
5'. 10 liters of flour [...]
6'. 1 liter [...]
7'. 1 liter of honey, 1 liter of (melted) butter.
8'. 1 liter of dried figs (?) 1 liter of raisins.
9'. 1 liter of [oil] (in) a jar
10'. 1 liter of good [... (some kind of grain?)]
11'. 1 normal sheep,
12'. and a fattened calf
13'. will be burned up to the spirit [of the god] (?).
14'. Monthly, daily, and yearly [...] I will bless him.
15'. O Ḫaḫarnum, ḫayašum, complete.
16'. I am Šulgi.
17'. According to the writing board. Copy of Babylon. Approved. Palace of Ashurbanipal, king of the universe, king of Assyria.

5

Chasing a Phantom

The Search for the Historical Marduk[1]

Introduction

I**F ONE ADOPTS FOR** the moment the ancient Near Eastern dictum, "As goes a divine patron, so goes a nation," tracing the ups and downs of Marduk's history should offer considerable insight into the way the ancient Babylonians perceived their own history, had they ever stopped to think about it. Therefore, I propose here to look at the history and civilization of Babylon through the eyes of the city's patron deity, Marduk.

I was not long into my research before I discovered that searching for the historical Marduk was like chasing a phantom. This is so, not only because of the consistent biblical perspective that gods such as Marduk were nothing more than the products of a vain human imagination; it is also so because the Babylonian Marduk is difficult to grasp. And just about the time you think you have caught him, he slithers out of your hands.

Nevertheless I shall attempt to provide a biography of this elusive god. In the process we should come to a better understanding, not only of ancient Babylonian religion, but also of this great city's self-understanding.

---

1. This article represents a revised version of a paper read at the Wheaton College Archaeology Conference, November 10, 1989. It was originally published in *Archaeology in the Biblical World* 2 (1992) 20–43.

Whatever is learned concerning her history turns out to be a most valuable bonus.

Figure 10: Marduk, the Serpent-Dragon of Babylon[2]

The Rise of Marduk

While the ultimate origins of Marduk remain a mystery, his roots go back to Sumerian times. The name, which is commonly written in Sumerian logograms as ᵈAMAR.UD, even in Akkadian texts, bears the sense, "bull calf of Utu."[3] (Utu is the sun god.) The deity was therefore perceived originally as a third rate god, the son of the sun god.

---

2. The image decorates the Ishtar Gate, now in the Vorderasiatisches Museum (Near East Museum), Berlin. Permission is granted to use this document under the terms of the GNU Free Documentation License, version 1.2. Copyright Einsamer Schütze. [GFDL (http://www.gnu.org/copyleft/fdl.html) or CC-BY-SA-3.0-2.5-2.0-1.0 (http://creativecommons.org/licenses/by-sa/3.0)], via Wikimedia Commons. The photograph was downloaded on January 26, 2013, from http://upload.wikimedia.org/wikipedia/commons/2/24/Vorderasiatisches_Museum_Berlin_001.jpg.

3. Lambert, "The Historical Development of the Mesopotamian Pantheon," 193; Lambert, "Studies in Marduk," 8. So also Sjöberg, "Ein Selbstpreis des Königs Hammurabi," 62; Sommerfeld, "Marduk," 361. Pettinato (*The Archives of Ebla*, 238) suggests that Mesopotamian deities like Marduk and Tiamat originated in a West Semitic ambience, but he produces no supporting evidence.

By the River Chebar

To recount the story of Marduk is to trace the history of his city, Babylon. The relative obscurity of the city in the third millennium BCE is reflected in the fact that the name of this god is attested in only three fragmentary tens.[4] Obviously Marduk was nothing more than a minor deity in the Sumerian pantheon. However, his star first began to shine in the second millennium BCE. An indication of Marduk's emergence as a significant Mesopotamian deity in the early second millennium is found in a god list from the Isin-Larsa period, in which his name appears following those of the great gods An, Enid, Ninhursaga Nanna Suen, Dumuzi, and Enki.[5] Especially significant is the association of Marduk with Asalluḫi, whose name appears immediately before, and the goddess, Sarpanitum, whose name comes immediately after his. By Hammurabi's time the identities of the former and Marduk had merged,[6] and the latter had become his consort.[7] At this time Marduk's name also began to appear in oaths, and as the theophoric (divine) element in personal names.[8] The first concrete evidence that his cult was being officially attended to is provided by a date notice from the reign of Sumulael (1880–1845 BCE), which reads: "Year in which he fashioned a throne of silver and gold for the great sanctuary of Marduk."[9] The name of Marduk's temple, Esagila occurs for the first time in a date notice of Sabium (1844–1831 BCE), who reports that he constructed this sanctuary in his tenth year.[10]

The turning point in Marduk's fortunes occurred when Hammurabi ascended to the throne of Babylon. During his reign (1792–1750 BCE), and that of his successor, Samsuiluna (1749–1712 BCE), Marduk's name began to appear in personal names and oath formulae in Borsippa, Lagaba, and Sippar, suggesting that Marduk had graduated from being a mere city deity to territorial god of northern Babylonia. Meanwhile, his influence was spreading southward as well, as Hammurabi's officials established themselves in Isin and Larsa.

---

4. Sommerfeld, "Marduk," 362–63.

5. Cf. Chiera, *Sumerian Lexical Texts*, 122, III:12; 124, IV:3. Cf. Nougayrol, "Textes Sumero-Accadiens," 214.

6. Cf. below.

7. On Sarpanitum, see Edzard, "Mesopotamien," 119.

8. Sommerfeld, *Der Aufstieg Marduks*, 24–26.

9. Cf. Ungnad, "Datenlisten," 165, line 37. The following date notice refers to the erection of a statue of Sarpanitum.

10. Ungnad, "Datenlisten," 166, line 60.

Hammurabi seems to have treasured the special relationship he had with Marduk. In the dedicatory inscription of the temple he built for Marduk in Borsippa he wrote:

> For Marduk, the great Lord, who bestows plenty on the gods, the Lord of Esagil and Ezida, his Lord. Hammurabi, the one called by An, who listens to Enlil, the favorite of Shamash, the shepherd, beloved of Marduk, mighty king, king of the lands of Sumer and Akkad, king of the four corners of the earth. When Enlil appointed him to rule the land and the people, when he handed the reins of rule into his hand, for Marduk, the god, his creator he has built in Borsippa his [Marduk's] beloved city, his pure temple Ezida.[11]

In a prayer for Hammurabi, Marduk was portrayed as a special intermediary between the great gods and the king.[12] The king's own epithets include: "the beloved of Marduk," "the shepherd of Marduk,"[13] "the one after Marduk's heart,"[14] "the one chosen by Marduk,"[15] "the one for whom Asalluḫi (Marduk) determines a good destiny,"[16] as "the one who secures the triumph of Marduk"[17]—Hammurabi functioned as the agent of Marduk. His military campaigns and the achievement of Babylon's hegemony over Mesopotamia were not accomplished in his own interests, but to advance the reputation of Marduk. In a self-laudatory hymn, Hammurabi declared, "Any country which does not submit to Marduk I destroy with my weapon."[18]

For Marduk's own story, his relationship with the other deities was more important than his involvement in earthly affairs. During the reign of Hammurabi he began to make his move up the pantheonic ladder. Symbolic of his new status was his merger with Asalluḫi, the son of Enki/Ea, the first-rank deity of Eridu, which then made possible the epithet, ^{d}AMAR.UD (^{d}*Marduk*) DUMU (*mârim*) *ri-es-ti-im ša* ^{d}EN.KI (^{d}Ea),

---

11. For the text see King, *Letters and Inscriptions*, 94; Borger, *Babylonisch-Assyrische Lesestücke*, 1; Sollberger and Kupper, *Inscriptions royales*, 216, IV c 6h.

12. CBS 4503 I:11', published by Sjöberg, "Prayers for King Hammurabi," 58–71.

13. Ibid.; cf. also the Borsippa Inscription above.

14. CBS 4503 I:11'.

15. Ibid. I:7'.

16. Ibid.

17. CH reverse xxv 27–29 (*ANET*, 178); Canal Inscription (*LIH* 95) 6–7, on which see Sjöberg, "Ein Selbstpreis des Königs Hammurabi," 66.

18. Ibid., A:12–13

By the River Chebar

"Marduk, firstborn of Enki."[19] This shift reflects Babylon's changing status among the cities of lower Mesopotamia.

The Prologue to the Law Code of Hammurabi specifically notes his promotion by Anu and Enlil to the status of one of the great gods and ties to it the ascendancy of Babylon:

> Lofty Anum, king of the Anunnaki, and Enlil, lord of heaven and earth, the determiner of the destinies of the land, determined for Marduk, the first born of Enki, the Enlil functions (^{d}en-lil-ut) over all man-kind, made him great among the Igigi, called Babylon by its exalted name, made it supreme in the world, established for him in its midst an enduring kingship, whose foundations are as firm as heaven and earth (CH I:II).[20]

Thereafter they (Anu and Enlil) rooted out all his enemies, made his destiny glorious, delivered into his hand "the life of the land," and then exalted Hammurabi, his (Asalluḫi's) shepherd, putting under him all the "black-headed."[21] It is apparent that Marduk's star had finally risen and that he was now firmly positioned among the great gods of the Mesopotamian pantheon.

Marduk's popularity continued during the reigns of Hammurabi's successors. Esagila was refurbished, and new golden thrones were constructed for him and his consort, Sarpanitum.[22] He began to be lauded in Babylonian hymnody, such as the following hymnic prayer for Abi-esuḫ:

> Your grandfather Anu, the king of the gods,
> has caused you to rule over the hosts of heaven and earth;
> He has given you responsibility for the exalted great decrees
> of heaven and earth;
> He has put into your head the ruler's staff that brings all
> [enemy] lands into submission.

---

19. CH i:8–10. Enki/Ea was acknowledged as lord of the life-giving fresh waters. Cf. Edzard, in *Götter und Mythen*, 56–57.

20. *ANET*, 164.

21. CBS 4503. Cf. Sjöberg, "Prayers for King Hammurabi," 61–67, I:31′–35′. As noted earlier in both the Borsippa (*LIH* 94) and Canal Inscriptions (*LIH* 95), Hammurabi credits Anu and Enlil with his rise. A first millennium edition of the Code of Hammurabi has replaced Babylon with Nippur (CH i:16) and Marduk with Enlil (xv: 15), thereby removing the references to the rise of Marduk and his city Babylon. The edition has the appearance of an anti-Babylon, Nippurian polemic. For the text see Wiseman, "Laws of Hammurabi Again," 161–71. For a discussion of and further bibliography on the text see Sommerfeld, *Der Aufstieg Marduks*, 76, n. 1.

22. Ungnad, "Datenlisten," 182–83.

> He has made you greater than all the gods.
> Furthermore, he has charged you to guide befittingly
> the royal scepter and the regulation of the gods.
> Enlil has determined the kingship over the entire heaven
> and earth as your destiny;
> He has permitted no one to be your equal.
> Among the Anunna-gods he has made you great;
> He has commissioned you to rule over them.[23]

Sommerfeld has correctly cautioned against over-interpretation of this hymn.[24] The fact that Anu and Enlil have granted him his power demonstrates that, while Marduk has been elevated to a position "greater than the gods," these two are to be excluded from this comparison.

The basis for Marduk's attractiveness seems to have been his special love for his subjects.[25] As one letter writer put it, "May Marduk, the one who loves you (*ra-im-ka*), be with you in your daily affairs." In fact, the participle *ra-im* + suffix, "the one who loves you," becomes a quasi-epithet for this deity,"[26] leading Sommerfeld to speak of a distinctive and emphatic *Menschenfreundlichkeit* (benevolence).[27] He was the kind of god who was particularly responsive to the needs and expectations of the people. The pain of failed expectations in one's personal deity and the trust that was placed in Marduk is poignantly expressed in a letter written by a certain Apil-Adad to his god:

> To the god, my father, speak!
> Thus says Apil-Adad thy servant:
> Why have you neglected me so?
> Who is going to give you one who can take my place?
> Write to the god Marduk, who is fond of you,
> that he may break my bondage;
> Then shall I see your face and kiss your feet!
> Consider also my family, grown-ups and little ones;
> Have mercy on me for their sake, and let your help reach me![28]

---

23. TCL 16, 81, on which see Falkenstein, "Ein sumerisches Kultlied auf Samsu'iluna," 214.

24. Sommerfeld, *Der Aufstieg Marduks*, 109.

25. On the personality of Marduk in literary texts see Sommerfeld, "Marduk," 367–70.

26. Only occasionally is it used of other deities. Sin, *ABPh* 120:10; Shamash, *AbB* 1, 18:13; 7, 153:3; *ABPh* 123:15.

27. Sommerfeld, *Der Aufstieg Marduks*, 125.

28. As translated by Jacobsen, *Treasures of Darkness*, 160. For the Akkadian text see Stamm, *Die akkadische Namengebung*, 54–55.

On the other hand, Lambert has rightly cautioned against too simplistic a view of Marduk's *Menschenfreundlichkeit*.[29] In *Ludlil bêl nêmeqi*, a sort of Babylonian Job account,[30] Marduk deprives his devoted, and apparently righteous, servant of everything he has—his wealth, status, family, friends, and health. Although the piece has a pious tone, and Marduk eventually restores the subject to his former status, Marduk's responsibility for the calamity is explicitly affirmed. As Lambert observes, this is a strange way to express love.

The Trials and Tribulations of an Ambitious God

The Old Babylonian period came to an abrupt end in the thirtieth year of Samsuditana when the Hittites under Mursilis I swept in from the north, took Aleppo in the Syrian heartland, sacked Mari on the mid-Euphrates, and finally reached Babylon in 1595 BCE. Though the Hittites' stay in Babylon was short-lived, it was long enough to disrupt the administration of the city and to open its gates to the Kassites. Upon Mursilis' retreat, the Kassite hordes burst out of the mountains to the northeast and overran the Babylon.

Although the Kassites were foreigners, and their kings claimed descent from their own god Shugamuna, they quickly adopted the native theological traditions.[31] The kings themselves seem to have adopted Anu and Enlil as their personal patrons,[32] but during their tenure (1595–1157 BCE) Marduk's hold on Babylon remained firm. In fact, the idea of Marduk's supremacy over the Babylonian pantheon began to be toyed with. This notion is reflected in the personal name, *Marduk-šar-ilî*, "Marduk, king of the gods,"[33] but the significance of this evidence should not be exaggerated. The source is unofficial and other divine names were also being used in the same way.[34] On the other hand, the increasing stature of

---

29. Lambert, "Studies in Marduk," 6.

30. Cf. Lambert, *Babylonian Wisdom Literature*, 21–62. For the previously missing lines 13–40 see Wiseman, "New Test of the Babylonian Poem," 101–7.

31. Cf. the Agum II inscription, Unger, *Babylon*, 276–77. On the Kassites see Brinkman, "Kassiten (*Kaššû*)," 464–73.

32. Cf. Kurigalzu I's self-introduction as "Favourite of Anu and Enlil, the one named by the gods." Ungnad, *Archiv für Keilschriftforschung*, 29ff.; Brinkman, *Materials and Studies*, 209, Q. 2.1. Also *ANET*, 57–59.

33. Cf. Clay, *Personal Names*, 106.

34. Lambert, "Studies in Marduk," 3, notes Nabu, Ea, Sin Adad, Ninurta, Nirah.

Marduk among the gods is suggested by the god-list An = *Anum*, which derives from the Kassite period. Although the segment that contains Marduk's names is incompletely preserved,[35] the fact that the number of names ascribed to him is fifty (the mystical number of Enlil) indicates that in the eyes of the compiler he has usurped Enlil's position.[36]

As a matter of fact, Babylon's growing influence at this time was reflected in the spreading fame of Marduk to other lands. In the fourteenth century, personal names bearing Marduk as the theophore began to appear in Assyria.[37] A clay tablet inscription from the time of Ashur-uballit I (1363–1338 BCE), a royal scribe, Marduk-nadin-aḫḫe, son of Marduk-uballit, son of Ush-shur-ana Marduk, reports that he built his house "in the shadow of the temple of the god Marduk." He also addresses Marduk as his patron and invokes his blessing upon the house and himself, as well as upon Ashuruballit the king.[38] Marduk's name even began to appear in faraway Hatti-land.[39]

But all was not roses for this upstart divinity. In fact, the Kassite period began with a serious crisis for Marduk. Among the booty hauled off by the Hittites to Hatti-land were the treasures of Esagila, including Marduk's own image and that of his consort, Sarpanitum. Similar tragedies happened on two occasions toward the end of the period.

In the late thirteenth century, the declining Kassite rulers were faced by the dynamic Assyrian king, Tukulti-Ninurta I (1243–1207 BCE). He defeated Kaštiliaš IV (1232–1225 BCE) in 1230 BCE and hauled off the statue of Marduk,[40] as the following excerpt from Chronicle P reports:

> He [Tukulti-Ninurta I] took out the property of Esagil and Babylon amid the booty. He removed the great lord Marduk [from] his [dais] and sent [him] to Assyria. . . . For [N] + six

35. Cf. Böhl, "Die fünfzig Namen des Marduk," 191–218.
36. So also Lambert, "Studies in Marduk," 3.
37. Cf. Fine, "Studies in Middle-Assyrian Chronology," 116–30.
38. For a translation of the text see Grayson, *Assyrian Royal Inscriptions*, 43–43. For discussion of this text see Willis, *Foundation Deposits*, 96–97. On the beginnings of Marduk's presence in Assyria see Brinkmann, "Notes on Mesopotamian History," 308, n. 82.
39. EKo 1:13. Cf. Laroche, *Catalogue des texts Hittites*, 786; Kammenhuber, "Marduk," 370. The transliterated text and a translation are also provided by Sommerfeld, *Der Aufstieg Marduks*, 198–99.
40. For a transcription and translation of the accounts of the event, see Weidner, *Die Inschriften Tukulti-Ninurtas I*, texts 5, 6, 16, 17. Cf. *Assyrian Royal Inscriptions* I, 197–10; 177–22.

> years—until [the time of] Tukulti-Ashur-Bel stayed in Assyria.
> In the time of Tukulti Ashur, Bel went to Babylon.[41]

The identity of Tukulti-Ashur is not clear. He is often equated with Ninurta-Tukulti-Ashur (1134 BCE),[42] but this creates considerable chronological problems. He may have been among the nobles who rebelled against Tukulti-Ninurta I seven years after his conquest of Babylon and put Adad-shuma-uṣur on the throne.[43]

After he was returned to Esagil by Tukulti-Ashur, Marduk hardly had time to settle before an even more serious threat appeared on the horizon. In about 1160 BCE, Kudur-Nahunte and the Elamites swept in from the plains of Susa to the east, plundered the city and deported much of the population, including the last Kassite king, Enlil-nadin-ahi. He too committed the ultimate sacrilege of razing Esagil and dragging off the image of Marduk. The event is reported as follows:

> [Kudur-nanhundi became angry] and swept away the whole population of Akkad like the deluge; [Babylon and the other] famous cult centres he transformed [into ruin heaps]. The great lord Marduk, he made rise from the throne of his majesty.[44]

This marks the third time the statue of Marduk had been purloined. The spoliation of the images of the patron deities of conquered cities was a common practice in the ancient Near East. The practice was intended to portray the abandonment of the foe by his gods in submission to the god of the conqueror. But viewed from the perspective of the deity, the departure of a deity from his city was understood as a sign of his extreme displeasure with his subjects.[45] This is explicitly stated in a fragmentary "historiographic" text dealing with the Elamite spoliation, K 4874 + Rm 1 255:[46]

> At that time, in the reign of a previous king, conditions changed.
> Good departed and evil was regular.
> The lord became angry and got furious.

---

41. As translated by Grayson, *Assyrian and Babylonian Chronicles*, 176.
42. Ibid., 176, 22:12; Grayson, *Assyrian Royal Inscriptions* I, 134.
43. Grayson, *Assyrian and Babylonian Chronicles* 22:iv:7–9
44. For the text and translation see Tadmor, "Historical Implications," 137–39.
45. See the discussion by Block, *Gods of the Nations*, 169–70.
46. For the text and translation see Lambert, "Enmeduranki and Related Matters," 128–31. Cf. the discussion in Block, *Gods of the Nations*, 136.

> He gave the command, and the gods of the land abandoned it
> [...]
> Its people were incited to commit crime.
> The guardians of peace became furious,
> and went up to the dome of heaven.
> The spirit of justice stood aside...,
> Who guards living beings, prostrated the people.
> They all became like those who have not god.
> Evil demons filled the land, the namtar-demon [...].
> They penetrated the cult centres.
> The land diminished, its fortunes changed (lines 15–22).

A slightly different perspective is presented by the so-called "Prophetic Speech of Marduk,"[47] which commemorates all three of these crises. The text is remarkable in several respects. First, with respect to genre, it represents the only extant ancient Near Eastern autobiography of a god. Second, in terms of substance, it presents a distinctive perspective on these events. In this portraiture of the patron of Babylon, Marduk's deportations are painted in totally positive strokes. Concerning his journey to Ḫatti-land, Marduk writes:

> I am Marduk, the Great Lord. I am always watching, walking watchfully over the mountains. I watch, a watchman, roaming the lands.[48] Throughout all the lands, from the rising of the sun to the setting of the sun, [...] I have roamed. I issued the order, and went out to the land of Ḫatti. I inquired of Ḫatti. In its midst I erected the throne of my divinity [Anum-dignity]. During the twenty-four years that I lived there I established there [lit. "in its midst"] the commerce of the citizens of Babylon. Its [i.e., the land of Ḫatti]. [...] Its merchandise and its goods [were sent] to (?) Sippar, Nippur, [and Babylo]n. [A king of Babylon(?)] arose and led me in procession [lit. "grasped my hand(?)"]. [... to] Babylon, which [...] was in good order. The processional street [?] of Babylon[?] was beautiful. The crown of my divinity (Anum-dignity) [...] and the image [...].[49]

---

47. For an English translation of the entire text, see Excursus A, above, 100–104. For transliteration, alternative translations, and commentary, see Neujahr, *Predicting the Past in the Ancient Near East*, 27–41; Borger, "Der Gott Marduk," 3–24 (German). For additional English translations, see Longman, *Fictional Akkadian Autobiography*, 132–42, 233–35; Longman, *COS*, 480–82; Foster, *Before the Muses*, 388–91. Longman provides a discussion of the text on pp. 132–42.

48. Lines 8–9 rendered according to *CAD* Ḫ 159b.

49. I:21'b–II:11. Cf. Block, *Gods of the Nations* (2013), 171–72.

By the River Chebar

Far from being *schleppt* off, Marduk, the world traveler, had decided to take a trip of his own free will. Combining business with pleasure he capitalized on the opportunity by establishing important trade relations with Hatti-land and his own city. The same is true of his other deportations.

Marduk's sojourn in Assyria, the result of Tukulti-Ninurta's absconding with the statue, is remembered as follows (I:12–21'):

> I completed (my days); I blessed Assyria. I handed him [. . . (the tablet)] of destinies. I established him. I returned home. With reference to Babylon I declared, "Bring your tribute, O lands, to Babylon!" I am Marduk, the Great Lord. I am the Lord of Destinies and Decrees. Who has undertaken such a journey [like this]? As I departed [?], so I have returned.[50]

Again, the stress was on the voluntary nature of the divine action.

The description of the Elamite exile contains the most detailed explanation for the god's abandonment of his city and the disastrous consequences of that abandonment:

> I issued the order. I went to the land of Elam, and all the gods went (with me). I issued the order myself. The meal offerings (*nindabê*) of the temples I terminated myself. Šakkan [the god of cattle] and Nisaba [the goddess of grain] I sent up to heaven. Siris [the god of beer] made the heart of the country sick. The corpses of the people blocked the doorways. Brothers consumed one another. Friends beat each other up with weapons. The nobles (*mārū bani*) stretched out their hands against the poor. The scepter was shortened. Disaster struck the land. Kings (*šarrānū*) reduced the land. Lions blocked the roads. Dogs [went mad] and bit people. None whom they bit recovered; they died.[51]

Again, the text observes that while in exile Marduk worked energetically on behalf of his city, establishing trade connections between Babylon and Elam. However, an actual change for the better in the city's fortunes occurred only after Marduk had a change of heart regarding Babylon. After he had fulfilled his (predetermined?) days in exile his heart longed for Ekur Sagila. He called for the goddesses and announced the arrival of a new king of Babylon, who would give proper attention to his cult once again:

---

50. Cf. Block, *Gods of the Nations*, 171.
51. I:21'b–II:11. Cf. ibid., 171–72.

A king of Babylon will arise. The amazing temple, Ekur-Sagila, he will restore. In Ekur-Sagila he will redraw the plans of heaven and earth. He will increase [?] its height. In my city, Babylon, he will establish exemption from taxes. He will lead me in procession [lit. "grasp my hand"] into my city, Babylon, and bring me into the Ekur-Sagila forever. He will restore the [procession] ship, Matusha. He will repair its rudder with ṣāriru-gold. He will [plate?] its bow with *pašallu*-metal. Sailors who man it, he will bring on board. They will be stationed to the right and to the left. A king [?], who like the star [?] of Ekur-Sagila. . . .[52]

Marduk's Reach for the Top

The identity of the king spoken of in the foregoing text is well known. The reign of Nebuchadnezzar I (1125–1104 BCE), the fourth ruler in the second dynasty of Isin, marked a major turning point, not only in the history of Babylon,[53] but also in the fortunes of Marduk.[54] It fell to Nebuchadnezzar to rescue Marduk's statue from "the wicked Elamites."[55] This achievement is described in a *kudurru* inscription from this period:

> Nebuchadnezzar, the king, undertook an expedition on their behalf, and they went with him to Elam and he overthrew Elam. The hand of Bêl he took, and Erija together with Bêl he carried into Babylon, and from Babylon he brought Erija into the city of Khussi.[56]

The last phrase of the "Prophetic Speech" represents an *ex eventu* report and theological interpretation of this event. The text is dated by most to the time of Nebuchadnezzar I.

In perceiving himself as the specially chosen agent of Marduk, the one who raised his weapon to avenge Akkad, "the prince, the beloved of

---

52. II:19–34. Cf. ibid., 172.

53. On his reign see Brinkman, *Political History of Post-Kassite Babylonia*, 104–18.

54. On the religious significance of Nebuchadnezzar's achievements see Lambert, "The Reign of Nebuchadnezzar I," 3–11.

55. The expression *se-e-nu e-la-mú* occurs in K 4874:23. Grayson, *Babylonian Historical-Literary Texts*, 42–43, has recently identified as text fragment from Kouyunjik which narrates Nebuchadnezzar's lament over the absence of Marduk. He suggests the remainder contained an epic account of the rescue of the image.

56. King, *Babylonian Boundary Stones*, 96, 24:7–14 (hereafter cited as *BBSt*).

Marduk," the one sent forth by the god,[57] Nebuchadnezzar was simply continuing the tradition of his predecessors. However, during his reign a most remarkable revolution was occurring in the heavens. Hints of the new situation may be found already in the use of the title for Marduk in royal and literary inscriptions,[58] and the increasing occurrence in the Isin II documents of universalistic epithets for Marduk, like *bêlu rabû*, "great lord,"[59] *bêl mâtâti*, "lord of the lands,"[60] *sar same u erṣeti*, "king of heaven and earth,"[61] *asarêd gimri*, "the foremost of the universe."[62] However, most striking are the new claims being made for the Babylonian deity in such epithets as *ur-sag-dingir-re-e-[ne]*, "hero of the gods,"[63] and especially *sar ilî*, "king of the gods,"[64] *Bêl bêl* [*bêlêXXX*], "lord of lords,"[65] and *en-lil ilâniXXX*.[66]

But the changes in the relationships among the gods are expressed most eloquently in Enuma Elish. The date of this document is disputed, but if Lambert's interpretation is correct, this text was composed during the reign of Nebuchadnezzar I to provide theological justification for the changes in the pantheonic relationships.[67] The epic opens by recounting

---

57. 6:11–12. Nebuchadnezzar's self-conscious dependence upon Marduk is reflected in a hatchet inscription translated by Brinkman, *Political History of Post-Kassite Babylonia*, 106, n. 575, as follows:

> Marduk, you are able to make the pious [man] . . . , who frequents your shrines, stand over [his] enemies. [. . .] Strengthen my Weapons so that I may cause my foes to fall. Belonging to Nebuchadnezzar, king of the world.

For the transliterated text see Dossin, "Bronzes inscrits," 158, #14.

58. Cf. the Adad-shuma-uṣur Epic, i:10, ii:16, 20, 25 (assuming a Nebuchadnezzar I dating with Grayson, *Babylonian Historical-Literary Texts*, 65, 69); *BBSt* 24:11–12.

59. *BBSt* 8:iii:31.

60. *BBSt* 11 iv:5.

61. *BBSt* 7 ii:25; Reschid and Wilcke, "Ein Grensztein," 56, lines 64–65.

62. Ibid.

63. Böhl, "Eine zweisprachige Weihinschrift," 42–46.

64. *BBSt* 6 i:12; K 4874 25.

65. Adad-shuma-uṣur Epic ii:16, 20.

66. K 4874:32.

67. Lambert, "Studies in Marduk," 4; Lambert, "The Reign of Nebuchadnezzar I," 3–4; Sommerfeld, *Der Aufstieg Marduks*, 174–76, follows von Soden ("Der hymnische Dialekt," 125–30) in arguing for a Kassite date. So also Jacobsen, *Treasures of Darkness*, 189–980, who associates Marduk's victory over Tiamat with Ulamburiash's conquest of the "Sealand," i.e., southern Babylonia, and his reunion of Sumer and Akkad. Speiser, *ANET*, 60, accepts an Old Babylonian provenance.

Chasing a Phantom

the origins of the gods. Premonitions of Marduk's coming role appear early in the birth narrative of this remarkable deity:[68]

> He who begot him was Ea, his father;
> She who bore him was Damkina, his mother.
> The breasts of the goddesses he did suck.
> The nurse that nursed him filled him with awesomeness.
> Alluring was his figure, sparkling the lift of his eyes.
> Lordly was his gait, commanding from of old.
> When Ea saw him, the father who begot him.
> He exulted and glowed,
> His heart filled with gladness.
> He rendered him perfect and endowed him
> with a double godhead.
> Greatly exalted was he above them, exceeding throughout.
> Perfect were his members beyond comprehension,
> Unsuited for understanding, difficult to perceive.
> Four were his eyes; four were his ears,
> When he moved his lips, fire blazed forth.
> Large were all four hearing organs,
> And the eyes in like manner, scanned all things.
> He was the loftiest of the gods, surpassing was his stature;
> His members were enormous, he was exceeding tall.
> "My little son, my little son!
> "My son, the Sun! Sun of the heavens!" (I:83–102)

However, by this time the conflict between Tiamat's forces and the rest of the divinities had begun. After Ann and Nudimmud had failed to challenge Tiamat, Marduk was chosen to champion the cause of the great gods and put down the rebellion. But like Jephthah in Judges 11, he was not oblivious to the political gain to be made. As a reward for his efforts, he demanded full authority over all the gods:

> Creator of the gods, destiny of the great gods.
> If I indeed, as your avenger,
> Am to vanquish Tiamat and save your lives,
> Set up the Assembly, proclaim supreme my destiny!
> When jointly in the Ubshukinna you have sat down rejoicing,
> Let my word, instead of you, determine the fates.
> Unalterable shall be what I may bring into being;
> Neither recalled nor changed shall be the command of my lips!"
> (II:122–29)

---

68. The translations follow that of Speiser.

The Assembly was called, and at the banquet, at the height of their inebriation, the gods conferred on Marduk all that he requested:

> They erected for him a princely throne.
> Facing his fathers he sat down, presiding.
> Thou art the most honored of the great gods,
> Thy decree is unrivaled, thy command is Anu.
> Thou, Marduk, art the most honored among the great gods,
> Thy decree is unrivaled, thy word is Anu.
> From this day unchangeable shall be thy pronouncements,
> To raise or bring low—these shall be in thy hand.
> Thy utterance shall be true, thy command shall be unimpeachable.
> No one among the gods shall transgress thy bounds!
> Adornment being wanted for the seats of the gods,
> Let the place of their shrines ever be in thy place.
> O Marduk, thou art indeed our avenger.
> We have granted thee kingship over the universe entire.
> When in Assembly thou sittest, thy word shall be supreme.
> (IV:1–15)

The following lines report that after Marduk had passed the test of the power of his word by creating and destroying a constellation, the proclamation was issued: "Marduk is King!" Having accepted the promotion, Marduk launched his attack on Tiamat. He was able to inflict a mortal blow on her rebellious forces, and upon Tiamat herself, from whose body he proceeded to create the universe. As a symbol of his newly won pantheonic authority he allocated to the triad of great gods their respective spheres: for Anu, the heavens; for Enlil, the earth; for Ea/Apsu, the waters below the earth. He then went on to create man, whom he charged with "the service of the gods that they might be at ease" (VI:8). The lesser gods, the Anunnaki, he rewarded with their own areas of jurisdiction. In gratitude they constructed the city of Babylon and Esagila as his permanent residence. The elevation of Marduk reached its climax with the conferral upon him of the fifty names of the great gods, beginning with Anu and ending with Enlil, who offers him his own title, "Lord of the lands." The significance of this final act is explained in EE VII:143–44: "With the title 'Fifty' the great gods proclaimed him whose names are fifty and made his way supreme." Marduk had truly reached the top.

This newly won position atop the Babylonian pantheon is reflected elsewhere as well. Increasingly Marduk's apologists saw the other deities merging with their own patron. In a triple-column god-list the name

Chasing a Phantom

Marduk is flanked on the left by a series of names of other deities and on the right by the respective deities' functions:

    Urash   is Marduk of planting.
    Lugalidda is Marduk of the abyss.
    Ninurta   is Marduk of strength.
    Nergal   is Marduk of battle.
    Zamama is Marduk of warfare.
    Elm   is Marduk of lordship and consultations.
    Nabu   is Marduk of accounting.
    Sin   is Marduk who lights up the night.
    Shamash is Marduk of justice.
    Adad   is Marduk of rain.
    Tishku   is Marduk of troops.[69]

In another document, a prayer to Marduk, various members of the pantheon are referred to as aspects of Marduk:

> I will pay homage to your great divinity.
> Oath(s) by the raising of hands to Marduk:
> You shall carry them out either offering utensils or incense.
> Oath:
> Sin is your divinity;
> Ann is your royalty;
> Dagan is your lordship;
> Enlil is your royalty;
> Ada is your strength;
> Ea the wise, is your ears;
> The one who holds the stylus, Nabu, is your skill;
> Your leadership is Ninurta;
> Your power is Nergal;
> The council of your heart is Nusku, your vizier;
> Your judgeship is Shamash, the shining one, who prevents enmity from arising.
> Your glorious name is "The Wise One" among the gods, Marduk.[70]

---

69. CT 24 50. Cf. the translation by Lambert, "The Historical Development of the Mesopotamian Pantheon," 197–98, as well as Rogers, *Cuneiform Parallels*, 193, and the discussion on p. 191.

70. *KAR* 25 ii:1–10. Cf. Ebeling, *Die akkadische Gebetsserie*, 14–15. Another fragmentary text reflecting similar notions is published by Lambert, "Reign of Nebuchadnezzar I," 11–13.

By the River Chebar

To the theologians of Babylon Marduk had not simply replaced another deity; he had swallowed them up, and in so doing posed as the sole power of the universe. As Lambert observes, "all other powers of nature were but aspects of him."[71] More recently Lambert has interpreted this identification of all the male deities of the pantheon with Marduk as "a kind of monotheism."[72] While this is still a far cry from the Israelite belief in the existence of only one god, it represents an unambiguous affirmation that Marduk had indeed reached the pinnacle.[73]

The Challenge of Maintaining Power

But, like Babylon's position among cities of Mesopotamia, Marduk's hold on the throne of the gods was never secure. After the death of Nebuchadnezzar, the city's (Babylon's) fortunes, and with them Marduk's, declined rapidly. In 1068, Adad-apla-iddina (1068–47 BCE), who is described in the chronicles as "an Aramaean, a usurper,"[74] and "a son of nobody,"[75] seized the throne. In the meantime, the Sutians had begun their raiding incursions into Babylonia,[76] sacking old cult centers and carrying off their spoils. In the process the cult statue of Shamash at Sippar was lost,[77] and that of Enlil was hauled off from Nippur.[78]

The fate of Marduk during these troubled times is uncertain. The textual sources note that the entire country was ravaged and all the temples leveled,[79] which would suggest a similar fate for the Babylonian deity. However, if the Erra Epic reflects these historical events,[80] then Marduk's

71. "The Historical Development of the Mesopotamian Pantheon," 198.

72. Lambert, "Ancient Mesopotamian Gods," 121.

73. According to Abusch, "The Form and Meaning of a Babylonian Prayer to Marduk," 3–15, the rise of Marduk from a local deity to a nation god is commemorated in the Babylonian prayer BMS9, which he dates to the reign of Adad-apla-iddina (1067–1047 BCE).

74. ^{kur}A-ra-mu-u šarru ḫammā'u, Assyrian and Babylonian Chronicles 24:8'. Gratitude is expressed to A. R. Millard for his reminder of this reference.

75. mār la ma-ma-n[A], Assyrian and Babylonian Chronicles 21:ii:31' (Synchronistic History).

76. Assyrian and Babylonian Chronicles 24:10'11'.

77. BBSt 36 i:20–23.

78. Goetze, "An Inscription of Simbar-Sihu," 121–22, lines 10–14.

79. Ibid.; BBSt 36 ii:29–30.

80. So Lambert, in a review of Gössmann, Das Era-Epos, 395–401, followed by Brinkman, Political History of Post-Kassite Babylonia, 139. The text itself was probably written later. Cf. Cagni, The Poem of Erra, 20–21.

lot may have been less severe. In the account, Erra, the pest god, persuades Marduk to get off his throne and vacate Esagila. The voluntary departure of the deity signifies his abandonment of his statue as well.[81] However, when Marduk leaves, the equilibrium of the entire universe is upset and a disaster analogous to the Great Deluge many generations earlier (which had also been brought on by Marduk's getting off his throne) ensues. The image of Marduk painted by this literary piece is not optimistic. To be sure, he is still the king on the throne, but he is presented as a weak willed, if not senile personality, unaware of the state of his domain and apparently powerless before Erra. The latter must incite him to be angry over the rebellion (*ḫuburru*) of his subjects.[82]

But the real threat to Babylon during this period was posed by the neo-Assyrians. At the beginning of the twelfth century, Tiglath-Pileser I (1114–1076 BCE) had managed to wage a campaign southward that took him as far as the city of Babylon.[83] With the rise of Assyria came the most severe challenge yet to Marduk's position among the Mesopotamian gods, the increasing might of Ashur. Marduk's troubles at home are reported in The Religious Chronicle which says that between 1033 and 943 BCE the Babylonian *akitu* festival was frequently suspended.[84] "Bel did not come out," that is, he did not go forth in the annual procession.[85] In one instance the reason for the disruption is explicitly stated, the Aramaeans were belligerent (iii:4, 7).

Meanwhile, all kinds of bizarre phenomena were being observed within the city, including unusual animals (a lion [i:17, cf. iii:11], a wolf [ii:6, iii:1], a panther [ii:9], two deer [ii:12, cf. iii:3]), fire in the sky (ii:14), the movement of the outer wall of the Urash-gate (ii:19), the movement of an image (iii:16), and a demon in a bed chamber (iii:16). These were auspicious signs that something was awry in the universe. Marduk's control was in serious question.

But Marduk experienced the ultimate indignity in the seventh century. Beginning with Merodach-Baladan II (Marduk-apla-iddina, 721–710 BCE), a series of Babylonian rulers had attempted to regain independence

81. Cf. Lambert, review of F. Gössmann, *Das Era-Epos*, 399.

82. Cagni, *Poem of Erra*, 28–29, I:42, 73, 82.

83. *Assyrian and Babylonian Chronicles* 21 ii:18'–21'. On the dates and circumstances of the campaign see Brinkman, *Political History of Post-Kassite Babylonia*, 126.

84. For the text see Grayson, *Assyrian and Babylonian Chronicles*, 133–38, Chronicle 17. For a discussion of the nature and significance of the document see pp. 36–39.

85. On which see Black, "New Year Ceremonies," "Taking Bel by the Hand," and "Cultic Picnic," 39–59.

from Assyria. Finally, in 689 BCE Sennacherib had had enough. Infuriated by their revolt at the death of Sargon, and their delivery of his son into the hands of the Elamites,[86] he mercilessly razed the city, and inundated the sacred precinct with water brought in by freshly dug canals. The Assyrian's intentions are explicitly stated in the Bavian Inscription: "That in days to come the site of the city, and its temples and gods, might not be remembered, I completely blotted it out with (floods) of water and made it like a meadow."[87] Sennacherib's problems with Babylon are chronicled in ABC 1 ii:19–iii:36.

However, from the inscriptions of Esarhaddon we learn that Marduk's statue had escaped destruction and had been purloined to Ashur. One text speaks of the gods "flying off like birds" and going up to heaven,[88] leaving the impression that Marduk had simply left his statue, as had been the case in the Erra Epic. However, several chronicles relate the event more concretely:

> For eight years [during the reign of] Sennacherib,
> For twelve years [during the reign of] Esarhaddon—
> Twenty years [altogether]—
> Bel stayed [in B]altil [Ashur]
> And the Akitu festival did not take place.
> Nabu did not come from Borsippa for the procession of Bel. . . .
> The accession year of Shamash-shumaukin:
> In the month Iyyar Bel and the gods of [Akkad] went out from Baltil [Ashur]
> And on the twenty-fifth day of the month Iyyar [they entered] Babylon.
> Nabu and the gods of Borsippa [went] to Babylon.[89]

Esarhaddon's building inscriptions provide a full theological interpretation of the collapse of this proud city.[90] The crisis had been precipitated by "evil forces" in Sumer and Akkad expressed in a series of moral and cultic offenses by the Babylonians. In his rage Marduk himself plotted

86. Brinkman, "Through a Glass Darkly," 35.

87. Luckenbill, *Ancient Records* 2.341 (hereafter cited as *ARAB*).

88. See Borger, *Die Inschriften Asarhaddons*, 14, Ep. 8; cf. *ARAB* 2, 649.

89. Esarhaddon Chronicle, *Assyrian and Babylonian Chronicles* 14:31–27. Cf. parallel accounts in the Babylonian Chronicle, *Assyrian and Babylonian Chronicles* 1 iv:34–36, and the Akitu Chronicle, *Assyrian and Babylonian Chronicles* 16:1–8.

90. Borger, *Die Inschriften Asarhaddons*, 11–15. Cf. Block, *Gods of the Nations*, 139–44. On this theological interpretation of the event see Brinkman, "Through a Glass Darkly," 35–42.

evil against the land, determining to level it and to bring its population to ruin. The city found itself under the curse of its patron deity, who had abandoned her, and at the mercy of the Assyrians. Writing the sentence down on the tablets of fate, Marduk decreed that this ruinous state should exist for seventy (𒐕𒌋) years.

However, Marduk had a change of heart. By transposing the digits in the number (𒌋𒐕), the apparently immutable decree of a seventy year devastation was cleverly transformed into an eleven year sentence. Having come upon a solution that was legally satisfying, he appointed Esarhaddon as the shepherd over the Assyrians and commissioned him with the task of rebuilding Babylon. The astrological signs suggested a return to normalcy in the heavens and the angered gods were reconciled to Akkad. An omen was given and Esarhaddon was charged to prepare for the return of Marduk by rebuilding Esagila. The king hesitated, and Marduk had to reassure him with a second sign. Finally the project was completed, and the citizens of Babylon could return home. The divine statues were redecorated, the cult rituals reinstituted, and images returned from exile.[91]

But Esarhaddon was an Assyrian. Even so, his disposition toward Marduk differed radically from that of his predecessor. To be sure, in the description of his fight for the throne he referred to Ashur as "king of the gods," whereas Marduk was "the merciful one,"[92] but he was also quite aware of the Babylonian tradition that viewed Marduk as "the lord of lords."[93] In fact, in a letter to the god Ashur, he identifies Marduk as "king of the gods!"[94] His theologically eclectic policies, designed not to cause offence to any of the gods, were continued by his successor, Ashurbanipal, the one who is actually to be credited with the return of the Marduk statue.[95]

91. KAR 143+ and parallels appear to constitute a special ritual text intended to commemorate Marduk's experiences during the past two decades and to celebrate his return to Esagila and his vindication in the annual Akitu festival in Babylon. Thus Frymer-Kensky, "The Tribulations of Marduk," 131–41. This interpretation is preferable to that of von Soden, "Gibt es ein Zeugnis?" 130–66, who sees in this text an anti-Marduk polemic in which the god is subjected to a judicial ordeal and punished for some crime he has committed by spending some time in the nether world, but in the end rising again from the dead.

92. ANET, 289.

93. ARAB 2.576. Cf. 667, "Marduk, the first-born, lord of the gods."

94. ARAB 2.600. Cf. also 657.

95. On Ashurbanipal and Marduk, see Landsberger, *Brief eines Bischofs von Esagila*, 66–69. Cf. also the review of this column by Borger in his review of Landsberger, *Brief eines Bischofs von Esagila*, 33–36; Millard, "Another Babylonian Chronicle Text," 19–23.

By the River Chebar

Marduk's attitude toward the neo-Assyrian period was probably ambivalent. The times were troubled at the beginning, and a nadir was experienced under Sennacherib. But he should have been satisfied with his rehabilitation under Esarhaddon and the continued support he received from the last Assyrian kings. However, the references to him as "king of the gods," began to sound hollow, and seem to have been motivated by sheer political pragmatism. After all, how many gods can be king at one time?

Marduk's Last Chance

Marduk had one more day in the sun. A new era was ushered in by Nabopolassar (625–605 BCE), a Chaldaean, who was able to capitalize on the decline of Assyria after the death of Ashurbanipal and reassert Babylonian independence. He was followed by his more illustrious son, Nebuchadnezzar (604–562 BCE), who succeeded in bringing the city and Babylonian culture to unprecedented heights. However, though incorporating much of the territory previously held by the neo-Assyrians, the neo-Babylonian empire was short-lived. Within less than twenty-five years of his death, the greatness that was Babylon had given way to the Persian colossus.

The question that concerns us is how Marduk fared in this brief period of Babylonian renaissance. The onomastic data suggest that he continued to receive stiff competition from his son Nabu, the patron of Borsippa. Among the neo-Babylonian rulers, the three major ones all bore Nabu-names (Nabopolassar, Nebuchadnezzar, Nabonidus). However, these names should be balanced off with those of Nebuchadnezzar's own family. Of his six known sons, four bore Marduk names.[96] This alternation of Nabu and Marduk names is echoed in the royal inscriptions, where both names appear repeatedly in the epithets of the Babylonian kings. *Tiris qāt Nabûm u Marduk*, "whose hand is held by Nabu and Marduk," seems to have been Nabopolassar's standard epithet,[97] but other phrases involving these two, usually with Nabu first, also occur.[98] Nevertheless, the tifle, *mi-gir* DN, "darling of DN," is restricted to Marduk,[99] and the com-

---

96. Evil Merodach/Amel-Marduk, Marduk-shuma-uṣur, Marduk-nadin-ahi, Mushezib-Marduk, Marduk-nadin-shumi. Cf. Wiseman (*Nebuchadnezzar and Babylon*, 9–12) for a discussion of Nebuchadnezzar's family.

97. So Berger, *Neubabylonischen Königsinschriften*, 72.

98. Cf. ibid., 72–82.

99. Weissbach, *Das Hauptheiligtum in Babylon*, 42–43 (i:21–28).

mon expression *Marduk bê-li-ar*, "Marduk my lord," reflected the locus of primary allegiance.[100] The following stamped brick inscription illustrates Nebuchadnezar's view of his special relationship with Marduk:

> Nebuchadnezzar, king of Babylon, who fears the great gods cares for Esagila and Ezida, son of Nabopolassar, King of Babylon am I. When Marduk the great lord, had raised my head, I offered reverent praise to Marduk the god, my creator.[101]

However, more important for our purposes than the kings' own relationships to Marduk was their perception of Marduk's status among the gods. The first clues may be found in the epithets ascribed to Marduk. Nabopolassar viewed him as:

> Marduk the great lord, Enlil of the gods the mighty one, supervisor of the Igigi, who holds the Anunnaki together, the light of the gods his fathers, who inhabits Esagila, the lord of Babylon, my lord.[102]

Nebuchadnezzar used similarly lofty titles:

> Enlil of the gods, the lofty one, the shining light, who exceeds the gods, his fathers, who inhabits the lord of Babylon, the great lord.[103]

In keeping with this status, the kings engaged in magnificent construction projects for the glory of Marduk. Included in these projects were Etemenanki, the temple tower, whose top was to reach into the heavens,[104] and whose splendor was to evoke amazement in all who saw it. When it was finally completed by Nebuchadnezzar, and the room for Marduk at the top had been decorated with blue-glazed enamel brick, making the topmost stage look like the sky itself,[105] there was great celebration.[106]

---

100. Cf. the building inscriptions of Nabolassar and Nebuchadnezzar in Weissbach, *Das Hauptheiligtum in Babylon*, 42–49.

101. Ibid., 48–49.

102. Ibid., 42–43, i:1–7.

103. Ibid., 46–47, 3:1–6.

104. Ibid., 43, i:26. For more on the tower see, AO.6555, translated by Unger, *Babylon*, 237–42. Lines 37–42 describe the tower itself. Cf. Herodotus' description of the tower in i.181, identified as the temple of Bel, whom he calls the Babylonian Zeus.

105. Cf. Langdon, *Neubabylonische Königsinschriften*, 98 (11 i:23; 114, 14 i:28; 12b, 15 iii:15).

106. Ibid., 90, 1:39.

Among numerous other building projects,[107] Esagil was also rebuilt, as the marvelous new residence befitting the status of Marduk.[108] Nebuchadnezzar spared nothing in his effort to honor Marduk.[109]

How Have the Mighty Fallen!

Long before Marduk's star had even reached its zenith, Judaean prophets had predicted the demise of the divine lord of Babylon. Jeremiah had announced:

> Declare among the nations and proclaim;
> Set up a banner and proclaim;
> Do not conceal it, say:
> "Babylon is taken; Bel is put to shame;
> Merodach [Marduk] is dismayed.
> Her images are put to shame;
> Her idols are dismayed."
> For out of the north a nation has come up against her;
> it shall make her land a desolation, and no one shall live in it;
> both human beings and animals shall flee away. (50:2–3 adapted from *NRSV*)

In another oracle against Babylon he declared:

> I will punish Bel in Babylon,
> And make him disgorge what he has swallowed.
> The nations shall no longer stream to him;
> The wall of Babylon has fallen.
> ...
> Therefore, the time is surely coming says YHWH,
> When I will punish her idols;
> Throughout her land her wounded shall groan. (51:44, 47; cf. vv. 52–23)

---

107. Cf. Berger, *Neubabylonischen Königsinschriften*, 104–8, who lists fifty-eight building projects in which Nebuchadnezzar was engaged. Eleven of these were temples to deities other than Marduk in Babylon; eighteen were temples to the divine patrons of other cities of Babylonia. For a map of Babylon with all its temples see Wiseman, *Nebuchadrezzar*, 52–53; Wiseman, "Babylon," 159.

108. *maḫazi bābal*[ki] *ama tabrātim us šepî*, Langdon, 18, §7 ii:11. Cf. the Esagila Tablet for the dimensions of the building. Unger, *Babylon*, 237–40; Weissbach, *Das Hauptheiligtum in Babylon*, 52–55. For a full discussion of these sacred structures see ibid., 57–84. Cf. the briefer treatment in Wiseman, *Nebuchadrezzar*, 64–73.

109. Even Nebuchadnezzar's Royal Gardens, which Strabo identified as one of "the seven wonders of the world," (*Geography* 16.1.5), will have advanced the reputation of Marduk, the patron of this great city.

With hindsight, the heights to which Nebuchadnezzar had brought Babylonian culture, and with it Marduk's reputation, seem only to have set the deity up for the incredible crash that was to follow. The death of Nebuchadnezzar was followed by a period of political instability in Babylon, and when Nabonidus had finally secured the throne, Marduk's fate was sealed. The way for this humiliation was prepared by Nabonidus, the last neo-Babylonian king.

Nabonidus' paternal origins are obscure, but the course of his life was set by his mother, the long-lived Adad-guppi, who early in his life, had dedicated him to Sin, the divine patron of Harran.[110] Although Nabonidus followed at least one of his predecessors, Nabopolassar, in referring to himself as *nibit Marduk*, "called by Marduk," and claimed the epithet *zānin Esagila u Ezida*, "Provider for Esagila and Ezida,"[111] those titles were largely propagandistic window dressing. Nabopolassar appears to have had no real affection for the lord of Esagila and insisted on putting ideological agendas ahead of political considerations. Ultimately it would cost him his throne and Babylon her independence.[112]

Several lines of evidence demonstrate that Adad-guppi's apparently heterodox dedicatory act was never forgotten. First, the epithets formerly associated with Marduk were transferred to Sin. The closing lines of one of the Harran Inscriptions illustrates this shift in allegiance:

> O Sin, lord of gods, whose name on the first day (of his appearance) is "Weapon-of-Anu," (you) who are able to illuminate the heaven and crush the netherworld, who hold in your hands the power of the Anu-office, who wield all the power of the Enlil office, who have taken over the power of the Ea-office, holding thus in your own hand all the heavenly powers; Enlil among the gods, king of kings, lord of lords, whose commands they do not contradict you who do not have to repeat your order, of whose great awe the heaven and the netherworld are covered—who can do anything without you? You are the one whose utterance all the gods and goddesses living in heaven observe; they execute the command of the Divine Crescent, their own father, who wields the powers of heaven and the nether world without whose exalted command, which is given in heaven every day no country can rest in security and no light can be in the world; the

---

110. "The Prayer of Adad-guppi," in Gadd, "Harran Inscriptions of Nabonidus," 46–56, cf. also *ANET*, 560–62.

111. Cf. Berger, *Neubabylonische Königsinschriften*, 80, 82.

112. So also Weisberg, "Royal Women of the Neo-Babylonian Period," 450.

> gods shake like reeds and the Anunnaki quiver; those who bow down before his command which cannot be changed.[113]

Second, Nabonidus' temple reconstruction projects tended to concentrate on the sacred sites of Sin, the moon god, including Ehulhul in Harran[114] and Ekish-nugul in Ur in southern Babylonia.[115] In fact, in his second year he went so far as to dedicate his only daughter to the lunar cult practiced in Ur.[116] Third, during the reign of Nabonidus, the cult of Marduk in Babylon suffered from wanton neglect. The Nabonidus Chronicle observes that from his seventh to eleventh years, while he was in Teima, "Nabu did not come to Babylon; Bel did not come out; the Akitu festival did not take place."[117] Fourth, Marduk suffered the ultimate ignominy when Nabonidus attempted to convert Esagila into an Ehulhul, a temple of Nanna (Sin). In a vitriolic attack on Nabonidus, apparently written near the end of the Babylonian independence, the king is portrayed as a "mad man," who oppressed his subjects and offended the city's divine patron:

> [He had made the image of a deity] which nobody had (ever) seen in (this) country; [He introduced it into the temple]; He placed (it) upon a pedestal; [. . .] he called it by the name of Nanna.[118]

The text goes on to describe the appearance of the statue, the redecoration of Esagila, and the substitution of the normal cult with that of the new deity. The pro-Marduk composers of the verse account characterized the entire enterprise as "a work of utter deceit," "an abomination," "a work of unholiness," and "blasphemous."[119]

---

113. ii:14–42, as translated by Oppenheim, *ANET*, 563. Cf. Gadd, "Harran Inscriptions of Nabonidus," 60–61.

114. This is anticipated in his mother's prayer, *ANET*, 561, and confirmed in his own testimony, *ANET*, 311–12; 562–63.

115. Cf. Nabonidus Cylinder published by Clay, *Miscellanneous Inscriptions*, 66–75, §45.

116. Cf. the Nabonidus Cylinder referred to in the previous note, on which see Weisberg, "Royal Women," 449.

117. Grayson, *Assyrian and Babylonian Chronicles* 7:ii:5–ii:24. Some suggest that this prolonged stay in the Arabian oasis of Teima was motivated by his passion for the moon cult. Cf. Lewy, "The Late Assyro-Babylonian Cult of the Moon," 434–49; Tadmor, "Inscriptions of Nabunaid," 351–64.

118. The fragmentary "Verse Account of Nabonidus," as translated by Oppenheim, *ANET*, 313. Cf. S. Smith, *Babylon Historical Texts*, 83–91.

119. *ANET*, 313 14. Nabonidus' offenses against the population and the cult are also "predicted" in "The Dynastic Prophecy"; Grayson, *Babylonian Historical-Literary Texts*, 32–33.

Chasing a Phantom

These offenses against Marduk are also remembered in the famous Cyrus Cylinder:

> a weakling has been installed as the *enû* of the country; [the correct images of the gods he removed from their thrones, imi]tations he order to place upon them. A replica of the temple Esagila he has ... for Ur and the other sacred cities inappropriate rituals ... daily he did blabber [incorrect prayers]. He (furthermore) interrupted in a fiendish way the regular offerings, he did ... he established within the sacred cities. The worship of Marduk the king of the gods, he [chang]ed into an abomination, daily he used to do evil against his (Marduk's) city. ... He [tormented] its [inhabitant]s with corvée-work without relief, he ruined them all.[120]

The fortunes of Marduk had obviously fallen on hard times. The one "called by Marduk the caretaker of Esagila and Ezida," the one for whose coming Marduk could hardly wait,[121] had become the deity's greatest enemy. The religion of Marduk was rotting from within.

Marduk's response to the terrible indignity he had suffered at the hands of his own appointed king is described in detail in the Cyrus Cylinder:

> He scanned and looked (through) all the countries, searching for a righteous ruler willing to lead him (i.e., Marduk) (in the annual procession). (Then) he pronounced the name of Cyrus (*Ku-ra-aš*), king of Anshan, declared him to become the ruler of all the world. He made the Guti country and all the Manda-hordes bow in submission to his (Cyrus') feet. And he (Cyrus) did always endeavor to treat according to justice the blackheaded whom he (Marduk) has made him conquer. Marduk, the great lord, a protector of his people/worshipers beheld with pleasure his (Cyrus') good deeds and his upright mind (lit. heart) (and therefore) ordered him to march against his city Babylon. He made him set out on the road to Babylon going at his side like a real friend.

The account goes on to describe how Babylon was taken without a battle. In fact, the residents of the city and the entire region celebrated the coming of Cyrus and his deliverance of them from death.

---

120. *ANET*, 315. For the text in transliteration, translation, and commentary, see Berger, "Der Kyros-Zylinder," 192–234. In "The Dynastic Prophecy" Cyrus is referred to as "the Elamite." Grayson, *Babylonian Historical-Literary Texts*, 32–33.

121. Cf. Langdon, *Neubabylonische Königsinschriften*, 18–19, 86ff.

The relationship between this foreign king and the divine patron of Babylon was painted in glowing, almost euphoric terms. He viewed himself as the one whose rule Bel and Nebo love, "whom they want as king to please their hearts," to whom Marduk the great lord responded with pleasure and blessing. For his part, Cyrus was faithful in attending to the worship of the great lord of Babylon. He also prided himself in having pleased all of the other gods whom Nabonidus had enraged by bringing their images to Babylon, by restoring the latter to their native chapels.[122] It would seem that Marduk had found another champion who would ensure his supremacy in the Babylonian assembly of the gods (*puḫur ilāni*). But these accounts must be taken with a healthy dose of salt. Expediency demanded that Cyrus secure the support of the local population. After the alienation caused by Nabonidus' religious policies, the Babylonian priesthood was eager to stand behind one who would promote their cult. Furthermore, this tolerance, nay sponsorship, of foreign cults was a fundamental element of Persian policy.

Nevertheless, Marduk's days of glory were over. Cyrus' stay in Babylon was brief. The city was left in the charge of his son, Cambyses II, who supervised Babylonian affairs from nearby Sippar. Relative calm seems to have prevailed throughout Cyrus' and Cambyses' emperorships. However, after the death of the latter in 522 BCE, turmoil set in. The new Achaemenid ruler, Darius finally squelched the rebellion of the Babylonians by establishing a Persian arsenal in the city. We know little about the fate of Marduk during the following decades. However, the accession of Xerxes to the Persian throne in 485 BCE created a new crisis for the god. Politically, it spawned revolts in many parts of the empire, including Babylon. But the rebellion was brutally crushed. The temple tower was destroyed[123] and the statue of Marduk carried off.[124] Theologically, the arrival of Xerxes presented Marduk with a brand new situation: an ideologue on the imperial throne who was determined to root out any challenges to Ahuramazda. Xerxes' own inscription reads:

---

122. *ANET*, 315–16. This picture of conquest without battle, reinstitution of the rites of Esagila, and the return of the statues, agrees with the Nabonidus Chronicle iii:15–22 (*Assyrian and Babylonian Chronicles*, 109–110). Cf. Herodotous, *Histories*, i.190–91.

123. Strabo, *Geography* 16.1.5, reports, "Here too is the tomb of Belus, now in ruins, having been demolished by Xerxes, it is said." Cf. also Arrian, *Anabasis of Alexander* 7.17.2.

124. Herodotus in 1.181 notes that a fifteen foot solid gold statue of a man in erect pose had been purloined by Xerxes.

> After I became king, there were (some) among these countries (names of which) are written above, which revolted, but I crushed these countries after Ahuramazda had given me his support, under the shadow of Ahuramazda and I put them (again) into their (former political) status. Furthermore, there were among these countries (some) which performed (religious) service to the "Evil (God)s" and proclaimed (as follows): "You must not perform (religious) service to the 'Evil (God)s' anymore!" Wherever formerly (religious) service was performed to the "Evil (God)s," I myself, performed a (religious) service to Ahura-mazda and the *arta* (cosmic order) reverently.[125]

But Marduk refused to give up easily. At the time of Herodotus' visit to Babylon (ca. 460 BCE), "the great sitting figure of Bel, all of gold on a golden throne," was still inside the temple.[126] During the Persian period, personal names incorporating Marduk or Bel as the theophore indicated that the Babylonian deity still had a significant following a century after Babylon's fall to the Persians.[127]

The arrival of Alexander the Great in 331 BCE raised new questions concerning the viability of Marduk. According to the second-century CE Greek historian, Arrian, when Alexander had crossed the Tigris and was approaching Babylon, he was met by Chaldaean seers who, on the basis of an oracle from their god Belus, begged him not to advance any farther or he would meet with disaster. Suspecting that they were merely trying to protect the rich temple revenues for themselves he responded smartly with a quotation from the Greek dramatist, Euripides: "Prophets who prophesy the best, are best." Thereupon they appealed to him not to advance westward, but to move on to the east. However, in the words of

---

125. *ANET*, 316–17. Cf. R. G. Kent, *Old Persian*, 150–51, lines 28–41.

126. Herodotus 1.181.

127. Cf. Nidinti-Bêl of Nippur, an official of Darius, 421 BCE, named in BE X 97. Cf. Eilers, *Iranische Beamtennamen I*, 10–11. Cf. Porten, *Archives from Elephantine*, 53–54. In a fourth–fifth century BCE inscription from Arebsun, Cappadocia, Bel is used as a title for Ahuramazda. See *KAI* 264. A late fifth century BCE papyrus from Saqqara in Egypt refers to Bel as the god of a certain Tabah. Cf. Segal, *Aramaic Texts*, 38, §23:5. The personal name Marduk appears in text 44 (ibid., 63). Other examples are given on p. 64. The Murašu business documents from the same general period contain more than sixty names beginning with Bel and at least nine that begin with Marduk, not to mention those in which these elements appear later in the names. Cf. Clay, *Business Documents II*, 42–46, 55. Among the latter are two hypocoristic forms, *Mar-duk* and *Mar-duk-a*, which are reminiscent of a certain מרדך in a fifth-century letter in Egypt. Cf. Driver, *Aramaic Documents*, 27, 6:1; cf. 56, for discussion.

Arrian, "Fate led him on the way in which he was doomed to die."[128] But Alexander refused to listen. In fact, reminiscent of Cyrus' account of his arrival in Babylon, Arrian reports that the Babylonians came out *en masse*, with their priests and other leaders. They lavished him with gifts and surrendered to him the city, the citadel, and the treasure.[129]

Like Cyrus two centuries earlier, Alexander dutifully performed the traditional Babylonian religious rituals according to the counsel of the Chaldaeans, paying particular attention to the cult of Bel.[130] He also ordered his soldiers to begin immediately to gather materials for the reconstruction of the temple of Bel, which had lain in ruins since the time of Xerxes.[131]

What the fate of Marduk would have been had Alexander survived we shall never know. His untimely death in 323 BCE left Babylon in a state of confusion. When the smoke had cleared some ten years later, the Seleucids were in firm control of Babylon. According to Strabo, none of Alexander's successors was interested in reconstructing Babylon. In fact, the founder of the dynasty, Seleucus Nicator (305–281 BCE) fortified a new site, Seleuceia on the Tigris 300 stadia from Babylon, to which he then transferred the capital. Eventually this new city even outstripped Babylon in size, the latter having become almost deserted.[132] However an Akkadian inscription of his successor, Antiochus Soter (281–261 BCE), commemorating the commencement of the rebuilding of the temple of Nebo at Borsippa suggests that this man perceived himself as the heir to all of the previous kings of Babylon. His epithets, including *zānin Esagila u Ezida*, "provider for Esagila and Ezida," had been copied deliberately from his neo-Babylonian predecessors. He boasted about having conceived the idea of reconstructing these sacred temples, and of having prepared the first brick with the finest oil with his own hands while he was still in the land of Hatti. The opening lines hold out great promise for Marduk.

128. Arrian, *Anabasis* 7.16.5–7

129. *Anabasis* 3.16.3. A fragmentary text recently published by Wiseman, BM 3676, may provide Babylonian confirmation of this reception. Wiseman, *Nebuchadrezzar*, 116–21. Cf. also "The Dynastic Prophecy," iii:15–23, which "predicts" that Enlil, Shamash, and [Marduk] will come to the aid of the unnamed king. Grayson, *Babylonian Historical-Literary Texts*, 34–35.

130. *Anabasis* 3.16.5.

131. *Anabasis* 7.17.2–3; Strabo, *Geography* 16.1.15. A similar account by Pseudo-Hecataeus is found in Josephus, *Contra Apion* 1.192, reports that the Jews in Alexander's army were the only ones who refused to comply. Cf. Doran, translator, "Pseudo-Hecataeus," 2.917–9.

132. *Geography* 16.1.5 On Babylon in the Seleucid period, see Bevan, *The House of Seleucus*, 246–57.

Nevertheless, as the text proceeds it becomes obvious that the patron of Babylon had been supplanted in the king's imagination by his son, Nebo. In fact, judging by the epithets ascribed to this god, Nebo had been raised to the top of the pantheon.[133]

The fate of Esagila and its divine host in the remainder of the Seleucid era is largely unknown. But the policy of the Hellenistic rulers toward the temples of Babylon seems to have been magnanimous. The latest datable Babylonian chronicle, from the second regnal year of Seleucus III (225–223 BCE), notes that this king presented offerings to Bêl and Beltiia and the great gods in Esagila.[134] Personal names with Bêl and Marduk as the theophores continued,[135] and in general Esagila and its cult seem to have been reasonably well maintained.[136] This is confirmed by the evidence for the existence of the temple of Bel Marduk in post-Seleucid documents.[137]

However, there is some evidence of syncretism of the Greek and Babylonian pantheons, so that Marduk could be identified as Zeus.[138] Since Zeus was also identified with other city patrons (e.g., Anu at Uruk), we should not exaggerate the significance of this equation with Marduk. In the meantime, the practice of replacing the name of the deity, Marduk with the title Bel, seems to have continued.[139] In fact, as Bel, this Babylonian deity resurfaced in the first-century CE oasis of Palmyra (Tadmor) on the northwestern edge of the Arabian desert, 200 miles northeast of Damascus. As the foremost god of this place, he had become a cosmic deity, elevated to the status of supreme god, and flanked by two acolytes, the sun god Yarhibol and the moon god Aglibol.[140]

133. For the text see *ANET*, 317.

134. *Assyrian and Babylonian Chronicles*, 283–84 (13b:3–8). Cf. van der Spek, "The Babylonian Temple," 547.

135. Cf. McEwan, *Priest and Temple in Hellenistic Babylon*, 203–5, for names beginning with Bêl and Marduk. These divine names also occur as later elements in personal names.

136. Cf. ibid., 193–201; Spek, "The Babylonian Temple," 546–50.

137. Cf. Musti, "Syria and the East," 197.

138. Cf. Berossus, *Babyloniaca* 1.2.3.b, according to the edition by Burstein, *Babyloniaca*, 15. According to the prologue of Berossus' work, this man was a priest of Bel/Marduk, a Chaldaean. The book was supposedly dedicated to Antiochus I. Cf. Burstein, *Babyloniaca of Berossus* 13 n. 2.

139. One of the soldiers in the battle of Raphia (217 BCE), in which Antiochus III (222–187 BCE) was defeated, was named Zabdibel, "gift of Bel." Polybius, *Histories* 5.79.8. Teixidor, *The Pagan God*, 105, concludes from the name that this person was a Palmyrene Arab Sheikh.

140. Dussaud, *Pénetration des Arabes*, 90–104, maintains that Bel is to be identified

By the River Chebar

CONCLUSION

Like water in a desert wadi, so Bel/Marduk virtually disappeared from the scene after this. This may be due in large measure to the accidents of preservation and discovery of ancient records. However, the growing silence reflects the decreasing role of Babylon in ancient Near Eastern affairs, and with this the decreasing significance of her divine patron, Marduk. The decision of Seleucus to move his official residence out of the ancient city to the new site of Seleucia seems to have made this fate inevitable. For two millennia Marduk had struggled to establish a significant place for himself in the Mesopotamian pantheon. However, the reach for the top was satisfied only to a limited extent and for brief periods of time. Always, it seemed, there were other gods with the identical ambition, anxious to have their moment in the sun.

The ups-and-downs of Marduk's story mirror exactly the fluctuating fortunes of his native city Babylon, as illustrated (Figure 11). Her moments of greatness were few and far between. However, because of her significance for the history of another people and their relationship with their own deity, YHWH, this city has captured the imagination of students of the Scriptures out of all proportion to the duration of her moment in the sun. This is particularly true of the neo-Babylonian dynasty, whose three-quarters of a century were but a flash in the drama of Ancient Mesopotamian history. For the most part, the real movers and shakers were elsewhere, in Assyria or Egypt, and later in Persia and Rome. However, by then Babylon had been reduced to a symbol of arrogance and vanity, and her deity had been all but forgotten (Rev 14:8; 16:19; 17:5; 18:2, 10, 21). We may stand back and watch in amazement the sudden rise of Marduk's fortunes under the great Hammurabi and Nebuchadnezzar I, or his renaissance under Nebuchadnezzar II, but our surprise is no less at the sudden and total collapse of this deity's influence after Nebuchadnezzar. In the words of Isaiah 46:1-2:

> Bel has bowed down; Nebo stoops;
> Their idols are on beasts and cattle;
> These things you carry are loaded as burdens on weary beasts.

---

with Baalshamin. However, among other arguments against this identification is the fact that these two deities had separate temples in the city. For further discussion see Teixidor, *The Pagan God*, 100-42; Drijvers, *The Religion of Palmyra*, 5-22; cf. also Höfner, "Stammesgruppen Nord- und Zentralarabiens," 431. Bel was also prominent at Dura Europos, a Palmyrene colony to the northeast on the Euphrates. Cf. Drijvers, *The Religion of Palmyra*, 13.

They stoop; they bow down together;
They cannot save the burden,
But themselves go into captivity.
The phantom had vanished.[141]

Figure 11: The Fluctuating Fortunes of a Divine Phantom

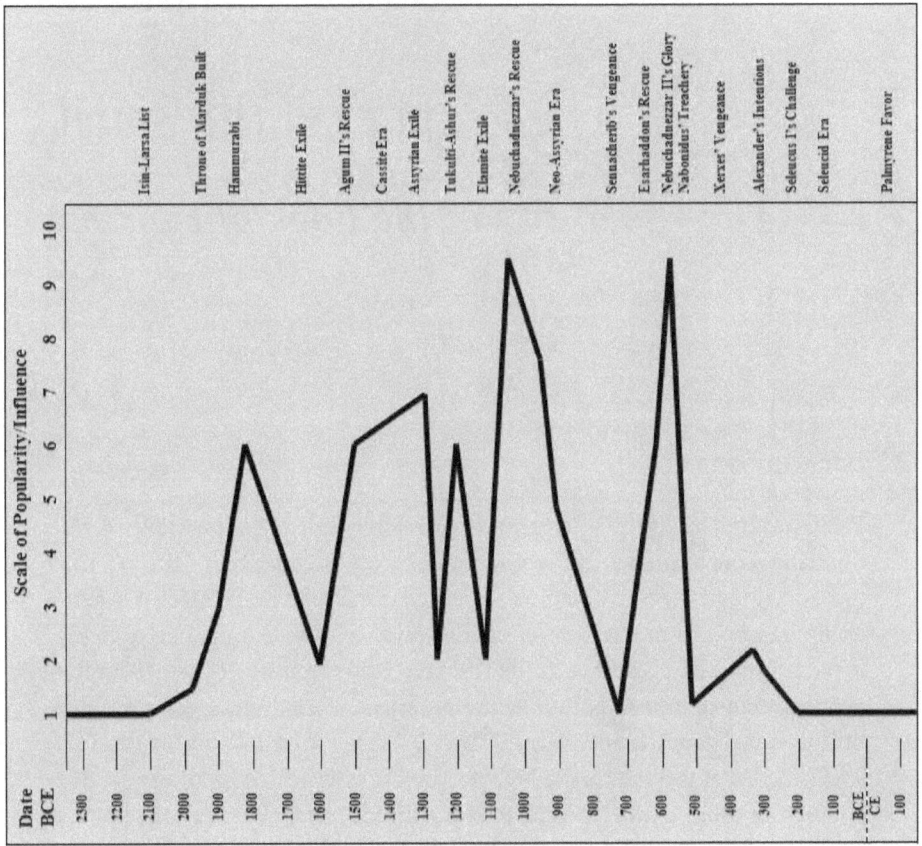

141. I am grateful to Alan Millard of the University of Liverpool for his reading of an earlier draft of this article and his numerous helpful comments.

6

The Prophet of the Spirit

The Use of רוּחַ in the Book of Ezekiel[1]

Introduction

Pneumatology, "the doctrine of the Holy Spirit," is essentially a NT doctrine. Few branches of theology suffer from the neglect of the OT like the doctrine of the Spirit. When reference is made to this source it is generally handled in one of the following ways: (1) The OT data are quickly summarized as a preamble to the real stuff, the teaching of the NT. In the process, one senses impatience, the enterprise being engaged more out of duty than genuine interest. (2) The OT is referred to only in passing, while the focus is fixed on the NT. (3) The OT is appealed to for the sake of analogy, as often as not to emphasize the discontinuity between the Spirit's operation in the two Testaments.

Some of the reasons for this wanton neglect are obvious. (1) For many, the expression "Holy Spirit" is a slogan. Since the phrase appears only three times in the OT (Ps 51:13[11]; Isa 63:10, 11), it seems to be assumed that little interest or information is to be found there. (2) Our theological systems have denigrated the value of the OT as a whole, with the result that a general ignorance pervades all of evangelical Christendom at many levels. (3) We have made little effort to master either the

---

1. The essay was originally published in *The Journal of the Evangelical Theological Society* 32 (1988) 27–50.

The Prophet of the Spirit

language or the thought patterns of the Hebrews. Consequently, we have little comprehension of the forms of expression and idioms used in the OT. We do not recognize the Holy Spirit when we see him at work.

These are but a few of the hurdles that the next generation of biblical scholars and theologians will need to overcome. The problem will not be resolved overnight. One of the first steps in recovering the OT for contemporary pneumatology, however, will be to examine systematically and deliberately each of the OT documents that has so much as a whisper to contribute to the subject. I offer this study as a modest proposal in that direction.

The Vocabulary of the Spirit

The richness of Hebrew vocabulary is reflected in the employment of three different expressions for "spirit" in the OT: אוֹב, נְשָׁמָה, and רוּחַ. The first of these is relatively rare, and its etymology remains obscure. The word אוֹב denotes "a bottle made of skins" in Job 32:19, but this usage is exceptional.[2] Elsewhere the word is always associated with the spirits of the departed dead, being applied to (1) the ghosts themselves (Isa 29:4), (2) the pit used to call up departed spirits (1 Sam 28:7–8), and (3) the necromancer who makes contact with departed spirits to acquire information.[3]

The second term, נְשָׁמָה, is only slightly more common, occurring twenty-four times.[4] The verb נשׁם means "to pant," as in a woman in travail (Isa 42:14). The noun נְשָׁמָה refers most commonly to "breath," whether of humans,[5] or of God,[6] or of breathing creatures/persons.[7] It is used in particular of the principle that gives life to the body. As such it has its origin in God[8] and may be withdrawn by him (Job 34:14 // רוּחַ).

By far the most common designation for "spirit" in the OT is רוּחַ. The term appears 378 times in the Hebrew text and an additional eleven in the

---

2. Cf. Even-Shoshan, *A New Concordance*, 23, for references.

3. Cf. Lev 19:31; 20:6, 27; Deut 18:11; 1 Sam 28:3, 9; 2 Kgs 21:6 (= 2 Chr 33:6); 23:24; Isa 8:19. For a study of the term see Hoffner, "אוֹב *ōbh*," 130–34.

4. Cf. Even-Shoshan, *A New Concordance*, 787.

5. 1 Kgs 17:17; Isa 2:22; 42:5; Job 27:3; Dan 10:17.

6. Isa 30:33; 2 Sam 22:16 = Ps 18:16[15]; Job 4:9.

7. Josh 10:40; Ps 150:6; Isa 57:16; cf. the phrase "every breathing thing," Deut 20:16; Josh 11:11, 14; 1 Kgs 15:29.

8. Gen 2:7; Job 32:8; 33:4; 34:14 // רוּחַ.

Aramaic parts of Daniel.[9] The word has been the subject of many previous studies.[10] Its semantic range includes breath, wind, direction, spirit, mind (//לֵב). LXX translates רוּחַ as πνεῦμα in three-fourths of its occurrences. The remainder alternate among ἄνεμος, "wind," πνοή, "wind, vapor," and other anthropological terms such as θυμός, ὀλιγόψυχο, αἷμα, νοῦς, ψυχή.[11] Of these three Hebrew words for "spirit," רוּחַ is the only one to occur in Ezekiel. We turn now to a closer study of its usage in this book.

Ezekiel: The Prophet of the Spirit

Ezekiel may well be described as the most "spiritual" prophet of the OT. Indeed he may be designated "the prophet of the spirit," and that for more than one reason. First, the term רוּחַ appears more often in his prophecy than in any other. To be sure, the fifty-two occurrences of the expression are almost matched by the fifty-one in Isaiah. The contrast with Jeremiah's eighteen occurrences, however, could hardly be greater. This is especially remarkable when one takes into account the strong influence Jeremiah's ministry had on Ezekiel in other respects. Even more remarkable is the total absence of רוּחַ from Leviticus, from which many thematic and stylistic features are borrowed. With his emphasis on the spirit Ezekiel is obviously going his own way.

Second, the expression is distributed widely throughout the book. As illustrated in Table 2, the occurrences of רוּחַ are scattered throughout the messages of judgment upon Judah in part 1 (chaps. 1–24) and words of hope for the nation in part 3 (chaps. 33–48). However, except for Ezekiel 27:26, where רוּחַ functions in a non-theological sense, it is conspicuously absent from part 2, the oracles against the nations (chaps. 25–32). This may be due to the nature of the material. On the other hand, it is remarkable that the prophet can go for eight chapters without once referring either to the spirit of man or God. One might speculate either that the Hebrew conception of the spirit was incomprehensible to foreigners, or that it differed so radically from that of her neighbors that it would have seemed incongruous for the prophet to speak of רוּחַ in such contexts.

---

9. Cf. the tabulation of these and related forms by Albertz and Westermann, "רוּחַ *rūaḥ Geist*," 727. A full discussion of רוּחַ is provided on pp. 726–53.

10. For bibliography see Albertz and Westermann, "רוּחַ *rūaḥ Geist*."

11. For these and others see Hatch and Redpath, *Concordance to the Septuagint*, 3:263, for references; Baumgärtel, "Spirit in the OT," 367–68.

Table 2: The Forms and Distribution of רוּחַ in Ezekiel

Forms	1	2	3	4	5	6	7	8	9	10	11	12	13	14	15	16	17	18	19	20	21	22	23	24
רוּחַ		1	3		2			1			3	1					1	1			1			
הָרוּחַ	3				1														1					
־רוּחַ	3									1	2		2				1							
רוּחִי																				1				
רוּחֲכֶם			1								1													
רוּחָם																								
רוּחוֹת																								
Totals	6	1	4		3			1		1	6	1	3				2	1	1	1	1			

Forms	25	26	27	28	29	30	31	32	33	34	35	36	37	38	39	40	41	42	43	44	45	46	47	48	Totals
רוּחַ												1	3		1				1						19
הָרוּחַ													4												8
־רוּחַ			1										1					4							16
רוּחִי												1	1	1											4
רוּחֲכֶם																									2
רוּחָם																									1
רוּחוֹת																		1							2
Totals			1									2	10	1	1			5	1						52

The Prophet of the Spirit

Table 3: The Semantic Range of רוּחַ in Ezekiel

Meaning	1	2	3	4	5	6	7	8	9	10	11	12	13	14	15	16	17	18	19	20	21	22	23	24
Wind	1				1								2						1					
Direction					2							1					1							
Agency of Conveyance			1					1			3													
Agency of Animation	5	1	2							1														
Agency of Inspiration											1													
Mind			1								2		1					1		1	1			
Sign of Divine Ownership																								
Totals	6	1	4		3			1		1	6	1	3			2	1	1	1	1	1			

Meaning	25	26	27	28	29	30	31	32	33	34	35	36	37	38	39	40	41	42	43	44	45	46	47	48	Totals
Wind			1																						7
Direction													1												5
Agency of Conveyance													1						1						7
Agency of Animation													8												17
Agency of Inspiration																									1
Mind												2			1										9
Sign of Divine Ownership															1										1
Totals			1									2	10		1			5	1						52

THE USES OF רוּחַ IN EZEKIEL

The identification of Ezekiel as "the prophet of the spirit" must be qualified in accordance with the range of meanings he attaches to the term. As Table 3 suggests, he was much more than "the prophet of the spirit."

One of the marks of Ezekiel's literary genius is his mastery of ambiguity. He uses many words with different meanings, frequently making the switch within the same context. In some of those instances one cannot be sure whether he intends a singular sense or if both possibilities are in mind. We will observe this to be true with his usage of רוּחַ as well. Indeed the usage of רוּחַ seems to move in two different directions, as reflected in Figure 12. In order to comprehend the scope of Ezekiel's use of רוּחַ, each of these dimensions deserves separate study.

Figure 12: The Usage of רוּחַ in Ezekiel

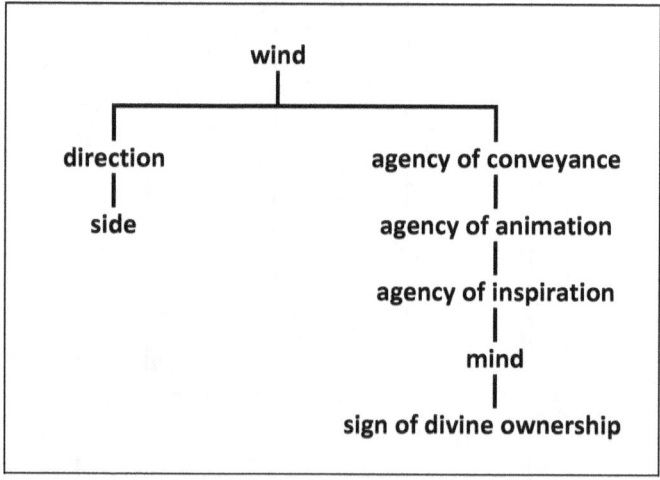

1. רוּחַ as "wind."

Since רוּחַ denotes "wind" more than one hundred times in the OT, it is not surprising that Ezekiel should employ the word this way as well. Whenever he does so, however, רוּחַ appears in association with another term. Three times רוּחַ הַקָּדִים, "the east wind," occurs. In 27:26 the east wind is a violent gale that destroys Tyrian galleys in the Mediterranean. In 17:10; 19:12, where רוּחַ is rendered ἄνεμος by LXX, the phrase applies to the scorching sirocco that blows in off the desert causing the plants to dry up and wither. A third weather phenomenon is suggested by the expression רוּחַ סְעָרָה/סְעָרוֹת. In 1:4, as in Job 38:1; 40:6, סְעָרָה refers to a theophanic storm cloud.[12] The wind is described as coming from the north,[13] bringing with it a fiery cloud out of which emerges the prophet's inaugural vision. The plural form occurs twice in Ezekiel 13:11–13 where רוּחַ־סְעָרוֹת denotes hurricane force winds that, along with deluging rain (גֶּשֶׁם שֹׁטֵף) and pounding hailstones (אַבְנֵי אֶלְגָּבִישׁ),[14] function as destructive agents of YHWH's wrath.

2. רוּחַ as "direction."

The use of רוּחַ in 5:2 represents the first stage along one of the two branches of the semantic tree. The prophet is commanded to chop up one-third of his hair and scatter it "to the wind" (זָרָה לָרוּחַ), symbolic of divine judgment. The sense seems plain enough, but in the interpretation of the action in verses 10–12 לָרוּחַ is expanded to לְכָל־רוּחַ, "to every wind." In spite of LXX εἰς πάντα ἄνεμον, this phrase is probably better rendered "in every direction."[15] The same is true of 12:14, where זָרָה לְכָל־רוּחַ recurs, as well as 17:21, in which the verb פָּרַשׂ replaces זָרָה. In each instance being scattered "in every direction" is an act of divine judgment upon the nation. The directional interpretation is even clearer in 37:9c, which makes reference to אַרְבַּע רוּחוֹת, "the four winds." The expression finds a close parallel in Akkadian *šari erbetti*[16] and reflects the hypothetical division of the earth

---

12. סְעָרָה serves as a nearer definition of רוּחַ, identifying the specific genus of wind, i.e., "tempest wind." Cf. GKC §131*b*; Joüon §131*b*.

13. צָפוֹן is frequently interpreted mythologically here as Mount Zaphon. But this interpretation is unlikely for several reasons: (1) This usage is absent elsewhere in Ezekiel (even though of the 152 occurrences of צָפוֹן in the OT forty-six are in this book). (2) As the name of the sacred mountain, צָפוֹן occurs only four times in the OT, always in poetry (Isa 14:13–14; Ps 48:3[2]; 89:13[12]; Job 26:7). Cf. Roberts, "Mount Zaphon," 977. For a recent refutation of the mythological interpretation of even these verses, however, see de Savignac, "Le sense du terme Saphon," 273–78. (3) The imagery in the present chapter derives primarily from Babylonian iconography, whereas Zaphon was the residence of the Canaanite storm-god Baal. (4) According to verse 1, it is the heavens that are opened to the prophet, not Zaphon. (5) The concern of the text is not to identify the place from which the deity proceeds but the direction from which the vision appears.

14. אֶלְגָּבִישׁ is a loanword cognate to Egyptian *irqbš* (translated "crystals of emery" by Driver, "Ezekiel," 151), Akkadian *algameš/šu* (*AHW*, 35; *CAD*, 1/1.337–338), and Ugaritic *algbt* (cf. *UT* 358 #168), all of which refer to a type of hard stone.

15. So *NJV*.

16. Cf. *AHW*, 1192; *CAD*, 4.256.

into quadrants. In this connection, especially instructive for understanding the relationship between winds and directions is Jer 49:36:

וְהֵבֵאתִי אֶל־עֵילָם אַרְבַּע רוּחוֹת	I shall bring upon Elam the four winds,
מֵאַרְבַּע קְצוֹת הַשָּׁמַיִם	From the four ends of the heavens;
וְזֵרִתִים לְכֹל הָרֻחוֹת הָאֵלֶּה	And I shall scatter them in all these directions.

Even more picturesque is the NT text, Rev 7:1, which speaks of four angels standing at the four corners of the earth holding back the four winds of the earth.[17]

3. רוּחַ as "side."

The tendency for רוּחַ to denote a point on the compass culminates in Ezekiel 42:16–20, where the word is used of the sides of the sanctuary. These sides are defined more specifically as the measured east side (רוּחַ הַקָּדִים), the north side (רוּחַ הַצָּפוֹן), the south side (רוּחַ הַדָּרוֹם) and the west side (רוּחַ הַיָּם) respectively. A summary statement is provided in verse 20: "He measured it on the four sides" (לְאַרְבַּע רוּחוֹת).[18]

4. רוּחַ as "agency of conveyance."

The first stage in the evolution of the second semantic branch of רוּחַ is represented by the use of the term to describe divine control over a person, specifically his supernatural transportation from place to place. Of the several figures employed by Ezekiel to describe YHWH's control over him perhaps the most graphic is the portrayal of the hand of YHWH coming upon him. Variations of וַתְּהִי עָלָיו שָׁם יַד־יְהוָה recur repeatedly in the book (1:3; 3:14, 22; 8:1 [with נָפַל instead of הָיָה]; 33:22; 37:1; 40:1). "Hand" is here used metaphorically of power, the overwhelming force with which God operates, as when he rescued Israel from the clutches of Egypt (cf. Deut 4:34; 5:15; 6:21; Ps 136:12). It describes the power with which God grips and energizes a person such as Elijah so that he is able to outrun the chariots of Ahab (1 Kgs 18:46). But in Ezekiel the "hand of YHWH" gains complete mastery over his movements (Ezek 3:22; cf. 33:22) and transports him back and forth to distant places (8:1ff.; 37:1; 40:1ff.). As

---

17. See further Dan 7:2 (Aramaic אַרְבַּע רוּחֵי שְׁמַיָּא); 8:8; 11:4; Zech 2:10[6]; 6:5 (all אַרְבַּע רוּחוֹת הַשָּׁמָיִם). Cf. also Matt 24:31.

18. Cf. also 1 Chr 9:24. See farther Albertz and Westermann, "רוּחַ rūᵃḥ Geist," 728–29.

The Prophet of the Spirit

Heschel observes, this expression describes "the urgency, pressure, and compulsion by which he is stunned and overwhelmed."[19] Ezekiel is a man seized by God. This more than any other quality distinguishes him from the other prophets. It accounts for his mobility and immobility, the apparent lunacy of some of his actions, and his stoic response to rejection, opposition, and grief.

But the prophet is also under the control of a רוּחַ. In no fewer than a half–dozen instances he is described as being picked up by a רוּחַ and wafted away to another location. In 3:12, 14 he is picked up and carried off to the exiles at Tel Abib. The pressure of YHWH upon him is emphasized with the additional comment that the hand of YHWH was strong upon him. In 8:3 he is picked up between heaven and earth and borne away to Jerusalem. The additional comment, בְּמַרְאוֹת אֱלֹהִים, "in divine visions," suggests that the experience is not to be interpreted literally. The prophet appears not to have actually left his room. As the vision nears its end he is picked up and brought to the east gate of YHWH's house. When it is over he is raised once more and returned to the exiles in Chaldea. In 43:5 he is picked up and brought to the court of the visionary temple.

The anarthrous form of רוּחַ in each of these texts highlights the ambiguity of the statements and renders the classification of this use of רוּחַ difficult. The nature of its activity might suggest that it is merely a gust of wind that comes along (at the command of YHWH, to be sure) and picks him up like a scrap of paper. However, several considerations point more specifically to the spirit of God. The temple vision is framed by references to the locomotion of the prophet by the spirit (8:1; 11:24) and contains one internal note of this experience (11:1). Moreover, in chapter 8, after Ezekiel has witnessed the first scene of the abominations being perpetrated in the temple precincts, each of the following three is introduced with the comment: "He brought me to . . ." On the basis of verse 3, and in the absence of any possible intervening antecedents, we should have expected a feminine form of the verb agreeing with the nearest subject רוּחַ. But in each instance the verb is masculine (vv. 7, 14, 16), suggesting that the one conveying him about is the same as the person who speaks to him and interprets the observations (vv. 5, 6, etc.) The nearest masculine antecedent is the Lord YHWH in verse 1. Similar considerations apply to the broader context of 43:5.

The interpretation of this רוּחַ as YHWH's רוּחַ is supported by two additional texts. In 11:24b the comment that the prophet was brought

---

19. Heschel, *Prophets*, 444. For a full discussion of the expression in its ancient Near Eastern context see Roberts, "Hand of YHWH," 244–51.

back to Babylon in a vision בַּמַּרְאֶה is expanded with בְּרוּחַ אֱלֹהִים. In this instance, however, אֱלֹהִים need not signify God any more than it does in the expression מַרְאוֹת אֱלֹהִים (1:1; 8:3), "divine visions."[20] Nevertheless, even this understanding raises it from the level of an ordinary wind to one that is controlled directly by God. If the previous texts leave the question open, the issue seems to be answered in 37:1. This time it is specified that, when Ezekiel feels the hand of YHWH upon him, he is brought out to the valley of the dry bones בְּרוּחַ יְהוָה, "by the רוּחַ of YHWH." Although even here the expression retains a certain ambiguity, it ties the conveying spirit directly to YHWH. The phrase רוּחַ יְהוָה occurs elsewhere in the book only in 11:5. Its significance in this case is quite different, however, as we shall see below.

5. רוּחַ as "agency of animation."

Judging by frequency, for Ezekiel the employment of רוּחַ to denote the animating, vitalizing force was more important than any other. The primary difference between this usage and that described in the preceding is the locus of the influence. When the רוּחַ lifts someone/something up and wafts him/it from place to place it operates upon the object from the outside. As "agency of animation," however, the רוּחַ operates internally, like the breath of a living creature. But the distinction between "wind" and "breath" is not absolute and should not be pressed in each instance. In fact the process of breathing involves the making of wind. But it is the effect of this רוּחַ upon a recipient that is our present concern.

In Hebrew thought it is the wind or breath of God that gives life to creatures. This notion is reflected in the expression נִשְׁמַת חַיִּים, "breath of life,"[21] and finds its anthropological paradigm in Gen 2:7: "When YHWH Elohim formed the man of dust from the ground and breathed into his

---

20. מַרְאוֹת אֱלֹהִים is usually translated "visions of God." Three considerations argue against this reading, however: (1) In the book אֱלֹהִים usually functions as an appellative rather than a proper noun. If visions of God had been intended, מַרְאוֹת אֲדֹנָי אֱלֹהִים would have been used. So also Greenberg, *Ezekiel 1–20*, 41. For a full discussion of the names of God in Ezekiel, see Zimmerli, *Ezekiel 2*, 556–62. (2) What the prophet witnesses is not so much a vision of God (only the last few verses of chapter 1 refer to the deity himself) but a vision of divine, heavenly realities. (3) The form מַרְאוֹת אֱלֹהִים is not a true plural but a "plural of generalization." Cf. Joüon § 136j, GKC §124e. As in 8:3 the expression is better translated as "divine visions" or "supernatural visions."

21. The expression finds its counterpart in Akkadian *šaru balaṭi*. In Amarna Letter 143, Ammunin of Berytus considers himself to be mere "dust" in the presence of his Egyptian overlord, who is "the breath of life."

nostrils the breath of life, the man became a living being." Some may object that the term for breath in this instance is נְשָׁמָה and not רוּחַ. But the close semantic relationship between the terms is demonstrated by their frequent conjunction in construct associations[22] and as a coordinate[23] and parallel pair.[24] The critical animating effect of the infusion and presence of the divine spirit is reflected in several texts. Isaiah 42:5 describes YHWH the Creator as the one "who gives breath (נְשָׁמָה) to people on it [the earth] and spirit (רוּחַ) to those who walk on it." In Job 27:3 the beleaguered saint vows to retain his integrity "as long as breath (נְשָׁמָה) is in me, and the spirit of God (רוּחַ אֱלוֹהַּ) is in my nostrils," which is clarified in verses 5–6 as "until I die" and "all my days." The notion is expressed negatively in Job 34:14–15:

> If he should decide,
> He can recall his spirit (רוּחַ)—that is, his breath (נְשָׁמָה).
> Then all flesh would expire at once,
> And mankind would return to the dust.

Even more picturesque is Psalm 104:29–30:

> You hide your face, they are terrified;
> You recall their spirit (רוּחַ), they expire and return to the dust.
> You send back your spirit (רוּחַ), they are created (בָּרָא);
> And you renew the face of the ground.[25]

This animating sense of רוּחַ is common in Ezekiel, being frequently signaled by the presence of the preposition -בְּ. When the רוּחַ enters an object it comes to life. Whoever opens the book of Ezekiel is immediately confronted with the animating effect of the presence of the spirit in the opening vision. The divine throne-chariot is borne by four cherubim, each having eagles' wings and four different kinds of heads (Ezek 1:5–14). Although he is unable to identify the creatures precisely at first, the prophet is impressed by their vitality and refers to them with the general designation חַיּוֹת, "living beings." (When the vision returns in chapter 10 he is able to identify them more precisely as cherubim.) These creatures

---

22. Cf. Gen 7:22, כֹּל אֲשֶׁר נִשְׁמַת־רוּחַ חַיִּים בְּאַפָּיו, "all in whose nostrils is the breath of the spirit of life"; 2 Sam 22:16, בְּגַעֲרַת יְהוָה מִנִּשְׁמַת רוּחַ אַפּוֹ, "by the rebuke of YHWH from the breath of the spirit of his nostrils." Cf. the parallel text in Ps 18:16[15].

23. Job 34:14.

24. Isa 42:5; 57:16; Job 4:9; 27:3; 32:8; 33:4.

25. For further discussion of רוּחַ as the animating principle of life see Hill, *Greek Words*, 212–15.

are described as capable of moving about effortlessly in any direction and without turning in the process. The inspiration and direction for this motion is attributed in verse 12 to the presence of the רוּחַ: "Wherever the רוּחַ wanted to go, they went; they would not turn as they went."

The presence of the article on הָרוּחַ here and in verse 20 calls for explanation. Which spirit? The only previous reference to the רוּחַ is found in verse 4. As we have observed, however, there the word had denoted "wind," a sense that is impossible at this point. One may only conclude that "the רוּחַ" that animates these "living creatures" is none other than the vitalizing principle of life that comes from God himself.

This interpretation finds support in verses 19–21, where each of the living creatures is associated with a complex system of wheels with which they moved about in perfect synchronism: "When the living beings moved, the wheels next to them would move, and when the living beings rose off the ground, the wheels would rise beside them, since the רוּחַ of the living being was in the wheels. Whenever the former moved, the latter would move, and whenever the former rose off the ground, the latter would rise alongside them, for the רוּחַ of the living being was in the wheels."

The use of the singular רוּחַ הַחַיָּה is striking in a context in which the creatures have otherwise been consistently referred to with the plural חַיּוֹת. Most scholars have tended to understand הַחַיָּה as a collective singular or distributive, "each living creature"—that is, the one beside each wheel.[26] Others see here an emphasis on the unity of the entire phenomenon.[27] Elsewhere I have argued that this incongruity of number is of a piece with the profusion of stylistic inconsistencies in the account of the vision and that it reflects the heightened emotional state of the prophet.[28] But if one be permitted to change his mind, I would now propose a different interpretation. It now appears rather significant that the singular form הַחַיָּה should have been preserved in 10:17. Although the account of the second vision of the throne-chariot in chapter 10 has smoothed out most of the stylistic problems raised by chapter 1, רוּחַ הַחַיָּה remains in verse 17. I would now argue that this is intentional and that the expression should be understood as "the spirit of life"—that is, the divine animating principle.[29] The twofold

26. Cooke, *Ezekiel*, 27; Zimmerli, *Ezekiel 1*, 20.

27. Greenberg, *Ezekiel*, 48.

28. Block, "Text and Emotion," 1–25; reproduced below.

29. Cf. LXX πνεῦμα ζωῆς, Vg *spintus vitae* Ezekiel uses חַיָּה instead of חַיִּים for "life" also in 7:13. Elsewhere this usage occurs only in poetry. Cf. Pss 74:19; 78:50; 143:3; Job 33:18, 20, 22, 28 (as a synonym of נֶפֶשׁ); 36:14. Cf. Gerleman, "חָיָה *ḥjh* leben," 553.

occurrence of the explanatory clause, כִּי רוּחַ הַחַיָּה בָּאוֹפַנִּים, "for the spirit of life was in the wheels," in 1:20–21 and again in 10:17, seems to emphasize that these normally inanimate objects appear to the prophet to be as alive as the "living creatures" themselves. For him the unusual phenomenon may be attributed only to the presence of the life-giving spirit of God.

This vivifying, energizing effect of the spirit of God is also felt by the prophet personally. Twice he speaks of the spirit entering him. According to 1:28 Ezekiel had responded to the vision of YHWH's glory by falling on his face. In his state of prostration, however, he had heard a voice, commanding him to rise in order that whoever was speaking might converse with him (2:1).[30] Simultaneous with this command, the revitalizing and energizing spirit entered him (2:2) and set him on his feet. Again the reader is frustrated by the refusal of the narrative to identify the source or nature of this spirit. Is it a sudden gust of wind that sets him upright? Or is it the spirit of YHWH? The fact that the raising of the prophet occurs concurrently with[31] the sound of the voice suggests a dynamic and enabling power in that voice. We should probably associate the רוּחַ that vitalizes the wheels with the רוּחַ that energizes the prophet.

Ezekiel's experience is described in royal court language. Having been ushered into the presence of a monarch, a person would signify his subjection with the act of prostration.[32] Only when the king had authorized one to arise would one dare to do so. Ezekiel realized that he had been ushered into the court of the divine king and that YHWH was seeking an audience with him. But only the divine spirit could give him the authority or the energy to stand erect before God. To fall before a god is appropriate, but to remain on one's face once he has indicated a desire to speak is insulting to the deity. Ezekiel may have been a בֶּן־אָדָם, "mere mortal," but infused with the רוּחַ he may—yea, he *must*—stand in God's presence. A second similar experience is recounted in 3:23–24.

No text in the entire OT portrays the vivifying power of the divine spirit as dramatically as 37:1–14. The unit is dominated by the tenfold recurrence of the *Leitwort* רוּחַ. But the use of רוּחַ is not uniform in this context. Impelled by the רוּחַ of YHWH, the prophet is brought to a valley that he observes to be full of very dry bones. The central issue in the chapter

---

30. The ambiguity of וַיֹּאמֶר is intentional, making it uncertain whether we should translate "it (i.e., the voice) said" or "he said."

31. Note the construction in 2:2 וַתָּבֹא בִי רוּחַ כַּאֲשֶׁר דִּבֶּר אֵלַי, "And the רוּחַ entered me while he spoke to me."

32. On which see Kreuzer, "Zur Bedeutung und Etymologie," 39–54; Gruber, *Aspects of Nonverbal Communication*, 187–251.

is introduced by the question that YHWH poses to the prophet: "Mortal, can these bones live?"[33] In reply to the prophet's agnostic answer, YHWH commands him to prophesy over the bones as follows: "I will cause רוּחַ to enter you that you may live. I will overlay you with sinews, cover you with flesh, and form skin over you. I will infuse you with רוּחַ and you shall live. Then you shall know that I am YHWH" (vv. 5–6). Ezekiel complies, and the bones come together with a mighty rattling, sinews overlay them, they are covered with flesh, and skin is formed over them. But alas! The prophet notes the absence of רוּחַ (v. 8).

The six-fold clustering of רוּחַ in verses 8b–10a suggests that we have now arrived at the heart of the unit. The solution to the absence of the רוּחַ is announced in verse 9:

> Prophesy to הָרוּחַ. Prophesy, mortal. Announce to הָרוּחַ: "Thus has the Lord YHWH declared: 'From the four רוּחוֹת come, O רוּחַ. Breathe[34] into these slain that they may live."

At the prophet's word the bodies are vitalized and, like Ezekiel himself in an earlier context (2:2; 3:24), they rise to their feet.

The play on רוּחַ in verse 9 is obvious. The רוּחַ that the prophet has summoned is the breath of life, the life-force that animates all living creatures. Here, however, it is being called from the four רוּחוֹת, which, as observed above, refers either to the four "winds" or the four "directions." The text is intentionally ambiguous. The interpretation of the dramatic parable is provided in verses 11–14. We now learn that the bones do not simply represent dead persons in general but the nation of Israel, which YHWH will bring back to life like people resurrected from their graves. They will be reclaimed as YHWH's people and brought back to the land of Israel. Perhaps necessitated by the demands of the figure, in verses 8–10 the רוּחַ is portrayed as something external to God and that can be summoned by him.[35] If the role of the prophet had really been to represent YHWH, he should have breathed over them his own breath.[36] But by merely adding the first-person singular suffix to רוּחַ in verse 14, Ezekiel produces an extremely significant shift in meaning. The רוּחַ that will revitalize Israel is not the ordinary, natural life-breath common to all living things; it is the

---

33. For a helpful discussion of the rhetorical strategy employed in the development of this theme see M. V. Fox, "Rhetoric of Ezekiel's Vision," 1–15.

34. The same verb נָפַח, "to breathe, blow," is used in Gen 2:7.

35. Cf. Fox, "Rhetoric," 15.

36. Cf. Ezekiel's role in the sign action involving the steel plate in 4:3.

The Prophet of the Spirit

spirit of God himself. Only he is able to restore to life a nation that has been destroyed and whose remnant now languishes hopelessly in exile.

We turn back now to a related text, 36:26–27. Here רוּחַ is juxtaposed with לֵב, which might suggest that "spirit" and "mind" are to be treated synonymously. The parallelism of the first two cola of verse 26 is readily recognized when they are set out as poetry:

וְנָתַתִּי לָכֶם לֵב חָדָשׁ   And I will give to you a new mind;
וְרוּחַ חֲדָשָׁה אֶתֵּן בְּקִרְבְּכֶם   And a new spirit I will put within you.

The common elements in the lines are the verb נָתַן, "to give," and the adjective "new," which is applied to both לֵב and רוּחַ. The chiastic structure is common in synonymous parallelism and may be merely stylistic. When examined more closely, however, the synonymous interpretation may be questioned on several counts. (1) As Robert Alter has convincingly argued, in poetic parallelism synonymity is seldom exact.[37] (2) The prepositions associated with the verbs are different. Whereas the new mind is given *to* (-לְ) Israel, the new spirit is placed *within* (בְּקֶרֶב) her. As we have seen, the placing of the spirit within someone or something has an animating, vivifying effect on the recipient. (3) The manner in which the two statements are elaborated upon in verses 26b–27 differs. The provision of the new heart is explained as a removal of the heart of stone from their flesh and its replacement with a heart of flesh. Which or whose heart is not specified. On the other hand, in verse 27 YHWH announces: וְאֶת־רוּחִי אֶתֵּן בְּקִרְבְּכֶם, "And I will put my spirit within you." Now we learn that the רוּחַ referred to in verse 26 is indeed YHWH's spirit. Furthermore, the transforming effect of the infusion of this רוּחַ is described: YHWH thereby causes them to walk in his statutes and to observe his covenant standards. This suggests a radical spiritual revitalization of the nation. (4) The announcement of YHWH's infusion of his own רוּחַ is repeated in 37:14, suggesting that the entire unit (37:1–14) is an exposition of the notion introduced in 36:26–27. This is not surprising, since it is characteristic of Ezekiel to announce a theme briefly and then to drop it, only to return to it later with a fuller development.[38]

But here Ezekiel again appears to have been influenced by Jeremiah. By juxtaposing Ezekiel's announcement of the infused רוּחַ with Jeremiah's

---

37. Alter, *The Art of Biblical Poetry*, 13–26.

38. Cf. 5:11, which is expounded in 8:5–18; 37:26–28, which is developed in chapters 40–48; 3:16–21 and expanded in 18:1–32; 33:1–20.

description of the new covenant in Jer 31:33, the similarities between the two texts become obvious:

Jeremiah 31:33	Ezekiel 36:27–28
נָתַתִּי אֶת־תּוֹרָתִי בְּקִרְבָּם	וְאֶת־רוּחִי אֶתֵּן בְּקִרְבְּכֶם
. . .	. . .
וְהָיִיתִי לָהֶם לֵאלֹהִים	וְהָיִיתֶם לִי לְעָם
וְהֵמָּה יִהְיוּ־לִי לְעָם	וְאָנֹכִי אֶהְיֶה לָכֶם לֵאלֹהִים
I will have put my Torah within them,	And my spirit I will put within you,
. . .	. . .
And I will be their God,	And you shall be my people,
And they shall be my people.	And I will be your God.

It would appear that at these points they are describing the same event. What Jeremiah attributes to the infusion of the divine Torah, Ezekiel ascribes to the infusion of the רוּחַ. In both the result is the renewal of the covenant relationship.

Before we leave this subject, we must ask whether and how Ezekiel's vision of the role of the רוּחַ in the future restored Israel differs from the operation of the Holy Spirit under the Old Covenant, as he understood it from his own tradition and experience. Some have argued that in ancient Israel the Holy Spirit came upon persons, whereas in the NT era he indwells the believer.[39] If this is so, then Ezekiel is predicting a phenomenon here of which he had heretofore no personal knowledge or experience. This interpretation, however, is questionable for several reasons.

First, it overlooks the indispensable animating role of the divine רוּחַ in effecting spiritual renewal. It seems to assume that an ancient saint became a member of the people of God by merely attending to the Torah. But Israelite religion was from the beginning a heart religion. Jeremiah's call for a circumcision of the heart in Jeremiah 4:4 was not an innovation but a recollection of a notion expressed in Deuteronomy 10:16, where the appeal is made to the Israelites to "circumcise their heart." Later, in 30:6, the divine role in this transforming work is emphasized: "YHWH your God will circumcise your heart and the heart of your descendants, to love YHWH with all your heart and with all your being, in order that you may live." Ezekiel's anticipation of a fundamental internal transformation (as described in Ezekiel 36:22–32) effected by the infusion of the divine רוּחַ rests upon ancient foundations.

---

39. Walvoord, *The Holy Spirit*, 152.

The Prophet of the Spirit

Second, it disregards the explicit witness of Psalm 51:12–13[10–11], one of only three OT occurrences of the expression רוּחַ הַקֹּדֶשׁ, "the holy spirit":[40]

> Create for me a clean heart, O God!
> And a steadfast רוּחַ renew within me.
> Do not cast me out of your presence,
> Nor take your holy spirit (רוּחַ קָדְשְׁךָ) from within me (מִמֶּנִּי).

In the context David stands before God fearing rejection, the loss of his salvation (יֶשַׁע), and the sentence of death (דָּמִים). His continued acceptance in the divine presence and the divine presence within him in the form of the רוּחַ represent his only hope.

Third, it evades the evidence of the NT. When Nicodemus requests of Jesus an explanation for his ministry, the discussion quickly digresses to a lecture on the role of the spirit in the life of one who would enter the kingdom of God:

> No one can enter the kingdom of God unless he is born of water and the spirit. Flesh gives birth to flesh, but the Spirit gives birth to spirit. You should not be surprised at my saying, "You must be born again." The wind blows wherever it pleases. You hear its sound, but you cannot tell where it comes from or where it is going. So it is with everyone born of the Spirit. (John 3:5–8)

One could interpret this statement as an innovative description of the work of the Holy Spirit in the new era, except that Jesus rebukes Nicodemus for being ignorant of these principles even though he was one of the leading theologians of the time. As far as Jesus is concerned, he is introducing nothing new. There can be little doubt that his statements here are based upon Ezekiel 36:25–29, a text with which the rabbi should have been familiar.[41]

Fourth, and most critically, the perception of radical discontinuity between the Holy Spirit's work in the two Testaments misses the point of the present context. It is unlikely that Ezekiel was self-consciously introducing a new notion with his promise of the transforming work of the indwelling רוּחַ of YHWH. He will have been well aware of Psalm 51. What concerns him, however, is the fundamental incongruity between the idealistic designation of his own people as "the people of God" and the reality that he observed. The problem was not the absence of the Holy Spirit to

---

40. Cf. also רוּחַ קָדְשׁוֹ, "the spirit of his holiness," Isa 63:10, 11.
41. So also Ewert, *The Holy Spirit*, 66.

transform lives, but that this was not occurring on a national scale. The issue was one of scope. The emphasis in the present text, as in the broader context of Ezekiel 34–39 in general, is on national renewal and revival, not individual regeneration. In 36:25–29 Ezekiel anticipates the day when the boundaries of the physical Israel will be coterminous with the spiritual people of God. In his day a vast gulf separated the two.

6. רוּחַ as "agency of prophetic inspiration."

The involvement of the spirit of God in the inspiration of the OT prophets is well known. The notion is given classic expression in 2 Peter 1:21: "No prophecy ever had its origin in the will of man, but men spoke from God as they were carried along by the Holy Spirit." The involvement of the רוּחַ in Ezekiel's prophetic inspiration is hinted at in several places, particularly where his influence is associated with the verbal utterance of YHWH. Examples of this phenomenon are found in Ezekiel 2:2, "The spirit entered me as he spoke to me," and 3:24, "The spirit entered me and set me on my feet, and he said to me." The most explicit statement of his prophetic inspiration is found in 11:5a, וַתִּפֹּל עָלַי רוּחַ יְהוָה וַיֹּאמֶר אֵלַי, "The spirit of YHWH fell upon me, and he said to me." Like his comment concerning the hand of YHWH falling upon him (8:1), this expression occurs nowhere else.

The role of the רוּחַ as agency of prophetic inspiration receives its most explicit statement in chapter 13. This text represents a woe oracle against false prophets, who posed as proclaimers of the will of God. Their authority and credibility as spokesmen for deity depended upon the presence of the divine רוּחַ. When the services of the prophets were required they would employ special techniques and instruments to work themselves into an ecstatic frenzy that was interpreted as seizure by the spirit of God. Once in this state, whatever utterances they might make would be interpreted as an expression of the will of God.[42]

The great prophets of Israel deliberately rejected all such artificial methods for determining the divine will. Their messages were based instead upon direct and personal encounters with YHWH at his own initiative. Instead of emphasizing the role of the רוּחַ, whose apparent influence could be manipulated or coerced (cf. 1 Kgs 22), they based their authority on דְּבַר יְהוָה, "the word of YHWH," which came to them almost as an objective concrete entity directly from God himself. However, as Fohrer

---

42. The classic texts on the false prophets are 1 Kgs 22:19–23; Jer 23:13–40. For a discussion of false prophecy in Israel see G. V. Smith, "Prophecy, False," 984–86.

The Prophet of the Spirit

has pointed out,[43] in his response Ezekiel deliberately distances himself from the false prophets. Being keenly aware of the control of the רוּחַ of YHWH over his own life, he dares to challenge head-on the fundamental premise on which false prophets operated: their claim to the divine spirit. Genuine and free charismatics, on the one hand, and officially accredited announcers, on the other, are to be distinguished. Calling and profession are not the same. This is not to say that the two were necessarily contradictory. Ezekiel may well have acknowledged some professional prophets as legitimate.

But it is apparent from the text that the prophets addressed by Ezekiel in 13:1–16 were charlatans. First, they are tautologically identified as "prophets who are prophesying." The redundancy betrays a sarcastic tone. As Davidson observed: "They prophesied and that without limit; their mouths were always full of Thus saith the Lord."[44] Apparently the people took their ranting seriously (cf. Jer 18:18). Second, they are "prophets from their own hearts." In verse 2 the preposition מִן on נְבִיאֵי מִלִּבָּם is a *min* of source.[45] The expression finds analogies in several OT texts. According to Num 16:28, in response to the challenge to his leadership by Korah and his followers Moses declared: "Thus you shall know that YHWH has commissioned me to do all of these things, for this was not my own idea" (כִּי־לֹא מִלִּבִּי). Similarly, Jeroboam's religious innovations are described as his own idea (מִלִּבּוֹ, 1 Kgs 12:33, *qere*). Since Ezekiel's oracle displays many other affinities with Jeremiah he may have been influenced by his contemporary's own invective against false prophets (Jer 23:9–40), particularly the latter's use of the phrase חֲזוֹן לִבָּם, "They pronounce a vision of their own heart" (23:16). In each of these instances לֵב probably signifies "mind," suggesting that the false prophets' inspiration was no higher than that of ordinary human wisdom. Their messages were their own concoction, based upon their own evaluation of the situation and their own private judgment. They were merely spouting off private opinions while posing as spokesmen for God.

This charge receives further elaboration in the opening volley of the oracle itself (Ezek 13:3). Here Ezekiel charges the professional prophets

---

43. Fohrer, *Ezechiel*, 69.

44. Davidson, *The Prophet Ezekiel*, 84.

45. MT לִנְבִיאֵי מִלִּבָּם represents an unusual case of the construct form before a preposition. GKC §130a suggests that this is a sign of elevated style. Cf. Gen 3:22; Isa 28:9; Jer 23:23; Hos 7:5 (all with מִן). The shorter text of LXX reads πρὸς αὐτούς = אֲלֵיהֶם, as in 34:2; 37:4, a reading preferred by *BHS* and many commentators.

with being fools. The adjective נָבָל is used in the wisdom literature of a special kind of fool, one who is arrogant (Prov 30:32), crude of speech (17:7), spiritually and morally obtuse (Job 2:10), a scoundrel (30:8).[46] Isaiah describes such a person in Isa 32:5–6:

> A villain (נָבָל) shall no longer be called noble,
> Nor a knave be spoken of as a gentleman;
> For the villain (נָבָל) utters villainous speech (נְבָלָה),
> And his mind (לִבּוֹ) plots evil, to act impiously
> And to express deviance (תּוֹעָה) toward YHWH.

Ezekiel's description of the prophets as נְבָלִים emphasizes their perverse and impious character.

Third, the false prophets "walk according to their own Spirit" (הֹלְכִים אַחַר רוּחָם, Ezek 13:3).[47] Here רוּחַ is employed ambiguously. On the one hand, the reference is to their own "spirit," their auto-animation that inspires them to prophesy, as opposed to the רוּחַ of YHWH, whose inspiration they claim. On the other hand, as we shall see in the discussion to follow, רוּחַ may also refer to their minds, functioning as a synonym for לֵב in verse 2. The expression הֹלְכִים אַחַר differs slightly from the more conventional הָלַךְ אַחֲרֵי, "to walk after" (cf. 20:16; 33:31). אַחַר is used in the sense of norm, standard, yielding "in accordance with."[48] In other words, far from taking their cues from YHWH, these false prophets were merely giving vent to their own imaginations. Their self-inspired messages were a delusion.

Fourth, they lack divine insight. The expression לְבִלְתִּי רָאוּ is awkward. It seems to mean something like "without seeing,"[49] which could be interpreted in several ways. Since prophets are identified elsewhere as

---

46. The classic illustration is found in Nabal, the husband of Abigail (1 Sam 25:25). In the Psalms the *nbl* denies God (14:1; 53:2 [3]) and blasphemes him (74:22). Guilt-incurring foolish acts included sexual sins (Gen 34:7; Deut 22:21; Judg 20:6; Jer 29:23; cf. also Judg 19:23–24; 2 Sam 13:12) as well as cultic irreverence (Josh 7:15).

47. LXX abbreviates and changes הַנְּבִיאִים הַנְּבָלִים אֲשֶׁר הֹלְכִים אַחַר רוּחָם with its rendering τοῖς προφητεύουσιν ἀπὸ καρδίας αὐτῶν. The last phrase seems to read לִנְבִיא מִלִּבָּם. Cf. Cooke, *Ezekiel*, 138, 142; Zimmerli, *Ezekiel* 1, 285. For an explanation of how MT might have arisen see Parunak, *Structural Studies*, 223–24.

48. Cf. Williams, *Hebrew Syntax*, §362. Note also 2 Kgs 13:2; 23:3; Isa 65:2; Job 31:7.

49. "The Prayer of Adad-guppi," in Gadd, "Harran Inscriptions of Nabonidus," 46–56, cf. also *ANET*, 560–62.

The Prophet of the Spirit

רֹאִים, "seers,"[50] and a vision could be called a רֹאֶה (Isa 28:7) or a מַרְאֶה,[51] this amounts to another denial of their genuineness. Moreover, the statement may also be an attack against their own lack of spiritual perception. However the false prophets "looked" upon themselves, the present situation, or their answer for it, it did not represent the perspective of YHWH.

7. רוּחַ as "mind."

The discussion of Ezek 13:3 has intimated that Ezekiel could also employ רוּחַ psychically as a synonym for לֵב, the seat of the emotions, the intellect and the will. This reflects a rather common usage in the OT.[52] Ezekiel 3:14–15 provides a rare window into the emotional reactions of the prophet to his work. The enigmatic clause in verse 14, וָאֵלֵךְ מַר בַּחֲמַת רוּחִי, has been rendered traditionally as "I went embittered in the rage of my spirit," or the like. However, the matter is not that simple.

חֵמָה occurs thirty-two times in Ezekiel. Elsewhere it always bears the sense "rage, wrath" (often parallel to אַף). Except for 23:25 it refers exclusively to divine anger. If "anger" were the intended sense here, however, the need for the preceding מַר is questionable.[53] LXX renders חֲמַת רוּחִי as ὁρμῇ τοῦ πνεύματός μου, suggesting a spiritual rather than psychological impulse, perhaps a form of spirit possession.[54] This is certainly possible on the basis of the root חמם, which means primarily "to be hot," and the related חמם, "to be warm," which yields the substantive חֵמָה, "glow."[55] In our text חֲמַת רוּחִי could therefore be understood something like "the heat of my excitement, the ecstasy of my spirit." The choice of the unparalleled compound expression in place of חֲמָתִי may have been intentional, to distinguish the significance of the word here from its usage elsewhere in the book. The addition of רוּחַ provides a pleasant play on the word, which

---

50. Cf. 1 Sam 9:9, 11, 18, 19; Isa 30:10; 1 Chr 9:22; 26:28; 29:29; 2 Chr 16:7, 10.

51. Ezek 1:1; 8:3; 40:2; 43:3; cf. Num 12:6; 1 Sam 3:15; Dan 10:16.

52. It may also serve as a synonym for נֶפֶשׁ. For studies of the psychological use of the term see Hill, *Greek Words,* 215–16; Robinson, "Hebrew Psychology," 360–61; Albertz and Westermann, "רוּחַ rûᵃḥ Geist," 739–42; Jacob, *Theology of the Old Testament,* 161–63.

53. Perhaps this is why LXX omits מַר.

54. So Bertram, "ὁρμή, ὅρμημα, ὁρμάω," 469

55. Secondarily יחם may refer to the sexual impulse of animals in heat. Occasionally חֵמָה is used of venom (Deut 32:24, 33; Pss 58:5[4]; 140:4[3]; Job 6:4). Cf. Akkadian *imtu,* "poison, wrath," *AHW,* 379, *CAD* 7.139–141, Ugaritic *ḥmy,* "venom," *UT* 397 #869a; In Hos 7:5 it denotes fever from wine.

for the first time in the book refers to human disposition rather than the divine spirit. The reference then seems to be to the "glow of his spirit,"[56] which arose as a consequence of seizure by the spirit/hand of YHWH. מַר, which precedes, is usually derived from מָרַר, "to be bitter."[57] It may be intended as an abbreviation for מַר־נֶפֶשׁ, "bitterness of soul," which occurs in 27:31[58] and which is related semantically to חֲמַת רוּחַ.[59] The term may have been inserted here for emphasis and/or as a wordplay on מָרַד and מְרִי, both of which have appeared earlier.

The cause of the prophet's bitterness is not indicated, though several suggestions may be proposed. (1) He may have come to share the feeling of God over the hardened disposition of his countrymen.[60] (2) He may have begun to show the effects of the incorporation of his message—namely, the "lamentations, moaning and woe." (3) He may be responding to the predicted thanklessness of his task. Or all three may have been involved, since they are not mutually exclusive.

Even so, the traditional interpretation of the phrase seems awkward in the context. An alternative is to understand מַר as deriving from מרר, "to be strengthened, empowered," as in Ugaritic. In 1 Aqht 194-195 *mrr* is paired with *brk*:

| *ltbrkn alk brkt* | Do bless me and I shall go blessed; |
| *tmrn alkn mrrt* | Strengthen me and I shall go forth strengthened. |

Our text may then be translated: "I went forth strengthened in the fervor of my spirit."[61] Besides changing the entire significance of מַר בַּחֲמַת רוּחִי, the following comment is rendered more comprehensible: "Now the strong hand of YHWH was upon me" (which otherwise looks strangely out of place) and brought into closer harmony with verse 15. By this interpretation, as the רוּחַ is bearing Ezekiel aloft and wafting him away he

---

56. Cf. Vogt, *Untersuchungen zum Buche Ezechiel*, 18, "die Glut seines Geistes."

57. BDB, 600. The word is attested in Aramaic (*DISO*, 168), cf. Akkadian *marāru* (*AHW*, 609; *CAD* 10/1.267-68).

58. Also 1 Sam 22:2; Isa 38:15; Job 7:11; 10:1.

59. The dropping of נֶפֶשׁ has necessitated the elimination of a preceding בְּ, thus creating an adverbial accusative, as in 27:30.

60. So Heschel, *Prophets*, 307-22.

61. Cf. Dahood, "Qoheleth and Recent Discoveries," 308-10; *UT* 438 #1556. Ward, "Egypto-Semitic *MR*," 357-60, has argued for an Egyptian derivation of the root. This "strong" interpretation has been cautiously rejected by Kutler, "A 'Strong' Case," 114; Pardee, "The Semitic Root *mrr*," 259-60.

The Prophet of the Spirit

is energized in a special way in the excitement of his spirit, an energizing power attributed in the following phrase to "the strong hand of YHWH."

In several texts רוּחַ is clearly the seat of mental activity. In 11:5–6 Ezekiel is called upon to expose the true and evil effects of the perverse thinking of the leaders of Jerusalem. As in verse 3, the verb אָמַר describes a cognitive function that precedes decision and action: "to consider, reflect, think over." The full form of the expression is אָמַר עַל־לֵב/בְּלֵב, "to speak in/to one's heart," which has reference to internal communication, the nonverbalized speech that passes through one's mind. This interpretation is confirmed by the following idiom, מַעֲלוֹת רוּחֲכֶם, "the things that arise in your mind." The former term is a *hapax* derived from the verb עָלָה, which occurs in a related idiom in 20:32, הָעֹלָה עַל־רוּחֲכֶם, "what comes to your mind," and 38:10, יַעֲלוּ דְבָרִים עַל־לְבָבְךָ, "words that come into your mind." It is apparent from the idiom that רוּחַ and לֵב are interchangeable. The use of רוּחַ as the organ of mental activity constitutes just one of several clever wordplays in this chapter by which different nuances are introduced without expanding the vocabulary (cf. רוּחַ = "agency of conveyance" in verse 1; "agency of divine inspiration" in v. 5a). The point of verse 5b is that YHWH is aware of the motives of the leaders without their mouths even opening to declare them. His gaze is able to penetrate the human mind.[62] In 20:32 he is able to predict that their aspirations to be like the nations will not transpire.

Unfortunately not all texts are as clear as these. 11:19 contains Ezekiel's first announcement of YHWH's predicted heart transplant and his infusion of a new רוּחַ. The use of רוּחַ appears to be intentionally ambiguous. Two considerations argue for treating it as the seat of one's mental activity. (1) The context has been dealing with people with a perverse רוּחַ (v. 5). The only effective cure for such perversion is the implantation of a new mind. (2) The parallel idiom, לֵב אֶחָד, "a single heart," deals with the seat of the intellect and the will. The present text may be viewed as an exposition of Jeremiah 32:39, וְנָתַתִּי לָהֶם לֵב אֶחָד וְדֶרֶךְ אֶחָד, "I will grant to them a single heart and a single way."[63] As this text suggests, YHWH's goal is to instill in his people a singleness of mind that expresses itself in singleness of conduct. The antithesis of לֵב אֶחָד, "single heart," is insincerity, the possession of two hearts, a double heart (לֵב וָלֵב), as described in Psalm 12:3[2]. David's loyal followers are commended in 1 Chronicles 12:34[33] as those who assisted him בְּלֹא־לֵב וָלֵב, "with undivided heart," and in verse

---

62. Cf. the use of עָלָה with לֵב in 14:3, 4, 7.
63. Cf. Jer 11:20; 12:3; 17:10; Pss 26:2; 139:1–6, 23.

39[38] as men of לֵבָב שָׁלֵם, "perfect heart." In Psalm 86:11 the psalmist prays that YHWH would cause his heart to be united to fear his name (יַחֵד לְבָבִי לְיִרְאָה שְׁמֶךָ). This demonstration of the single heart in the fear of YHWH is echoed in the Jeremiah text, where the words quoted above are followed up with לְיִרְאָה אוֹתִי כָּל־הַיָּמִים, "to fear me all the days."

The use of רוּחַ and לֵב for the seat of the will and the mental organ is reminiscent of David's penitential psalm referred to earlier. His plea for the renewal of a "right spirit" (וְרוּחַ נָכוֹן חַדֵּשׁ בְּקִרְבִּי; Ps 51:12[10]) is a plea for steadfastness and stability of disposition. The source and nature of the new רוּחַ spoken of by Ezekiel are not described. The absence of the article leaves the way open for several possibilities. As we have already noted, when the present theme resurfaces in Ezekiel 36:26–27 the nuance of seat of intellect and will recedes in רוּחַ and gives way to YHWH's own spirit, which will be infused into the nation.

One final text deserves comment in this context. In 21:12[7] the prophet is commanded to groan publicly with broken heart and in bitter grief over the news of Jerusalem's impending doom. In response to the people's questions regarding the reason for his groaning, the prophet is to say:

אֶל־שְׁמוּעָה	Because of the news,
כִּי־בָאָה	for it is coming,
וְנָמֵס כָּל־לֵב	every heart will melt,
וְרָפוּ כָל־יָדַיִם	and all hands will be feeble,
וְכִהֲתָה כָל־רוּחַ	and every spirit will be faint,
וְכָל־בִּרְכַּיִם תֵּלַכְנָה מָּיִם	and every knee will run with water.

Here רוּחַ clearly refers to the seat of the emotions. The fainting רוּחַ represents but one symptom along with several others of the utter demoralization of the population.

8. רוּחַ as "sign of divine ownership."

We conclude our discussion of Ezekiel's use of the term רוּחַ with a brief look at 39:29, according to which YHWH's preservation of Israel from the threat of Gog is said to be based upon his having poured out his spirit upon his people. The full discussion of this text that I have published elsewhere need not be repeated here.[64] I wish only to make some observations relevant to the present topic.

---

64. For a more detailed analysis of this text and its significance in its context see Block, "Gog and the Pouring Out of the Spirit," 257–70 (reprinted in the second volume of my Ezekiel essays, *Beyond the River Chebar*, 141–54).

The Prophet of the Spirit

Although this is the only occurrence of the notion of "pouring (שָׁפַךְ) the divine spirit upon" someone in Ezekiel, the idea recalls several other prophetic statements. In Joel 3:1[2:28], as in our text, the concept appears in a salvation oracle, specifically in the context of the renewal of the covenant and the restoration of prosperity and peace for Israel.[65] In Zechariah 12:10 the pouring of the spirit of grace and supplication occurs in the context of the restoration of the dynasty of David and God's renewed activity on behalf of Jerusalem and, in the broader context, of the renewal of the covenant.[66] Although a different verb is used in Isaiah 32:15 (עָרָה), once again the pouring out of the רוּחַ from on high represents the divine activity that immediately precedes the restoration of peace and prosperity in Israel. These are normally the consequences of the reestablishment of the covenant. The covenantal context is unmistakable in Isaiah 44:1–4:

> But now listen, O Jacob, my servant,
> And Israel, whom I have chosen.
> Thus says YHWH who made you
> And formed you in the womb,
> Who will aid you:
> "Do not fear, O Jacob my servant,
> And you, O Jeshurun, whom I have chosen,
> For I will pour (יָצַק) water on the thirsty land
> And streams on the dry ground;
> I will pour (יָצַק) my spirit on your descendants,
> And they will spring up among the grass
> Like poplars by streams of water."
> This one will say, "I belong to YHWH,"

---

65. Cf. Joel 2:18—3:2[2:29], specifically the first verse, "Then YHWH will be zealous for his land and will have pity on his people," and 2:27, which immediately precedes the reference to the pouring out of the spirit, "Thus you shall know that I am in the midst of Israel, and that I am YHWH your God, and there is no other; and my people will never be put to shame." In agreement with Wolff (*Joel and Amos*, 67) the context requires that כָּל־בָּשָׂר, "all flesh," not be interpreted universally, as it is commonly understood, but for all Israel. In Peter's Pentecost sermon this original sense is respected. Acts 2:5 notes that the people gathered on the occasion were Jews from all parts of the empire. Peter himself emphasizes that he is speaking to the men/house of Israel. Cf. vv. 22, 36. That he understood it in this restricted sense is confirmed by the need for a special revelation in Acts 10 to convince him to go outside the house of Israel.

66. Note the reference to the covenant formula in 13:9, "I will say, 'They are my people,' and they will say, 'YHWH is my God.'" Admittedly there is some distance between these two verses, and it may be argued that originally these were uttered as separate oracles. But the repeated references to "in that day" (12:11; 13:1, 2, 4) as well as the editorial juxtaposing of the oracles suggest some connection.

And that one will call on the name of Jacob;
And another will write on his hand "Belonging to YHWH,"
And will name Israel's name with honor.

The idea of pouring out the divine spirit is rooted in the perception of the רוּחַ as a sort of divine fluid that covers the object.[67] In each of the texts cited, the pouring out of YHWH's רוּחַ signified the ratification and sealing of the covenant relationship. This represented the guarantee of new life, peace, and prosperity. It served as the definitive act whereby YHWH claimed and sealed the newly gathered nation of Israel as his own.

In the context of Ezekiel 39:29 the causal clause, "For I shall have poured out my spirit upon the house of Israel," explains more than just the events described in the preceding verses—that is, the regathering of the nation. It also explains YHWH's fulfillment of his covenant with his people. The presence of the רוּחַ of YHWH, poured out upon his people, served as the permanent witness and seal of the בְּרִית שָׁלוֹם and the בְּרִית עוֹלָם. The pouring out of YHWH's רוּחַ upon the returned exiles guaranteed that he would never leave any of the house of Israel at the mercy of her enemies and that he would never hide his face from them again, as Ezekiel and his contemporaries had witnessed. In short, Gog becomes the agent through whom YHWH declares concretely that 587 BC shall never repeat itself again.

The implications of this covenantal interpretation of the pouring out of the רוּחַ for the progress of the Holy Spirit's activity in the book of Acts are tantalizing but may be touched upon only briefly. It hardly seems accidental that with the commencement of every new stage in the advance of the gospel and the incorporation of new groups of people into the covenant people reference is made to the manifestation of the Spirit. The Spirit comes upon the Jews in Jerusalem (Acts 2:4, 33, 38), the Samaritans (8:14–17), the Gentile proselytes of Judea (10:44–48; cf. 11:16), and the Gentiles of Asia Minor (19:6). It might also be noted that when Paul speaks of being sealed with/by the Holy Spirit (2 Cor 1:22; Eph 1:13; 4:30) he seems also to be speaking of the divine confirmation of the covenant.

Conclusion

It is clear that in the OT the word רוּחַ bears many different meanings. The nuances intended by the authors vary greatly, and the requirements of the

---

67. Cf. Clines, "The Image of God in Man," 82.

context must determine the interpretation in each instance. Fundamentally the term signified "wind" or "breath." But in the hands of Hebrew psychologists (if one may speak of them as such) and theologians רוּחַ seemed to open up numerous possibilities. When we are attempting to formulate a biblical doctrine of the Holy Spirit we can ill afford to do so without paying more careful attention to the OT understanding than we have done heretofore. After all, the outlook of the theologians of the NT was determined primarily by their sacred Scriptures and not by prevailing Greek notions. This applied to their anthropology and their pneumatology no less than their theology, their soteriology, and their Christology.

When we think in terms of the OT understanding of the רוּחַ of YHWH, of which τὸ πνεῦμα τὸ ἅγιόν is the counterpart, we should think first and foremost of the divine presence on earth. It was on this basis that the psalmist could cry out: "Where can I escape from your רוּחַ? / Where can I flee from your presence?" (Ps 139:7[6]). The רוּחַ is the agency through which God's will is exercised, whether it be in creation, his dispensing of life, his guidance and providential care, the revelation of his will, his salvation (Isa 63), his renewal of unregenerate hearts and minds, or his sealing of his covenant people as his own. The spirit of YHWH is not a self-existent agent operating independently. In the words of A. R. Johnson, the divine spirit is an "extension of YHWH's personality" by which he exercises his influence over the world.[68] The רוּחַ is the power of God at work among humankind. It is his creating, animating, energizing force. The רוּחַ can hardly be identified as one other than God himself.

This does not mean that the Hebrews could not speak of the רוּחַ as a concrete (or, better, fluid) entity, separable from YHWH, as in Psalm 104:30: "When you send forth your רוּחַ . . ." This, however, is anthropomorphic language. YHWH's sending out his רוּחַ, "breath," is analogous to his extending his arm, his smelling of an offering, his utterance of words with his mouth, his seeing, and his hearing. Consequently, just as the activity of YHWH's right arm represents YHWH's own actions, so the work of his רוּחַ signifies his own direct involvement. If a prophet could be so identified with YHWH that what the prophet said God said, surely such an identification between the Spirit and YHWH himself is not inconceivable. When the divine רוּחַ acts, God acts.

The instruction provided by the prophets concerning God's activity in this world is both rich and complex. Ezekiel has served as the model

---

68. Johnson, *The One and the Many*, 36.

teacher in this regard, for he not only spoke of the power of the spirit, but also embodied it in his own person.[69]

---

69. Appreciation is expressed to Bruce Ware for his many helpful interpretive comments and to my assistants, Bradley Soukup and William Odermann, for their proofreading of the manuscript.

7

Beyond the Grave

Ezekiel's Vision of Death and Afterlife[1]

INTRODUCTION

MR. CHAIRMAN AND FELLOW scholars. I am honored to have been invited to read this year's Old Testament paper. For the past eight years or so the prophet Ezekiel and I have developed a very special relationship. But as I have been poring over the collection of his prophecies found in the Old Testament, I have often found myself wishing that he were personally present to answer some of my questions. Among the many intriguing issues that the book of Ezekiel raises is the nature of death and especially the prophet's vision of life beyond the grave. Around the turn of the year I suggested to Professor Hawthorne that this topic might be worth exploring in a paper to this gathering of scholars. At the time I had no idea how in tune with the times my own questions were. However, when the June 3, 1991 issue of *Time* magazine headlined its feature article on show business, "Hollywood Goes to Heaven," I realized we were on to something.[2] This year will see the release of no fewer than a dozen films dealing with the afterlife. The supernatural, death, and the afterlife are "in." The renaissance of

---

1. This is a revised version of the paper delivered to the Institute of Biblical Research in Kansas City, Missouri, 23 November, 1991. It was originally published in *Bulletin for Biblical Research* 2 (1992) 113–41.

2. Smilgis, "Hollywood Goes to Heaven," 70–71.

popular fascination with the subject has caused me to wonder if scholarly interest will match it. Perhaps an investigation such as this will provide a catalyst for some of us to wrestle more earnestly with a matter that was of great concern to the ancients.

Several problems confront anyone interested in pursuing Ezekiel's vision of death and afterlife: (1) How many of the ideas represented in the book that goes by his name are the prophet's own, and how many derive from later interpreters?[3] (2) What is the source of Ezekiel's images of postmortem realities? (3) To what extent do the images reflect reality, or are these to be interpreted merely as figures of speech? For those of us who are concerned to develop a Christian doctrine of the afterlife, this issue is of more than academic interest.

In this short study we cannot possibly answer all of these questions. However, it does seem to me that Ezekiel's vision of death and afterlife deserves a little more respect than it has received in the past.[4] Our aim is to assemble the data that reflect this prophet's vision of death and to synthesize them in an ordered picture. We shall do so by first exploring Ezekiel's vocabulary of death; then examining his perception of the nature of death itself, the state of the dead, and their relationship to the living, and finally summarizing his view of life beyond the grave.

The Vocabulary of Death in Ezekiel

Many casual readers stumble over the overwhelmingly judgmental character of three-fourths of the book of Ezekiel. The prophet himself might also have, had YHWH not prepared him for this type of ministry. At the time of Ezekiel's commissioning YHWH had commanded him to swallow a scroll received from his hand on which were written "lamentations, dirges, and woes" (2:10).[5] These three expressions capture in a nutshell

---

3. The differences in perspective are illustrated by Walther Zimmerli, who distinguishes between the prophet's own work and that of the "Ezekielian school" (*Ezekiel*; also Garscha, *Studien zum Ezechielbuch*), and Moshe Greenberg, who attributes virtually the entire book to the prophet himself (*Ezekiel 1–20*). For Greenberg's critique of the Zimmerlian approach see "What Are Valid Criteria?," 123–35.

4. Apart from passing references to Ezek 37:1–14, the prophet's contributions to the subject tend to be largely ignored by theologians, even in discussions of Sheol/Hades. Cf. Berkhof, *Systematic Theology*, 1.276–308; K. Barth, *Church Dogmatics* 3/2:587–640; Buswell, Jr., *Systematic Theology*, 2.304–23; Hodge, *Systematic Theology*, 3.713–32; Thielicke, *Evangelical Faith*, 3.400–403; Erickson, *Christian Theology*, 3.1167–84.

5. קִנִים וָהֶגֶה וָהִי, as rendered by *NJPSV*.

Beyond the Grave

the nature of the messages that he was to pass on to the house of Israel, particularly in the years leading up to the fall of Jerusalem in 586 BC. But I admit that the overtly mortuary nature of his ministry had not gripped me until I conducted a systematic tabulation of the expressions relating to death and dying used in the book.

The common Semitic root מות occurs fifty-one times in Ezekiel,[6] two-thirds (33) of these occurrences being clustered in three stylistically related texts: 3:1–20 [6x]; 18:1–32 [15x]; 33:1–20 [12x].[7] But other words for the dead and for dying also occur. פְּגָרִים is used of corpses in 6:5.[8] Euphemistic expressions for the dead include הַנֹּפְלִים, "those who have fallen" (32:22–24 [3x]);[9] הַיֹּרְדִים, "those who go down" (26x), especially to Sheol,[10] where they lie;[11] חֲלָלִים, "the mortally wounded" (36x);[12] הַהֲרוּגִים, "the slain," in 37:9.[13] To this list we may add a series of verbs for "killing," including הָרַג, "to kill";[14] רָצַח, "to slaughter" (21:27[22]); רָצַח, "to butcher,

---

6. Including בְּמוֹתָם in 43:7. Of the prophets only Jeremiah uses the root more often (61x). For a study of מות, see Gerleman, "מות *mût*, sterben" 1.893–97.

7. The remainder are found in 5:12; 6:12 [*bis*]; 7:15; 11:13; 12:13; 13:19 [*bis*]; 17:16; 24:17, 18; 28:8–10 [4x]; 31:14; 43:7; 44:25.

8. Cf. 43:7, 9, where the word denotes a stela erected in honor of the dead. While others use גְּוִיָּה for a cadaver, Ezekiel uses the term only for visionary living creatures (1:11, 23).

9. The root נפל occurs sixty times. More than two-thirds of these refer to the violent fall of persons. The experience of death is their מַפֶּלֶת, "fall" (26:15, 18; 27:27; 32:10. Cf. the fall of a tree in 31:13, 16).

10. Except for 26:16, 27:11, 29, 30:6, 31:12, and 47:1, 8, the verb always describes the descent of the dead to their nether abode, identified variously as Sheol (31:15, 16, 17; 32:27), "the pit" (26:20: בּוֹר [*bis*]; 31:14, 16; 32:18, 24, 25, 29, 30; שַׁחַת 28:8), "the netherworld" (אֶרֶץ תַּחְתִּיּוֹת: 32:18, 24; cf. 31:18, אֶל־אֶרֶץ תַּחְתִּית). 28:8 associates "going down to the pit" with "dying the death of the slain" (וָמַתָּה מְמוֹתֵי חָלָל).

11. In 31:18, 32:19, 21 and 32:32, those who are sent down lie (שָׁכַב) among the uncircumcised and those who have fallen to the sword.

12. In 26:15 and 30:24 חֲלָלִים refers simply to "the wounded," but in most other cases the expression denotes "the mortally wounded," those slain in battle or executed. See further below. In 32:22, 23, 24 the חֲלָלִים are more closely defined as הַנֹּפְלִים בַּחֶרֶב, "those who fall by the sword." חָלָל and נָפַל are also conjoined in 6:4, 7, 28:23, and 30:4. The expression חַלְלֵי־חֶרֶב, "those slain by the sword," is typically Ezekielian (31:17, 18; 32:20, 21, 25, 28, 29, 30, 31, 32; 35:8). Cf. also the *pual* form, מְחֻלְלֵי חֶרֶב in 32:26, and the expression, חֲלַל רָשָׁע, "mortal sinner," in 21:30, 34[25, 29].

13. Cf. also the abstract noun הֶרֶג, "slaughter," in 26:15. Four of these associate the slaughter directly with the sword (23:10; 26:6, 8, 11).

14. 9:6; 21:16[11]; 23:10, 47; 26:6, 8, 11, 15; 28:9.

slay,"[15] שָׁחַט, "to slay [children] for sacrifice" (16:21; 23:39);[16] הִשְׁמִיד, of YHWH destroying persons;[17] הִכְרִית, of "cutting off" from the living or from the earth;[18] אָבַד, "to destroy," used of persons in 22:27;[19] שִׁחֵת, "to ruin, destroy," of persons in 5:16 and 20:17; כִּלָּה,[20] "to exterminate, annihilate," with the accusative of persons in 20:13, 22:31, and 43:8.[21]

This list is not exhaustive, but it is sufficient to capture the somber tone of Ezekiel's ministry. Despite YHWH's affirmation that he takes no delight in death, not even the death of the wicked (18:32), in the first twenty-four chapters its shadow hangs like a cloud over the inhabitants of Jerusalem and Judah. However, once the divine judgment has fallen upon his own people, the cloud lifts and assumes new positions over the foreign nations, who take their turns as the objects of God's lethal wrath. In the meantime the sun may shine again upon Israel. We should not be surprised that the vocabulary of death disappears almost completely in Ezekiel's oracles and visions of restoration in chapters 32–34 and 36–48.

15. Cf. the description of the sword as טֶבַח הוּחַדָּה טָבֹחַ, "sharpened for slaughter" (21:15[10]); פְּתוּחָה לְטָבַח, "polished for slaughter" (21:33[28]); מְעֻטָּה לְטָבַח, "wrapped for slaughter" (21:20[15]).

16. Cf. 40:39, 41, 42, and 44:11, where the word is used of killing a sacrificial animal.

17. 14:9; 25:7; 34:16. Cf. 32:12, where the *niphal* is used of a devastated multitude (הָמוֹן).

18. 17:17 speaks of Nebuchadnezzar "cutting off many lives" (לְהַכְרִית נְפָשׁוֹת רַבּוֹת). In most instances, however, YHWH is the subject: 14:8, 13, 17; 21:8, 9[3, 4]; 25:1, 7, 13, 16; 29:8; 30:7, 15. Cf. the literal sense of cutting in 31:12 (*qal*, of a tree), 16:4 (*piel*, of an umbilical cord), and the idiom כָּרַת בְּרִית, "to cut a covenant" (34:25; 37:26).

19. לְאַבֵּד נְפָשׁוֹת. The verse compares the greedy princes of Jerusalem to wolves tearing prey (זְאֵבִים טֹרְפֵי טָרֶף), and shedding blood (שָׁפָךְ־דָּם). Cf. the use of the *qal*, אָבַד, "to perish" (7:26, of Torah; 12:22, of a vision; 19:5, 37:11, of hope; 26:17, of Tyre). In 34:4, 16 lost sheep are referred to as הָאֹבֶדֶת, "the perishing."

20. The root is used most often of ruining inanimate entities: of ruinous deeds (20:44); ruined walls (22:30; 26:4); corrupting wisdom (28:17); the land (30:11); the city (43:3). Cf. 16:47 and 23:11, where the *hiphil* form means "to act corruptly." In 20:17 שִׁחֵת functions antithetically to חוּס, "to spare," and synonymously with עָשָׂה כָלָה, "to effect annihilation." The form מַשְׁחִית, "destruction," is applied to persons in 5:16; 9:1 (מַשְׁחֵת), 6; 21:36[31], and 25:15. The noun שַׁחַת, is used of "the place of ruin," that is a trap used to catch lions (19:4, 8), as well as the grave, where humans go to ruin (28:8).

21. The *qal* form in 5:12 (alongside מוּת and נָפַל) and 13:14 speaks of humans perishing. The root denotes fundamentally "to cease, to be at, come to an end" (Gerleman, "מוּת *mût*, sterben," 831–33). Ezekiel often uses it of YHWH's satisfaction of his fury against humans: *qal*: 5:13a (cf. כַּלּוֹתִי in 13b); *piel* + בְּ: 5:13; 6:12; 7:8; 13:15; 20:8, 21. To this list should be added the occurrences of the noun form כָּלָה, which carries the sense "annihilation" in 11:13; 13:13, and 20:17.

The Way of Death in Ezekiel

Modern cartoonists often portray death as a skeletal grim reaper dressed in black with scythe in hand. This image bears little resemblance to the way ancient Near Easterners perceived death. Outside of Israel, death itself was personalized as a divine figure, the ruler of the netherworld, whom Mesopotamians identified as Nergal,[22] and Northwestern Semites as Mot (from the same root as Hebrew מוּת, "to die").[23] In Ugaritic mythology the perpetual struggle between the forces of death and life, which played itself out primarily in the annual seasonal cycles of nature, was personified in the conflict between Mot and Baal, the life and fertility dispensing deity. But Mot's influence was also evident in non-routine calamities: war, famine, plague, and pestilence.[24] Although we may have difficulty at times distinguishing between the deity of death and personalized forces of death,[25] it was often thought that behind these evils lay malevolent spirits, demons,[26] who came up from the netherworld and stalked the land in search of victims. In fact, like Death itself, they too were personalized, bearing names like *Resheph*,[27] *Deber*,[28] and *Qeteb*.[29]

The doctrine of malevolent spirits remains remarkably undeveloped in the Old Testament. To be sure, some have found demons in the שֵׁדִים of Deuteronomy 32:17 and Psalm 106:37, the שְׂעִירִם of Leviticus 17:7

22. On Nergal see Römer, "Religion of Ancient Mesopotamia," 137–37; Weiherr, *Der babylonische Gott Nergal*; as well as the review of this volume by Lambert, "Studies in Nergal," 355–63.

23. On the Ugaritic deity Mot, see Pope and Röllig, "Mythologie der Ugariter und Phönizier," 300–2; Pope and Röllig, "Mot," 607–8; Tromp, *Primitive Conceptions of Death and the Netherworld*, 99–107; M. Smith, *The Early History of God*, 53 and notes.

24. For a recent study of plagues in the ancient Near East and the peoples' perceptions thereof see Martinez, "Epidemic Disease, Ecology, and Culture," 413–58.

25. Cf. the Mesopotamian equation of Nergal = Erra, the god of pestilence. For an account of the activities of Erra see Cagni, *The Poem of Erra*.

26. On demons in Mesopotamia see Ebeling, "Dämonen," 107–12.

27. On this deity see Pope and Röllig, *Götter und Mythen*, 305–6; Fulco, *The Canaanite God Rešep*; Yadin, "New Gleanings on Resheph," 259–73; Weinfeld, "Divine Intervention," 124–31. J. Day interprets the title *b'l ḥẓ ršp* in *UT* 1001:3 as Resheph the archer ("New Light," 259–74).

28. An Eblaite deity, whose name survives in Ugaritic only as a common word for "fatal pestilence" (*UT* 67 VI:6–7). Cf. Dahood, *Ras Shamra Parallels* 3.54–55 §84; Caquot, "Sur quelques démons," 57–58. According to Pettinato the title *ᵈda-bi-ir* dingir-*eb-la* in Ebla tablet TM.75.G.1464 suggests that Dabir was the patron deity of the city (*The Archives of Ebla*, 247).

29. Cf. Caquot, "Sur quelques démons," 66–68; Fulco, *Canaanite God Rešep*, 57; Tromp, *Primitive Conceptions of Death and the Netherworld*, 161–66.

and 2 Chronicles 11:15, the לִילִית of Isaiah 34:14, and the Azazel figure of Leviticus 16:8, 10, 26, but the force of the evidence varies for each of these.[30] Actually, if the Old Testament writers recognized demons at all, they remain faint and indefinite figures, and the influence of malevolent spirits has been almost if not totally expunged.[31] YHWH has assumed all power over life and death, health and illness, fortune and misfortune.[32]

In this regard Ezekiel follows traditional Jewish thinking, according to which the threat to human life is not to be found in some sort of Mot figure, nor in demons, but in God alone.[33] But this does not mean that YHWH is always perceived as being directly responsible when death occurs. On the contrary, the prophet recognized at least four ways in which people died.

First, Ezekiel actually witnesses the death of two persons, apparently from natural causes—Pelatiah, in visionary form (11:13), and his own wife, in person (24:16-24).

Second, people die as victims of other persons' violence, often without a hint of divine involvement. The human participants operate on their own accord and for their own reasons.[34]

Third, YHWH employs a variety of agents to carry out his deadly mission. The prophet's perspective is summarized in several scattered texts, most notably 5:17: "I will send famine and wild animals against you, and they will rob you of your children; pestilence and bloodshed shall pass through you; and I will bring the sword upon you" (*NRSV*).[35] A sixth agent is referred to in 39:6, "I will send fire on Magog and on those who live securely in the coastlands." What distinguishes these calamities as divinely

---

30. The literature on the subject is vast. For general overviews see Gaster, "Demon, Demonology," 818-22; Ringgren, *Israelite Religion*, 101-3; Eichrodt, *Theology of the Old Testament*, 2.223-28; Aune, "Demon, Demonology," 919-22.

31. Eichrodt proposed that some of the Israelite cultic and ritual laws originated in apotropaic rites against demons (*Theology of the Old Testament*, 2.226).

32. The notion of an "evil spirit" (רוּחַ רָעָה) sent by YHWH is perhaps the nearest counterpart to the demons (Judg 9:23; 1 Sam 16:14).

33. See several Old Testament texts which seem to personify death: Isa 25:8; 28:15, 18; Jer 9:20[21]; Hos 13:14; Hab 2:5; Ps 18:5-6[4-5] (= 2 Sam 22:5-6); Job 18:14.

34. This finds graphic expression in the idiom, "to shed blood," always with humans as subjects (16:38; 18:10; 22:3, 4, 6, 9, 12; 23:45; 33:25; 36:18). Elsewhere the Israelites slaughter their (YHWH's) children (16:21; 23:39); her princes destroy lives (22:27); the Philistines take vengeance on Israel by destroying them (25:15); Nebuchadnezzar opens his mouth for slaughter (21:27[22]), and his forces carry out a siege to cut off many lives (17:17); the Assyrians slay Oholah with the sword (23:10).

35. Cf. similar catalogues in 6:11, 7:15, 12:16, 14:21, and 28:23.

authorized agents is the use of the verb שָׁלַח, "to send," or more precisely the *piel* form, שִׁלַּח, "to let loose," with YHWH as the subject.³⁶ This feature strengthens the view that the inspiration for Ezekiel's understanding of YHWH's agents of destruction lies in Israel's covenant curse traditions, preserved in Leviticus 26 and Deuteronomy 28.³⁷

Fourth, YHWH is directly involved in issues of life and death. While he takes his stand firmly on the side of life (18:23, 32; 33:11), he is the divine judge who sentences the wicked and the sinner to death,³⁸ he executes the sentence,³⁹ he wields the sword in his own hand,⁴⁰ he cuts people off,⁴¹ he destroys,⁴² he causes to perish,⁴³ in his fury he consumes,⁴⁴ he causes people to fall,⁴⁵ he sends them down to Sheol/the Pit.⁴⁶ A vivid illustration

---

36. 5:16 (hunger); 14:13 (famine); 14:19 (pestilence); 14:21 (sword, famine, wild animals, plague); 28:23 (pestilence, blood, sword); 39:6 (fire); but also אַף, "rage," in 7:3. But Ezekiel employs the customary *qal* stem when he describes his personal commissioning (2:3, 4; 3:6; cf. 2 Kgs 2:2, 4, 6; Isa 6:8; Jer 1:7. Cf. also Hag 1:12; Zech 1:12-13, 15[8-9, 11]; 4:9; 6:15), as well as in his denunciation of false prophets for never having been formally sent by YHWH (13:6). This usage applies also to the dispatching of an acknowledged prophet on a specific mission. E.g., 1 Sam 15:1; 16:1; 2 Sam 12:1; etc. For discussion of this use of שָׁלַח, see Richter, *Die sogenannten vorprophetischen Berufungsberichte*, 156-58. For a fuller study of the root see Delcor and Jenni, "שָׁלַח *šlḥ* senden," 909-16.

37. Lev 26:25; Deut 28:20; 32:24. On comparable lists of curses in ancient Near Eastern documents see Fensham, "Common Trends," 155-75; Hillers, *Treaty-Curses*.

38. Cf. "I will judge/pass sentence according to their ways" in 18:30 and 33:20, as well as the generally quasi-legal formulae "You/he shall surely die" (מוֹת יָמוּת/תָּמוּת) and "for his guilt/iniquity he shall die" (בַּעֲוֺנוֹ יָמוּת) in 3:16-21; 18:1-32; 33:1-20. On the form and usage of these expressions in Ezekiel see Reventlow, *Wächter über Israel*, 108-34; Schulz, *Das Todesrecht*, 162-92; Zimmerli, *Ezekiel* 2, 374-77, 383-84.

39. שָׁפַט means "to execute judgment" in 11:10, 11; 21:25[30]; 35:11 (perhaps 7:27). Cf. עָשָׂה שְׁפָטִים, "to execute judgments," in 5:10, 15; 11:9; 16:41; 25:11; 28:22, 26; 30:14, 19. Only in 25:11 does the "execution" not necessarily involve death.

40. Cf. 21:8-10[3-5], where YHWH "unsheathes" his sword (וְהוֹצֵאתִי חַרְבִּי מִתַּעְרָהּ), and 32:10, where he "brandishes" his sword (בְּעוֹפְפִי חַרְבִּי). The form חַרְבִּי, "my sword," occurs elsewhere in 30:24, 25.

41. YHWH is the subject of הִכְרִית in 14:8, 13, 17; 21:8[3], 9[4]; 25:7, 13, 16; 29:8; 30:15; 35:7.

42. YHWH is the subject of הִשְׁמִיד in 14:9; 25:7; 34:16.

43. YHWH is the subject of הָאֱבִיד in 6:3; 25:7, 16; 28:16; 30:13 (of idols); 32:13 (of cattle).

44. YHWH is the subject of כִּלָּה in 20:13; 22:31; 43:8. Cf. also 11:13; 20:17.

45. YHWH is the subject of הִפִּיל in 6:4; 32:12.

46. YHWH is the subject of הוֹרִיד in 26:20; 31:16.

of YHWH's direct involvement is found in 17:19–21, where he poses as a hunter out to capture prey.

Ezekiel's Vision of the Netherworld

But what happens to people when they die? The increasing interest in Israelite views of death and the netherworld is reflected in a growing bibliography of studies on the subject.[47] Earlier discussions tended to concentrate on references to Sheol in the Psalms and in the outbursts of Job, with occasional appeal to Isaiah (Isa 14; 26:7–19). But scholars have paid little attention to Ezekiel, despite the fact that his collection of prophecies probably devotes as much space to the subject as any other biblical book.

Three texts provide most of the information on Ezekiel's views concerning the state of the dead: 26:19–21 represents the conclusion to the first of three redactional units that make up Ezekiel's oracles against Tyre; 31:14b–18 serves as the conclusion to the fifth of seven oracles against Egypt; and 32:17–32, the longest of this triad, brings the entire complex of oracles against Egypt to a conclusion.

These texts are closely related in both style and substance. In fact, the plethora of lexical links between 32:17–32 and 31:14–18[48] suggests that this text presents another example of the typically Ezekielian pattern of *Wiederaufname*, "resumption."[49] Especially intriguing is the notice in 31:16 that YHWH would cause the nations to shake (הִרְעַשְׁתִּי גוֹיִם) over the fall of the tree and that they would take comfort (וַיִּנָּחֲמוּ) at its descent into Sheol. In 32:17–32 Ezekiel provides a representative sampling of those nations, and describes in greater detail their relationship to the

---

47. Cf. McDannell and Lang, *Heaven*; Spronk, *Beatific Afterlife*; Tromp, *Primitive Conceptions of Death and the Netherworld*; Wächter, *Der Tod*; C. Barth, *Errettung vom Tode*.

48. Expressions that are repeated include נָתַן, "to hand over" (to death, 31:14; to the sword, 32:20); אֶרֶץ תַּחְתִּית, "netherworld" (31:14, 16, 18; 32:18, 24); יוֹרְדֵי בוֹר, "those who go down to the pit" (31:14, 16; 32:18, 24, 25, 29, 30); יָרַד שְׁאוֹלָה, "to go down to Sheol" (31:15, 16, 17; 32:27); חַלְלֵי־חֶרֶב, "victims of the sword" (31:17, 18; 32:20, 21, 25, 28, 29, 30, 31, 32); עֲרֵלִים, "uncircumcised" (31:18; 32:19, 21, etc.); שָׁכַב בְּתוֹךְ, "to lie with/among" (31:18; 32:19, 27, 28, 29, 30, 32); הָמוֹן, "pomp, horde" (31:18; 32:18, 20, 24, 25, 26, 31, 32).

49. According to which a subject is raised in an early text, only to be dropped immediately without further development, but then picked up and given fuller exposition in a later text. We use the term *Wiederaufname* somewhat differently from Kuhl, for whom *Wiederaufname* serves to distinguish interpolations from the original *traditum* ("Die 'Wiederaufname,'" 1–11). Cf. also Fishbane, *Biblical Interpretation*, 84–86.

Beyond the Grave

Egyptian newcomer. The shoe of comfort, however, has been placed on the other foot. Instead of the nations finding consolation in the arrival of Egypt, Egypt may take comfort in the fact that she is not alone in the netherworld. Other nations, great and small, have experienced the same fate (32:31). In view of the expository nature of 32:17-32, we may focus our attention here.

Structurally 32:17-32 is complex.[50] Following the opening date notice, YHWH commands Ezekiel to wail for the hordes of Egypt and to bring them down to the netherworld (vv. 17-18). This charge serves as a thesis-type statement, introducing the reader to the theme of the oracle. Verses 19-21 constitute a general announcement of judgment upon the nation, highlighting the depths to which she shall fall. The bulk of the oracle (vv. 22-30) is taken up with a roll call of nations that greet Egypt upon her arrival in Sheol. The passage concludes with a statement of the significance of the previous scenes for Pharaoh (v. 31), and a theological interpretation of the descent of the king of Egypt (v. 32).

The problematic state of the text complicates the interpretation of the prophecy. Not since the prophet's opening vision have truncated sentences and inconsistencies of gender, number, and tense so plagued a passage.[51] Compounding the issue is a stylistic monotony, which some would say ill befits the prophet so renowned for his literary power. The pool of words and expressions is limited, but its heavy dependence upon stock phrases associated with death and burial contributes to its morbid tone. But the issue for us is, what does this text tell us about Ezekiel's view of life after death?

The Topography of the Netherworld

We do well to begin our discussion of Ezekiel's understanding of the netherworld with a look at its relationship to the rest of the universe. Like his fellow Israelites, Ezekiel assumed a universe divided into three tiers (Fig. 13):[52]

---

50. Perhaps a consequence of the grief poem (נְהִי) genre, on which see Hals, *Ezekiel*, 228-29.

51. Cf. the number of divergences from MT in LXX.

52. Cf. Lang's discussion of the relationships among the tiers ("Life after Death," 145-48).

Figure 13: Ezekiel's Three Tiers of Existence

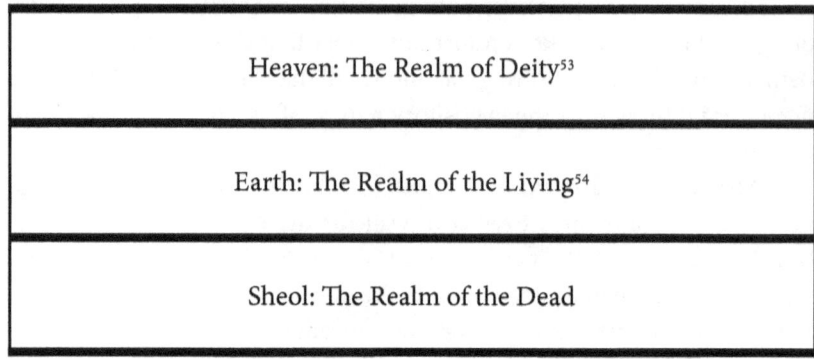

Heaven: The Realm of Deity[53]
Earth: The Realm of the Living[54]
Sheol: The Realm of the Dead

Ezekiel 32 uses several different expressions for the netherworld. Of special interest is its use of אֶרֶץ. In Ezekiel this term usually denotes "earth" in contrast to "the heavens" (see 8:3). However, it is clear from phrases like אֶרֶץ תַּחְתִּיּוֹת, "land of the depths" (vv. 18, 24; cf. 26:20), a distinctly Ezekielian variation of אֶרֶץ תַּחְתִּית, "the lower world" (cf. 31:14, 16, 18),[55] that in this context it refers to the netherworld. As such it represents a counterpart to אֶרֶץ הַחַיִּים, "land of the living" (vv. 23, 24, 25, 26, 27, 32; cf. 26:20).[56] The subterranean location of the realm of the dead is reflected in the frequent occurrence of the verb יָרַד, "to go down,"[57] as well as the specific terms used to identify the place: בּוֹר, "pit, cistern" (vv. 18, 23, 24,

---

53. The word שָׁמַיִם occurs eight times in the book, but only in 1:1 does it denote the realm of deity.

54. Identified in Ezekiel as אֶרֶץ הַחַיִּים, "the land of the living" (26:20; 32:23, 24, 25, 26, 27, 32). This is the sphere in which humans live and in which they inflict terror upon one another (cf. 32:23, 24, 25, 26, 27, 30, 32).

55. Cf. תַּחְתִּיּוֹת אֶרֶץ, "depths of the earth" (Isa 44:23; Pss 63:10[9]; 139:15); בּוֹר תַּחְתִּיּוֹת (Ps 88:7[6]; Lam 3:55); שְׁאוֹל תַּחְתִּית (Deut 32:22).

56. Cf. the absolute use of אֶרֶץ for "netherworld" elsewhere in the Old Testament (Isa 26:19; Jonah 2:7[6]; Ps 22:30[29]), as well as Ugaritic 'rṣ, and the Akkadian cognate erṣetu. On these terms as designations for the netherworld see Stadelmann, *The Hebrew Conception of the World*, 167.

57. Hence the identification of the deceased as יוֹרְדֵי בוֹר, "those who go down to the pit" (26:20 [2x]; 31:14, 16; 32:18, 24, 25, 29, 30), and references to "going/bringing down to Sheol" (הוֹרִיד/יָרַד שְׁאוֹלָה) in 31:15, 16, 17; 32:27; as well as the use of הוֹרִיד/יָרַד alone in 26:20; 31:18; 32:18,19, 21, 24, 30.

25, 29, 30),[58] and its semantic cognate שַׁחַת, "pit, trap" (28:8),[59] as well as the distinctly Hebrew expression, שְׁאוֹל (vv. 21, 27; cf. 31:15, 16).[60] Since all of these terms are used elsewhere for "grave," it is not surprising that they should have assumed this netherworldly significance.

Ezekiel offers few details of the design of the netherworld. Nowhere does he describe how one enters, whether by "the gates of Sheol" (Isa 38:10) or "the gates of death" (Job 38:17; Pss 9:14[13]; 107:18). However, his description creates the impression of a massive communal cemetery, in which the graves are arranged by nationality and organized in such a way that the principal grave is located in the center, surrounded by the graves of the attendants.[61] The residents themselves are all reclining on their own beds (מִשְׁכָּב).[62]

The expression יַרְכְּתֵי־בוֹר, "the remotest parts of the Pit" (v. 23), suggests a gradation of assignments in Sheol, with the most dishonorable occupants being sent to the farthest recesses. The fact that the uncircumcised and the victims of the sword are separated from the "mighty men of old," who receive an honorable burial with their weapons of war at their sides, reinforces this impression. It is unclear whether these compartments are arranged horizontally or vertically. The plural form אֶרֶץ תַּחְתִּיּוֹת, "land of depths," may point in the latter direction.

---

58. Cf. also 26:20a, 20b; 31:14, 16. On the range of meanings for בוֹר, a by-form of בְּאֵר, see Heintz, "בְּאֵר beʾēr," 463–66.

59. The word's primary sense is reflected in 19:4, 8, where שַׁחַת denotes a pit dug for trapping game. On this term see further Tromp, *Primitive Conceptions of Death and the Netherworld*, 69–71; Pope, "The Word שַׁחַת in Job 9:31," 269–78; Pope, "A Little Soul-Searching," 25–31. Cf. also Held, "Pits and Pitfalls," 173–90, who distinguishes between שַׁחַת I, "pit, netherworld," and שַׁחַת II, "net."

60. While the etymology of the word remains unknown, the fact that it always occurs without the article suggests that it was considered a proper name. For discussions cf. Spronk, *Beatific Afterlife*, 66–71; Tromp, *Primitive Conceptions of Death and the Netherworld*, 21–23; Gerleman, "שְׁאוֹל šeʾōl Totenreich," 837–41; Stadelmann, *The Hebrew Conception of the World*, 165–67.

61. The word קְבָרֹת, "graves," appears six times in 32:22–26.

62. The verb שָׁכַב, "to lie," occurs seven times in verses 22–32. Another image of the netherworld is suggested by 26:20, which, though textually problematic, speaks of Tyre as dwelling in the lower parts of the earth like חֳרָבוֹת מֵעוֹלָם, "waste places from eternity." Here Sheol seems to have taken on the character of a massive wasteland filled with the refuse of collapsed civilizations, an image which is reminiscent of a Mesopotamian view reflected in one of Nergal's titles, "King of the Wasteland" (*šar šēri*). Cf. *AHW*, 1095; Tallqvist, *Sumerisch-akkadische Namen*, 17, 22–23. On the netherworld as a wasteland see further Pedersen, *Israel*, 464; C. Barth, *Errettung vom Tode*, 86–87.

Ezekiel's picture of the netherworld is reminiscent of two well-known ancient mortuary customs. First, the arrangement of the grave complexes resembles that of a royal tomb, with the king's (in this instance the queen's) crypt (sarcophagus?) in the middle, and his (her) nobles all around. In fact, this oracle displays some deliberate local coloring. The pyramid complexes, in which the Pharaoh's tomb (the pyramid itself) was surrounded by the tombs of his princes, courtiers, and other high officials, provides the closest analogue to Ezekiel's portrayal of Sheol.[63] Second, the image of the beds recalls the pattern of ancient Near Eastern tombs in which the place where the corpse was laid was designed as a bed, often complete with headrest.[64]

The Inhabitants of the Netherworld

But who are these יוֹרְדֵי בוֹר, "who go down to the pit"? Earlier, in 31:16, 18 the prophet had identified the occupants of Sheol as כָּל־עֲצֵי־עֵדֶן, "all the trees of Eden." The dendroid imagery is appropriate for an oracle in which Assyria is presented as a tall tree that is cut down and sent to the netherworld. Assyria will be one of many nations as wholes that have been assigned their places in Sheol, a notion chapter 32 picks up and develops more fully.

In 32:17–32 Ezekiel refers repeatedly to חֲלָלִים and עֲרֵלִים. The former expression is filled out with חַלְלֵי־חֶרֶב, a typically Ezekielian phrase, which translates literally as "those slain by the sword."[65] However, as Eissfeldt has shown, the persons so designated are not simply passive victims of violence nor soldiers who have died valiant deaths on the battlefield. In the book of Ezekiel the expression generally refers to executed murderers and evildoers,[66] whose bodies may have been tossed in a heap in a separate burial place, or even left out in the open,[67] instead of being given an honorable burial. Ezekiel 28:10 implies that no death is more ignominious than

---

63. On Egyptian burial patterns see Montet, *Eternal Egypt*, 199–234, esp. 212–23; Aldred, "Grablage, Auszeichnung durch," 859–62.

64. On Judahite bench tombs see Bloch-Smith, *Judahite Burial Practices*, 41–52. Cf. the superbly illustrated presentation of a complex Israelite family tomb by Barkay and Kloner, "Jerusalem Tombs," 22–39.

65. חֲלָלִים and derivatives occur fourteen times in 32:17–32.

66. Eissfeldt, "Schwerterschlagene bei Hesekiel," 73–81; cf. Dommershausen, "חָלָל *chālal* II," 417–21. Note the pejorative connotations in 28:8.

67. On the ignominy of being denied a proper burial or exhumation see Deut 28:25–26; 1 Kgs 13:22; 14:10–11; Jer 16:4.

the death of the חַלְלֵי־חֶרֶב, an interpretation which the frequent pairing of עֲרֵלִים and חֲלָלִים confirms.

In 31:18 Ezekiel had mentioned עֲרֵלִים, "the uncircumcised," only in passing, but the expression appears no fewer than ten times in 32:17–32. It is somewhat surprising to see the Egyptians among the uncircumcised in Sheol, especially since they (as well as Edomites and Sidonians from this list) practiced the rite of circumcision.[68] Obviously Ezekiel's usage of the term is metaphorical and culturally determined. In Israel, circumcision was the sign and seal of membership in the covenant community (Gen 17), which in time became a symbol of cultural superiority. To call anyone "uncircumcised" was the ultimate insult. Those who did not bear this mark at the time of their deaths were excluded from the family grave. For Ezekiel this meant being sentenced to the most undesirable compartment of the netherworld along with other vile and unclean persons.[69]

A third designation for the residents of Sheol is חִתִּית בְּאֶרֶץ חַיִּים, "those who spread terror in the land of the living" (32:23). The distinctly Ezekielian expression חִתִּית, occurs seven times in verses 17–32.[70] It derives from a root meaning "to be filled with terror," and refers to the fear, confusion, and anguish created by a powerful foe.[71] In this text those nations who have created such *Angst* in others discover that their violent conduct while in the land of the living has determined their status in the realm of the dead.

Verse 21 identifies another group in Sheol, אֵלֵי גִבּוֹרִים, literally "the rams of mighty men."[72] In verse 27 they are referred to as "the fallen heroes from ancient times."[73] This phrase is reminiscent of Genesis 6:4, which labels the antediluvian progeny of the "sons of God" (בְּנֵי הָאֱלֹהִים) and hu-

---

68. On circumcision in the ancient Near East see Sasson, "Circumcision," 473–76; Lewis and Armerding, "Circumcision," 700–2. For primary evidence see the illustration in *ANEP* §629; the inscription dealing with the rite, *ANET*, 326; Herodotus, *Histories* 2.104; Josephus, *Ant.* 8.10.3.

69. Cf. Lods, "La 'mort des incirconcis," 271–83.

70. Cf. 26:21. This expression is not to be confused with its homonym "Hittite" in 16:3, 45.

71. On the expression see Maas, "חָתַת *ḥātat*," 277–83.

72. אַיִל occurs also in 17:13; 30:13; 31:11, 14; 39:18. For a discussion of this expression see Miller, "Animal Names as Designations in Ugaritic and Hebrew," 181–82.

73. Assuming the originality of LXX ἀπὸ αἰῶνος, which reflects an original מֵעוֹלָם, a form which has occurred earlier in 26:20. MT's נֹפְלִים מֵעֲרֵלִים, "the fallen from the uncircumcised," is not only unattested elsewhere; it makes no sense. Allen suggests MT arose as a result of a r/w confusion and assimilation with the recurring עֲרֵלִים (*Ezekiel 20–48*, 135).

man daughters (בְּנוֹת הָאָדָם) Nephilim,[74] and identifies them more closely as הַגִּבֹּרִים אֲשֶׁר מֵעוֹלָם אַנְשֵׁי הַשֵּׁם, "the heroes who were from ancient times, the men of renown."

According to Ezekiel 32:21, these heroic personages speak from the midst of Sheol, which may suggest that they are located in the heart of the netherworld, perhaps a more honorable assignment than "the remotest recesses of the pit," where the uncircumcised and those who have fallen by the sword lie. The description in verse 27 indicates that these individuals have indeed been afforded noble burials. There they lie with their weapons of war, their swords laid under their heads and their shields[75] placed upon their bones. Ancient burial customs in which personal items and symbols of status were buried with the corpses of the deceased provide the source of this image.[76]

Ezekiel's use of the antediluvian heroic traditions at this point is shocking. How could the prophet possibly perceive these men as noble and hold them up as honorable residents of Sheol, when his own religious tradition presents them as the epitome of wickedness, corruption, and violence (Gen 6:5, 11–12)?[77] To be sure, as he himself recognizes, they too had terrorized the land of the living. But why should they be granted special status in Sheol? Three explanations may be considered. First, Ezekiel's picture might be inspired by some independent Israelite tradition that actually perceived the antediluvians as noble figures, *à la* Gilgamesh of Mesopotamia, the hero of the Great Deluge, of whom it was said that two-thirds of him was god and one-third was human.[78] But this view flounders for lack of evidence. Second, the present image might derive from extra-Israelite traditions in which departed kings were viewed as divinized heroes. However, according to the picture of the netherworld painted in verses 22–26, the kings are surrounded by their courtiers in "the farthest recesses of the pit." Furthermore, this interpretation overlooks the allusions to Genesis 6:4 in verses 21 and 27. Third, this description might

74. *BHS*, Eichrodt (*Ezekiel*, 436), and many others repoint נֹפְלִים as נְפִלִים.

75. Even though MT עֲוֹנֹתָם, "their iniquity," is reflected in all the versions, the context requires emendation to צִנֹּתָם, "their shields" (thus *BHS* and most translations: *RSV, NRSV, NJB, NEB*, following Cornill, *Das Buch des Propheten Ezechiel*, 390). For an explanation of the error see Allen, *Ezekiel 20–48*, 135.

76. On the practice in Judah and its significance see Bloch-Smith, *Judahite Burial Practices*, 75-93.

77. For a discussion of the relationship between these texts see Hanson, "Rebellion in Heaven," 208–9.

78. *ANET*, 73.

Beyond the Grave

represent another example of Ezekielian revisionism, according to which authentic Israelite traditions are reinterpreted for rhetorical effect.[79] The present aim is to highlight the ignominy of Meshech-Tubal. No matter how negatively the tradition might have considered the antediluvians, they were noble compared to the Meshech-Tubalites, and by extension the Egyptians, who will join them in the nether recesses of the underworld.

Some have seen references to the occupants of the netherworld in two additional expressions that occur outside this passage. In 26:20 the prophet announces that Tyre shall join the עַם עוֹלָם. The literary context suggests some relationship between this phrase and מְתֵי עוֹלָם, which in Psalms 143:3 and Lamentations 3:6 denotes the departed dead from long ago who dwell in dark places.[80] On the other hand, if we understand עוֹלָם substantively, viz., as a designation for "eternity," or more specifically the netherworld,[81] then the עַם עוֹלָם may be the inhabitants of the בֵּית עוֹלָם, "eternal house," referred to in Ecclesiastes 12:5,[82] that is, "the people of the netherworld."

In 39:11, 14 the phrase, גֵּי הָעֹבְרִים identifies the place of Gog's burial. Scholars have interpreted this expression in several ways, most notably

---

79. Cf. 16:44–59, where Jerusalem is shamed not only for being more wicked than her sister but for abominations that exceeded those of Sodom, and 20:25, according to which YHWH had given Israel statutes that were not good and ordinances by which they could not live.

80. Cf. Dahood, *Psalms III*, 323, who repoints מְתֵי as מֻתֵי, and translates "men of the eternal home."

81. Cf. A. Cooper ("*MLK 'lm*: 'Eternal King' or 'King of Eternity,'" 1–8) and Pope (in a review of Spronk, *Beatific Afterlife*, 458), who interpret the Ugaritic expression *mlk 'lm*, "king of eternity," as "king of the underworld." According to Cooper and Jenni ("עוֹלָם *'ōlām* Ewigkeit," 242), this spatial understanding of "eternity" derives from Egypt, where Osiris bore the title, "Lord of Eternity" (*ḥk3 d.t* or *nb nḥḥ*), which alluded to his domain (the realm of the dead), as well as the duration of his reign.

82. The expression בית עלם, signifying "grave," has also surfaced in the Deir 'Allā texts (11:6, on which see Hackett, *The Balaam Text*, 59), and other Northwest Semitic inscriptions (on which see cf. Jenni, "Das Wort עוֹלָם," 217; Hoftijzer and Kooij, *Aramaic Texts*, 224–25), and is well known in the Rabbinic writings (cf. Jastrow, *Dictionary of the Targumim*, 1084–85). Jenni compares the expression to the Egyptian reference to a tomb as *niwt nt nḥḥ*, "the city of eternity" ("עוֹלָם *'ōlām* Ewigkeit," 242). בֵּית עוֹלָם finds a semantic equivalent also in Akkadian *šubat dārati/dārat*, "the dwelling place of eternity," and *ēkal salāli kimaḫ tapšuḫti šubat dārati*, "a palace of sleeping, a resting tomb, a dwelling place of eternity." On these see Tawil, "A Note on the Ahiram Inscription," 36.

as "Valley of the Travelers,"⁸³ a variant spelling of Abarim,⁸⁴ or as a new name, "the Valley of Hamon-Gog," which plays on גֵּי־הִנֹּם, "the valley of Hinnom."⁸⁵ However, drawing on the support of the Ugaritic text *KTU* 1:22, 1:12–17, some have recently argued that הָעֹבְרִים represent the inhabitants of the netherworld.⁸⁶ This mortuary cultic document associates the עברם with *mlkm*, departed kings who are identified elsewhere as *rpim*.⁸⁷ According to this interpretation, הָעֹבְרִים refers to these departed heroes,⁸⁸ and the "valley of those who have passed on" is a cemetery where people disposed of their dead.

In surveying Ezekiel's references to the inhabitants of the netherworld one observes two glaring omissions. First, nowhere does he identify these individuals as רְפָאִים, a term used elsewhere for the chthonic shades.⁸⁹ Is the word loaded with too many pagan associations? Is it too closely tied to the cult of the dead? Perhaps we should see here another illustration of the prophet's historicizing and de-mythologizing style. For him the occupants of Sheol are real people: Assyrians, Elamites, Sidonians, Egyptians, antediluvians. They are not divinized kings.

Second, Ezekiel provides no information on the state of the righteous in death. The persons he describes in 32:17–32 are all wicked individuals or nations. Not a word is said about the righteous. Would they also have been in Sheol? If so, where would their beds have been located? On the other hand, we note that all of his depictions of the netherworld occur in oracles against foreign nations (cf. Isa 14:9–20). But where is Israel in all of this? We know from chapter 37 that the prophet's own nation was considered deceased, but in these accounts they are completely out of the

---

83. Thus *NRSV* and *NJPS*, treating הָעֹבְרִים as a participle from עָבַר, "to pass over." For possible locations of this valley see Zimmerli, *Ezekiel 2*, 317.

84. Cf. KB, 1000; Allen, *Ezekiel 20–48*, 201. The Old Testament knows of two Abarims, one east of Galilee (Jer 22:20), and another in the Moabite highlands (Num 27:12). However, this interpretation is weakened by the fact that the place of Gog's burial is explicitly located "in Israel."

85. This valley was the site of Molech worship (Jer 2:23; etc.) and the place where the bodies of animals and criminals were burned. Cf. Zimmerli, *Ezekiel 2*, 317.

86. So Ribichini and Xella, "La valle dei passanti," 434–47; Spronk, *Beatific Afterlife*, 229–30; Pope, "Rephaim Texts," 173–75; Pope, review of Spronk, *Beatific Afterlife*, 462.

87. On which see Levine and Tarragon, "Dead Kings and Rephaim," 649–59; Healey, "*MLKM/ RP'UM* and the *Kispum*," 89–91.

88. Pope describes the עֹבְרִים as "those who cross over the boundary separating them from the living so that from the viewpoint of the living they 'go over' rather than 'come over,'" in review of Spronk, *Beatific* Afterlife, 462.

89. Isa 14:9; 26:14, 19; Job 26:5; Ps 88:10[11]; Prov 2:18.

Beyond the Grave

picture. Whether he would have located them among these foreign nations or reserved a compartment separate from them we may only speculate.

The State of the Dead

Ancient Mesopotamians perceived the netherworld as an inhospitable place, dark and dingy, especially for those who had been killed in battle and/or who had not been afforded a proper burial.[90] How familiar Ezekiel was with these notions we cannot say. His own comments on the state of the dead are not entirely consistent. On the one hand, the oracles against Tyre present death as the termination of existence. Three times in roughly equivalent terms the prophet announces, "I shall bring terrors upon you and you will be no more."[91] In fact, according to 26:21, any efforts by search parties to find the lost city would prove futile. However, the broader context of this verse shows that we should not interpret these statements literally. The language is phenomenological; no one ever returns from the realm of the dead.

On the other hand, our primary text, 32:17–32, clearly recognizes a continued existence for the deceased. Several observations on their condition in the afterlife may be made. First, that which survives of the deceased is not simply the spiritual component of the human being, but a shadowy image of the whole person, complete with head and skeleton.[92] Second, as we have already noted, the deceased lie שָׁכַב[93] on beds (מִשְׁכָּב) in their respective wards, arranged according to nationality. Third, the inhabitants of Sheol are not asleep, but fully conscious.[94] They are not only aware of one another and their relative positions; they also know that their conduct

---

90. Cf. the poetic account of the descent of Ishtar into the netherworld *(ANET,* 107); "The Vision of the Netherworld" (ibid, 109–10); and Enkidu's description of the fate of the dead ("Epic of Gilgamesh," ibid, 99).

91. Cf. 26:21: בַּלָּהוֹת אֶתְּנֵךְ וְאֵינֵךְ, "To a dreadful end I will bring you, and you shall be no more."

27:36: בַּלָּהוֹת הָיִיתָ וְאֵינְךָ עַד־עוֹלָם, "To a dreadful end you have come and you shall be no more forever."

28:19: בַּלָּהוֹת הָיִיתָ וְאֵינְךָ עַד־עוֹלָם, "To a dreadful end you have come and you shall be no more forever."

92. Eichrodt, *Theology of the Old Testament,* 2.214. NEB renders אֱלֹהִים as "ghostly form" in 1 Sam 28:13.

93. 32:21, 27, 28, 29, 30, 32.

94. Cf. Job's desire as expressed in 3:13, 18, 7:9, and the phenomenological language of Dan 12:2; Matt 9:24; John 11:11; 1 Cor 11:30; 15:51; 1 Thess 4:14; 5:10.

during their tenure "in the land of the living" has determined their respective positions in Sheol. Those who were high and mighty on earth express grief over their loss of status and power (32:31). They consciously bear the disgrace (נָשְׂאוּ כְלִמָּתָם) of those who have been dishonorably buried (32:24, 25, 30). This description agrees with Israelite burial practices,[95] which suggest that the tomb was not considered the permanent resting place of the deceased. While the physical flesh decomposed, the person was thought to descend to the vast subterranean mausoleum in which the dead continued to live in a remarkably real sense as "living corpses."[96]

The Cult of the Dead

One further question remains. What is Ezekiel's understanding of the relationship between the dead and the living? In the ancient world outside Israel, it was commonly assumed that the deceased continued to exercise both beneficent and malevolent power over the living. The favorable influence of departed ancestors could be won through necromancy, which required the engagement of mediums, and through mortuary cults involving propitiatory sacrifices by a specially designated member of the family,[97] and through urgent pleas for their blessing. In the light of explicit prohibitions on such activity in the Old Testament (Deut 14:1; 26:14), scholars have tended to deny the existence of any such practices in Israel.[98] However, scholars are uncovering more and more evidence that mortuary cult

---

95. Bloch-Smith, *Judahite Burial Practices*, 25–59, 140–41.
96. Cooley, "Gathered to His People," 47–58.
97. On the role of the *pāqidu* see Bayliss, "The Cult of Dead Kin," 115–25.
98. Cf. G. E. Wright, "Deuteronomy," 487; de Vaux, *Ancient Israel*, 60; Kaufmann, *Religion of Israel*, 312.

activities persisted throughout the nation's history, not only in the biblical writings,⁹⁹ but in the archaeological records as well.¹⁰⁰

Given Ezekiel's denunciation of so many pagan features in Judah's religious life, his silence on mortuary cult practices in his judgment oracles (chapters 1–24) is striking. Only once in the entire book, in 43:7–9, is there any allusion to the veneration of the dead.¹⁰¹ Here Ezekiel refers to a series of past abominable practices, including "the corpses of their kings at their death,"¹⁰² and calls upon the Israelites to put away their idolatry and the "corpses of their kings." There is some dispute among scholars about the meaning of פִּגְרֵי מַלְכֵיהֶם,¹⁰³ but it seems best to associate Ezekiel's פְּגָרִים with the pagan practices referred to in Leviticus 26:30. Here פִּגְרֵי

---

99. (1) Psalm 106:28 condemns זִבְחֵי מֵתִים, "sacrificial meals for the dead." Cf. vv. 37–38. The dependence of the phrase on זִבְחֵי אֱלֹהֵיהֶן, "sacrifices of their gods" in Num 25:2 is widely recognized. Cf. Heider, *The Cult of Molek*, 388–89; M. Smith and Bloch-Smith, "Death and Afterlife," 282. (2) Isaiah 65:3–5a describes people as spending the night in rock-cut tombs; (3) Amos 6:7 and Jer 16:5 refer to the מַרְזֵחַ, a funerary feast, on which see Heider, *The Cult of Molek*, 389. (4) Second Chronicles 16:12 has the diseased Asa seeking (דָּרַשׁ) aid from the Rephaim instead of YHWH. So also Pope, in his review of Spronk, *Beatific Afterlife*, 461. Neither Dillard, *2 Chronicles*, 126–27, nor Williamson, *1 and 2 Chronicles*, 276–77, considers this possibility. (5) Psalm 16:3–4 speaks of pouring out libations of blood to the "saints who are in the earth" (קְדוֹשִׁים אֲשֶׁר־בָּאָרֶץ) and to the "mighty ones" (אַדִּירִים). So Pope, in his review of Spronk, *Beatific Afterlife*, 462–63, approving of Spronk, *Beatific Afterlife*, 249. For additional possible allusions to the mortuary cult see Bloch-Smith, *Judahite Burial Practices*, 109–32. For a recent caution on some of these texts see Pitard, "Post-Funeral Offerings," 76–77.

100. Cf. Bloch-Smith, *Judahite Burial Practices*; Lewis, *Cults of the Dead*, etc.

101. The prohibition on "eating the bread of men" in 24:17, 22 is not to be associated with mortuary cult rituals but customary mourning rites.

102. Thus *NRSV*, repointing MT's בְּמוֹתָם, "on their high places," as בְּמוֹתָם, "in their death," with most moderns. On the textual problems see Zimmerli, *Ezekiel 2*, 402; Allen, *Ezekiel 20–48*, 243.

103. The use of פְּגָרִים in 6:5 to denote corpses of idolaters strewn about their idols accords with the common Old Testament usage and corresponds to the meaning of the Akkadian cognate, *pagrum* (*AHW*, 809), leading many to see here an allusion to royal graves located in the vicinity of the temple precinct. Cf. Taylor, *Ezekiel*, 265; Wevers, *Ezekiel*, 312; Cody, *Ezekiel*, 219; Alexander, "Ezekiel," 969; Spronk, *Beatific Afterlife*, 250. However, this interpretation is weakened by the absence of archaeological evidence for such tombs near enough to the temple grounds to have been considered defiling, and the fact that most of Judah's kings were buried "in the city of David," some distance removed from the temple. Cf. Simons, *Jerusalem*, 194–225; Galling, "Nekropole," 73–101. The apostate kings, Manasseh (2 Kgs 21:18; 2 Chr 33:20) and Amon (2 Kgs 21:26), who were interred "in the garden of Uzza," apparently on the palace grounds, and Josiah, who was buried in his own tomb (2 Kgs 23:30), were exceptions. Cf. Bloch-Smith, *Judahite Burial Practices*, 116–19.

גִּלּוּלֵיכֶם, refers not to the corpses themselves, but to some element of the cult of the dead. Appealing to the Ugaritic usage of the same root, *pgr*, D. Neiman proposed that in both these texts the פְּגָרִים were memorial stelae to the gods erected in honor of the kings.[104] More recently scholars have removed the divine connection and seen here stelae erected in memory of the dead,[105] or special offerings involved in the cult of the dead, in which case they would be related to the *pagru*-offering found in Akkadian texts.[106] In either case, Ezekiel is attacking some sort of Israelite royal ancestor cult,[107] comparable perhaps to the cult of the dead at Ugarit, which was designed to ensure the positive influence of the deceased on the fortunes of the living.

If this interpretation is correct, in keeping with orthodox Yahwism, Ezekiel is calling for the strict maintenance of the boundaries between the land of the living and the realm of the dead.[108] Although the deceased retained consciousness, memory, emotion, awareness of their relationship to others in Sheol, and even a measure of form,[109] mortuary cult activity is forbidden. Undoubtedly he would also have repudiated any necromantic consultation of the dead as well.

---

104. Neiman, "*PGR*: Canaanite Cult-object," 55–60. Cf. the pillar set up by Absalom for himself in the King's Valley in 2 Sam 18:18.

105. Cf. Galling, "Erwägungen," 11; Albright, *Archaeology and Religion*, 201–2 n. 29, "mortuary stelae"; Lust, "Exegesis and Theology," 217. For a fuller discussion see Lewis, *Cults of the Dead*, 72–79.

106. Cf. the identification of Dagan as *b'l pagrê* in the Mari texts, on which see Healey, "Underworld Character," 43–51; Ebach, "*PGR* = (Toten-) Opfer?," 365–68; Heider, *Cult of Molek*, 392–94; KB, 861–62.

107. Most commentators interpret מְלָכִים in its usual sense, "kings," in which case Ezekiel's ban is on some sort of royal ancestor cult. However, some have seen in the expression a reference to the rephaim, which in Canaanite usage could apply to deceased and divinized kings. This sense of מְלָכִים is admittedly rare in the Old Testament (cf. Isaiah 24:21, on which see Heider, *Cult of Molek*, 392), but it accords with the usage of *mlkm* in the Ugaritic texts. Cf. Dietrich and Loretz, who conclude that like the *mlkm*, the *rp'ym* belong to the beneficent spirits of the dead worshiped by the living ("Neue Studien," 69–74). See also Healey, "*MLKM/RPUM* and the *KISPUM*," 89–91; Xella, "Aspekte religiöser Vorstellungen," 288, who finds a singular Eblaite counterpart in *'il 'ib*.

108. This principle also informed Israel's strict taboos on contact with corpses. See Lang, "Life after Death," 149–51.

109. Cf. the notion of a "living corpse" in Egypt, as discussed by Morenz, *Egyptian Religion*, 198–204.

Ezekiel's Vision of Life after Death

So far we have been focusing on the realm of the dead and the state of the deceased within that sphere. But does the absolute severance of ties between the living and the dead mean that Ezekiel viewed death as final? That there was no hope beyond the grave and Sheol? To answer this question we turn to one more text, the well-known vision of the dry bones (37:1–14).

No prophecy in the entire book of Ezekiel has captured the imagination of readers down through the centuries like the account of the revivification of the dry bones in chapter 37.[110] Few have consumed so much scholarly energy. Unfortunately, time and space constraints force us to limit our comments to conclusions that relate directly to our topic.

At the outset we acknowledge that 32:17–32 and 37:1–14 bear little if any relationship to one another. These texts differ in respect to genre (judgment oracle vs. divine vision), style (formal pronouncement vs. narrative), prophetic involvement (passive recipient vs. active participant), focus of attention (Egypt vs. Israel), result (Pharaoh will take comfort vs. Israel will acknowledge YHWH), aim (pronounce judgment vs. inspire hope), the location of the dead (persons in Sheol vs. dry bones on the surface of the ground and/or corpses in physical graves[111]), the sphere in which the afterlife is experienced ("the land below" vs. "the land of Israel"), and language.[112] One hesitates, therefore, to draw two texts, which display such total disparity, into the same discussion. Nevertheless, since they both deal with the issue of life beyond the grave, we shall proceed.

Although the literary integrity of 37:1–14 continues to be questioned by some,[113] we follow an increasing number of scholars in treating the entire passage as a unity.[114] With respect to genre, the text represents a mixed form, being cast (1) as an account of a vision, complete with the vision proper (vv. 1–10) and its interpretation (vv. 11–14); (2) as a dramatic

---

110. Cf. the lower frieze of the third-century CE synagogue of Dura Europos, on which see Kraeling, *Synagogue*, 178–207, and plates LXIX–LXXI.

111. The קְבָרוֹת ("graves") in 32:22–26 are portrayed as resting places in Sheol, in 37:12–13 the term is used in its literal sense, "graves."

112. None of the technical terms relating to Sheol that occur in 32:17–32 is found in 37:1–14.

113. Cf. Höffken, "Beobachtungen," 305–17; Bartelmus, "Ez 37,1–14," 366–89, idem, "Textkritik," 55–64.

114. Cf. Zimmerli, *Ezekiel 2*, 256–58; M. V. Fox, "Rhetoric of Ezekiel's Vision," 1–15; Fishbane, *Biblical Interpretation*, 451–52.

autobiographical narrative, with the prophet's actions playing a more significant role than in any previous vision (cf. 1:1—3:15; 8:1—11:25; 40:1—48:35); (3) and as a salvation oracle. Although the occasion for this prophecy is declared in verse 11—viz., the loss of hope by the prophet's fellow exiles—the seeds of this vision have actually been planted earlier. In fact, in this passage we recognize another example of Ezekielian *Wiederaufname*, with 37:1-14 offering an expansion on 36:26-27, where the subject of YHWH's infusion of his Spirit (רוּחַ) had been first introduced.

The prophet begins by recounting how he is brought in visionary form to a vast valley, white with the bones of humans long deceased. The issue of the vision is presented in direct interrogatory form by YHWH himself: "Can these bones live?" (v. 3). After deferring to YHWH for the answer, through a series of miraculous events the prophets discovers that the question is to be answered with an enthusiastic, "Indeed!" Infused with the breath of YHWH, Israel can—nay, she will live again!

But the question for us is, what does this text say about Ezekiel's perception of death and afterlife? Without entering into a detailed discussion, we offer the following brief observations:

First, for Ezekiel (as for other prophets) death represents the punishment for spiritual infidelity. Because Israel had not kept YHWH's covenant, he had imposed its curses upon them.[115] Second, the Israelites may take hope because there is life after death. God sees their present hopeless condition and cares about their welfare. And he has the power to revive them and to return them to their native soil.[116] Death and the grave need not keep their sting (see Hos 13:14) because the Creator of life and the divine patron of Israel, not Nebuchadnezzar, holds the key to the nation's future. Third, the means whereby the corpses are revitalized is by being infused with YHWH's own life-giving spirit.[117] This is how the first lump

---

115. Verse 9 indicates the bones are the remains of הַהֲרוּגִים, "the slain," that is victims of battle; hence Baumgartner's designation of this text as a *Schlachtfeldsage* (*Zum Alten Testament und seiner Umwelt*, 361). The fact that the corpses had been left exposed for the vultures and hyenas suggests that they were the objects of some horrendous curse. Cf. Fensham, "Curse of the Dry Bones," 59–60. One of the curses in Esarhaddon's vassal-treaty with Ramataya of Urakazabanu provides an extrabiblical analogue: "May Ninurta, leader of the gods, fell you with his fierce arrow, and fill the plain with your corpses, give your flesh to eagles and vultures (Fensham translates "jackal") to feed upon" (*ANET*, 538). Similar curses hung over the Israelites if they should break their covenant oath with YHWH. Cf. Deut 28:25–26; Jer 34:17–20.

116. Cf. Demson, "Divine Power Politics," 97–110.

117. Cf. our discussion of the role of YHWH's רוּחַ in "Prophet of the Spirit," 27–49, especially pp. 34–41 (reprinted above, pp. 150–58) on the רוּחַ as "agency of animation."

of clay became a living being; this is how these dry bones will come to life. Fourth, this miraculous act of God will result in YHWH's people recognizing his person and the power of his word. In fact, this is YHWH's primary objective in the event.

Theological Implications

Having gathered the data that reflect Ezekiel's understanding of the afterlife, several major questions remain. First, what is the doctrinal value of his picture of the netherworld? Does it represent the beliefs of the Israelites, or has the prophet simply created a metaphor for rhetorical effect? Several considerations seem to support the latter view.

First, since Ezekiel's picture is heavily influenced by ancient burial practices (see the inferior location of the realm of the dead, the stratification, the reclining posture, the burial objects), it seems natural that he would describe the netherworld as an extension of the grave, a massive communal mausoleum in which the departed continue to exist as "living corpses."

Second, all of Ezekiel's images of the netherworld are found in judgment oracles against foreign nations.[118] The fact that such pictures are absent in prophecies condemnatory of his own people may suggest they were uniquely relevant for non-Israelites, perhaps because of their distinctive perceptions of the afterlife.

Third, Ezekiel regularly borrows images from outside Israel to craft his own oracles, without thereby giving assent to their reality.[119] Not only do several features of his netherworld recall Canaanite and Egyptian models (the three-tiered universe, the designations for the realm of the dead, the presence of "heroes" and kings in the netherworld), the incorporation of local coloring in 32:17-32 (the arrangement of the tombs of lesser

---

118. The same is true of the closest extra-Ezekielan analogue, Isaiah's taunt of the "King of Babylon" in 14:9-11, 15-20. The links between this text and Ezek 32:17-32 are obvious: (1) The designations for the netherworld (Sheol, the Pit); (2) The physical stratification of Sheol (cf. the references to יוֹרְדֵי בוֹר, "the farthest recesses of the Pit"); (3) The social ordering of its residents, with the more wicked inhabitants (like the "King of Babylon" in Isaiah), who were never afforded an honorable burial, being confined to the farthest recesses of the Pit; (4) The state of the dead (a shadowy existence, as "living corpses," lying on their beds, but fully conscious of their relative positions). On the date of Isaiah 14 see Erlandsson, *Burden of Babylon*, esp. 160-66.

119. Cf. the iconographic features of his inaugural vision (1:4-28); the description of the king of Tyre's hubris and fall (28:1-10); the comparison of the king of Egypt to a sea monster (תַּנִּים), 29:3-5; 32:2-8.

individuals around that of the king) is quite appropriate for the principal subject of the oracle.

Fourth, the intention of this oracle is not doctrinal, but rhetorical—to inspire hope in the hearts of the prophet's fellow exiles by announcing the eventual demise of their foreign enemies. The caricatured and contrary-to-fact features in the prophecy (e.g., Egypt, Sidon, Edom lie among the uncircumcised) suggest that it should be interpreted as a literary cartoon rather than a literary photograph.

Fifth, the doctrinal value of related texts is not always clear. Like our text, the nearest prophetic analogue, Isaiah 14, concerns a foreign nation. Comments on the netherworld in the book of Job and in the Psalter represent human responses to reality from the lips of persons experiencing intense trauma, rather than didactic expressions of belief or divine affirmations of reality. Nor is the issue resolved when Jesus takes up the metaphor in Luke 16:19-31. The Old Testament background helps to explain the distinct fates of Lazarus and the rich man in the afterlife. But with his reference to the impenetrable gulf between "Abraham's Bosom" nd "Hades,"[120] Jesus has not only taken the stratification in Sheol one step farther; if Abraham's Bosom is actually to be located in the netherworld he has also found a place there for the righteous. However, as in the prophetic utterances, Jesus' discussion of the afterlife occurs in story form in a polemic against his opponents.

It is tempting to conclude, therefore, that the Israelites had no doctrine of the netherworld; they just told stories about it.[121] However, the doctrinal implications of oracles like this should not be discounted too quickly. Admittedly Ezekiel's prophecy deals with a foreign nation, but to base the claim that the Israelites shared none of these views on their absence in oracles concerning their own judgment is to argue from silence. Moreover, although the oracles against the foreign nations by definition dealt primarily with Israel's enemies, they were intended first of all for

---

120. The New Testament use of "Hades" is inconsistent. On the one hand, it identifies the location of the ungodly in the netherworld at their decease (as in Luke 16:23; cf. 1 Pet 3:19), in contrast to Abraham's Bosom (Luke 16:23), Paradise (23:23), the presence of the Lord (2 Cor 5:8), union with Christ (Phil 1:23), the heavenly Jerusalem (Heb 12:22). On the other hand, Acts 2:27, 31 seems to envision Hades as the place of assembly for all souls. This inconsistency of usage is also evident in Josephus. Hades is the place of both the righteous and the wicked in *Ant* 18.14 and *Jewish Wars* 2.163; of the temporary sojourn of the wicked only in *Wars* 3.375. Cf. Jeremias, "ᾅδης," 146-49.

121. According to von Rad, "Apart from isolated questionings (e.g., Job xiv.13-22), it [the realm of the dead] was not a subject of real interest to faith. Poetic fancy alone took it up now and then (Isa xiv. 9ff.; Ezek xxxii.20ff.)" (*Old Testament Theology*, 2.350).

the prophet's own people's consumption. His primary audience consisted of fellow Israelites in exile with whom he shared a particular worldview, but whose minds he was seeking to change. Given the apostate condition of his countrymen, it is conceivable that many of them had bought into pagan beliefs concerning the netherworld, and many of them will have interpreted the details of his oracle literally. But this does not preclude the normativeness of the underlying theological truths: life continues after death; YHWH is the supreme ruler of the entire universe, including the netherworld; a person's status in the afterlife is affected by conduct in the realm of the living.

But we should not be surprised that there are still many gaps in Ezekiel's presentation of the afterlife. His occasional use of the term עוֹלָם creates the impression of an enduring stay, but he provides no clear indication of how permanent the assignments in Sheol are. His Sheol is not to be confused with Gehenna/hell. There are no hints yet of a final eschatological judgment, or of an eternal fiery punishment of the wicked. All of these developments must await a later day.[122]

The second major doctrinal question is raised by chapter 37. It is clear that the primary concern of this vision is the revival of the nation of Israel, but does the prophet hereby imply a belief in individual resurrection? In addressing the issue two types of evidence may be considered, viz., the witness of comparative ancient Near Eastern religion, and inner biblical data.

Some have found the roots of Ezekiel's ideas in Egyptian beliefs about the deceased rising as stars and taking their place in the heavens.[123]

---

122. Cf. Dan 12:2. However, there is still no specific mention of torment or the fires of Gehenna. On the development of this notion in early Jewish thought see Bauckham, "Early Jewish Visions," 355-85. Cf. also S. J. Fox, *Hell in Jewish Literature*. On the growth of the Christian doctrine see Bromiley, "Hell, History of the Doctrine of," 677-79.

123. On which see Frankfort, *Ancient Egyptian Religion*, 100-123; Cf. Spronk, *Beatific Afterlife*, 86-95; Morenz, *Egyptian Religion*, 204-13. In some Old Kingdom texts hope for a beatific afterlife was held out only for the king, who in his identification with a star, or later the sun-god Re, crossed the heavens each day and entered the netherworld at night. Some texts identify the king with Osiris, the ruler of the dead, but this role offered him no possibility of leaving that realm. Later these two notions merged, and Osiris took his place in the heavens, being associated with Orion or the moon, as a nightly counterpart to Re. The custom of mummification was designed to enable the deceased to live on as a "living corpse" and to protect him on his nightly journey to the world of the dead and the daily journey through heaven. With the decline of the Egyptian kingdom, some democratization of the hope of beatific afterlife made possible by identification with Osiris after death becomes apparent. On the role of Osiris see Kees, *Totenglauben*, 132-59.

Others have recognized a belief in personal resurrection in ancient Mesopotamian and Syrian festivals celebrating the annual revivification of the storm god, and/or the annual New Year's festival which commemorated the storm god's victory over death (Mot).[124] K. Spronk argues that the hope for a beatific afterlife, which he defines as "being forever with God (or the gods) in heaven (cf. 1 Thess 4:17)," was an important element in Israelite "folk religion" (as opposed to "official Yahwistic religion").[125] He concludes, "The Israelites were clearly familiar with the Canaanite belief in Baal rising from the netherworld every year and taking the deified spirits of the royal dead with him."[126] These royal dead, known as Rephaim, are thereby entitled to celebrate with Baal at the New Year's Festival, and as "divine ancestors" ('*il 'ib*, *KTU* 1.17:1, 26).

However, neither the Egyptian nor the Near Year's festival theory is convincing.[127] Nor does Ezekiel's vision of the resuscitation of the dead have anything to do with a beatific afterlife "forever with God in heaven," as Spronk defines it.[128] The theory of Zoroastrian influence seems more likely.[129] B. Lang is especially impressed by the sight of the dry bones lying

---

124. Cf. Spronk, *Beatific Afterlife*, 195–96. On the issue of the Ugaritic New Year's festival see Marcus, Review of *New Year*, 589–91; Grabbe, "Seasonal Pattern," 57–63. On the New Year's festival background to Ezekielian ideas see Riesenfeld, *Resurrection in Ezekiel XXXVII*. But cf. Birkeland, "Belief in Resurrection," 60–78; Zimmerli, *Ezekiel 2*, 264.

125. Spronk, *Beatific Afterlife*, 85.

126. Ibid., 344.

127. There are no hints of Egyptian influence at all in Ezek 37. The resuscitation of the dry bones is presented as a one-time event, the graves actually open and return their occupants to the land of the living (not to heaven), and YHWH, at once the patron of Israel and sovereign Lord of life and death, imbues the corpses with his breath. Not only is it doubtful that a New Year's festival based on the Mesopotamian or Canaanite model was ever a part of the Yahwist cult (cf. Block, "New Year," 529–32), orthodox Yahwism viewed notions of fertility deities and their conflicts with the god of death as pagan and tended to react against them rather than to incorporate them into its cult. Cf. also Birkeland, "Belief in Resurrection," 60–78, and Zimmerli, *Ezekiel 2*, 264, for rejection of this connection.

128. Cf. the critique of Spronk by M. Smith and Bloch-Smith, "Death and Afterlife," 277–84.

129. See Lang, "Street Theater," 307–16; Lang, "Life after Death," 144–56, esp. 154–55; Lang, "Afterlife," 12–23, esp. 19–20 (a popular treatment); McDannell and Lang, *Heaven*, 12–13. For a survey of the history of this view and a more cautious understanding of the relationship see Martin-Achard, *From Death to Life*, 186–95; Spronk, *Beatific Afterlife*, 57–59. Cf. also Widengren, "Israelite-Jewish Religion," 311–12; Birkeland, "Belief in Resurrection," 60–78. Cf. also Nobile, who relates the

Beyond the Grave

exposed on the surface of the ground, which he relates to the Zoroastrian practice of exposing human corpses to the elements, rather than burying them.[130] He surmises that Ezekiel might have visited or heard of funeral grounds such as these, and that the prophet's vision echoes the Zoroastrian belief that one day the bones will be reassembled and revived.

There is no a priori reason why Ezekiel could not have incorporated Iranian notions into his message for rhetorical effect, even as he makes use of Mesopotamian, Syrian, and Phoenician ideas elsewhere. In fact, the monotheism and ethical character of this religion render it much more compatible with Yahwism than the other pagan ideologies. However, not only does Lang not answer the chronological[131] and conceptual[132] objections to the theory of Iranian influence that have been raised previously,[133] his suggestion that Ezekiel may have been familiar with, and may even have visited Zoroastrian funeral grounds is speculative wishful thinking. This would have required visionary translocation far to the northeast of the exilic community to the land of Persia, a land which no other Israelite had ever visited. Furthermore, the reference to הַהֲרוּגִים, "the slain," in 37:9 rules out the possibility of Ezekiel's valley of dry bones being a cemetery of

---

motif of resurrection in Ezek 37 to the annual Iranian festival of *Farvardigān* ("Influssi Iranici?" 449–57).

130. Lang, "Street Theater," 310–12. Cf. Herodotus, *Histories* 1.140. For a description of Zoroastrian funeral practices see Boyce, *History of Zoroastrianism*, 325–30. Cf. also Rüssel, "Burial iii. In Zoroastrianism," 561–63.

131. It is unclear when the doctrine of the resurrection of the dead was developed in Persian religion. The earliest certain reference derives from the Greek Theopompus (born *circa* 380 BCE). The citation by Aeneas of Gaza in Theophrastus 77 reads as follows:

> And yet even Plato brings back Armenius in bodily form from Hades to the land of the living. And Zoroaster prophesies that someday there will be a resurrection of all dead. Theopompus knows of this and is himself the source of information concerning it for the other writers.

No explicit contemporary Persian attestation is known.

132. Whereas the Old Testament concentrates on life before death, the Persian attention is focused on life after death. The Old Testament has no counterpart to the Persian view of the separation of body and soul. The Persian focus on judgment immediately after death contrasts with the Israelite, and specifically Ezekielian view of Sheol as a place of shadowy existence. When the doctrine of judgment emerges it is seen as an eschatological event. Perhaps the most important difference is the Israelite interest in reconciliation with God and the remission of sins, notions which have no parallel in Persian thought.

133. See the critique of König, *Zarathustras Jenseitsvorstellungen*, 271–85. Cf. also Spronk, *Beatific Afterlife*, 58.

any kind, Israelite, Babylonian, or Persian. What Ezekiel sees in the bones is a graphic portrayal of the effects of the covenant curse upon his people. If there is any connection with Persian notions at all, rather than adopting Zoroastrian ideas, in verses 11–14 in particular, Ezekiel has presented a powerful polemic against them.[134]

Native Israelite soil provides a more likely seedbed for Ezekiel's notions of resurrection. First, the doctrine of resurrection could have developed as a natural corollary to Israelite anthropological views. The Hebrews looked upon man as a unity, a נֶפֶשׁ חַיָּה ("living being"), constituted by the infusion of divine life breath into the physical form (Gen 2:7).[135] At death, which was viewed as the divine sentence for sin (Gen 2:17; 3:19), the physical matter and life-giving breath are divorced and the נֶפֶשׁ dissolves (Job 34:14–15; Ps 104:29; Qoh 3:18–21; 12:7). It follows then that any hope of victory over death and a beatific afterlife would require a reunion of the divorced components, which is exactly what happens in Ezekiel 37.[136]

Second, the revivification of the dry bones is reminiscent of the life-giving power of his predecessors, Elijah and Elisha (1 Kgs 17:17–24; 2 Kgs 4:18–37; and 13:20–21). To be sure, these cases could be interpreted simply as postmortem healings, inasmuch as the raised persons had recently died and their flesh was certainly still on the bones. But the fact is that as was the case with Elijah and Elisha, through the involvement of a prophet, the dead come to life.

Third, the psalmists regarded having one's life threatened as being in the grip of Sheol, and to be delivered from this dangerous situation as being brought back to life (e.g., 16:11–12; 49:15–16[14–15]).[137] Admittedly, the concern is for an early, if not immediate, rescue rather than an

---

134. This Zoroastrian connection is also rejected by di Lella, in Hartman and di Lella, *Daniel*, 308.

135. Cf. נֶפֶשׁ מֵת, Num 6:6; Lev 21:11. On the expression see Johnson, *Vitality of the Individual*, 19; Wolff, *Anthropology*, 22; Eichrodt, *Theology of the Old Testament*, 2.134–42.

136. Cf. the discussion of Greenspoon, "Origin of the Idea of Resurrection," 249–53 (Greenspoon argues that the doctrine arises out of the image of YHWH as a divine warrior); Rost, "Alttestamentliche Wurzeln," 66–72. But this interpretation is rejected by di Lella, *Daniel*, 308.

137. Cf. Andersen and Freedman, *Hosea*, 421. For discussion of the relevant texts in the Psalms, as well as several from Proverbs see Dahood, *Psalms III*, xlii–lii. Dahood's recognition of this "obvious meaning" (p. xlv) contrasts with that of earlier scholars like C. Barth, who maintained that the belief in YHWH's ability to rescue one from death has nothing to do with a belief in a beatific afterlife *(Errettung vom Tode,* 166).

eschatological deliverance from Sheol, but the language of resurrection can scarcely be denied.

Fourth, earlier prophets anticipate Ezekiel's vision of a national resurrection. The fact that Hosea (6:1-3[138]) and Isaiah (26:19)[139] had already toyed with the idea suggests that in chapter 37 an idea that had germinated at least one and a half centuries earlier has begun to bud.[140] On the other hand, although scholars are reluctant to acknowledge the creative contributions of any prophet, we should not overlook the significance of internal evidence. This message comes to Ezekiel as a direct revelation from God. In a new and dramatic way, the conviction that the grave need not be the end provided a powerful vehicle for announcing the full restoration of Israel. The curse would be lifted. YHWH would bring his people back to life. To be sure, the form of Ezekiel's message is striking, but his concept of resurrection need not have caught his audience by surprise.[141] Even so, it

---

138. Note the resurrection language in the verbs in verse 2: חִיָה, "to make alive," and הֵקִים, "to raise up," with which may be compared Ezekiel's חָיָה, "to live," and עָמַד, "to stand" (37:10). Recent scholars have tended to view this penitential song as a reflex of the Canaanite myth of Baal, whose death and resurrection are celebrated annually in the cult. Wolff speaks of "the Canaanization of the YHWH cult" (*Hosea*, 117). Cf. Martin-Achard, *From Death to Life*, 74-86; Spronk, *Beatific Afterlife*, 62-63. Since it is doubtful that Hosea himself would have composed such a song, it has become fashionable to see here the words of Hosea's opponents, perhaps the priests, who found in the pagan myth cheap grounds for hope. Cf. Eichrodt, *Theology of the Old Testament*, 2.504-5; Wolff, *Hosea*, 109, 117. But the style of the text is genuinely Hoseanic, and its placement in the context follows the doom-hope alternation characteristic of the book as a whole. Cf. Andersen and Freedman, *Hosea*, 417-25; Stuart, *Hosea-Jonah*, 106-9.

139. This text provides one of the clearest statements of resurrection in the Old Testament, whether one interprets it as a prayer (Martin-Achard, *From Death to Life*, 131; *NJPS*; etc.) or an affirmation of certainty (Kaiser, *Isaiah 13-39*, 2315; Watts, *Isaiah 1-33*, 337; Spronk, *Beatific Afterlife*, 299; etc.). On the passage see Hasel, "Resurrection," 268 n. 8. For defenses of an early date for this text see Oswalt, *Isaiah 1-39*, 441; idem, "Recent Studies," 289-302. Cf. also Coggins, "Problem of Isaiah 24-27," 329-33.

140. Other texts that have been drawn into the discussion of resurrection include Deut 32:39; Hos 13:4; Isa 53:10-12; Jer 51:39, 57.

141. Cf. the overstatement of M. Fox, "Ezekiel's primary strategy is boldly to affirm the absurd. . . . He will seek to make them expect the unexpectable" ("Rhetoric of Ezekiel's Vision," 10). While Ezek 37 may represent *a* determinative moment for the Old Testament belief in the resurrection of the dead (cf. Haag, "Ez 37 und der Glaube," 78-92), contra many (e.g., Hanson, *Method and Message*, 368), it is highly unlikely that this passage provides the first reference to the resurrection of the dead in Hebrew literature.

remained for his successors to develop a clearer picture of an eschatological individualized revivification.[142]

Conclusion

It is remarkable that as recently as 1985 biblical scholars were still maintaining that "in ancient Israel there was no belief in a life after death."[143] Many believe that the Pharisaic acceptance of the doctrine (see Acts 23:6–9) derives from a limited number of late texts which reflect Persian influence, and that the Sadduceans, who rejected the notion, were the true heirs of Old Testament belief. It is encouraging to see that some have reversed the roles of these two parties and are now insisting that the Sadducean position represented a conscious departure from both Hebrew and common Semitic beliefs.[144]

In his oracles against Egypt and in his vision of the resuscitated dry bones, Ezekiel offered his countrymen powerful declarations of hope. There is life after death, and there is hope beyond the grave. YHWH remains the incontestable Lord, not only of the living, but also of the dead. He alone determines the moment and nature of a person's decease. He alone has the keys to the gates of Sheol, and he faces no challenge from Mot or any other chthonic power. In this regard Ezekiel, like all other orthodox Yahwists, distances himself from the prevailing notions of his day. But this vision of resuscitation of dry bones is not only for the nation of Israel. It holds out hope for all who offer themselves to YHWH in covenant commitment. With good reason we who are heirs of the glorious message of the prophets and apostles may find in this text a dramatic affirmation that the sting of death may—nay, it will be overcome by the animating power of YHWH's Spirit. After all, as Ezekiel had witnessed, and as he had heard on dozens of occasions, the Lord is YHWH. He has spoken. He will make good his word.

---

142. Cf. Muller, "Resurrection," 145–50.

143. Neyrey, "Eternal Life," 282. Cf. the reaction to this statement by Lang, "Life after Death," 144.

144. Lang, *Monotheism*, 25; Lang, "Life after Death," 144–45 (cf. his citation of other scholars who have come to similar conclusions).

8

Text and Emotion

A Study in the "Corruptions" in Ezekiel's Inaugural Vision (Ezekiel 1:4–28)[1]

Introduction

THE OBSCURITIES AND DIFFICULTIES presented by the text of Ezekiel have almost become proverbial and undoubtedly account for the relatively little popular and scholarly interest there has been in this book of prophecy. Centuries ago Jerome admitted his inability to deal with the "obscuritates" of the book. In fact, he compared its difficulties with those of the Song of Songs and the opening chapters of Genesis. He observed, furthermore, that Jews under thirty years of age were forbidden to read its beginning and its ending.[2] With this we should compare the comments of the renowned Puritan scholar, William Greenhill, who bemoaned the fact that Ezekiel had "been past over, both by Writers and Readers, as dark, difficult, and lesse useful."[3] Recourse to the Hebrew text does not relieve the

---

1. This essay was originally published in *Catholic Biblical Quarterly* 50 (1988) 1–25.

2. Jerome, "Epistula LIII," 460–61; cf. Jerome, *Opera. Pars I*, 3–4. See Spiegel, "Ezekiel or Pseudo-Ezekiel?," 256–57; reprinted in *Pseudo-Ezekiel*, 123–24. For a fuller discussion of Jerome's treatment of Ezekiel's prophecy, see Neuss, *Das Buch Ezechiel*, 65–75.

3. Greenhill (*Exposition of the Five First Chapters of the Prophet Ezekiel*, iv), as

difficulties; on the contrary, it compounds them sevenfold. A quick scan of *BHS* reveals that only chapter 41 has elicited more textual notes by the editors than chapter 1.

Scholars studying the prophet's inaugural vision have used many different approaches in attempting to account for the present shape of the text. More often than not, in this century efforts have concentrated on isolating the original kernel and describing the evolution of the text. However, the lack of consensus in its interpretation and reconstruction attests to the generally unsatisfactory nature of the results. R. R. Wilson aptly observes: "To date no single reconstruction has proven to be totally convincing."[4] With similar pessimism, M. Greenberg laments that the criteria employed in the search for the hypothetical original are arbitrary, and the creativity credited to editors and copyists excessive.[5] In the light of scholarly inability to come to a satisfactory interpretation of Ezekiel 1, it may appear presumptuous to enter the arena. However, an explanation for the present state of the text may (and the tentative nature of the hypothesis is emphasized here) be nearer to hand than expected.

The investigation pursued in this article will consist of three parts: (1) a review of the difficulties posed by the text; (2) a survey of recent interpretations; (3) a proposal for an alternative approach. The study will be restricted to the actual vision itself, i.e., 1:4–28. The introductory verses present great difficulties on their own, as does the sequel to the vision.

Problems in the Text of Ezekiel's Inaugural Vision

Difficulties in Ezekiel's inaugural vision may be classified under three heads: problems of grammar, style, and substance. We shall deal with each of these in turn.

Problems of Grammar

The grammatical difficulties encountered in the text are legion. They may be grouped under several general categories.

---

quoted in the introduction to the commentary by Sheppard, et al. (eds.) (*English Protestant Biblical Commentary*).

4. Wilson, "Prophecy in Crisis," 123.

5. Greenberg, *Ezekiel 1–20*, 52.

Text and Emotion

(1) *Confusion of Gender.* The most obvious grammatical problem is the ubiquitous confusion of gender. The seemingly irrational interchange of masculine and feminine forms permeates the entire text and every conceivable context.

The ways in which pronominal suffixes are used, at least up to verse 26, appear to be totally arbitrary. Although the subject in verses 15–18 is the masculine אופנים ("wheels") and here masculine suffixes referring to this antecedent are expected,[6] throughout most of the remaining text the subject is stated or assumed to be the feminine אש ("fire")[7] or חיות ("creatures").[8] Nevertheless, the pronouns referring to these antecedents are inconsistent, whether they are attached to prepositions,[9] nouns,[10] or verbal forms.[11] Often the switch will occur within the same verse, even the same sentence.[12]

The gender of verbs is also discordant. The form תרפינה ("they relaxed") in verses 24–25 indicates that the author is aware of the normal shape of the second person feminine plural imperfect. However, in every other instance the masculine forms of the verbs are used, again regardless of the gender of the subject.[13] The participial forms are more regular. The

---

6. But even here feminine pronominal suffixes appear alongside masculine; cf. the nouns לארבעתן ("their four"; 16, 18), רביעיהן ("their four"; 17), and גביה ("their rims"; 18), juxtaposed with מעשיהם ("their construction"; 16 *bis*), מראיהם ("their appearance"; 16), and גבתם ("their rims"; 18); also the infinitive construct בלכתן ("as they went"), which follows immediately on בלכתם ("as they went") in verse 17.

7. Vv. 4–5a.

8. Vv. 5b–15, 19–26. The feminine noun כנף/כנפים ("wing"/"wings") also occurs as antecedent to prepositions in verses 9, 23. In each of these instances, the pronoun on אחות ("sisters") is appropriately feminine.

9. Feminine: מתוכה ("from its midst"; 4, 5); להנה ("to them"; 5, 23 *bis*); לאחת ("to one"; 6 *bis*).
Masculine: לו ("to it"; 4); להם ("to them"; 6); אצלם ("beside them"; 19); לעמתם ("alongside them"; 20, 21).

10. Feminine: מראיהן ("their appearance"; 5); לארבעתן ("for their four"; 10 *bis*, 16); גויתיהנה ("their bodies"; 11); כנפיהן ("their wings"; 24, 25).
Masculine: רגליהם ("their feet"; 7 *bis*); כנפיהם ("their wings"; 8 *bis*, 9, 11, 23, 24); רבעיהם ("their sides") and פניהם ("their faces"; 8, 10, 11; cf. פניו ["his face"; 12, 15]); ארבעתם ("their four"; 8, 10); מראיהם ("their appearance"; 13); ראשיהם ("their heads"; 22; cf. ראש ["head"]; 25, 26); גויתיהם ("their bodies; 23).

11. Feminine: בלכתן ("as they went"; 9, 12, 17). Masculine: בלכתם ("as they went"; 17, 21, 24); בעמדם ("as they stood"; 21, 24, 25); בהנשאם ("as they rose"; 21).

12. Cf. vv. 8, 10, 11, 16, 17, 18, 23, 24, 25.

13. Note the following verb forms (their subjects are given in the brackets): יסבו ("they turned"; 9, 12 [חיות, "creatures"], 17 [האופנים, "the wheels"]); ילכו ("they went";

only instances in which genders are crossed occur in verse 7, where נצצים ("sparkling") follows רגליהם ("their feet"), and in verse 13 where בערות ("burning") follows גחלי־אש ("coals of fire").[14]

Some confusion is apparent also in the use of nouns. In verse 9a the feminine אשה ("each") referring back to feminine כנפיהם ("their wings"), is used in the distributive sense. However, within the same verse the masculine איש ("each") is used in the very same sense. The masculine form recurs in verse 11, again with a feminine antecedent. However, in verse 23 both masculine and feminine forms reappear, again within the same verse.

(2) *Confusion of Number.* The clause ורגליהם רגל ישרה, literally, "and their feet were/was a straight foot," in verse 7 is awkward. It is not possible to tell whether the singular "leg" means each of two legs or each creature had only one leg. The adjective ישרה ("straight") occurs in Ezekiel only once more, in verse 23, where the feminine form refers to the "outstretched" wings of the living creatures.[15] Here the number of adjective and antecedent agrees.

Although it may be argued that in this case the singular may be deliberately used after the plural, the appearance of the singular החיה ("the creature"), employed in verses 20–22 as the designation for what in chapter 10 is/are identified as the cherubim, catches one totally off guard. G. A. Cooke suggests that חיה is either a collective singular or distributive, "each living creature," i.e., the one beside each wheel.[16] However, it is difficult to explain why now the unity of the creatures should become significant.

9, 12a, 12b [חיות, "creatures"], 17, 19, 20, 21 [האופנים, "the wheels"]); ינשאו ("they rose"; 19, 20, 21 [האופנים, "the wheels"]); יעמדו ("they stood"; 21 [האופנים, "the wheels"]); יהיה ("it was"; 12, 20 [רוח], 16 [האופן, "the wheel"], 28 [קשת, "bow"]).

14. Note the following participles (their subjects are given in the brackets): באה ("it came"; 4 [רוח, "wind"]); מתלקחת ("flashing"; 4 [אש, "fire"]); נצצים ("sparkling"; 7 [רגליהם, "their feet"]); חברת ("touching"; 9 [אשה, "each wing"]); פרדות ("spreading"; 11 [כנפיהם, "their wings"]); חברות ("touching"; 11 [כנפיהם, "their wings"]); מכסות ("covering"; 11 [כנפיהם, "their wings"]); בערות ("burning"; 13 [גחלי־אש, "coals of fire"]); מתהלכת ("moving"; 13 [החיות, "the creatures"]); יוצא ("going"; 13 [ברק, "lightning"]); מלאת ("being full"; 18 [גבתם, "their rims"]); נטוי ("stretching out"; 22 [רקיע, "expanse"]); מכסות ("covering"; 23a, 23b [כנפיהם, "their wings"]).

15. Barrick ("Straight-Legged Cherubim," 543–50) suggests that the legs were straight because they did not use their legs for locomotion.

16. Cooke, *Ezekiel*, 27; so also Zimmerli, *Ezekiel 1*, 20. Compare Greenberg (*Ezekiel 1–20*, 48), who sees here an emphasis on the unity of the entire phenomenon.

Text and Emotion

In any case, this interpretation escaped the translators of most modern English versions, which translate the term as a plural.¹⁷

Finally, reference must be made to the alternation of singular and plural forms of ראש ("head") in verses 22 (plural *bis*) and 25, 26 (singular *bis*). The singular antecedent חיה ("creature") in the former would have led us to expect the singular form of ראש ("head"). All in all, one is left bewildered. Is there one creature with one head, or one creature with more than one head? Or is there more than one creature with one head for the whole, or does each have its own head?

(3) *Use of the Infinitive Absolute as Finite Verb.* The forms רצוא ("run") and שוב ("return") in verse 14 are pointed as infinitives absolute by the Masoretes.¹⁸ This usage presents several difficulties. In the first place, infinitives functioning as finite verbs regularly precede the subject.¹⁹ Here the subject החיות ("the creatures") comes first. The second problem is lexical. The word ראש ("head"), which appears to serve as a biform of רוץ, "to run," here represents a *hapax* occurrence. The verb may be related to the Aramaic רחט ²⁰ and Akkadian *raṣum*.²¹ The expression then means "to dart to and fro." The Vg's *ibant* assumes a textual error for יצוא ("to go out").²²

(4) *Inconsistency in the use of* שם/שמה *("there").* In the first occurrence of the clause אל/על אשר יהיה־שמה הרוח ללכת ילכו, "wherever the spirit would go, they went," in verse 12, the *hē*-directive is attached to the adverb שם. However, when the expression recurs in virtually the same form in verse 20, the directive is omitted, only to resurface in the immediately following redundant recurrence of the phrase. Most emend the shortened form to harmonize with the others.

(5) על ("upon, to") *used in the sense of* אל ("to"). In the second occurrence of the phrase noted above, על is used in the sense of "to," normally

---

17. So *RSV, NEB, JB, NIV*, contra the *Authorized Version*, which renders it in the singular.

18. The verse is omitted entirely by the LXX.

19. See GKC §113*aa–gg*; Joüon, §123*u–y*.

20. So BDB, 952, cf. 930; KB, 905, cf. 882. See also Jean and Hoftijzer, *DISO*, 275. There are eight instances in the Hebrew OT in which או is written as וא, but this is the only example in Ezekiel. All of the remaining seven are postexilic. For a discussion of these forms, see Kutscher, *Language and Linguistic Background*, 173–74.

21. See *AHW* 2.960, "(zur Hilfe) laufen."

22. So also Zimmerli (*Ezekiel 1*, 85), following Bauer and Leander (*Historische Grammatik*, 405).

expected of אל. It is true that in Ezekiel these two prepositions are often interchanged. However, as G. R. Berry pointed out long ago, this is rare in the early chapters.[23]

Problems of Style

Several features of the account are not necessarily grammatically wrong, but they are stylistically irregular.

(1) *Morphology*. Although the masculine plural pronominal suffix is represented characteristically as -הם or -ם, this is not true of the feminine counterpart. In verses 5 and 23 (*bis*), the form attached to the preposition ל is that of the independent personal pronoun, הנה. This is attested elsewhere only in 42:9 and Zechariah 5:9. But גויתיהנה ("their bodies") in 1:11 is unique.[24] The masculine counterpart in verse 23, גויתיהם, is normal.

(2) *Asyndetic Constructions*. On four occasions an expected conjunction is missing in the text: before ענן ("cloud"; v 4), לא יסבו ("they did not turn"; v. 12), מראה ("appearance"; v. 16), and בעמדם ("when they stood"; v. 24). In each instance the LXX presents a smoother reading of the text by the insertion of καὶ.

(3) *Dittography*. In several places the account appears to contain dittographic errors. The reference to ופניהם ("and their faces") in verse 11 looks suspiciously secondary, influenced perhaps by the three preceding expressions, all of which have begun with ופני ("and the face of"). It may also have been added to וכנפיהם ("and their wings") as an echo of verse 8b, where the two are also conjoined. The word ומעשיהם ("and their construction") in 1:16a seems out of place and redundant in the light of verse 16b, where it reappears after מראה ("appearance"). As already noted, שמה הרוח ללכת ("there the spirit would go") appears twice in immediate succession in verse 20. A similar phenomenon occurs in verse 23, where ולאיש שתים מכסות להנה ("and each creature has two wings") is duplicated for no apparent reason. Verses 25b–26a read בעמדם תרפינה כנפיהן וממעל לרקיע אשר על־ראשם, "when they stood still they let down their wings, and above the firmament that was over their head." But a slightly modified form of this comment has already been

---

23. Berry, "The Authorship of Ezekiel," 25.
24. See Joüon, §94*h–i*.

Text and Emotion

given in the immediately preceding verses 24b–25a. By omitting the repeated word or phrase the LXX presents a smoother reading.²⁵

(4) *Difficult Constructions.* Although the places in the text that cry out for explanation are numerous, four major ones should be cited. In each instance, the LXX presents an abbreviated and easier reading, causing most commentators to argue for the priority of the latter.²⁶ In verses 8–9, after אדם מתחת כנפיהם וידי ²⁷ ("hands of a human under their wings") the MT adds a long note: על ארבעת רבעיהם ופניהם וכנפיהם לארבעתם חברת אשה אל־אחותה, "on their four sides, and the faces and wings of the four of them touched one another." How this comment entered the text is hard to explain. The entire verse 14 is difficult: והחיות רצוא ושוב כמראה הבזק, "and the living creatures darted back and forth like sparks." The word בזק, translated "sparks" by Greenberg,²⁸ is a *hapax* in biblical Hebrew. The Targum apparently mistook it for ברק, ("lightning"), which appears at the end of verse 13.²⁹ Added to כקול מים רבים, "like the sound of many waters," in verse 24 the MT has כקול־שדי בלכתם קול המלה כקול מחנה, "like the voice of the Almighty when they went, the sound of tumult like the sound of a camp." The heaping up of similes appears laborious and catches the reader by surprise. Finally, in verse 27 כמראה־אש בית־לה סביב, "like the appearance of fire enclosing it round about," after וארא כעין חשמל, "and I saw [ ] like the gleam of metal." This comment introduces to the upper part of the body the appearance of fire, which belongs more appropriately to the lower half.

(5) *Difficult insertions.* Scattered throughout the text are small details whose presence is difficult to explain. The phrase מתוך האש ("from the

---

25. A helpful study of these verses (except for verse 23) is provided by Lind, "A Text-Critical Note," 137. His comment, "These cases exhaust the possibilities of dittography," overlooks the most obvious example.

26. Lind (ibid., 138) discusses all of these, arguing that in each of these instances the principle of *lectio difficilior* supersedes that of preference for the shorter reading. It is difficult to imagine a scribe having the *Vorlage* of the LXX before him and then adding the extra phrases found in the MT. Far from clarifying, they becloud the texts.

27. So Qere. Ketib וידי is obviously a scribal lapse.

28. Greenberg, *Ezekiel 1–20*, 46.

29. The text is commonly emended accordingly; see Zimmerli, *Ezekiel 1*, 85. Halperin ("Merkabah Midrash," 355 n. 22) questions the common preference for the LXX, which omits this verse, arguing that the omission may be attributed to homoioteleuton. The translator's eye skipped from ברק ("lightning") at the end of verse 13 in the *Vorlage* to the similar הבזק ("the lightning") at the end of verse 14.

midst of the fire") in verse 4 seems unnecessary after ומתוכה in the preceding phrase. The word להם ("to them") at the end of verse 6 is unnecessary after לאחת ("to each"). Furthermore, if it is intended as a repetition of להנה earlier (v. 5), it changes the gender. Verse 13 begins with a problematic ודמות ("and the likeness"), which most emend to ומתוך or ובתוך after the LXX's καὶ ἐν μέσῳ.³⁰ The article on הבזק ("the lightning") in verse 14 is unexpected. Ezekiel's normal introduction to a new section or subsection, וארא והנה ("and I looked and behold") is interrupted by an intrusive החיות ("the creatures") in verse 15. The word וגבתם ("and their rims") in verse 18 looks redundant and defies satisfactory interpretation.³¹ The adjective הנורא ("awesome") modifying הקרח ("the crystal") in verse 22 seems awkward and is missing in the LXX. The verb ויהי ("and it happened"), a common form in continuous narrative, occurs for the first time in verse 25. But here it seems strangely out of place. The LXX's καὶ ἰδοὺ appears to read והנה ("and behold").

(6) *General Narrative Style.* Beyond all of these problems of detail, the literary style of the account is cumbersome and difficult. Sentences are short and constructed in a choppy, staccato mode. A rhythm is never established. The flow characteristic of narrative, even of Ezekiel's own writings, is lacking. Verbless clauses abound. In these, subjects and predicates are often only tentatively identifiable. The first finite verb occurs in verse 9b. All in all, despite Wilson's observation that the general outline of Ezekiel's vision is clear,³² coming to grips with the details is an extremely arduous task. The problems raised by the text itself are so numerous that it is difficult even to know where one should begin.³³

Problems of Substance

The account of Ezekiel's inaugural vision breaks down into five basic sections: (1) the introductory notice of the fiery cloud out of which the details emerge (v. 4); (2) the description of the four חיות ("creatures"; vv. 5–14); (3) the description of the mysterious wheels (vv. 15–21); (4) the

---

30. See *BHS.*

31. For a helpful study of this verse, interpreted in the light of Sumerian and Akkadian expressions, see Waldman, "Note on Ezekiel 1:18," 614–18.

32. Wilson, "Call of Ezekiel," 123.

33. See Zimmerli (*Ezekiel 1*, 101–6) for a discussion of the seemingly innumerable problems raised by the text.

Text and Emotion

description of the enthroned figure (vv. 22–27); (5) the concluding summary statement (v. 28).

Each of the three major sections presents difficulties to those of us moderns who expect narratives to flow smoothly, coherently, and logically from one idea to another. After introducing the reader to the living creatures in verse 5, verses 6–9 deal successively with their faces, legs, wings, and manner of locomotion. But the same four subjects are redundantly taken up again in verses 10–12.

Verses 13–14 are full of motion, but the scene shifts from the lightning in the midst of the fiery vehicle to the lightning-like motion of the living creatures themselves, giving the impression of some confusion in the description. We are left wondering in which context the image of lightning is at home. Some have noted that the burning coals in the midst of the living beings have no functional purpose in the context of this chapter.[34]

The account of the enigmatic wheels given in verses 15–21 has the appearance of a self-contained unit. It is introduced with the common introductory formula וארא והנה ("And I looked and behold"), suggesting that what follows is a new theme.[35] Furthermore, if this section is removed, verses 22–25 seem to follow quite naturally after verse 14. Finally, although the elements described in the first part of the vision take on special significance in verses 22–25, the wheels disappear entirely from view. Many suggest, therefore, that this paragraph is a secondary intrusion into the account of the vision.

The last section, verses 22–27, also presents its puzzles. The paragraph opens with a reference to the platform (רקיע) that appeared above the living creatures. We would expect the following verses to elaborate this aspect of the vision. Instead, the account goes off in another direction, describing the functions and motions of the wings beneath the platform and emphasizing the sound effects accompanying the entire phenomenon. Only in verse 26 does the narrator return to the matter of what was witnessed above the platform.

To sum up, the disorganized nature of the account is of a piece with the difficulties encountered in its grammar and literary style.

---

34. See Cody, *Ezekiel*, 25.

35. The expression is used to introduce new units in 1:4; 2:9; 8:2, 7, 10; 10:1, 9; 44:4; cf. Zech 1:8; 2:1[1:18], 5[1]; 5:9; Dan 10:5; cf. also the perfect form of the first verb in the expression (והנה . . . ראיתי; Jer 4:23). On the irregular intrusion of החיות ("creatures") between the two elements, see above.

By the River Chebar

Recent Treatments of Ezekiel's Inaugural Vision

The responses of scholars to the problems in Ezekiel 1:4–28 have varied greatly. Several of the more important solutions are summarized here. Some would attribute many of the problems to lapses in scribal transmission. Thus W. Eichrodt, for example, sees no reason to look elsewhere for an explanation of the gender inconsistencies.[36] A detailed examination of the text of Ezekiel by K. S. Freedy has sought to account for many of the difficulties in chapter 1 by appealing to scribal glosses. The incongruities posed by the reverse genders he labels "cue glosses," which were designed intentionally to identify a word as a gloss and are not to be treated as part of the text.[37] "Explicative glosses" account for כמראה הלפדים היא ("It was like the appearance of torches") in verse 13a, על־ראשיהם ("on their heads") in verse 22b, and עליו ("on it") in verse 26b. Their function is to explicate the meaning or significance of words found in the text.[38] A "rubrical gloss," which originally served as a theme notation in the margin but found its way into the text, is recognized in החיות ("creatures") in verse 15a.[39] Freedy has identified as exegetical glosses those annotations that have no direct bearing on the meaning but highlight ethical or theological qualities of the traditions with which they are associated. An example is found in הנורא ("awesome"; v. 22).[40]

Although G. Fohrer shares this interest in identifying the glosses in the text,[41] his division of the entire account of the call of Ezekiel into strophes adds another dimension. He sees the call narrative as being divided into two main parts, each ten strophes in length (1:1–28a; 1:28b—3:9), followed by a short conclusion to the entire event (3:12–15).[42] The concern here is his treatment of the first part. His ten strophes in 1:1–28a consist (minus the glosses) respectively of 1:1–3, 4–5, 6–7, 10, 11, 13, 15–16, 22–23, 26, 27–28a.[43] The result is that the essential unity of the account is maintained, and the theories of two separate experiences or accounts are rejected.

---

36. Eichrodt, *Ezekiel*, 55–56. So also Houk, "The Final Redaction of Ezekiel 10," 46.
37. Freedy, "Glosses in Ezekiel," 131–36.
38. Ibid., 137–41, 150.
39. Ibid., 142, 151.
40. Ibid., 147.
41. See Fohrer, "Glossen," 204–21; Fohrer, *Ezechiel*, 7–14.
42. Ibid., 6.
43. Ibid., 8–16; cf. See Fohrer, *Hauptprobleme*, 60–66, for a discussion of poetry, meter, and strophes in Ezekiel.

Text and Emotion

These approaches are attractive, especially for dealing with the questionable textual features of the account. However, they do not explain the intrusion of unexpected subjects, such as the wheels in verse 15. Some have seen verses 15–21 as secondary, having entered chapter 1 under the influence of chapter 10.[44] However, it is unlikely that a second edition of the vision would have so many textual problems, and most would reject this interpretation as untenable.[45]

W. Zimmerli, who provides the most exhaustive search for the original text of the call of Ezekiel,[46] marshals the irregular use of suffixes to isolate the original from secondary material. He assumes that in 1:5–12 the correct feminine suffixes point to the original, whereas the erroneous masculine suffixes signal secondary additions. This observation confirms for him the secondary nature of the entire paragraph verses 15–21, the difficulties of which have already been noted. The result for Zimmerli is that the original text of Ezekiel's inaugural vision consisted of 1:4a, 5, 6b, 12, 13, 22, 26–28. All of the remainder represents commentary and expansions on the original "in the circles of the school who transmitted Ezekiel's words."[47] He rejects the use of catchwords like "redaction" or "gloss" to describe this elaboration. Rather, these additions represent successive serious attempts to understand and clarify the meaning of the vision.

The inconsistency in Zimmerli's use of pronominal suffixes as a literary criterion has been noted by C. B. Houk.[48] To his comments it should be added that, as has been observed, the confusion of gender extends beyond the use of suffixes. Surely, if the suffixes are employed, the search for the original text should also consider the incorrect genders of verbs and nouns as well, to say nothing of the confusion in number.

The conflicting results of these attempts to unravel the mystery of Ezekiel 1 raise questions concerning the methods that have been employed.[49]

---

44. So Eichrodt, *Ezekiel*, 118, following Sprank, *Studien zu Ezechiel*, 52–54, 68–69, 74; Baumann, "Die Hauptvisionen Hesekiels," 57; cf. Cody (*Ezekiel*, 25), who sees the reference to the burning coals as having been inserted in anticipation of chapter 10.

45. Zimmerli, *Ezekiel 1*, 105, 232; Houk, "The Final Redaction of Ezekiel 10," 44–47; Halperin, "Exegetical Character," 129–41. Halperin concludes that "from a very early period, therefore, ch. i was a sacred, and, to this extent, 'fixed' text: its obscurities were to be treated in separate exegetical essays, but its own text was not to be tampered with."

46. Zimmerli, *Ezekiel 1*, 100–10.

47. Ibid., 124.

48. Houk, "The Final Redaction of Ezekiel 10," 46.

49. See the comments of Wilson and Greenberg, in the Introduction *supra*.

Since the evidence cited is often mutually contradictory, disagreement may be inevitable. Perhaps the time has come to stand back and take a more holistic look at the description of Ezekiel's inaugural vision, one that takes into account all of the obscurities found in the text.

An Alternative Approach

Any explanation for the confused nature of the description must take into account all of the difficulties that it presents: grammatical, stylistic, substantive. While no difficulty exists in accepting that this passage may have suffered from inadvertent errors in copying (e.g., errors of dittography, spelling, homoioteleuton, etc.), it seems that to lay the burden of all of the irregularities on the shoulders of either scribes or redactors is to impose upon them a load that they might have been both unwilling and unable to bear.[50] In view of the remarkable agreement between most of the copies of biblical texts found at Qumran and the MT, it is hard to imagine that all of the proposed scribal influences would have crept into the text in the centuries between the composition of the original text of Ezekiel and the production of the Qumran texts. Furthermore, to attribute so many irregularities to later editors is hardly a solution. The more authoritative a text was considered to be, the more carefully the scribes would operate. As D. J. Halperin has suggested, Ezekiel 1 must have been accepted as "canonical," hence basically inviolable, early, i.e., by the time chapter 10 was written.[51] While obscurities may have been smoothed out in a later rendition, one would not expect later redactors to "mess up" so badly an authoritative and unproblematic original. It seems more likely that redactors would preserve problematic features of an inherited text.

The Nature of Ezekiel's Experience

The call narrative of Ezekiel may yet contain the clues to the obscurities of the inaugural vision. In the first place, the genre of the experience requires identification. Verse 1 speaks of נפתחו השמים ("the heavens were opened") and the prophet seeing מראות אלהים ("divine visions"). Although elsewhere

---

50. On ancient scribal techniques, see Millard, "Text and Comment," 245–52; Millard, "In Praise of Ancient Scribes," 143–53.

51. See n. 72 above.

God is spoken of as "rending the heavens,"⁵² this use of the expression "to open the heavens" is unique.⁵³ The image is that of the opening of a gate to the temple/palace of a god, permitting full view of the statue of the divinity in all its splendor. In this instance, it is not an earthly residence of the deity that is being exposed, but the heavenly throne room of God.⁵⁴

The second expression is commonly translated, "visions of God,"⁵⁵ but this understanding seems unlikely. The word אלהים ("God") is seldom, if ever, used as a proper noun in Ezekiel. Usually it serves as an appellative.⁵⁶ Furthermore, מראות ("vision") is not a true plural, but a "plural of generalization."⁵⁷ As in 8:3 and 40:2, the expression should therefore be interpreted as a "divine or supernatural vision," one that is inaccessible to ordinary mortals apart from the revelation of God. This interpretation is supported by what follows inasmuch as what the prophet witnesses is not so much a vision of God (only the last few verses refer to the divinity himself), but rather a vision of divine, heavenly realities.

Verse 3 employs another expression to describe the prophetic experience, ותהי עליו שם יד־יהוה, "the hand of YHWH came upon him there."⁵⁸ Here "hand" is used metaphorically of power, the overwhelming force with which God grips the prophet. In 1 Kings 18:46 the same experience energizes Elijah with remarkable strength so that he is able to outrun the chariots of Ahab. Speaking of divine compulsion, Isaiah 8:11 and Jeremiah 15:17 employ the phrase with a somewhat milder significance. But in Ezekiel the "hand of YHWH" gains complete mastery over his movements (3:22; cf. 33:22) and transports him in spirit back and forth to distant places (8:1; 37:1; 40:1). As A. J. Heschel observes, this expression

---

52. See 2 Sam 22:10, נטה שמים, "to sweep aside the heavens" (so *NEB*); Isa 63:19, קרע שמים, "to rend the heavens."

53. The expression occurs also in Gen 7:11, but with a quite different meaning.

54. In the NT, cf. Matt 3:16; Luke 3:21; John 1:51; Acts 7:56; Rev 19:11, all with similar sense. Rev 4:1–11 actually speaks of a door of heaven that opens up to the throne room of God. Acts 10:11 is somewhat different in sense.

55. *RSV, NIV*; cf. *JB*, "visions from God"; *NEB*, "a vision of God." The expression recurs in 8:3 and 40:2.

56. So also Greenberg, *Ezekiel 1–20*, 41. For a full discussion of the names of God in Ezekiel, see Zimmerli, *Ezekiel 25–48*, 556–62, esp. 556–57.

57. See Joüon, §136j; GKC §124e.

58. This is a favorite expression for Ezekiel, recurring in 3:22; 33:22; 37:1; 40:1. Ezek 8:1 uses a variant of the same, ותפל עלי שם יד אדני יהוה, "And the hand of the Lord YHWH fell on me there."

describes "the urgency, pressure, and compulsion by which he is stunned and overwhelmed."[59]

These, then, represent the nature of the prophet's experience. What transpires is an unusual, unprecedented, unexpected encounter with divinity. Is it possible that this may have influenced the shape of the description?

Second, the language of the description may reflect the nature of the experience. It is apparent from the account that, although Ezekiel has a clear view of what he is seeing, he is at a loss to find words that will describe the vision adequately. Thus he is forced to use the language of analogy. He cannot say "the wheels" (v. 16), "the brightness around" (v. 28), the כבוד of YHWH (v. 28), but only "the appearance (מראה) of the wheels, the appearance (מראה) of the brightness around, the appearance (מראה) of the likeness of the כבוד of YHWH" respectively. He cannot even say "the appearance of torches (v. 13), lightning (v. 14), sapphire stones (v. 26), man (v. 26), fire (v. 27 bis), rainbow (v. 28)"; he must resort to "like the appearance (כמראה) of torches, lightning, etc." In verse 27, with respect to the body of the human-like figure he uses the expression "from the appearance (ממראה) of his loins and upward/ downward." "Their appearance" (מראיהן/מראיהם) is used absolutely three times (vv. 5, 13, 16).

The language of analogy is also seen in the frequent occurrence of דמות, "likeness." Unable to express himself definitively with the man (v. 5), their faces (v. 10), the living beings (v. 13), the כבוד of YHWH (v. 28), he refers obliquely to "the likeness" of the man, their faces, the living beings, the כבוד of YHWH, respectively. The noun דמות is used absolutely in verse 16 ("all four had one likeness"), verse 22 ("the likeness over the heads of the living beings was an expanse"), and verse 26 ("a likeness, like the appearance of man was over it").

The description of the vision is also replete with expressions connoting brilliance, magnificence, brightness. "Fire" (אש) occurs in verses 4 (2x), 13 (3x), 27; "brilliance" (נגה) in verses 4, 13, 27, 28; "like the sparkle" (כעין) in verse 4 (of חשמל),[60] 7 (of bronze), 16 (of tarshish), 22 (of crystal), 27 (of חשמל, cf. 8:2); "burning coals of fire" (גחלי־אש) in verse 13; "torches" (לפדים) in verse 13; "lightning" (ברק) in the same verse, and "lightning" (בזק) in the next. He also speaks of the rims of the wheels as

---

59. Heschel, *Prophets*, 444. For a full discussion of the significance of the expression in its ancient Near Eastern context, see Roberts, "Hand of YHWH," 244–51.

60. On which see Greenberg, *Ezekiel 1–20*, 43.

being "majestic and awesome" (גבה להם ויראה להם) in verse 18,[61] and the crystal in verse 22 as being "awesome" (הנורא).

The climax of the account, verse 28, heaps up a series of analogical expressions: "Such was the appearance of the surrounding brilliance. It was the appearance of the likeness of the glory of YHWH" (כן מראה הנגה סביב הוא מראה דמות כבוד יהוה).

It is apparent that the vocabulary and forms of expression available to the prophet fall far short of the requirements of this vision, which transcends all of the bounds of normal human experience. Things cannot be described for what they are; the vision can be recounted only in relation to ideas and concepts familiar to the prophet. Could not the prophet's grasping for appropriate forms of expression, and his frustration with the inadequacy of human language for the depiction of supernatural realities, have left its imprint on the shape of the description in other ways as well?

Third, we note Ezekiel's response to the event. According to 1:28b—2:2, he falls down on his face, stunned. The apparition is awesome and overwhelming. As Zimmerli aptly observes, "No vague presence of deity passed him by, but YHWH, the God of Israel, in the glory of the כבוד יהוה met him as he had met with Israel in the great events of the wilderness period."[62] Ezekiel's response was appropriate for one who had been ushered into the heavenly court, into the presence of the divine king. In Isaiah's parallel vision of YHWH in his heavenly palace, the focus had been on the deity's holiness, causing the prophet to fear for his life in view of his own contrasting sinfulness (Isa 6:1–5). But this vision has concentrated on the awesome splendor and indescribable majesty of the divine king and his surroundings. This produced in Ezekiel not a recognition of sinfulness but an overwhelming sense of awe. Where Isaiah's sense of sinfulness had been responded to with a divine act of cleansing, here the divine king invites the prophet to arise, to stand in his presence. Not that Ezekiel is able or dares to do this of himself; it requires a special infusion of the spirit of YHWH and a specific divine act to get him back on his feet. Furthermore, although this appears to have restored him to full alertness for the rest of the vision and the commissioning, according to Ezekiel 3:15, the entire experience left him awestruck, unable to speak for seven days.

The experience had left the prophet stunned. Is it possible that the recollection of the event at the time the account was recorded could still have produced a similar state, to the extent that it affected the shape of the description?

61. On which see n. 31 above.
62. Zimmerli, *Ezekiel 1*, 124.

Fourth, and finally, reference is made to the reappearance of the theophany in chapter 10. Although the first part of the chapter introduces some new notions, the connection between the two accounts is obvious, as may be witnessed by juxtaposing parallel passages from each.[63] Regrettably, we must forgo here a detailed discussion of the relationship of these two chapters.[64] Nevertheless, a few observations must be made. (1) Where chapter 10 repeats the material found in chapter 1, the grammatical difficulties of the latter have been completely smoothed out: על ("upon, to"; 1:17) is replaced with the more conventional אל ("to"; 10:11), and the irregularities of gender and number have been corrected. (2) The narrator now seems to know what he is describing; the abstract has become concrete. Much of the analogical language has disappeared; the indefinite expression החיות ("the creatures") has been replaced by the specific הכרובים ("the cherubim"); the האופנים ("the wheels") are identified specifically as גלגל (10:13); the sheer brilliance of the first vision has been toned down. (3) The description of the creatures' faces has been rationalized (10:14; cf. 1:10). (4) Details that seem out of place in chapter 1 now have vital parts to play. Thus, the burning coals in the midst of the living creatures, whose function is unclear in 1:13, become symbols of judgment in 10:2. The wheels, which seemed to be an unnatural intrusion into the inaugural vision, are now at home, serving in a vital role as bearers of the כבוד ("glory") of YHWH as it exits from Jerusalem.

How these modifications are to be accounted for is a matter of some discussion. In 1924 Gustav Hölscher recognized the original kernel of the text in 10:2, 7, which tie in with 9:11. The remainder represents at least four different interpolations plus further additions (10:1, 8–17, 20–22), all of which were heavily dependent on chapter 1.[65] Zimmerli proposes that apart from 10:2, 18a this description derives from "the apparatus of a school, a 'teaching house,'" which took up the words and ideas of Ezekiel and elaborated these themes.[66] In this instance, the aim of the editorial school was twofold: (1) a zealous concern for the freedom of YHWH; (2) a desire to show that the glory of YHWH was as real in judgment as it had been in the vision of chapter 1.[67] Houk argues that the two come from

---

63. See the Appendix of this article.

64. For such studies see the articles by Houk, "The Final Redaction of Ezekiel 10," 42–54; and Halperin, "The Exegetical Character of Ezek. X 9–17," 129–41.

65. Hölscher, *Hesekiel*, 78–79.

66. Zimmerli, "Message of the Prophet Ezekiel," 133.

67. Zimmerli, *Ezekiel* 1, 256; cf. Greenberg's critical evaluation of Zimmerli

different hands entirely. He writes: "The vision of the cherubim obviously depends on the vision of the החיות. Someone freely copied from that vision to compose what is presently chapter 10, a purposeful redactional effort."[68] Halperin sees 10:9–22 as the work of a "commentator," whose purpose was exegetical. By deliberately omitting unnecessary and confusing repetitions, paraphrasing, and expansion, he sought to make the אופנים ("wheels") of chapter 1 clear, his specific interest being angelological.[69]

It seems that there must be another way of understanding the relationship between the two accounts. It is proposed here that the key is to be found in those comments in chapter 10, which many consider to be secondary, viz., those statements that deliberately link this vision with chapter 1, i.e., verses 15b, 20, 22a. However, the comments concerning scribal techniques that were made above in relation to the glosses in chapter 1 apply here as well. These should not be dismissed too readily as secondary insertions designed to ensure cohesion for the book as a whole. Rather, the text itself seems to identify the recipient of this vision and the author of this text with the author of the first chapter. If we view the statements of identification here as authentic, this may explain the differences between the two chapters.

According to 8:1, the vision of the departure of the כבוד ("glory") of YHWH from Jerusalem (8:1—11:25), of which chapter 10 is a part, was received in the sixth year, on the fifth day of the month, i.e., in September of 592 BCE. This date is more than a year later than that given for the inaugural vision in 1:1–2, the fifth year, on the fifth day of the fourth month, i.e., July of 593.[70] This means that Ezekiel has had more than a year to reflect on the inaugural vision by the time he receives the vision of the destruction of Jerusalem. This also means that the images that came to him like a bolt out of the blue at the time of his inauguration, images that he had had extreme difficulty in describing and identifying, have now settled in his mind. A year later the experience is no longer as startling, and he is able to describe what he sees in composed and coherent fashion.

In other words, the reason why the account of the inaugural vision appears so garbled and contains so many obscurities lies in the emotional state of the recipient, who by internal data is purported to have been the

---

("Ezekiel," 1090): "The common assumption that a circle of disciple-transmitters existed who had a large part in the shaping of the present text and its disjunctures lacks any evidential basis."

68. Houk, "The Final Redaction of Ezekiel 10," 47.
69. Halperin, "Merkabah Midrash," 133–41.
70. We are here following the dates suggested by Greenberg (*Ezekiel 1-20*, 8–11).

narrator of the experience as well. This may well account for the nature of the description that, as W. A. Irwin observed, "more than once oversteps the thin line that separates the sublime from the ridiculous."[71] We all know from common experience that attempts to describe mental pictures while in a state of high excitement often come out garbled with incomplete sentences, erratic grammar, confused vocabulary, and incoherent structure. One could well imagine that a transcript of such efforts would have many similarities with our text.

Analogous Texts

Our thesis, which argues for a connection between the nature of the visionary experience and the shape of the text, would be greatly enhanced if similar occurrences, biblical or otherwise, could be adduced. The overwhelming nature of Ezekiel's inaugural vision has been seen by some to have parallels in several other accounts of prophetic calls.[72]

In 1 Kings 22:19-20, the Hebrew historian preserves an account of a visionary experience of one Micaiah ben Imlah, in which he, too, sees YHWH the king enthroned and surrounded by his heavenly entourage. However, this is no proper prophetic call-narrative. The prophet is a third party witnessing the commissioning of one of the divine king's heavenly messengers. The text is silent on the prophet's emotional response to the vision. As for the nature of the record, the text is perfectly comprehensible and clear.

The call of Isaiah (Isa 6:1-8) provides the closest parallel to Ezekiel's experience. Similarities in the narratives include: the vision of YHWH enthroned, the attendant angelic creatures, the vividness of the imagery and the amount of movement in the scene, the references to coals of fire, the notes on the responses of the respective prophets, and the reaction to those responses by YHWH. However, the accounts differ dramatically in other respects, in particular with regard to the nature of the prophets' responses. In Ezekiel's inaugural vision, the sharp contrast between divine majesty and human impotence leaves him paralyzed, requiring specific divine action to restore the prophet to full alertness. In Isaiah's experience,

---

71. Irwin, *Problem of Ezekiel*, 233.

72. Form critics distinguish between the "protested call" (e.g., Moses, Exod 3:1—4:17; Gideon, Judg 6:1-24; Jeremiah, Jer 1:4-10) and the "overwhelming call." For discussions see Zimmerli, *Ezekiel 1*, 97-100; Habel, "The Form and Significance of the Call Narratives," 297-323.

Text and Emotion

what impresses the prophet is the holiness of YHWH, which casts into such sharp relief his own and his people's sinfulness. But Isaiah remains in full control of his senses. He is impressed, but he is not physically overwhelmed. As G. B. Gray aptly stated, "Isaiah becomes a prophet owing to no physical compulsion, but by a perfectly free choice, or at least all that compels him is his sympathy with the purposes of YHWH."[73] It could therefore be argued that, although the prophets' emotional states differ after having witnessed YHWH on his throne, in each instance the shape of the text is in keeping with the experience.

These differences in response are mirrored in the nature of the narratives. Where the description of Ezekiel's call is beset with grammatical and textual difficulties, that of Isaiah is virtually problem-free;[74] where the former is cast in a convoluted, cumbersome prose, the latter is characterized by a lofty poetic grandeur; where the former is weighted down with wordiness and repetition, the latter displays extreme verbal economy; where the former can speak only periphrastically by analogy, the latter is direct. In short, the call of Isaiah is described in an exalted style quite appropriate for so sublime an experience.[75]

Zimmerli has also pointed to the call of Saul/Paul as an example in which the commissioning of the person is connected with a vision of the divine glory (Acts 9:1–9; 22:4–8; 26:12–18).[76] Like Ezekiel, Paul falls to the ground at the sight of the exalted Christ. However, since the experience is recorded by a third party in Acts 9, and Paul has had years to reflect upon the event by Acts 22 and 26, one would not expect irregularities in the text like those found in Ezekiel 1.

Decades ago, R. H. Charles recognized and discussed the irregularities in the text of the Revelation of John.[77] It might be argued that this type of language is determined by the literary genre of the text, i.e., apocalyptic writings have a tendency to become stylistically erratic. Could it not also be suggested that the genre of the experience, rather than the genre of its transcription, determines the nature of the text? As in the case of Ezekiel's vision of the divine majesty, so in the vision of the glorious "one like a son of man," the recipient is left stunned (1:17).[78] Like Ezekiel's vision,

---

73. Gray, *Isaiah I–XXVII*, 109.

74. The apparatus of *BHS* does not have a single note on this text.

75. See von Rad, *Old Testament Theology*, 2:64.

76. Zimmerli, *Ezekiel 1*, 100.

77. Charles, *The Revelation of St. John*, 1:cxvii–clix.

78. On the thematic and literary connections between Ezekiel and Revelation, see Vanhoye, "L'utilisation du livre d'Ezéchiel," 436–76.

this apocalyptic message is also cast in autobiographical form. Perhaps, therefore, the emotional impact of the experience itself may have left its mark on the shape of the text.

Several additional texts, which do not involve inaugural visions, but which nonetheless indicate the effect of divine revelations upon the recipient, might be noted. According to Daniel 8:27, the visionary experience had left Daniel sick for days; and, even after he was going about his business once more, he remained appalled and perplexed. Even more instructive is Daniel 10:7-9:

> And I, Daniel, alone saw the vision, for the men who were with me did not see the vision, but a great trembling fell upon them, and they fled to hide themselves. So I was left alone and saw this great vision, and no strength was left in me; my radiant appearance was fearfully changed, and I retained no strength. Then I heard the sound of his words; and when I heard the sound of his words, I fell on my face in a deep sleep with my face to the ground. (*RSV*)

Like Ezekiel, Daniel requires the divine touch to be set on his feet again.

No text provides a picture of the agitated and tormented state of a prophet after receiving a divine revelation as transparently as Isaiah 21:1-10. In verses 3-4 the prophet declares:

> Therefore my loins are filled with anguish;
> pangs have seized me,
> like the pangs of a woman in travail; I am bowed down so that
> I cannot hear,
> I am dismayed so that I cannot see.
> My mind reels, horror has appalled me;
> the twilight I longed for
> has been turned for me into trembling. (*RSV*)

The expression עַל־כֵּן, with which the description of the prophet's disturbed state of mind begins, ties it directly to the preceding oracle. Is it not possible that this agitation may have left its mark on the text of the oracle, which poses a host of problems and which A. Bruno describes as "ganz verworren."[79]

Finally, reference may be made to Habakkuk 3. This psalm of Habakkuk represents a closer parallel to Ezekiel 1 than does Isaiah 21:1-10

---

79. Bruno, *Jesaja*, 284. For a survey of many of the exegetical problems raised by the text, see Kaiser, *Isaiah 13-39*, 121. For recent textual studies of the oracle, see Erlandsson, *The Burden of Babylon*, 81-85; Macintosh, *Isaiah xxi*.

inasmuch as it involves an actual majestic theophany. The psalm concludes by providing the reader with another remarkable window into the emotions of the prophet:

> I hear, and my body trembles,
> my lips quiver at the sound;
> rottenness enters into my bones,
> my steps totter beneath me. (3:16, RSV)

Quite apart from questions of the relationship of this psalm to the rest of the book, the exegetical and textual problems are legion.[80] While several gallant attempts have been made recently to reconstruct the poem and to make sense out of it,[81] a connection between the prophet's emotional condition and the shape of the text has not yet been proposed. Although to suggest such a connection does not render the text any more intelligible, it may help to account for some of the difficulties it poses.

Extra-biblical support for our thesis is difficult to produce for lack of true parallels to the visionary call experience of Ezekiel. Divine revelations are well attested, especially in the eighteenth-century BCE Mari letters.[82] In these letters, rather than the divine messages being given directly to the intended addressee, they pass through four stages:

$$\text{Divinity} \rightarrow \text{Prophet} \rightarrow \text{Governor} \rightarrow \text{King (Zimri-Lim)}$$

However, no hint of the emotional response of the prophet[83] to the revelation received is given. One of the letters serves notice of the recipient prostrating himself before the deity.[84] But this genuflection precedes the revelation; it is not the response. In any case, even if the prophets' reports of the revelations are quoted verbatim, since they are committed to writing

---

80. See the plethora of notes in *BHS*.

81. See Albright, "Psalm of Habakkuk," 1–18; Mowinckel, "Zum Psalm des Habakkuk," 1–23; Eaton, "The Origin and Meaning of Habakkuk 3," 144–71; Margulis, "The Psalm of Habakkuk," 409–42.

82. *ANET*, 623–25.

83. The prophetic officials are variously identified as *āpilu muḫḫtu*, or *assinu* (in the case of females). For discussions of these terms, see Huffmon, "Prophecy in the Mari Letters," 199–224; Huffmon, "Prophecy in the Ancient Near East," 698; Malamat, "Mari Prophecy," 76–78. For additional studies of prophecy in Mari, see Malamat, "Prophetic Revelations," 207–27; Moran, "New Evidence," 15–56; Ringgren, "Prophecy in the Ancient Near East," 1–11.

84. *ANET*, 623, letter a.

by a third party (the governor), one would not expect the emotions that attended the revelatory event to be preserved in the written account.

Much nearer to Ezekiel chronologically are several interesting neo-Assyrian oracle reports deriving from the times of Esarhaddon and Ashurbanipal.[85] In these oracles there is no reference to a prophetic intermediary; the god/goddess speaks directly to the king. In each instance the divinity commences his/her address with "Fear not!"[86] It is possible that the oracles are intended to provide reassurance for the respective kings with a positive word concerning the near future. However, it seems more likely that these words are a response to the agitated state of the recipient's mind at being addressed by the deity and are uttered to calm him. Beyond this, the accounts leave no indication of the emotional state of the recipient.

Unfortunately, none of the examples cited, biblical or otherwise, provides a clear parallel to the experience of Ezekiel or the record of the experience. However, Isaiah's vision and the Revelation of John may yet hint at some connection between the nature of the event and the shape of the text. Nevertheless, although true parallels would be desirable to make our thesis more convincing, their absence should not prevent us from considering seriously the evidence of a single witness.

The major problem facing this interpretation is the lack of information concerning the circumstances of the transcription of Ezekiel's experience. There is no compelling reason for doubting the account as genuinely autobiographical.[87] The *terminus ad quem* for the transcription of the inaugural vision would be the recording, if not the vision itself, of the reappearance of the theophany in chapter 10. This would mean that no more than one year separated event and text. However, the greater the distance between event and text, the greater would be the likelihood for the smoothing out of the account. Our interpretation assumes that the emotion accompanying the theophany was present also at the time of recording. This would suggest that the prophet put his experience to writing almost immediately after he had had his inaugural vision.

From other prophetic texts we learn that the recording of prophetic messages as soon as they were received was a common practice. In Isaiah 8:1, Isaiah is commanded to write down his cryptic message. Isaiah 8:16–18 implies the preservation of written prophetic transcripts of some

---

85. *ANET*, 449–51.
86. See Ringgren, "Prophecy," 5–8.
87. See Greenberg ("Ezekiel," 1091), who finds in the book no post-571 BCE anachronism that requires a hand other than Ezekiel's.

type, apparently in the hands of disciples. In 30:8, the prophet is instructed to record his oracle so that, in the absence of response by the people to the message, the written word may stand as a witness to the prophetic nature of the oracle. Habakkuk is commanded by YHWH in 2:2 to record the vision of judgment so that the messenger may have written documentation of the authority and certainty of the oracle. Nahum, in 1:1, speaks of a "book of the vision" (ספר חזון).

Jeremiah, Ezekiel's contemporary, provides the most information on the nature of the transcription of prophetic materials. In 22:30, the prophet is to "write this man [Jehoiachin] down as childless." Jeremiah 25:13 speaks of Jeremiah's oracles against the nations being written down "in this book." In 30:2, he is instructed to commit to writing all the words that YHWH had spoken to him. The events described in chapter 36 indicate that the prophetic message was so imprinted on the prophet's mind that it could be recalled, not only once, but twice, many years later. Jeremiah 45:1 provides the fullest statement of how this transcription was achieved. Jeremiah dictated the words to his trusted scribe Baruch ben Neraiah, who recorded them in a book. Admittedly, these examples do not demonstrate an immediate recording of a message, but they do affirm the prophet's involvement in the process.

This chronological proximity of the reception of a divine revelation to the commitment of the vision to writing has a clear analogy in the NT, viz., the Revelation of John. The recipient of this vision represents the nearest NT counterpart to the OT prophet. According to 1:19, he too is commanded to commit the revelation to writing. The conclusion to the book confirms the fulfillment of this command.

Ample extra-biblical evidence may be cited to demonstrate the recording of visions soon after their reception. The revelations described in the Mari letters cited above are reported to have been committed to writing by the respective governors prior to being transmitted to the king. Since the revelations concern immediate crises, there is no reason to doubt that they were written down immediately.[88] Several Neo-Assyrian oracles (for Esarhaddon and Ashurbanipal) summarize the occasions by referring sequentially to the crisis, the complaint, the divine message of reassurance, the deposit of the written oracle, and the presentation of the written oracle to the king.[89]

---

88. See *ANET*, 623–25.

89. See S. A. Strong, "Some Oracles," 625–45; Streck, *Assurbanipal*, 2:32–33, 112–19, 343–51. A relevant part of one of Esarhaddon's oracles is reproduced by Huffmon, "Prophecy in the Ancient Near East," 700.

By the River Chebar

Ezekiel himself, on two occasions, is said to have produced written copies of his message for the sake of the public. The message is cryptic, but in 37:16–20 he is instructed to write down his messages on two "writing boards" (עֵצִים).[90] In 43:10–12, he is commanded to record the plan of the temple.

But these messages are all different from the inaugural vision under discussion. They are intended for the public, or at least for a third party, whereas the theophany described in chapter 1 was an intensely private affair. What would motivate its transcription can only be speculated upon. It is predicted at the time of the call of Ezekiel that his message would fall on stone-deaf ears (2:4–7; 3:6–11). The absence of an immediate recognition of his prophetic authority may have made it important for him to transcribe the vision. His moments of doubt could be answered by the presence of a written account of his original call.

On the other hand, the extraordinary nature of the experience of this man far away in Babylon, receiving a vision of the living God still seated on his throne in all his splendor and power (in spite of all appearances to the contrary), was justification enough for the preservation of the moment in written form. But this was a heavenly vision, a rare glimpse of eternal realities afforded to a mortal on alien soil. No human language was sufficient to capture the scene. Nor could it be captured without the excitement of the moment leaving its indelible mark on the shape of the written record itself. An encounter with the living God must be a moving experience.

---

90. So interpreted by Driver, *Semitic Writing*, 76.

EXCURSUS B

Ezekiel 1:6, 8–10, 15–21, and 10:9–22 in Parallel

Ezekiel 10:9–22		Ezekiel 1:6, 8–10, 15–21	
וָאֶרְאֶה וְהִנֵּה	10:9	וָאֵרֶא הַחַיּוֹת וְהִנֵּה אוֹפַן אֶחָד בָּאָרֶץ	1:15
אַרְבָּעָה אוֹפַנִּים אֵצֶל הַכְּרוּבִים		אֵצֶל הַחַיּוֹת לְאַרְבַּעַת פָּנָיו:	
אוֹפַן אֶחָד אֵצֶל הַכְּרוּב אֶחָד וְאוֹפַן אֶחָד אֵצֶל הַכְּרוּב אֶחָד וּמַרְאֵה הָאוֹפַנִּים		מַרְאֵה הָאוֹפַנִּים וּמַעֲשֵׂיהֶם כְּעֵין תַּרְשִׁישׁ	1:16
כְּעֵין אֶבֶן תַּרְשִׁישׁ: וּמַרְאֵיהֶם דְּמוּת אֶחָד לְאַרְבַּעְתָּם	10:10	וּדְמוּת אֶחָד לְאַרְבַּעְתָּן וּמַרְאֵיהֶם וּמַעֲשֵׂיהֶם	
כַּאֲשֶׁר יִהְיֶה הָאוֹפַן בְּתוֹךְ הָאוֹפָן:	10:11	כַּאֲשֶׁר יִהְיֶה הָאוֹפַן בְּתוֹךְ הָאוֹפָן:	
בְּלֶכְתָּם אֶל־אַרְבַּעַת רִבְעֵיהֶם יֵלֵכוּ לֹא יִסַּבּוּ בְּלֶכְתָּם כִּי הַמָּקוֹם אֲשֶׁר־יִפְנֶה הָרֹאשׁ אַחֲרָיו יֵלֵכוּ לֹא יִסַּבּוּ בְּלֶכְתָּם:		עַל־אַרְבַּעַת רִבְעֵיהֶן בְּלֶכְתָּם יֵלֵכוּ לֹא יִסַּבּוּ בְּלֶכְתָּן:	1:17
וְכָל־בְּשָׂרָם וְגַבֵּהֶם וִידֵיהֶם וְכַנְפֵיהֶם וְהָאוֹפַנִּים מְלֵאִים עֵינַיִם סָבִיב לְאַרְבַּעְתָּם אוֹפַנֵּיהֶם:	10:12	וְגַבֵּיהֶן וְגֹבַהּ לָהֶם וְיִרְאָה לָהֶם וְגַבֹּתָם מְלֵאֹת עֵינַיִם סָבִיב לְאַרְבַּעְתָּן:	1:18

By the River Chebar

Ezekiel 10:9–22		Ezekiel 1:6, 8–10, 15–21	
לָאוֹפַנִּים לָהֶם קוֹרָא הַגַּלְגַּל בְּאָזְנָי:	10:13		
וְאַרְבָּעָה פָנִים לְאֶחָד פְּנֵי הָאֶחָד פְּנֵי הַכְּרוּב	10:14	וְאַרְבָּעָה פָנִים לְאֶחָת וְאַרְבַּע כְּנָפַיִם לְאַחַת לָהֶם:	1:6
וּפְנֵי הַשֵּׁנִי פְּנֵי אָדָם		וּדְמוּת פְּנֵיהֶם פְּנֵי אָדָם	1:10
וְהַשְּׁלִישִׁי פְּנֵי אַרְיֵה		וּפְנֵי אַרְיֵה אֶל־הַיָּמִין לְאַרְבַּעְתָּם	
וְהָרְבִיעִי פְּנֵי־נָשֶׁר:		וּפְנֵי־שׁוֹר מֵהַשְּׂמֹאול לְאַרְבַּעְתָּן	
וַיֵּרֹמּוּ הַכְּרוּבִים הִיא הַחַיָּה אֲשֶׁר רָאִיתִי בִּנְהַר־כְּבָר:	10:15	וּפְנֵי־נֶשֶׁר לְאַרְבַּעְתָּן:	
וּבְלֶכֶת הַכְּרוּבִים יֵלְכוּ הָאוֹפַנִּים אֶצְלָם וּבִשְׂאֵת הַכְּרוּבִים אֶת־כַּנְפֵיהֶם לָרוּם מֵעַל הָאָרֶץ לֹא־יִסַּבּוּ הָאוֹפַנִּים גַּם־הֵם מֵאֶצְלָם:	10:16	וּבְלֶכֶת הַחַיּוֹת יֵלְכוּ הָאוֹפַנִּים אֶצְלָם וּבְהִנָּשֵׂא הַחַיּוֹת	1:19

Text and Emotion

Ezekiel 10:9–22		Ezekiel 1:6, 8–10, 15–21	
		מֵעַל הָאָרֶץ	
		יִנָּשְׂאוּ הָאוֹפַנִּים:	
		עַל אֲשֶׁר יִהְיֶה־שָּׁם	1:20
		הָרוּחַ לָלֶכֶת	
		יֵלֵכוּ	
		שָׁמָּה הָרוּחַ לָלֶכֶת	
		וְהָאוֹפַנִּים יִנָּשְׂאוּ	
		לְעֻמָּתָם	
בְּעָמְדָם יַעֲמֹדוּ	10:17	כִּי רוּחַ הַחַיָּה	
וּבְרוֹמָם		בָּאוֹפַנִּים:	
יֵרוֹמּוּ		בְּלֶכְתָּם יֵלֵכוּ	1:21
אוֹתָם		וּבְעָמְדָם יַעֲמֹדוּ	
כִּי רוּחַ הַחַיָּה		וּבְהִנָּשְׂאָם מֵעַל הָאָרֶץ	
בָּהֶם:		יִנָּשְׂאוּ הָאוֹפַנִּים	
וַיֵּצֵא כְּבוֹד יְהוָה	10:18	לְעֻמָּתָם	
מֵעַל מִפְתַּן הַבָּיִת		כִּי רוּחַ הַחַיָּה	
וַיַּעֲמֹד		בָּאוֹפַנִּים:	
עַל־הַכְּרוּבִים:			
וַיִּשְׂאוּ הַכְּרוּבִים	10:19		
אֶת־כַּנְפֵיהֶם			
וַיֵּרוֹמּוּ			
מִן־הָאָרֶץ			
לְעֵינַי			
בְּצֵאתָם			
וְהָאוֹפַנִּים לְעֻמָּתָם			
וַיַּעֲמֹד			
פֶּתַח שַׁעַר בֵּית־יְהוָה			
הַקַּדְמוֹנִי			
וּכְבוֹד אֱלֹהֵי־יִשְׂרָאֵל			
עֲלֵיהֶם			
מִלְמָעְלָה:			
הִיא הַחַיָּה	10:20		
אֲשֶׁר רָאִיתִי			
תַּחַת אֱלֹהֵי־יִשְׂרָאֵל			
בִּנְהַר־כְּבָר			
וָאֵדַע			
כִּי כְרוּבִים הֵמָּה:			
אַרְבָּעָה	10:21		
אַרְבָּעָה			
פָּנִים לְאֶחָד			

225

By the River Chebar

Ezekiel 10:9-22		Ezekiel 1:6, 8-10, 15-21	
וְאַרְבַּע כְּנָפַיִם לְאֶחָד		וְאַרְבָּעָה	1:6
		פָּנִים לְאֶחָת	
וּדְמוּת יְדֵי אָדָם		וְאַרְבַּע כְּנָפַיִם לְאַחַת	
תַּחַת כַּנְפֵיהֶם:		לָהֶם: (*sic*; read וִידֵי with Qere)	
וּדְמוּת פְּנֵיהֶם	10:22	וִידֵו אָדָם	1:8
הֵמָּה הַפָּנִים		מִתַּחַת כַּנְפֵיהֶם	
אֲשֶׁר רָאִיתִי		עַל אַרְבַּעַת רִבְעֵיהֶם	
עַל־נְהַר־כְּבָר		וּפְנֵיהֶם	
מַרְאֵיהֶם			
וְאוֹתָם		וְכַנְפֵיהֶם	
		לְאַרְבַּעְתָּם:	
		חֹבְרֹת אִשָּׁה	1:9
		אֶל־אֲחוֹתָהּ כַּנְפֵיהֶם	
		לֹא־יִסַּבּוּ	
		בְלֶכְתָּן	
אִישׁ אֶל־עֵבֶר פָּנָיו		אִישׁ אֶל־עֵבֶר פָּנָיו	
יֵלֵכוּ:		יֵלֵכוּ:	

9

Ezekiel's Boiling Cauldron

A Form-Critical Solution to Ezekiel 24:1–14[1]

Introduction

SINCE THE APPEARANCE OF Claus Westermann's work on the basic forms of prophetic speech more than two decades ago,[2] form-critical considerations have become an indispensable part of the study of Old Testament prophecy. Although one type of prophetic utterance, the disputation speech, received brief mention in this volume,[3] in another work he questioned the existence of such a genre because of the lack of a clear common structure.[4] This skepticism has been challenged recently by Adrian Graffy, who claims that the reason for the apparent lack of structure is created by an imprecise definition of the genre. Once it is realized that "The name

---

1. This essay was originally published in *Vetus Testamentum* 41 (1991) 12–37. This is a revision of a paper presented to the Society of Biblical Literature in Chicago, November, 1988. Appreciation is expressed to Kelvin Friebel of the University of Michigan, my colleague Gary V. Smith, and Marvin A. Sweeney of the University of Miami, for their helpful comments on earlier drafts of the paper.

2. Westermann, *Grundformen prophetischer Rede* (English, *Basic Forms of Prophetic Speech*).

3. Ibid., 144–45; English translation, 201.

4. Westermann, "Sprache und Struktur," 124–34.

'disputation speech' can worthily be given to those texts where an opinion of the speakers is explicitly reported by the prophet and refuted by him,"[5] a clear pattern emerges. He finds that the texts of this genre typically consist of an introductory quotation of a popular saying, followed by a deliberately constructed refutation. In some instances the latter bifurcates into a double refutation; occasionally a programmatic refutation precedes a rejoinder and reply.[6]

Some have found Graffy's definition of a disputation speech too restrictive. In the most recent essay on the subject, D. F. Murray argues that Graffy's perspective reflects a fundamental misunderstanding of the nature of disputation in general.[7] What is determinative for the disputation genre is not the quotation-refutation rhetorical surface structure (though these elements will naturally frequently be present), but the tripartite logical deep structure involving thesis, counter-thesis, dispute (not necessarily in this order). He recognizes that the opponent's position need not be quoted verbatim; it may be inferred from other devices used by the disputant.

Naturally, if a disputation speech is defined as one that opens with some comment like "Do you hear what they are saying?" followed by a direct quotation, which in turn is succeeded by the refutation, the field of potential candidates from the Old Testament prophets is limited. But our preoccupation with the opening signal may have prevented us from recognizing oracles that function similarly but appear unannounced. D. J. McCarthy has rightly distinguished a genre from a schema with his observation that "A genre may use formulae, but it need not. It can be made up of elements, that is, parts which regularly enter into its composition though not expressed in a fixed set of words."[8] J. S. Ackerman criticizes W. Richter for overlooking Deborah's commissioning of Barak in his examination of pre-prophetic call narratives "because his methodology demands that a given set of formulae appear before a passage can be said to contain a 'schema.'"[9] Graffy and others may have made the same mistake in their identification of "disputation speeches."

5. Graffy, *A Prophet Confronts His People*, 23.

6. Cf. ibid., 107–18, for a discussion of the parts of the disputation speech.

7. Murray, "The Rhetoric of Disputation," 95–121, particularly pp. 96–99, for his response to Graffy and his own theoretical position. There is no need to mention the numerous other studies that have appeared on the subject of disputation speeches. The reader is referred to the bibliographies provided by Murray and Graffy.

8. McCarthy, "An Installation Genre?," 31.

9. J. S. Ackerman, "Prophecy and Warfare," 7. Cf. Richter, *Die sogenannten vorprophetischen Berufungsberichte*, 142–43.

Ezekiel's Boiling Cauldron

It will be proposed in this article that in Ezekiel 24:1–14 we are faced with one such unannounced disputation address. This oracle of the boiling cauldron remains one of many in Ezekiel that continue to defy clear understanding. The preserved record presents the interpreter with problems at every level: textual, grammatical, lexical, formal, theological. Not surprisingly, the solutions offered vary greatly and generally depend upon the hermeneutical stance of the commentator. It will be suggested here that, when the disputational nature of the prophecy is recognized, some of the perplexing interpretative problems are resolved. Specifically, by looking at the passage from this perspective we may have stumbled upon the solution to one of the key cruxes, the enigmatic חֶלְאָה, commonly interpreted as "rust."

The investigation will consist of three parts: (1) an examination of the unity and style of the account; (2) a discussion of its form and structure; (3) a summary interpretation.

The Unity and Style of Ezekiel 24:1–14

The borders of the major textual unit comprising 24:1–27 are clearly defined. It opens with the word event formula, וַיְהִי דְבַר־יְהוָה אֵלַי לֵאמֹר, "And the word of YHWH came to me as follows," followed by a date notice (v. 1), and concludes with the recognition formula וְיָדְעוּ כִּי־אֲנִי יְהוָה, "and they will know that I am YHWH," in verse 27, which in turn is followed by a new word-event formula in 24:1. However, this apparent unity is purely literary. The text subdivides into two halves, almost equal in length, verses 1–14 and 15–27. This division is indicated formally by the presence in verse 14 of the common Ezekielian formula, אֲנִי יְהוָה דִּבַּרְתִּי, "I am YHWH; I have spoken," and the concluding signatory formula, נְאֻם אֲדֹנָי יְהוִה, "the declaration of the Lord YHWH," followed by a new word-event formula in verse 15. This demarcation is confirmed by the nature and style of the two segments. Verses 1–14 consist of a formal oracle, an extended מָשָׁל (metaphor), and verses 15–27 revolve around a sign-act. Both were delivered immediately prior to the fall of Jerusalem. In fact, they could both have been presented on the same day, in which case the date notice in verse 1 would apply to the entire chapter.

Scholars have tended to view the oracle proper in 24:3b–14 as a conflation of two separate oracles, consisting of the cooking song and its interpretation (vv. 3b–5, 9–10), and the figure of the corroded pot (vv.

6–8, 11–14), respectively.[10] Most recently, Hans F. Fuhs[11] has argued that stylistically and kerygmatically verses 1, 3–5, 10b form a closed unit that possesses its own word-event formula, charge to the messenger, and messenger formula, followed by an adaptation of a popular work song and its interpretation. It therefore represents a *bona fide* משל (*māšāl*). This oracle may be reconstructed as follows:

1	(ויהי דבר יהוה אלי . . . לאמר)	(Now the word of YHWH came to me saying?)
	ו)משל אל בית המרי משל)	Utter a parable to the rebellious house,
3	ו)אמרת אליהם)	And say to them:
	כה אמר אדני יהוה	Thus has the Lord YHWH declared:
	שפת הסיר שפת	Put on the cauldron, put it on.
	וגם יצק בו מים	And pour in the water as well.
4	אסף נתחי(ם) אליה	Put into it the pieces of meat—
	כל נתח טוב ירך וכתף	every good piece, thigh and shoulder.
	מבחר עצמים מלא	Fill it with choice bones.
5	מבחר הצאן לקוח	Take the choicest one of the flock.
	וגם דור (העצמים) (מ)תחתיה	Also pile the logs under it.
	רתח (נת)חיה	Boil its pieces
	גם (בשל) עצמיה בתוכה	Also see the bones in it.
	א)תם הבשר)	I am boiling the flesh well,
10b	ו)הרקח המרקח)	Cooking up the broth
	והעצמות יחרו	So that the bones are burned up.

A second figure concerns the rusty cauldron, also with its own messenger formula in verse 6a, which is followed by the announcement of woe, and ended by the concluding formula in verse 14a. The basic text of this oracle is reconstructed as follows:

---

10. Cf. Wevers, *Ezekiel*, 188–92; Freedy, "Glosses in Ezekiel *i–xxiv*," 139, n. 2; Zimmerli, *Ezekiel 1*, 496–501.

11. Fuhs, "Ez 24: Überlegungen zu Tradition," 266–82.

6	כה אמר אדני יהוה	Thus has the Lord YHWH declared:
	אוי סיר אשר חלאתה בה	Woe, O Cauldron, on which rust is found!
9b	אני אגדיל המדורה	I will make the pyre large.
10a	הרבה העצים	Pile on the logs,
	הדלק האש	Kindle the fire,
11	והעמידה על־גחליה	And set it upon its coals,
	למען תחם	To heat it up,
	וחרה נחשתה	And make its copper glow,
	ונתכה בתוכה טמאתה	And melt away its filthiness inside it;
	תתם חלאתה	And remove its rust.
12	ולא תצא ממנה רבת חלאתה	But its abundance of rust will not depart.
13	בטמאתך זמה	On account of your lewd filthiness…
	יען טהרתיך עוד	You shall never be cleansed again,
	עד הניחי את חמתי בך	Until I have satisfied my fury against you
	אני יהוה דברתי	I, YHWH, have spoken,
14a	ועשיתי	And I will carry it out.

The omitted segments, particularly the allusions to the blood-guilt of Jerusalem (vv. 6, 7–8, 9a), and fragments of varying lengths in verses 12–14, are deleted as secondary. Fuhs maintains that both oracles serve as announcements of judgment, undoubtedly derived from before 587 BCE, probably even from Ezekiel himself.[12]

In response it must be admitted that it is possible that the prophet issued two separate oracles, involving the work song and the woe against the cauldron respectively. However, as Allen has demonstrated, in its present form the text exhibits numerous indications of coherence that cut across these divisions.[13] The passage is framed by a punning *inclusio* involving שְׁפֹת … שְׁפֹת, "set on [the cauldron], set on," and שְׁפָטַיךְ, "I will judge you."[14] Effective use is made of repetition, particularly the messenger formula (vv. 3, 6, 9), which resounds like drum beats of inescapable doom. The two-fold "Woe to the bloody city!" keeps the audience's or reader's attention focused on the fundamental causes of Jerusalem's demise. To postulate a secondary *Wiederaufnahme* for verse 9a, as some have

---

12. Ibid., 271, 273.

13. Allen, "Ezekiel 24:3–14," 404–14.

14. Following the versions and many manuscripts instead of the MT שפטוך. It seems unlikely that the versions have altered the text to harmonize with 11:10, 11. Only in 23:24 and 45 is someone other than YHWH or the prophet the subject of the verb שָׁפַט. More serious is the absence of any plural antecedent in this text that might serve as the subject. The first person is much more appropriate after אֲנִי יְהוָה in the opening line of the verse. Cf. 7:3, 8; 16:38; 36:19, etc. The MT may be explained as an erroneous copying of a *waw* for a *yodh*.

done,[15] destroys this rhetorical effect. Verse 6 should not be divorced from verses 7–8, since the latter verses not only expand on the bloodstains of Jerusalem; they also provide an explanation of the corruption introduced in verse 6. Similarly, verses 9–13 are to be interpreted as a unit. These verses describe the second stage of the judgment of the city. The first half (vv. 9–10) emphasizes YHWH's direct involvement, and the second half (vv. 11–13) his motivation. These halves are also tied together by common vocabulary (הַרְבֵּה/רַבַּת, "abundance," אֵשׁ, "fire") and assonance (וחרה/יחרו, רקה/והרקח, תתם/התם).

In addition to these internal connections, by reintroducing many of the themes that have been dealt with in earlier oracles, the prophet's messages of judgment are brought to a fitting climax. Familiar from previous prophecies are: the rebellious house (בֵּית־הַמֶּרִי),[16] Jerusalem as the bloody city (עִיר הַדָּמִים),[17] her uncleanness (טֻמְאָה),[18] and need of cleansing (טָהֵר),[19] her lewdness (זִמָּה),[20] burning coals of judgment (גֶּחָלֶת),[21] smelting/pouring out (נָתַךְ)[22] YHWH's wrath (חֵמָה),[23] the refusal to show pity (לֹא־אָחוּס and לֹא אֶנָּחֵם).[24] Even the charge to the prophet, מְשֹׁל ... מָשָׁל, "Issue a literary figure" (v. 3), recalls 17:2. The command in the preamble to record the message הַיּוֹם הַזֶּה, "this day," emphasizes explicitly that what follows represents the fulfillment and culmination of the prophecies of judgment preserved in chapters 4–23.

The unity of 24:3b–14 may also be defended on form-critical grounds, a subject we now address in greater detail.

Form and Structure

Inadequate attention has been given to the form of this unit as a literary whole. Fohrer interpreted the passage as a report of a symbolic action and

---

15. Fuhs, "Ez 24: Überlegungen zu Tradition," 268, following Lang, "A Neglected Method in Ezekiel Research," 39–40.
16. V. 3; cf. 2:3, 6, 8.
17. Vv. 6, 9; cf. 22:2, 3, 27.
18. Vv. 11, 13; cf. 22:15.
19. V. 13 (3x); cf. 22:24.
20. V. 13; cf. 16:27, 43, 58; 22:9, 11; 23:21, 27, 29, 35, 44, 48a, 48b, 49.
21. V. 11; cf. 1:13; 10:2.
22. V. 11; cf. 22:21.
23. V. 8; cf. v. 13 and an additional 27 times in Ezekiel.
24. V. 14; cf. v. 11; 8:18; 9:10.

its explanation,[25] but this seems forced, and not many have followed suit. Because the introduction fails to state specifically that a popular quotation is involved in the oracle, the disputational qualities of this prophecy have been overlooked. However, the moment this possibility is suggested, features shared with other disputation addresses become apparent.

First, like many disputation speeches, the opening lines, which appear to reflect popular opinion, have a metaphorical quality. From the relatively small sample of Graffy's narrowly defined disputation speeches found in the Old Testament,[26] the quotation that is to be refuted often had a parable-like (מָשָׁל) quality. Twice in Ezekiel a quotation is formally introduced as a מָשָׁל (12:22; 18:2), and on at least two other occasions the quotation sounds like a מָשָׁל even if it is not identified as such (11:3; 37:11b; perhaps also 33:24). Although Jeremiah does not announce it as a proverb, one of his three disputation addresses opens with what is known from Ezekiel 18:2 to have been a widely circulated proverb (Jer 31:29). The only certain speech of this type in Isaiah (28:14–19) opens with a מָשָׁל-like metaphor:

> We have made a covenant with Death,
> And with Sheol we have made a pact.

In fact, those who are charged with circulating this comment are identified as אַנְשֵׁי לָצוֹן מֹשְׁלֵי הָעָם הַזֶּה, which may be rendered, "scoffers, composers of taunt verses for this people."[27] Although מֹשְׁלִים may be translated as "rulers," לָצוֹן, from ליץ, "to scoff," suggests strong wisdom influence.[28] It is perhaps in the nature of the case that the types of comments that appeal to the people, circulate widely, and catch the prophet's ear, should have a picturesque quality.

This is certainly the case with our text. In fact, this one is identified as a מָשָׁל. According to most interpretations, in verse 3 YHWH commands the prophet to speak a parable to the rebellious house. However, one wonders if מְשֹׁל אֶל־בֵּית־הַמֶּרִי מָשָׁל, should not be rendered, "Quote a proverb to the rebellious house." To be sure, the same idiom occurs in 17:2, but there its meaning is determined by the preceding parallel command, חוּד חִידָה,

---

25. Fohrer, *Ezechiel*, 138–40.
26. Graffy, *A Prophet Confronts His People*, 21–23.
27. *NJPSV*, note.
28. Cf. Wildberger, *Jesaja*, 1064, 1072; Kaiser, *Der Prophet Jesaja* 13–39, 197, "Ihr Sprüchemacher" (English trans. *Isaiah 13–39*, 248, 250–51), "proverb-makers"; Watts, *Isaiah 1–33*, 365–66, 369, "speech-makers." W. H. Irwin's "reigning wits" (*Isaiah 28–33*, 25), combines the two meanings of מָשָׁל, "ruler," and "wit."

"Propound a riddle." Although the eagle and vine motifs developed in the parable that follows there have antecedents elsewhere, few would deny that the core of that text at least is authentically Ezekielian, and that the poem gives evidence of his own literary genius. Even as radical a scholar as G. Hölscher, who credits the prophet with fewer than 170 of the 1,273 verses, allowed the prophet most of 17:1–9.[29]

But the poem preserved in 24:3b–5 is quite different. To be sure, the verse is presented as the words of YHWH, but its secular tone gives it the ring of a popular work-song (*Arbeitslied*), such as would be sung in houses throughout Israel while performing routine household chores,[30] analogous to "Polly Put the Kettle On."[31] Comparable well-digging (Num 21:17–18) and vintage (Judg 9:27; 21:21; Isa 16:10; cf. 9:2) songs have been proposed.[32] However, the fact that this one is identified as a מָשָׁל suggests that the residents of Jerusalem may have been using it as a figure of speech as well.

Second, the classification of this oracle as a disputation speech is not excluded by any of the disclaimers that Graffy suggests rule out this genre.[33]

1. The popular saying is quoted to be refuted, not to illustrate guilt. Spiritually and theologically the parable of the boiling cauldron is neutral, and the nearest accusatory element is the reference to the addressees as בֵּית־הַמֶּרִי, "the rebellious house." Some would see the prophet to be responding to this quality,[34] but the distance between verses 3 and 6 renders this position unlikely.

2. If verses 3b–5 preserve a popular work song, this qualifies them as an actual quotation, not simply an implied opinion.

3. The oracle has a pronounced argumentative tone, but it cannot be classified as a normal judgment speech, or woe oracle, etc.

4. The refutation clearly answers the quotation. The two dominant motifs in the song are the pot and the piled up wood for the fire. The rebuttals occur in this order, with the first paying special attention to the pot and its contents, and the second to the wood and the fire. In fact the refutations themselves scarcely leave the figure.

29. Hölscher, *Hesekiel*, 97–102.
30. So van den Born, *Ezechiël*, 154.
31. Suggested by Taylor, *Ezekiel*, 178.
32. Eissfeldt, *The Old Testament: An Introduction*, 88–89.
33. *A Prophet Confronts His People*, 22–23.
34. Allen, "Ezekiel 24:3–14," 406.

5. The text does not reflect any dialogic interchange. YHWH (through his messenger) alone speaks.
6. The interchange is provoked by the people's comments, not YHWH's, as in Malachi. The aim is not to clarify points introduced in the beginning, but to dispute their opinions.
7. Although the refutations open with אוֹי, "Woe!," this "woe" does not determine the structure or style.
8. The opening and concluding formulae confirm this oracle as a self-contained unit, rather than part of a larger speech.

Third, in spite of the absence of a formal identification of a quotation to be rebutted, the text displays all of the structural and stylistic features which Graffy has observed to be characteristic of disputation oracles.[35] According to his scheme, the oracle divides structurally as follows:

Introduction	(1–3a)
The Popular Saying	(3b–5)
The Refutation	(6–13)
The First Rejoinder	(6–8)
The Second Rejoinder	(9–13)
Conclusion	(14)

Once verses 3b–5 have been identified as a מָשָׁל that is being widely quoted among the people, the refutational style of verses 6–13 becomes apparent. In fact, the rejoinders display close formal links with the rebuttals found in disputation addresses found elsewhere in Ezekiel. First, the refutation is divided into two parts, clearly set apart by identical introductions (vv. 6, 9):

לָכֵן כֹּה אָמַר אֲדֹנָי יְהוִה   Therefore, thus has the Lord YHWH declared:
אוֹי עִיר הַדָּמִים   Woe to the bloody city!

Rather than this redundancy being treated as a sign of secondary editorial involvement, as is commonly done, these lines should be recognized as rhetorical signals announcing the two parts of a geminated rejoinder to a popular saying. Similar double refutations are found in Ezekiel in 11:2–12; 11:14–17; 33:23–29 (also Isa 49:14–25; Hag 1:2–11); 18:3–20; and 20:34–44 contain three-part refutations.

The ways in which 24:6–8 and 9–13 are introduced also resemble the openings to Ezekiel's refutations elsewhere. It seems to have been characteristic for him to open his rejoinders with the particle לָכֵן, "Therefore," followed

---

35. Graffy, *A Prophet Confronts His People*, 107–18.

by the messenger formula, כֹּה אָמַר אֲדֹנָי יְהוִה, "Thus has the Lord YHWH declared."[36] The same phenomenon occurs here.

Fourth, the oracle has close ties with another disputation speech, 11:1–12. Structurally, both have twinned refutations. Rhetorically, in both the rebuttals open with לָכֵן plus כֹּה אָמַר אֲדֹנָי יְהוִה, "Therefore, thus has the Lord YHWH declared." Thematically, even if the vessel has a different significance in each oracle, the most obvious link is the common motif, the pot, referred to by סִיר. The expression occurs nowhere else in Ezekiel. Furthermore, theologically the notion of election and special status, vaguely hinted at in the two-fold reference to מִבְחַר, "choice," in 24:4–5, finds its analogue in the implied claim of the people of Jerusalem to divine protection, as represented by the flesh safely stored in the pot (11:3), and their overt declaration in the disputation speech immediately following (11:15) that they are the special objects of YHWH's favor. Finally, the announcement, אֶשְׁפּוֹט אֶתְכֶם, "I will judge you," which occurs twice in the earlier oracle (11:10, 11), finds an echo in שְׁפָטִיךְ in 24:14 (cf. n. 26 above).

Although scholars have noted some of these connections, it is surprising that the ties with 11:1–12 have not had a greater bearing on the interpretation of 24:1–14. Is it not possible that both preserve a popular slogan that was being parroted by the people in Jerusalem to celebrate their special status as the truly elect people of God? In this instance an everyday cooking song is being illegitimately exploited to buttress an illusory sense of security and privilege. In order to destroy these illusions the use of the song must be refuted directly.

In view of all these considerations it is tempting to identify Ezekiel 24:1–14 as another hitherto unrecognized disputation speech. The principal difficulty with this conclusion is the absence of a specific identification of the song as a quotation.[37] Perhaps some comment like "Do you hear what they are saying?" was originally included between the messenger formula and the song in verse 3, but in the course of transmission it has inadvertently fallen out. On the other hand, if the prophet is actually quoting a well-known figure, it would have been immediately recognized as such, and an ellipsis at this point would have been tolerable. In fact, it would connect stylistically with the sequel, in which the relationship between announced statements of having spoken and the actual speech is not entirely clear (cf. 24:18). The presence of the messenger formula

---

36. 11:7, 16, 17; 12:23, 28; 33:25; 37:12. Isaiah 28:14 is similar, but not identical.
37. Cf. 11:3, 15; 12:22, 27; 18:2; 20:32; 33:10; 37:11.

in verse 3 may suggest that even the prophet's quotation of the proverb is directed by YHWH.

On the other hand, our fascination with the resemblances between this text and Ezekiel's other disputation speeches may have led us up the proverbial garden path. The absence of an introductory announcement of a quotation may not have been accidental. The cooking song need not have been a popular verse that was circulating among the people. It may just as well have been an ad hoc composition by the prophet,[38] reflecting the viewpoint of the audience, and functioning as the thesis in this disputation oracle. The imagery of cooking meat over a hot fire may derive from Ezekiel's pre-exilic experience in preparing sacrificial meals in the temple.[39] However, by referring to the pot as a סִיר, the prophet deliberately alludes to the popular saying dealt with earlier in 11:1–12, thereby capturing their attention. The rhetorical strategy finds an analogue in Isaiah's "Song of the Vinedresser and his Vineyard" (vv. 1b–2a). Undoubtedly the opening lines of this "love song" will have been greeted with applause from the audience. Similarly, if Ezekiel's song ever managed to reach Jerusalem prior to the fall of the city, the residents will have cheered at the prophet's apparent celebration of their special status before YHWH.

Ezekiel's verse has its theological origin in one of the fundamental pillars upon which the security of the citizens of Jerusalem was being defended in official circles: the inviolability of the city. But, like Isaiah, this prophet is a clever rhetorician and his strategy is deliberate. Having gained the attention of his hearers, and having caught their imagination with a song that feeds their perverted manner of thinking, he proceeds immediately to destroy such false notions by systematically refuting the validity of his own composition. Since Ezekiel's purpose here is so similar to the oracles in which popular opinion is explicitly quoted, it is not surprising that he finds in the form of the disputation address an effective vehicle for refuting false notions of any kind, whether they are expressed in popular sayings, or captured in his own literary compositions. Furthermore, the refutation, which appears on the surface to conform to Graffy's pattern of bifurcated rejoinders, actually follows Murray's dispute (vv. 6–8), counter-thesis (vv. 9–14) structure. Once this is recognized it becomes even more apparent that Graffy's definition of a "disputation speech" should be

---

38. So also Marvin A. Sweeney, in private communication.

39. Cf. 1 Sam 2:12–28, which describes the abuses of Phinehas and Hophni in the preparation of sacrificial meals at the temple in Shiloh.

By the River Chebar

expanded to include any oracle that attacks prevailing opinion, whether that opinion is quoted or not.

Interpretation

Introduction

1 Now the word of YHWH came to me
   in the ninth year,
   in the tenth month,
   on the tenth [day] of the month,
   as follows:
2 Human being,
   Record[40] the date, this very day—[41]
      The king of Babylon has laid siege
         to Jerusalem on this very day—
      Compose a parable concerning[42] the rebellious house,
         and declare to them:

The oracle begins with Ezekiel's regular word-event formula, followed by a date notice.[43] On the basis of an early Nisan 597 BCE date for Jehoiachin's deportation, the tenth day of the tenth month of the ninth year would fix the date of the oracle (and the commencement of Nebuchadnezzar's siege of Jerusalem) at 15 January 588 BCE.[44] The charge to the prophet in verse 2 consists of three commands. First, he is ordered to put a matter in writing. The urgency of the situation is highlighted by the repetition of "this very day" (עֶצֶם הַיּוֹם הַזֶּה), which creates an envelope effect around the actual announcement of the event. Although the term עֶצֶם is used

---

40. *Kethib* כתוב, a rare occurrence of *plene* orthography in the imperative. Cf. *Qere* כתב, conforming to the defectively written imperatives in verses 3–4.

41. *BHS* deletes אֶת־עֶצֶם הַיּוֹם, following Syr and Vg. But cf. LXX and Tg.

42. אֶל in the sense of עַל.

43. Most scholars contend that it has been secondarily inserted under the influence of 2 Kgs 25:1. Cf. Kutsch, *Die chronologischen Daten*, 62–63; Wevers, *Ezekiel*, 189; Zimmerli, *Ezekiel 1*, 498–99; Lang, *Ezechiel*, 35; Eichrodt, *Ezekiel*, 336–37. However, as we hope to demonstrate in another context, this explanation is not entirely convincing.

44. Cf. Parker and Dubberstein, *Babylonian Chronology*, 27–28; Kutsch, *Die chronologischen Daten*, 83; Zimmerli, *Ezekiel 1*, 15, 498; Malamat, "Last Kings of Judah," 150–51; Malamat, "The Twilight of Judah," 145. Cf. Hayes and Hooker, *A New Chronology*, 97, who date the event one year later.

Ezekiel's Boiling Cauldron

demonstratively,[45] it provides an assonantal foreshadowing of the cooking of עֲצָמִים/עֲצָמוֹת, "bones," to follow. The "day of bones," i.e., death (cf. 37:1–14), is signaled by the arrival at Jerusalem of the king of Babylon. Coinciding with this momentous event, Ezekiel is charged to מְשֹׁל מָשָׁל, "compose a proverb." Like the disputation oracles in chapter 11, this message, although intended primarily for the exiles, finds its point of departure in popular opinion in the homeland. However, while the residents of this city continue to cling tenaciously to their illusions of special favor with YHWH, the reference to the exilic addressees as בֵּית־הַמֶּרִי, "the rebellious house" (cf. 2:5, 6, 8; 3:9) attests their own continued intransigent resistance of YHWH's divine lordship.

The Thesis

> 3 Thus has the Lord[46] YHWH declared:
> Put on the cauldron, put [it] on;[47]
> Then pour water into it.[48]
> 4 Gather into it the pieces[49] [of meat]—
> Every good piece, thigh and shoulder.
> Fill it[50] with the choicest cuts.[51]
> 5 Take[52] the choicest[53] of the flock.
> Furthermore, heap up the logs under it.[54]

45. Cf. Joüon, §143k.

46. אֲדֹנָי is missing in the LXX.

47. *BHS* suggests deletion of the second שְׁפֹת, after LXX, Syr. But Ezekiel displays a fondness for duplication in such contexts. Cf. 20:4; 21:14[9]; 22:2; 37:9.

48. Since סִיר is usually feminine (cf. v. 4; 2 Kgs 4:38, etc.), the masculine suffix on בוֹ looks like a scribal error for בָהּ. But cf. the masculine form in Jer 1:13, which seems to underlie the present oracle.

49. נְתָחֶיהָ looks like an error for נְתָחִים, perhaps under the influence of the following אֵלֶיהָ. The suffix is lacking in the LXX and Syr.

50. מִבְחַר is omitted in the LXX.

51. MT עֲצָמִים, literally, "bones," but the context suggests the large bones with their meat. The LXX ἐκσεσαρκισμένα ἀπὸ τῶν ὀστῶν, "fleshed off from the bones," and Syr *dšmyt grmh* are interpretations.

52. לָקוֹחַ, vocalized in the MT like an infinitive absolute, functions as an imperative within the sequence of imperatives, casting doubt on the correctness of the reading.

53. מבחר appears to be a haplographic error for ממבחר. Cf. LXX, Syr.

54. Read העצים with the LXX and verse 10, in place of MT העצמים, "the bones," which is meaningless. The extra מ seems to have been mistakenly taken from the

Bring it to a brisk boil.⁵⁵
Indeed boil⁵⁶ its cuts in it.

By means of a series of imperatives the artistically composed opening poem traces the actions of a cook in preparing a special meat dish: (1) Set up the apparatus.⁵⁷ The duplication of the verb reflects the cook's enthusiasm for the task. (2) Pour in the water.⁵⁸ (3) Put in the meat. While "flesh" (בָּשָׂר) will be used in the refutation (v. 10), the song uses a rare term נֵתַח for a cut of meat. עֲצָמִים, literally "bones," in verse 4c is to be interpreted broadly to include the meat attached to the bones. (4) Pile on the logs under the pot. The verb דּוּר, "to heap up," hints at the strength of the fire to be lit. (5) Boil the meat. The verb רָתַח, which occurs elsewhere only in Job 12:23 and 30:27, speaks of the turbulence of cooking water. The last line summarizes the entire process.

Earlier it was suggested that the poem could have derived from an everyday activity of preparing a meal. But the cook does not appear to be fixing an ordinary dinner. An extra-ordinarily sumptuous meal seems to be implied by the quality and amount of meat being prepared. Not only is the slaughtered animal to be the choicest (מִבְחַר) of the flock; the cauldron is to be filled (מַלֵּא) with "every good piece" (כָּל־נֵתַח טוֹב), with particular reference to the thigh and shoulder, and its choice cuts (מִבְחַר עֲצָמִים). The vividness of the verbs creates an atmosphere of excitement and anticipation.

The fact that this is no ordinary meal seems to be confirmed in the prophet's rebuttal. In the first place, the vessel is described as a bronze (נְחֹשֶׁת) cauldron (v. 11). Since the average household cooked with clay pots, this would suggest that either a court banquet or a cultic meal

---

original מחתיה, which followed. Cf. Driver, "Linguistic and Textual Problems," 175.

55. The redundancy of the MT רַתַּח רְתָחֶיהָ, "boil its boilings," is preserved in the LXX. But BHS and many commentators follow 2 mssKen and emend the second word to נתחיה, "its pieces." Cf. Fuhs, "Ez 24–Überlegungen," 272, n. 21, who anticipates the pair עֲצָמִים//נְתָחֶיהָ as in verse 4. But the Kennicott manuscripts may have followed the same reasoning and intentionally changed the reading.

56. The plural perfect form, בָּשְׁלוּ, disturbs the sequence of imperatives and should probably be revocalized as a *piel* imperative, בַּשֵּׁל. The *qal* occurs only in Joel 4:13[3:13], where the meaning, "to become ripe," is quite different. Allen, "Ezekiel 24 3–14," 405, 412, n. 27, emends to the *qal* jussive form, יבשלו. Cf. Tg.

57. Usually סִיר refers to a large wide-mouthed clay vessel. For an illustration, see *Illustrated Bible Dictionary*, 3.1251 §42; cf. Kelso, *Ceramic Vocabulary*, 27 and fig. 16. The present usage is illustrated in 2 Kgs 4:38–41 (cf. Job 12:31), where סִיר also occurs in conjunction with שָׁפַת, "to set (on the fire)," presumably on a three-stone tripod.

58. Cf. the Israelite prohibition, Exod 23:19; 34:26; Deut 14:21.

underlies the song. The prophet's concern with issues relating to purity and defilement in verses 11–12 may tip the scales in favor of the latter.[59] Perhaps the preparation of a *zebaḥ*-meal is in view. Given the prophet's priestly heritage and interests, this cultic derivation would not be surprising. Nevertheless, the song itself is secular in tone.

It was also noted earlier that this is not the first time the motif of a cooking pot has been employed in Ezekiel's prophecy. According to 11:2–12, three years earlier the prophet had been called upon to reinterpret a popular saying in which the pot (סִיר) had figured as a sign of the security of the residents of Jerusalem. This song should probably be interpreted similarly. On the surface, the song has been composed to bolster the people's sense of well-being before YHWH. For the Israelite, participation in the *zebaḥ*-meal signified acceptance by and fellowship with YHWH (cf. 20:41; 43:25–27).[60] The doctrine of election seems to be implicit in this poem. The flock (צֹאן) represents the nation, the people of YHWH.[61] To have been selected (מִבְחַר) as the fare for this banquet is viewed as a privilege. In keeping with chapter 11, in which the pot had represented Jerusalem and the elect were those inside the city, the choice cuts refer to those who remain behind after the deportation of 597 BCE. Undoubtedly, a Jerusalem audience would have received this song with great enthusiasm, and interpreted it in a positive sense[62] to celebrate their claims to special divine favor.

The Dispute

6 Therefore, thus has the Lord[63] YHWH declared:
Woe to the city of bloodshed—
The cauldron whose corruption[64] is inside it;
Whose corruption has not been removed.[65]

---

59. For proponents of a cultic interpretation of the pot see Fuhs, "Ez 24–Überlegungen," 269–71, following Fohrer *Ezechiel*, 140; Kelso, "Ezekiel's Parable," 391–93.

60. Cf. Lang, "זבח," 17–29.

61. Cf. ch. 34, which expands on Jer 23:1–8; 25:34–38.

62. This is not the case in Mic 3:2–3, where the prophet speaks of the rulers of Israel's cannibalistic exploitation of their subjects.

63. אֲדֹנָי is missing in the LXX.

64. Read חֶלְאָתָהּ with mappiq in the final ה, or without the *taw*. Cf. *BHS*.

65. לֹא יָצְאָה, literally, "has not gone out from it."

By the River Chebar

> Remove[66] it piece by piece;[67]
> No lot has fallen on it.
>
> 7 For her blood is within her;
> On the exposed rock she has put it;[68]
> She did not pour it out on the ground,
>   to cover it with dust.
>
> 8 In order to rouse wrath,
> To take vengeance,
> I have[69] placed her blood upon the bare rock,
> that it might not be covered.

The transition from song to dispute is formally marked by לָכֵן, followed by the messenger formula. The prophet's disposition toward popular opinion is reflected in his opening scathing pronouncement of woe upon the city. However, instead of following the form of a woe oracle, with its typical participial accusation (cf. 33:2), Ezekiel simply characterizes the object of the woe as "the city of bloodshed" (עִיר הַדָּמִים), that is, Jerusalem.[70] At issue is simply the fact of her guilt, not the manner in which it was incurred. For information on the latter, knowledge of previous charges involving bloodshed, such as those found in 7:23; 9:9; and 22:1–12, is assumed.

The actual dispute that follows consists of a shocking reinterpretation of the status of the meat and its significance within the cauldron. The appositional comment, סִיר אֲשֶׁר חֶלְאָתָה בָהּ, usually rendered "a pot whose corruption is inside it," is a crux. Most modern versions and interpreters follow LXX ἰὸς and interpret חֶלְאָה as "rust,"[71] assuming a derivation from a root, חלא, "to be rusty."[72] Although the image of oxidized iron, with its

---

66. MT הוֹצִיאָהּ is probably a perfect (used impersonally) with the third feminine suffix referring to חֶלְאָתָה. Allen, "Ezekiel 24:3–14," 408, n. 11, follows Davidson, *Ezekiel*, 175, and Cooke, *Ezekiel*, 274, in removing the *mappiq* and treating the form as an emphatic imperative. In view of the difficulty of verse 6b and the fact that verse 7 joins smoothly to verse 6a, Zimmerli (*Ezekiel 1*, 494) deletes these two lines as secondary.

67. The distributive sense is emphasized by the duplication and the use of the distributive *lamedh*. On the latter, see GKC §§134g, 123a. Cf. 4:6.

68. Influenced by verse 8, the LXX renders שמתהו and שפכתהו in the following line with the first person.

69. Brownlee, "Ezekiel's Copper Caldron," 31, n. 28, takes the ending of נתתי as a second feminine. This compels him also to emend דמה, "her blood," to דמך, "your blood." But, as Allen ("Ezekiel 24:3–14," 408, n. 14) observes, this destroys the *inclusio* of דמה. Cf. v. 7a.

70. Cf. chapter 23, where Oholibah is expressly equated with Jerusalem.

71. *RSV, NASB, JB, NIV*.

72. Cf. Driver, "Ancient Lore," 283–84; Driver, "Linguistic and Textual Problems," 176; Seybold, "חלה," 401.

reddish appearance, would be an appropriate representation of a bloody city, this interpretation is questionable on several counts.

First, verse 11 notes that the pot is made of copper or bronze (נְחֹשֶׁת). Copper does not rust; when it oxidizes it turns green, suggesting a verdigrised condition for this vessel.[73] "Rust" can be retained only if the term is generalized to metallic corrosion in a broad sense.[74]

Second, it assumes that חֶלְאָה is primarily a metallurgical term, and refers to a defect in the metal of which the pot is made.[75] However, etymologically, it is doubtful that חֶלְאָה should be treated as a technical metallurgical term. Although the root is relatively rare, חָלָא is never used of metal in the Old Testament.[76] In 2 Chronicles 16:12 the verb denotes "to be diseased," which answers to חָלָה, in the parallel text, 1 Kings 15:23. The noun from the same root, תַּחֲלֻאִים, "diseases," is attested five times.[77] For some of these Driver proposed the sense "to be gangrenous," alluding to the greening of the flesh.[78] חָלָא should therefore probably be viewed as an Aramaized by-form of חָלָה, and interpreted according to its normal usage, "to be sick."[79] At best one might speak of a kind of "copper disease."[80]

But the question of what is spoiled in the present context remains. Any interpretation that finds here a "rusty cauldron" would see the

---

73. Cf. Kelso, "Ezekiel's Parable," 391–93; Driver, "Ancient Lore," 283. The latter's influence is apparent in the *NEB*, "a pot green with corrosion."

74. Cf. Greek ἰός, which may refer to the corrosion of iron or brass, LSJ, s.v. In the New Testament ἰός also refers to the corrosion of gold and silver (Jas 5:2–3; cf. Matt 6:19–20).

75. Kelso, "Ezekiel's Parable," 391–93, has explained how this could occur. If the vessel was made of hammered copper, the corrosion might have occurred in a dent or a scratch that was inaccessible to scouring. On the other hand, if cast copper was used, the quality of the metal may have suffered from countless tiny air bubbles that appear when it is cast at too high a temperature. These holes give the metal a porous quality, and allow corrosion to set in "under the skin." To speak of the corrosion being "inside it" (בָהּ) suggests an internal corruption of the metal rendering the pot worthless and fit only to be melted down into scrap.

76. But cf. Sir. 12:10, which employs the *hiphil* of חָלָא in connection with bronze. Apart from Ezek 24:6, 11, this is the only occurrence of the metallurgical usage of the root cited by KB.

77. Deut 29:21[22]; Jer 14:18; 16:4; 2 Chr 21:19; Ps 103:3[2].

78. Driver, "Ancient Lore," 283–4.

79. Cf. the same alternation of חלא and חלה/חלי in rabbinic writings. Jastrow, *Dictionary of the Targumim*, 464, 467. On analogous Aramaized forms with *aleph* replacing *hē*, see Wagner, *Lexikalischen und grammatikalischen Aramäismen*, 128, §10; GKC §75*hh*.

80. Kelso, "Ezekiel's Parable," 392.

corruption in the metal itself. Zimmerli speaks of "a serious 'sickness' of the metal" that cannot be removed by cleansing.[81] But this interpretation of "a pot whose corruption is inside it" is awkward. It is more natural to view חֶלְאָה בָהּ as the contents of the pot, that is, the meat. The statement then represents a challenge to the people's mistaken perception of their status. Far from being YHWH's choice cuts, the residents of Jerusalem are nothing more than putrid flesh, fit only to be discarded as refuse.

This interpretation helps to clarify the difficulties posed by the last line of verse 6. In everyday life impartial decisions were often arrived at by casting the lot (גּוֹרָל). Although to the modern mind this appears to have the character of luck or chance, to the ancients, even in secular affairs, the way a dice fell was divinely determined (Prov 16:33). The notion of casting lots "before YHWH" highlighted the sacral nature of the act.[82] The best known use of the lot in the Old Testament involved the allocation of land among the tribes and families of Israel (Num 26:55–56; Josh 13:6; etc.), but it was also employed in cultic contexts. In the first-temple era the religious functionaries were assigned by lot (1 Chr 24–26). On the Day of Atonement the lot was used to determine which goats YHWH had chosen for the sin offering and the scapegoat (Lev 16:7–10). When Ezekiel declares that no lot has fallen on this piece of meat he is repudiating the people's claim to special status before YHWH.[83]

In verses 7–8 the prophet elaborates on the reasons why Jerusalem has been rejected. In the process he seems to be mixing his metaphors. The thought of cooking a meat dish reminds him of Leviticus 17:10–16, in which instructions for the preparation of kosher food are spelled out. The statement that Jerusalem's blood is within her alludes to the prescription of bleeding an animal that has been slain for food. Since the blood was viewed as sacred, and represented the life of the victim, the consumption of meat with the blood still in it was strictly prohibited. The people of Jerusalem may have thought they were choice cuts, but as far as Ezekiel was concerned they were unfit for consumption; no lot would fall on their city.

However, the figure changes in the reminder of the verse. Now Jerusalem is described as the offender, not the victim. At issue in verses 7b–8 is the violation of a second taboo cited in Leviticus 17:13, namely, leaving

---

81. Zimmerli, *Ezekiel 1*, 500.

82. Josh 18:6–10; 19:51. Cf. Dommershausen, "גורל," 450–56.

83. Allen's interpretation of the idiom גּוֹרָל נָפַל עַל, "a lot has fallen upon," as "retribution" ("Ezekiel 24:3–14," 409), is not convincing.

the blood of a slain animal exposed. It seems best, therefore, to understand דָּמָהּ, "her blood," as "the blood she has shed," or "her blood-guilt." The Levitical prescription required that, whenever a game animal or bird was slain, the blood was to be poured out and covered with earth. To leave it exposed was to provoke the wrath of God, the source and guarantor of all life. In the case of the murder of a fellow human being in particular, the blood of the victim cried out for vengeance (Gen 4:10). But the crime of the residents of Jerusalem was not merely one of neglect. Instead of covering the blood with dust, they had willfully poured it out on the smooth bare rock (צְחִיחַ סֶלַע), where there was no soil, as if to advertise their deeds. The allusion may be either to the sacrificial slaughter of children on the high places,[84] or to the blatant criminal activity, the judicial murder by the leaders in the city. The unatoned-for blood of innocent victims in the city calls out for vengeance.

In a surprising turn, the purpose clause of verse 8 introduces the hearers to YHWH's response to this blatant impiety. With pointed irony he declares in effect, "If you want to pour out the blood of your victims on the exposed rock [as an act of sacrilege], I shall see to it that it remains there." His motive is clear. In a way reminiscent of Job, who requested that his blood not be covered so that God might forever be reminded not to allow the offences committed against him to be forgotten (Job 16:18), YHWH determines to take vengeance on the city. He will ensure that the blood on the rock remains exposed as a perpetual witness to their crimes and a reminder to him to visit the criminal city with his judgment. For the first time in this oracle the prophet announces YHWH's personal response to the sins of Jerusalem. In so doing, he paves the way for the counter-thesis, where the stress will be placed on the fury of YHWH's judgment.

The Counter-Thesis

9 Therefore, thus has the Lord[85] YHWH declared:
Woe to the city of bloodshed![86]
Indeed I myself will make the pyre huge.

---

84. Cf. 16:20–21; 20:26, 31, particularly if the meal being prepared was intended for some cultic celebration. Thus Brownlee, "Ezekiel's Copper Caldron," 32. Cf. the wrath provoked when the king of Moab sacrificed his son on the wall, 2 Kgs 3:27.

85. אֲדֹנָי is missing in the LXX.

86. *BHS* follows the LXX in deleting this line. However, emphatic repetition is characteristic of Ezekielian style. Cf. שְׁפֹת in verse 3.

10 Pile⁸⁷ on the logs.
   Kindle the fire.
   Cook the meat thoroughly.
   Pour out the broth.⁸⁸
   Let the bones be charred.⁸⁹
11 Then let it stand⁹⁰ empty⁹¹ on the coals,⁹²
   So that it becomes hot,
   And its copper glows,
   And its filthiness inside it is poured out.
   Its corruption shall be consumed⁹³
12 Its corruption is troublesome,⁹⁴

87. Wevers, *Ezekiel*, 191, follows the LXX, Tg, in interpreting הַרְבֵּה, הַדְלֵק, הָתֵם, and הָרְקַח (MT) as infinitives absolute. אַגְדִּיל in verse 9 points to YHWH as the subject. But the series continues in verse 11 with a clear imperative, וְהַעֲמִידֶהָ.

88. וְהָרְקַח הַמֶּרְקָחָה, literally, "season with seasoning," is ill-suited to the progress of thought. On the assumption that ת has been confused with ק, Driver ("Linguistic and Textual Problems," 175) emends to והרתח המרתחה, "and stew the stew." So also *NJPS*, *BHS*, *RSV*, *NEB*, and many commentators since Kraetzschmar (*Ezechiel*, 196) have emended to והרחק המרק, or והרק המרק, "and pour out the broth," which finds support in the LXX καὶ ἐλαττωθῇ ὁ ζωμός, "and the broth becomes little."

89. וְהָעֲצָמוֹת יֵחָרוּ is suspicious. (1) It is missing in the LXX. (2) The imperfect replaces the previous imperatives. (3) The feminine עֲצָמוֹת is used elsewhere in Ezekiel only of "dead bones" (6:5; 32:27; 37:1, 3–5, 7, 11), while "pieces of bone" is rendered by the masculine, עֲצָמִים. Cf. vv. 4–5. (4) In the context חָרָה relates more correctly to the scorching of the pot, not the burning of bones. Cf. v. 11. Freedy ("Glosses in Ezekiel i–xxiv," 151) suggests the phrase was "probably inserted as a scruple to establish correctly the relevance of the figure of the pot song to the fate of Jerusalem." However, the charring of the bones is not out of place if the pot is allowed to cook until all the liquid has evaporated. Cf. the reference to the empty cauldron in verse 11. Nor is the jussive out of place in the context of imperatives. Cf. Tg.

90. MT imperatival וְהַעֲמִידֶהָ is rendered as an infinitive absolute in the LXX. *BHS* reads וְהֶאֱמַדְתִּיהָ or וְאַעֲמִידֶהָ, following Tg and Syr.

91. רֵקָה, missing in the LXX, is deleted by Zimmerli (*Ezekiel 1*, 495) on metric grounds. Freedy, "Glosses in Ezekiel i–xxiv," 139, argues the word was added after the two separate segments comprising verses 3–11 had become disjointed and interwoven to emphasize that the pot was "empty." Allen ("Ezekiel 24:3–14," 412) notes the word play with והרחק in the previous verse along with יֵחָרוּ and וְחָרָה here.

92. As with נְתָחֶיהָ in verse 4 above, the suffix on גֶּחָלֶיהָ appears superfluous.

93. תִּתֻּם is an Aramaized imperfect form of תָּמַם, "to be perfect, finished." Cf. *GKC* §67g, q; Bauer-Leander §58.

94. תְּאֻנִים חֶלְאָת is missing in the LXX and usually deleted as a dittographic gloss after תִּתֻּם חֶלְאָתָהּ in the previous verse. But Allen ("Ezekiel 24:3–14," 410, n. 23) suggests this results in too short a "line." Driver ("Linguistic and Textual Problems," 176) transposes the consonants of the second word to read תלאה, "you shall weary yourself with great toil." However, the flow of thought is retained if חֶלְאָת is read as חֶלְאָת, and

And the magnitude of its corruption will not leave.
Into the fire with its corruption[95]

13 On account of your lewd filthiness—[96]
Because I tried to cleanse you,
But you would not be cleansed of your filthiness—[97]
You shall never be cleansed again,
Until I have satisfied my fury against you.

14 I am YHWH.
I have spoken.
It is coming.[98]
And I will carry [it] out;
I will not hold back;
And I will not spare;
And I will not relent.[99]
According to your conduct
and your wanton behavior
I will judge you.[100]
The declaration of the Lord[101] YHWH.[102]

The number and nature of the textual notes reflect the textual difficulties involved in the counter-thesis. Nevertheless, the thrust of the argument seems clear enough. The opening of the counter-thesis is identical with that of the foregoing dispute, consisting of לָכֵן, followed by the

---

the vocalization reflected by a final hē is assumed. This interpretation is supported by verse 6, which follows the same word with a reference to the removal of the putrid meat.

95. LXX καταισχυνθήσεται ὁ ἰὸς αὐτῆς, "she who had rust was ashamed," misread בְּאֵשׁ as בּוֹשׁ. Most delete the entire last part of the verse.

96. As in 16:27, in the phrase בְּטֻמְאָתֵךְ זִמָּה an epexegetical substantive follows a substantive with a suffix. Cf. GKC §131r. The LXX ἀνθ' ὧν ἐμιαίνου σύ καὶ τί reflects an underlying בטמא אתה ומה.

97. The LXX smooths out the MT by omitting the intrusive יַעַן טִהַרְתִּיךְ וְלֹא טָהַרְתְּ מִטֻּמְאָתֵךְ.

98. BHS and most commentators delete בָּאָה as disruptive to the stereotypical formulation, דִּבַּרְתִּי וְעָשִׂיתִי. Cf. Brownlee, "Ezekiel's Copper Caldron," 39, n. 10a.

99. Most delete וְלֹא אֶנָּחֵם with the LXX as a variant gloss.

100. On שְׁפַטְתִּיךְ, "I judge you," for שְׁפָטוּךְ, "They judge you," see n. 26 above.

101. אֲדֹנָי is missing in the LXX.

102. The LXX assumes a long addition to the verse: διὰ τοῦτο ἐγὼ κρινῶ σε κατὰ τὰ αἵματά σου καὶ κατὰ τὰ ἐνθυμήματά σου κρινῶ σε ἡ ἀκάθαρτος ἡ ὀνομαστὴ καὶ πολλὴ τοῦ παραπικραίνειν, reflecting לכן אני אשפטך דמיך ובעלילותיך טמאת השם ורבת המרי, "Therefore I will judge you according to your bloodshed and your wanton behavior, the defilement of the name and the greatness of rebellion."

messenger formula, which in turn is succeeded by a pronouncement of woe. However, thereafter the prophet's change in strategy becomes immediately apparent. The emphatic construction in the first line, גַּם־אֲנִי אַגְדִּיל הַמְּדוּרָה, serves notice that the focus will now be on YHWH's direct intervention and reaction to those who would find in the prophet's מָשָׁל an affirmation of their own privileged status.

The refutation divides into two parts, the first of which deals with the manner in which YHWH's wrath will be vented (vv. 9b–12), and the second with a justification of his vengeance (vv. 13–14).[103] The first segment sub-divides further into two halves, verses 9–10 dealing with the destruction of the tainted meat, and verses 11–12 with the purifying of the pot which has been rendered unclean by its contents.

The imagery in verses 9b–12 derives directly from the מָשָׁל of the cooking pot. However, the opening statement announces in emphatic terms that YHWH has now taken charge and assumed the role of cook. His first task is to make a huge fire. The term, מְדוּרָה, "pyre," derives from דּוּר, which had been used in verse 5 of "heaping up a pile of firewood." The present punitive usage recalls the only other Old Testament occurrence of the noun in Isa 30:33:

> Topheth has long been ready;
> It has been prepared for the king.
> Its fire pit has been made deep and wide,
> Its pyre (מְדֻרָתָהּ), a fire with plenty of wood;
> The breath of YHWH—
> > like a stream of burning sulfur—
> > sets it ablaze.

A second link with this verse is found in the call to pile on the logs in verse 10.[104] The switch to imperatives poses no difficulty, inasmuch as YHWH may be either talking to himself, or calling on his assistant or servant. The first three actions in the series seem innocent enough: the logs are piled on, they are lit, and the meat is cooked. Even the choice of בָּשָׂר for meat is natural. Both the special מִבְחַר עֲצָמִים, "choice cuts," of verse 4, and the pejorative חֶלְאָה, "corruption," are avoided. Nevertheless, the audience might have become suspicious that the prophet has in mind

---

103. On the stylistic relationship between these parts see Allen, "Ezekiel 24:3–14," 410–13.

104. Cf. הַרְבֵּה הָעֵצִים here and וְעֵצִים הַרְבֵּה in Isaiah.

something more than the mere cooking of meat. Why is there such a stress on the size of the pile of logs? Why does the prophet use the word הָתֵם?[105]

The following lines are textually difficult, but a progression may be recognized. The liquid broth is to be poured out, leaving the bones (with their meat) to be charred into a useless mass of carbon. Since the feminine plural form, עֲצָמוֹת, is used elsewhere in Ezekiel only of human bones, an element of interpretation has already been introduced: the contents of the pot about to be destroyed are not animal bones; they are human.

But the process is not finished. In verse 11 it becomes apparent that the putrid flesh has had its effect on the vessel; it has been defiled and must now be cleansed before it can be used again. But this cannot be accomplished by superficial washing. The pot is to be heated red hot so that every remnant of the defiled meat may be destroyed. The use of the verb נָתַךְ in the following line is striking. Usually, it is interpreted as a metallurgical term for melting down metal, as in 22:15, the subject being the pot. However, it is preferable to treat the verb in its usual sense of "to pour out," the subject being טֻמְאָתָהּ, "its filthiness." Since the verb is used in connection with divine wrath elsewhere, a motif that appears in verse 13, its use in the present context is rendered all the more appropriate.[106] It has become clear that the prophet holds out no hope at all for the inhabitants of Jerusalem. The only solution is to pour them out into the fire (v. 10), and then to stoke up the flame so hot that every remnant of the stew inside the vessel is burned up.

To make explicit the refutation of the Jerusalemites' false claims of security and privilege, in verse 12 the prophet highlights again that YHWH's basic complaint is with the meat. The word תְּאֻנִים is a *hapax legomenon*, derived from a root אוֹן, meaning "trouble, sorrow." In 11:2 the phrase הַחֹשְׁבִים אָוֶן had been used of "wicked/troublesome thoughts."[107] The magnitude (רַבַּת) of the corruption prevented any solution other than "from the frying pan into the fire."

The oracle reaches its climax in verses 13–14. Now the prophet abandons the figure and concentrates on its theological significance. The third-person references to the meat and the city are replaced by the second

---

105. The phrase, הָתֵם הַבָּשָׂר, may indeed be interpreted as "Finish [the job of cooking] the meat," but it may also signify "Finish off (i.e., do away with) the meat."

106. Cf. the references to YHWH pouring out his wrath (נִתַּךְ אַפִּי וַחֲמָתִי) in Jer 42:18; 44:6; etc. Cf. BDB, 677.

107. Cf. the phrase, מַחְשְׁבוֹת אָוֶן in Isa 59:7; Jer 4:14; Prov 6:18.

person of direct address, the second-person feminine forms confirming that the judgment announced applies to "the bloody city" itself.

Verse 13 opens with a purpose clause that is never completed. The description of the city's corruption as "lewd filthiness" (בְּטֻמְאָתֵךְ זִמָּה) recalls 16:27. However, the prophet moves quickly to a justification of YHWH's harsh treatment of Jerusalem. All his past efforts at purifying the city had failed.[108] To which historical events he alludes we can only surmise. Most likely, Josiah's most recent attempts at reformation are in view (2 Kgs 22–23), but Hezekiah's earlier efforts may also be included (2 Kgs 18:4, 22; 2 Chr 31). The people's intransigence justified YHWH's resolve not to hold out another opportunity for cleansing and renewal until his wrath against the city has been satisfied.[109]

Postscript (v. 14)

The oracle concludes with the longest affirmation of YHWH's resolve in the book. The familiar parts of the verse stress that it is in YHWH's nature to fulfill his pronouncements. He who issues the word guarantees its fulfillment. The tri-partite form of his self-identification, אֲנִי יְהוָה דִּבַּרְתִּי וְעָשִׂיתִי, is characteristically Ezekielian.[110] The interruptive בָּאָה, "It is coming," inserts an ominous reference to Nebuchadnezzar, who is even now poised for attack. YHWH's refusal to reconsider is announced with three negative statements, whose reverberations sound the death knell of the city. The first, לֹא־אֶפְרַע, literally, "I will not refrain, leave alone," occurs only here in Ezekiel, and stresses that there will be no restraint to YHWH's judgment, nor his fulfillment of his word. The second, וְלֹא־אָחוּס, "I will not spare," is familiar from previous passages.[111] The third, וְלֹא אֶנָּחֵם, which means "I will not be sorry, be moved to pity," emphasizes that his mind has been irrevocably made up.[112]

The justification of YHWH's action toward Jerusalem concludes with a final statement of principle: the judgment pronounced corresponds to the wanton behavior (עֲלִילוֹת) of the city. The sentence is sealed with the customary signatory formula.

108. The new key word, טָהֵר, occurs three times in this verse.
109. On יָנִיחַ חֵמָה, cf. 5:13; 16:42; 21:22[17].
110. Cf. 12:25; 17:24; 22:14; 36:36; 37:14.
111. 5:11; 7:4, 9; 8:18; 9:5, 10; 16:5; 20:17.
112. Cf. the positive counterpart in Exod 32:12, 14; Jer 18:8; Joel 2:13; Jonah 3:10; 4:2.

Conclusion

The official theology on which the security of the Judaeans was based was deeply entrenched. So long as temple and city remained these convictions would not be abandoned. After the deportation in 597 BCE those who were left behind in Jerusalem interpreted their lot as a special mark of divine favor. The fact that many of their number had been exiled to Babylon was interpreted as a sign that these had been rejected by YHWH, and that only those residents who remained were his chosen remnant, entitled to all the privileges that went with this status, including the right to confiscate the property of those who had been removed (11:15). Ezekiel struggled hard to destroy such illusions, using a variety of rhetorical strategies to achieve this goal: sign-actions, parabolic speech, pronouncements of woe, judgment oracles, etc. However, in his disputation speeches he attacked prevailing opinions head-on.

Ezekiel's parable of the boiling cauldron challenges Jerusalemite illusions of security. The residents of the city (the pot) viewed themselves to be the choice portions of meat specially selected for a sumptuous banquet. The exiles in Babylon by implication represented the discarded offal. In refutation of this illusion, what will have been greeted as a favorable figure is turned into a frightening literary caricature. YHWH assumes the role of the cook who calls for the wood to be piled on and the fire to be stoked as hot as possible. But he is not interested in preparing a meal; his mind is only on destruction. In his rage he pours the contents of the pot on to the fire. Lest any shred of hope remain, the fire is stoked so hot that every vestige of meat or broth in the pot is burned and the vessel is purified of its defiling contents. Residence in Jerusalem offers no security; it guarantees only destruction and judgment. Even as he speaks (24:2) the fire is being stoked. Nebuchadnezzar has arrived and has begun to lay siege to the city. Her fate and that of her inhabitants is sealed. They may compose clever proverbs and relish songs that celebrate their special privilege, but they are deluded. YHWH has spoken. He will have the last word.

Appendix

In Praise of Moshe

A Tribute to Moshe Greenberg[1]

Mr. Chairman, colleagues and friends. I am deeply honored to be invited to participate in this tributary session for Professor Moshe Greenberg. Few scholars, if any, have influenced and inspired me in my own study of the Hebrew Scriptures the way he has. But I have been asked to speak specifically to his significance and influence in Ezekiel studies. Some of my response will be autobiographical; in other respects I will speak for all who have sat at his feet, either in person or through his work. I realize it is not very creative, but I would like to begin with a rather lengthy citation from Ben Sirach's preamble to his praise of the ancestors of his people:

> 1 Let us now sing the praises of famous men,
> our ancestors in their generations.
> 2 The Lord apportioned to them great glory,
> his majesty from the beginning.
> 3. There were those who ruled in their kingdoms,
> and made a name for themselves by their valor;
> those who gave counsel because they were intelligent;
> those who spoke in prophetic oracles;
> 4. those who led the people by their counsels
> and by their knowledge of the people's lore;
> they were wise in their words of instruction;
> 5 those who composed musical tunes,
> or put verses in writing;

---

1. Presented to the Society of Biblical Literature Annual Meeting in Atlanta, GA, November 22, 2010.

By the River Chebar

> 6   rich men endowed with resources,
>   living peacefully in their homes—
> 7   all these were honored in their generations,
>   and were the pride of their times.
> 8   Some of them have left behind a name,
>   so that others declare their praise.
>   . . .
> 10 But these also were godly men,
>   whose righteous deeds have not been forgotten;
> 11 their wealth will remain with their descendants,
>   and their inheritance with their children's children.
> 12 Their descendants stand by the covenants;
>   their children also, for their sake.
> 13 Their offspring will continue forever,
>   and their glory will never be blotted out.
> 14 Their bodies are buried in peace,
>   but their name lives on generation after generation.
> 15 The assembly declares their wisdom,
>   and the congregation proclaims their praise. (Sirach 44:1–15; NRSV)

That is what we have come to do for Moshe Greenberg today.

Many of you will have known this giant among us at the personal level much better than I did. I met professor Greenberg only once—well actually twice, separated by four days. In 1990 I had the great privilege of attending the Second International Congress on Biblical Archaeology in Jerusalem. By then I had been living with Ezekiel for about seven years, and not surprisingly my head was full of questions about this fascinating and mysterious prophet and the written record of his utterances—more accurately, God's utterances to him. By then I had also drunk deeply from the cup of Professor Greenberg's writings on this book, both in the form of his magnificent commentary on *Ezekiel 1–20* (Anchor Bible 22, 1983), and the steady stream of essays related to Ezekiel that came from his pen. On the whole, for my own work I found his work to be much more helpful than anyone else's. Like no other, his work reflected a profound awareness of the contents of the Hebrew Bible, the cultural and literary context from the writings of the Hebrew Bible emerged, and the history of Jewish interpretation of the Scriptures. For one not reared in the Jewish tradition the last of these was particularly important, opening up a world of perspectives that was both fresh and exciting. And his style was always warm.

But I must get back to my story. Several months before the Congress, I had the *chutzpa* to introduce myself to Professor Greenberg by letter,

In Praise of Moshe

letting him know that I was also working on Ezekiel, that I was coming to Jerusalem, and that I would be honored to meet him, perhaps over a cup of coffee. He wrote back immediately. By all means, he would like to meet me as well. He advised me, "After the first session of the conference I will be standing at the back of the room. You will recognize me by my red hair." But more than this, he invited me to his house for coffee at 3:00 P.M. on Friday, being careful to add, however, that I would need to leave at 6:00 because his children were coming for Shabbat supper.

Spending that afternoon with Professor Greenberg is one of the most delightful memories of my academic career. It was a special treat to discuss with this extraordinary scholar issues of mutual interest in the book of Ezekiel, and to get his feedback on some of my own conclusions regarding specific passages in the book. I expressed to him my gratitude for his clear vision and practice of what he called "holistic interpretation." After decades of atomizing approaches I found his treatment of the text so refreshing. While he held critical scholarship in high regard, ultimately he found preoccupation with sources and redactional layers behind the text less than satisfying. I recall asking him directly, "Professor Greenberg, in the guild of biblical scholarship how influential do you think your holistic method will be?" He expressed to me his own conviction that until we rediscover the biblical texts as largely coherent literary wholes, they will remain lifeless fossils. But then I was surprised by his pessimism regarding his own influence on the scholarly study of the Hebrew Scriptures. "I don't expect many to take my holistic approach seriously," he said. We who have gathered here this morning are testimony to how wrong was his assessment of his own work. I regret deeply that that was the last personal conversation I ever had with the esteemed Rabbi.

How should one judge the influence of this man in Ezekiel scholarship? I am not sure he would have claimed me as his student, but I am proud to claim him as my teacher. I suppose my presence here could be interpreted as a small witness to the pervasiveness of his influence beyond the world of Jewish scholars and Hebrew scholarship. But there are other evidences of his significance for Ezekiel scholarship.

First, we recognize his importance in his writings. Not only has Professor Greenberg produced two volumes of the finest commentary on the book of Ezekiel available in any language, but those commentaries also arise out of a depth of research that is reflected in dozens of essays on fine points of interpretation related to the book.

Second, we recognize it in the references to his work in other commentaries on the book of Ezekiel. Since the two volumes of his Anchor

By the River Chebar

Bible Commentary on Ezekiel were published we have welcomed a series of significant commentaries in English by Leslie Allen (Word Biblical Commentary, 1990, 1994), Iain M. Duguid (NIVAC, 1999), Christopher J. H. Wright (Bible Speaks Today, 2001), Katheryn Pfisterer Darr (New Interpreter's Bible, 2001), Margaret S. Odell (Smith & Helwys Bible Commentary, 2005), Steven Shawn Tuell (New International Biblical Commentary, 2009), Paul Joyce (Library of Hebrew Bible/Old Testament Studies, 2009). In these commentaries we find scores of references to Greenberg's work—indeed more references than to any other source.

Third, evidence of his influence extends beyond his interpretive insights to the tone with which he communicated his findings. His irenic spirit has characterized our conversations for more than twenty years in the Ezekiel Consultation/Seminar here at SBL. I was involved in this study group for many years, and found great delight in the interaction with other eccentrics who were as fascinated by this mysterious prophet as I was. I shall never forget one session in the early 90s when, after a panel conversation, Robert Carroll got up and expressed his amazement over the proceedings. He was impressed by two features of our conversation, both of which he contrasted with the discussions going on in Jeremiah studies. First, whereas the longer scholars worked with Jeremiah, the less confident they became of recovering the historical prophet from the book that bears his name, Ezekiel scholars seemed to understand this man, his context, and his message. This was a real historical figure. Second, whereas the folks working on Jeremiah seemed to have trouble working together, those participating in this seminar were actually friendly toward each other. Although I do not recall Moshe Greenberg participating in or even attending this seminar, all of us have been inspired by him, both for the vitality of his work and the respect with which he treated conversation partners, especially those with whom he disagreed. His spirit is evident in many of our works.

Fourth, we observe his influence in specific testimonials. In 2004, out of the blue I received an invitation from the Leopold-Franzens Universität in Innsbruck, Austria, to serve as external examiner and to read the Habilitationsschrift of Volkmar Premstaller, *Die Völkersprüche des Ezechielbuches*. Given the long history of diachronic redaction criticism in the German speaking world, I was puzzled that I should be invited to evaluate Professor Premstaller's work—until I read his preface. In his *Vorwort* the author thanks Professor Dr. Moshe Greenberg for conversations in the Ezekiel Seminar of the [International] Society of Biblical Literature, and

In Praise of Moshe

explicitly declares that he is following the "holistic interpretation" found in the commentaries of Greenberg and Block. Professor Greenberg should be proud.

Fifth, although much of Professor Greenberg's work was focused on Ezekiel, the hermeneutical principles that governed his work may be applied on a much wider scale. I have found two of his essays particularly helpful as I have launched into other areas: "The Vision of Jerusalem in Ezekiel 8–11: A Holistic Interpretation,"[2] and "What are Valid Criteria for Determining Inauthentic Matter in Ezekiel?"[3] Whether one is working in the prophets—former or latter—or in the Torah, the principles he espouses are valid far beyond this book. Commenting on his commentary, Kathe Darr's observed, "Greenberg's 'holistic' approach to the text pays enormous dividends for serious students of Ezekiel."[4] I would add that it pays enormous dividends even beyond the Hebrew Bible in my tradition to the Gospels and the book of Acts in the New Testament. In a review of Professor Greenberg's first volume in 1984, Jon Levenson compared his work with the magisterial two-volume work of Walther Zimmerli. He wrote,

> Whereas Zimmerli sees the book of Ezekiel as a puzzle which the exegete must put into an intelligible order, Moshe Greenberg sees it as a subtle work of art and the exegete's task as the demonstration of its intelligibility. Where Zimmerli is a plastic surgeon, Greenberg is a midwife, carefully uncovering even more order and symmetry in a text before which he stands in obvious reverence.[5]

While this is all true of Moshe's work, for me the last comment is particularly significant. Whatever ancient texts we choose to study, it strikes me that the best analysis derives from those whose disposition toward the text and its author is fundamentally positive and sympathetic, rather than negative and cynical. It is in this regard that I have found the greatest inspiration from Professor Greenberg. As it was for him, for me as a

---

2. In *The Divine Helmsman: Studies on God's Control of Human Events*, edited by J. L. Crenshaw and S. Sandmel, 143–64. New York: Ktav, 1980.

3. In *Ezekiel and His Book: Textual and Literary Criticism and their Interrelation*, edited by J. Lust, 123–35. Bibliotheca ephemeridum theologicarum lovaniensium 74. Leuven: Leuven University Press, 1986.

4. "Ezekiel," in *The New Interpreter's Bible*, Vol. 6, 1100. Nashville: Abingdon 2001.

5. Jon D. Levenson, "Ezekiel in the Perspective of Two Commentators," *Interpretation* 38.2 (1984) 213.

Christian interpreter the book of Ezekiel is not only a fascinating document placed before us for cold and distanced analysis; it is also a sacred text before which I need to stand with reverence. He has shown us the way.

We all lament that Professor Greenberg was unable to finish his Ezekiel project. And we regret that the work of his designated successor, Jacob Milgrom, has not seen the light of day.[6] However, for all of us who have made Ezekiel the focus of our own study, the spirit of Moshe lives on. May we continue to find inspiration in his written legacy and in the memory of this intellectual giant among us.

Professor Tigay, thank you for giving me a few brief moments, on behalf of the community of Ezekiel scholars to express publicly our profound admiration and respect for Professor Greenberg.

Respectfully submitted,
Daniel I. Block

---

6. The work has now appeared as Jacob Milgrom and Daniel I. Block in conversation, *Ezekiel's Hope: A Commentary on Ezekiel 38–48*. Eugene, OR: Cascade, 2012.

Bibliography

Abusch, T. "The Form and Meaning of a Babylonian Prayer to Marduk." *Journal of the American Oriental Society* 103 (1983) 3–15.
Ackerman, J. S. "Prophecy and Warfare in Early Israel: A Study of the Deborah-Barak Story." *Bulletin of the American Schools of Oriental Research* 220 (1975) 5–13.
Ackerman, Susan. "The Personal is Political: Covenantal and Affectionate Love (ʾāhēb ʾăhābâ) in the Hebrew Bible." *Vetus Testamentum* 52 (2002) 437–58.
Ackroyd, Peter R. *Exile and Restoration: A Study of Hebrew Thought of the Sixth Century B.C.* Old Testament Library. Philadelphia: Westminster, 1968.
———. "The 'Seventy Year' Period." *Journal of Near Eastern Studies* 77 (1958) 23–27.
Albertz, Rainer, and Claus Westermann. "רוּחַ rûaḥ Geist." In *Theologisches Handwörterbuch zum Altern Testament*, edited by E. Jenni and C. Westermann, 2:727. Munich: Kaiser, 1976.
Albright, William F. *Archaeology and the Religion of Israel*. 5th ed. Garden City, NY: Doubleday, 1968.
———. "The Psalm of Habakkuk." In *Studies in Old Testament Prophecy*, edited by H. H. Rowley, 1–18. New York: Scribner's Sons, 1950.
Aldred, C. "Grablage, Auszeichnung durch." *Lexikon der Ägyptologie*, edited by W. Helck and E. Otto, 2:859–62. Wiesbaden: Harrassowitz, 1977.
Alexander, R. H. "Ezekiel." *The Expositor's Bible Commentary*, edited by F. C. Gaebelein, 6:737–996. Grand Rapids: Zondervan, 1986.
Allen, Leslie C. *Ezekiel 20–48*. Word Biblical Commentary 29. Dallas: Word, 1990.
———. "Ezekiel 24:3–14: A Rhetorical Perspective." *Catholic Biblical Quarterly* 49 (1987) 404–14.
Alter, Robert. *The Art of Biblical Poetry*. New York: Harper, 1985.
Andersen F. I., and D. N. Freedman. *Hosea: A New Translation with Introduction and Notes*. Anchor Bible 24. Garden City: Doubleday, 1980.
Arrian. *Anabasis of Alexander*. Books 5–7. Translated by P. A. Brunt. Loeb Classical Library. Cambridge: Harvard University Press, 1983.
Aune, D. E. "Demon, Demonology." In *International Standard Bible Encyclopedia*, rev. ed, edited by G. Bromiley, 1:919–23. Grand Rapids: Eerdmans, 1979.
Balentine, Samuel E. *The Hidden God: The Hiding of the Face of God in the Old Testament*. Oxford: Oxford University Press, 1983.
Barkay, G. and A. Kloner. "Jerusalem Tombs from the Days of the First Temple." *Biblical Archaeology Review* 12.2 (1986) 22–39.
Barrick, W. Boyd. "The Straight-Legged Cherubim of Ezekiel's Inaugural Vision (Ezekiel 1:7a)." *Catholic Biblical Quarterly* 44 (1982) 543–50.
Bartelmus, R. "Ez 37,1–14, die Verbform wĕqāṭal und die Anfänge der Auferstehungshoffnung." *Zeitschrift für die alttestamentliche Wissenschaft* 97 (1985) 366–89.
———. "Textkritik, Literarkritik und Syntax. Anmerkungen zur neueren Diskussion um Ez 37,11." *Biblische Notizen* 25 (1984) 55–64.

Bibliography

Barth, Christoph. *Die Errettung vom Tode in den individuellen Klage- und Dankliedern des Alten Testaments*. Zollikon: Evangelischer, 1947.
Barth, Karl. *Church Dogmatics*. Vol. 3.2, *The Doctrine of Creation*. Edinburgh: T. & T. Clark, 1960.
Bauckham, Richard. "Early Jewish Visions of Hell." *Journal of Theological Studies*, n.s., 41 (1990) 355–85.
Bauer, H., and P. Leander. *Historische Grammatik der hebräischen Sprache des Alten Testaments*. 1922. Reprint. Hildesheim: Olms, 1962.
Baumann, E. "Die Hauptvisionen Hesekiels." *Zeitschrift für die altestamentliche Wissenschaft* 67 (1955) 56–67.
Baumgärtel, F. "Spirit in the Old Testament." In *Theological Dictionary of the New Testament*, edited by G. Kittel and G. Friedrich, and translated by G. W. Bromiley, 6.367–68. Grand Rapids: Eerdmans, 1968.
Baumgartner, W. *Zum Alten Testament und seiner Umwelt: Ausgewählte Aufsätze*. Leiden: Brill, 1959.
Bayliss, M. "The Cult of Dead Kin in Assyria and Babylonia." *Iraq* 35 (1973) 115–25.
Beale, G. K. *We Become What We Worship: A Biblical Theology of Idolatry*. Downers Grove, IL: InterVarsity, 2008.
Ben-Ze'ev, Aaron. "Envy and Jealousy." *Canadian Journal of Philosophy* 20 (1990) 487–516.
———. *The Subtlety of Emotions*. Cambridge, MA: MIT, 2000.
Berger, P. R. "Der Kyros-Zylinder mit dem Zusatzfragment BIN II Nr. 32 und die akkadischen Personennamen im Danielbuch." *Zeitschrift für Assyriologie* 64 (1875) 192–234.
———. *Die neubabylonischen Königsinschriften: Königsinschriften des ausgehenden babylonischen Reiches* (626–539 a. Chr.). Alter Orient und Altes Testament 4.1. Neukirchen-Vluyn: Neukirchener, 1973.
Berkhof, L. *Systematic Theology*. 2 vols. Grand Rapids: Eerdmans, 1938.
Berossus. *The Babyloniaca of Berossus*. Sources and Monographs: Monographs on the Ancient Near East 1.5. Malibu: Undena, 1978.
Berry, G. R. "The Authorship of Ezekiel 40–48." *Journal of Biblical Literature* 34 (1915) 17–40.
Bertram, G. "ὁρμή, ὅρμημα, ὁρμάω." In *Theological Dictionary of the New Testament*, edited by G. Kittel and G. Friedrich, and translated by G. W. Bromiley, 5.469. Grand Rapids: Eerdmans, 1967.
Betts, T. J. *Ezekiel the Priest: A Custodian of Torah*. Studies in Biblical Literature 74. New York: Lang, 2005.
Bevan, E. R. *The House of Seleucus*. 1902. Reprint. New York: Barnes & Noble, 1966.
Birkeland, H. "The Belief in the Resurrection of the Dead in the Old Testament." *Studia Theologica* 3 (1949) 60–78.
Black, J. A. "The New Year Ceremonies in Ancient Babylon: 'Taking Bel by the Hand' and a Cultic Picnic." *Religion* 11 (1981) 39–59.
Bloch-Smith, Elizabeth. *Judahite Burial Practices and Beliefs about the Dead*. Journal for the Study of the Old Testament Supplement Series 123. Sheffield, UK: JSOT, 1992.
Block, Daniel I., and Jacob Milgrom in Conversation. *Ezekiel's Hope: A Commentary on Ezekiel 38–48*. Eugene, OR: Wipf & Stock, 2012.

Bibliography

Block, Daniel I. "Bearing the Name of the LORD with Honor." In *How I Love Your Torah, O LORD: Studies in the Book of Deuteronomy*, 61–72. Eugene, OR: Cascade, 2011. Previously published in *Bibliotheca Sacra* 168 (2011) 20–31.

———. "Beyond the Grave: Ezekiel's Vision of Death and Afterlife." *Bulletin for Biblical Research* 2 (1992) 113–41.

———. *The Book of Ezekiel Chapters 1–24*. New International Commentary on the Old Testament. Grand Rapids: Eerdmans, 1997.

———. *The Book of Ezekiel Chapters 25–48*. New International Commentary on the Old Testament. Grand Rapids: Eerdmans, 1998.

———. "Ezekiel: Theology of." In *New International Dictionary of Old Testament Theology & Exegesis*, edited by Willem VanGemeren, 4:615–28. Grand Rapids: Zondervan, 1997.

———. "Ezekiel's Boiling Cauldron: A Form Critical Solution to Ezekiel XXIV 1–14." *Vetus Testamentum* 41 (1991) 12–37.

———. *The Gods of the Nations: Studies in Ancient Near Eastern National Theology*. Evangelical Theological Society Monographs 2. 2nd ed. 2000. Reprint. Eugene, OR: Cascade, 2013.

———. "Gog and the Pouring out of the Spirit: Reflections on Ezekiel xxxix 21–29." *Vetus Testamentum* 37 (1987) 257–70.

———. "New Year." In *International Standard Bible Encyclopedia*. Rev. ed, edited by G. Bromiley, 3.529–32. Grand Rapids: Eerdmans, 1986.

———. "No Other Gods: Bearing the Name of YHWH in a Polytheistic World." In *The Gospel according to Moses: Theological and Ethical Reflections on the Book of Deuteronomy*, 237–71. Eugene, OR: Cascade, 2012.

———. "Preaching Ezekiel." In *"He Began with Moses . . .": Preaching the Old Testament Today*, edited by G. J. R. Kent, P. J. Kissling, and L. A. Turner, 157–78. Nottingham, UK: InterVarsity, 2010.

———. "The Prophet of the Spirit: The Use of *rwḥ* in the Book of Ezekiel." *Journal of the Evangelical Theological Society* 32 (1989) 27–49.

———. "Text and Emotion: A Study in the 'Corruptions' in Ezekiel's Inaugural Vision." *Catholic Biblical Quarterly* 50 (1988) 1–25.

———. "The Prophet of the Spirit: The Use of *rwḥ* in the Book of Ezekiel." *The Journal of the Evangelical Theological Society* 32 (1988) 27–50.

———. Review of *Gog of Magog*, by William Tooman. *Biblica*, forthcoming.

———. "The Tender Cedar Sprig: Ezekiel on Jehoiachin." *Journal of Hebrew Bible and Ancient History* 2 (2012) 173–202.

Blumenthal, David R. *Facing the Abusing God: A Theology of Protest*. Louisville: Westminster John Knox, 1993.

Bodi, Daniel. *The Book of Ezekiel and the Poem of Erra*. Orbus biblicus et orientalis 104. Göttingen: Vandenhoeck & Ruprecht, 1991.

Böhl, F. M. Th. "Die fünfzig Namen des Marduk." *Archiv für Orientforschung* 11 (1936–37) 191–218.

———. "Eine zweisprachige Weihinschrift Nebukadnezars I." *Bibliotheca Orientalis* 7 (1950) 42–46.

Borger, Riekele [Rykle]. "An Additional Remark on P. R. Ackroyd, JOURNAL OF NEAR EASTERN STUDIES XVII 23–27." *Journal of Near Eastern Studies* 18 (1959) 74.

———. *Babylonisch-Assyrische Lesestücke*. 2nd ed. Analecta orientalia 54. Heft I, *Die Texte in Umschrift*. Rome: Pontifical Biblical Institute, 1963.

Bibliography

———. "Gott Marduk und Gott-König Šulgi als Propheten: Zwei prophetische Texte." *Bibliotheca Orientalis* 28 (1971) 3–24.

———. *Die Inschriften Asarhaddons Königs von Assyrien*. Archiv für Orientforschung Beiheft 9. Graz, Austria: Weidner, 1956.

———. Review of *Brief eines Bischofs von Esagila an König Asarhaddon*, by B. Landsberger. *Bibliotheca Orientalis* 29 (1972) 33–36.

Born, A. van den. *Ezechiël*. De Boeken van het Oude Testament. Roermond en Maaseik, Netherlands: Romen & Zonen, 1954.

Boyce, Mary. *A History of Zoroastrianism*. Handbuch der Orientalistik 1.8.1. Leiden: Brill, 1975.

Brinkman, John A. "Kassiten (*Kaššû*)." In *Reallexikon der Assyriologie und Vorderasiatischen Archäologie*, edited by M. P. Streck, 5:464–73. Berlin: DeGruyter, 1976.

———. *Materials and Studies for Kassite History* I. Chicago: University of Chicago Press, 1976.

———. "Notes on Mesopotamian History in the Thirteenth Century B.C." *Bibliotheca Orientalis* 27 (1970) 301–14.

———. *A Political History of Post-Kassite Babylonia 1158–722 B.C.* Analecta orientalia 43. Rome: Pontifical Biblical Institute, 1968.

———. "Through a Glass Darkly: Esarhaddon's Retrospects on the Downfall of Babylon." *Journal of the American Oriental Society* 103 (1983) 35–42.

Bromiley, G. W. "Hell, History of the Doctrine of." In *International Standard Bible Encyclopedia*, rev. ed, edited by G. Bromiley, 2.677–79. Grand Rapids: Eerdmans, 1979.

Brownlee, William H. "Ezekiel's Copper Caldron and Blood on the Rock (Chapter 24 1–14)." In *For Me to Live: Essays in Honor of James L. Kelso*, edited by R. A. Coughenhour, 21–43. Cleveland: Liederbach, 1972.

Bruno, A. *Jesaja: Eine rhythmische und textkritische Untersuchung*. Stockholm: Almqvist & Wiksell, 1953.

Burstein, S. M. *The Babyloniaca of Berossus*. Sources and Monographs: Monographs on the Ancient Near East, 1.5. Malibu: Undena, 1978.

Buswell, J. O. Jr. *A Systematic Theology of the Christian Religion*. 2 vols. Grand Rapids: Zondervan, 1962

Butterworth, Brian, Robert Reeve, Fiona Reynolds, and Delyth Lloyd. "Numerical Thought with and without Words: Evidence from Indigenous Australian Children." *Publications of the National Academy of Science* 105.35 (September 2, 2008) 13179–84.

Cagni, Luigi. *Das Erra-Epos, Keilschrifttext*. Studia Pohl 5. Rome: Pontifical Biblical Institute, 1970.

———. *The Poem of Erra*. Sources from the Ancient Near East, 1.3. Malibu: Undena, 1973.

Calvin, John. *Commentaries on the First Twenty Chapters of the Book of the Prophet Ezekiel*. 2 vols. Translated by T. Myers. Grand Rapids: Eerdmans, 1948.

Caquot, A. "Sur quelques démons de l'Ancien Testament (Reshep, Qeteb, Deber)." *Semitica* 6 (1956) 57–58.

Carroll, Robert P. "Desire under the Terebinths: On Pornographic Representation in the Prophets—A Response." In *A Feminist Companion to the Latter Prophets*, edited by Athalya Brenner, 275–307. The Feminist Companion to the Bible 8. Sheffield, UK: Sheffield Academic Press, 1995.

Bibliography

Charles, R. H. *A Critical and Exegetical Commentary on the Revelation of St. John*. International Critical Commentary. 2 vols. Edinburgh: T. & T. Clark, 1920.

Chiera, E. *Sumerian Lexical Texts from the Temple School of Nippur*. Oriental Institute Publications 11. Chicago: Oriental Institute Press, 1929.

Clay, A. T. *Business Documents of Murashû Sons of Nippur Dated in the Reign of Darius II (424-404 B.C.)*. Babylonian Expedition Series A: Cuneiform Texts 10. Philadelphia: University of Pennsylvania, 1904.

———. *Miscellaneous Inscriptions in the Yale Babylonian Collection*. Yale Oriental Series, Babylonian Texts 1. New Haven: Yale University Press, 1915.

———. *Personal Names from Cuneiform Inscriptions of the Cassite Period*. Yale Oriental Series, Texts 1. New Haven: Yale University Press, 1912.

Clines, D. J. A. "The Image of God in Man." *Tyndale Bulletin* 19 (1968) 53-103.

Cody, A. *Ezekiel*. Old Testament Message 11. Wilmington, DE: Glazier, 1984.

Cogan, Mordechai. *Imperialism and Religion: Assyria, Judah, and Israel in the Eighth and Seventh Centuries B.C.E*. Society of Biblical Literature Monograph Series 19. Missoula, MT: Scholars, 1974.

Coggins, R. J. "The Problem of Isaiah 24-27." *Expository Times* 90 (1978-79) 328-33.

The Compact Edition of the Oxford English Dictionary. Oxford: Oxford University Press, 1971.

Cooke, G. A. *A Critical and Exegetical Commentary on the Book of Ezekiel*. International Critical Commentary. Edinburgh: T. & T. Clark, 1936.

Cooley, Robert E. "Gathered to His People: A Study of a Dothan Family Tomb." In *The Living and Active Word of God: Studies in Honor of Samuel J. Schultz*, edited by M. Inch et al., 47-58. Winona Lake, IN: Eisenbrauns, 1983.

Cooper, A. "MLK 'lm: 'Eternal King' or 'King of Eternity.'" In *Love and Death in the Ancient Near East: Essays in Honor of Marvin H Pope*, edited by J. H. Marks and R. M. Good, 1-8. Guildford, UK: Four Quarters, 1987.

Cooper, Jerrold S. *The Curse of Agade*. Baltimore: Johns Hopkins University Press, 1983.

Cooper, Lamar. E. *Ezekiel*. New American Commentary. Nashville: Broadman & Holman, 1994.

Cornill, C. H. *Das Buch des Propheten Ezechiel*. Leipzig: Hinrichs, 1886.

Cuddon, J. A. *A Dictionary of Literary Terms and Literary Theory*. 3rd ed. Oxford: Blackwell, 1991.

Dahood, Mitchell. *Psalms III*. Anchor Bible 17A. Garden City, NY: Doubleday, 1970.

———. "Qoheleth and Recent Discoveries." *Biblica* 39 (1958) 308-10.

———. *Ras Shamra Parallels: The Texts from Ugarit and the Hebrew Bible*, edited by S. Rummel, 3.54-55. Analecta orientalia 51. Rome: Pontifical Biblical Institute, 1981.

Dalley, Stephanie. "Erra and Ishum." In *The Context of Scripture*, vol. 1: *Canonical Compositions from the Biblical World*, edited by William H. Hallo and Lawson K. Younger Jr., 404-16. Leiden: Brill, 1997.

———. *Myths from Mesopotamia: Creation, the Flood, Gilgamesh, and Others*. Oxford: Oxford University Press, 1989.

Darr, Katheryn Pfisterer. "Ezekiel." In *New Interpreter's Bible*, vol. 6, 1073-1607. Nashville: Abingdon, 2001.

Davidson, A. B. *The Book of the Prophet Ezekiel*. Cambridge: Cambridge University Press, 1900.

———. *Hebrew Syntax*. 3rd ed. Edinburgh: T. & T. Clark, 1901.

Bibliography

Day, John. "New Light on the Mythological Background of the Allusion to Resheph in Habakkuk III 5." *Vetus Testamentum* 29 (1979) 259–74.

Day, Linda. "Rhetoric and Domestic Violence in Ezekiel 16." *Biblical Interpretation* 8 (2000) 205–30.

Day, Peggy. "The Bitch Had it Coming to Her: Rhetoric and Interpretation in Ezekiel 16." *Biblical Interpretation* 8 (2000) 231–54.

Delcor, M., and E. Jenni. "שָׁלַח šlḥ senden." In *Theologisches Handwörterbuch zum Alten Testament*, edited by E. Jenni and C. Westerman, 2.909–16. Munich: Kaiser, 1976.

Dempsey, Carol J. "The 'Whore' of Ezekiel 16: The Impact and Ramifications of Gender-Specific Metaphors in Light of Biblical Law and Divine Judgment." In *Gender and Law in the Hebrew Bible and the Ancient Near East*, edited by Victor H. Matthews, Bernard M. Levinson, and Tikva Frymer-Kensky, 57–78. Journal for the Study of the Old Testament Supplements, 262. Sheffield, UK: Sheffield Academic Press, 1998.

Demson, D. E. "Divine Power Politics: Reflections on Ezekiel 37." In *Intergerini Perietis Septvm (Eph. 2:14): Essays Presented to Markus Barth on his Sixty-fifth Birthday*, edited by D. Y. Hadidian, 97–110. Pittsburgh: Pickwick, 1981.

Dietrich, M., and O. Loretz, "Neue Studien zu den Ritualtexten aus Ugarit." *Ugarit Forschungen* 13 (1981) 69–74.

Dijk-Hemmes, Fokkelien van. "The Metaphorization of Woman in Prophetic Speech: An Analysis of Ezekiel 23." In *On Gendering Texts: Female & Male Voices in the Hebrew Bible*, edited by Athalya Brenner and Fokkelien van Dijk-Hemmes, 167–76. Biblical Interpretation Series, 1. Leiden: Brill, 1996.

Dillard, R. B. *2 Chronicles*. Word Biblical Commentary 15. Waco: Word, 1987.

Dommershausen, W. "גּוֹרָל gôrāl." In *Theological Dictionary of the Old Testament*, edited by G. J. Botterweck and H. Ringgren, and translated by G. W. Bromiley, 2:450–56. Grand Rapids: Eerdmans, 1975.

———. "חָלַל chālal II." In *Theological Dictionary of the Old Testament*, edited by G. J. Botterweck and H. Ringgren, and translated by G. W. Bromiley, 4.417–21. Grand Rapids, Eerdmans, 1980.

Doran, R., translator. "Pseudo-Hecataeus." In *The Old Testament Pseudepigrapha*, edited by J. H. Charlesworth, 2:917–19. Garden City, NY: Doubleday, 1985.

Dossin, Georges. "Bronzes inscrits du Luristan de la collection Foroughi." *Iranica Antigua* 2 (1962) 149–64.

———. *La divination en Mésopotamie ancienne et dans les régions voisines*. Rencontre Assyriologique Internationale 14. Paris: Presses Universitaires de France, 1966.

Drijvers, H. J. W. *The Religion of Palmyra*. Iconography of Religions 15.15. Leiden: Brill, 1976.

Driver, G. R. "Ancient Lore and Modern Knowledge." In *Hommages a André Dupont-Sommer*, edited by A. Caquot, 283–84. Paris: Adrien-Maisonneuve, 1971.

———. *Aramaic Documents of the Fifth Century B.C*. Oxford: Clarendon, 1957.

———. "Ezekiel: Linguistic and Textual Problems." *Biblica* 35 (1954) 145–59; 299–312.

———. "Linguistic and Textual Problems: Ezekiel." *Biblica* 19 (1938) 60–69; 175–87.

———. *Semitic Writing from Pictograph to Alphabet*. 3rd ed. Edited by S. A. Hopkins. London: Oxford University, 1976.

Duguid, Iain M. *Ezekiel and the Leaders of Israel*. Vetus Testamentum Supplement Series 56. Leiden: Brill, 1994.

Bibliography

Dussaud, R. *La Pénetration des Arabes en Syrie avant l'Islam*. Bibliothéque archéologique et historique 59. Paris: Geuthner, 1955.

Eaton, J. H. "The Origin and Meaning of Habakkuk 3." *Zeitschrift für die altestamentliche Wissenschaft* 76 (1964) 144–71.

Ebach, J. H. *"PGR* = (Toten-) Opfer? Ein Vorschlag zum Verständnis von Ez. 43,7.9." *Ugarit Forschungen* 3 (1971) 365–68.

Ebeling, E. *Die akkadische Gebetsserie "Handerhebung."* Deutsche Akademie der Wissenschaften zu Berlin Institut für Orientforschung 20. Berlin: Akademie-Verlag, 1953.

———. "Dämonen." In *Reallexikon der Assyriologie und Vorderasiatischen Archäologie*, edited by E. Ebeling and B. Meissner, 2:107–12. Berlin: de Gruyter, 1938.

Edzard, D. O. "Mesopotamien. Die Mythologie der Sumerer und Akkader." In *Wörterbuch der Mythologie. Vol. 1, Götter und Mythen im Vonderen Orient*, 2nd ed., edited by H. W. Haussig, 17–140. Stuttgart: Klett-Cotta, 1983.

Eichrodt, Walther. *Ezekiel: A Commentary*. Old Testament Library. Philadelphia: Westminster, 1970.

———. *Theology of the Old Testament*. 2 vols. Philadelphia: Westminster, 1965/67.

Eilers, W. *Iranische Beamtennamen in der Keilschriftliche Überlieferung*. Vol 1. Leipzig: Deutsche Morgenländische Gesellschaft, 1940.

Eissfeldt, Otto. *The Old Testament: An Introduction*. New York: Harper & Row, 1965.

———. "Schwerterschlagene bei Hesekiel." In *Studies in Old Testament Prophecy*, edited by H. H. Rowley, 73–81. New York: Scribner's Sons, 1950.

Ellermeier, F. *Prophetie in Mari und Israel*. Herzberg, Germany: Jungfer, 1968.

Erickson, Millard J. *Christian Theology*. 3 vols. Grand Rapids: Baker, 1985.

Erlandsson, S. *The Burden of Babylon: A Study of Isaiah 13:2—14:23*. Coniectanea biblica: Old Testament Series 4. Lund: Gleerup, 1970.

Evans, John Frederick. "An Inner-Biblical Interpretation and Intertextual Reading of Ezekiel's Recognition Formulae with the Book of Exodus." ThD diss., University of Stellenbosch, 2006.

Even-Shoshan, A. *A New Concordance of the Bible*. Jerusalem: Kiryat Sepher, 1981.

Ewert, David. *The Holy Spirit in the New Testament*. Scottdale, PA: Herald, 1983.

Exum, J. Cheryl. "Prophetic Pornography." In *Plotted, Shot and Painted: Cultural Representations of Biblical Women*, 101–28. Journal for the Study of the Old Testament Supplements, 215/Gender, Culture, Theory 3. Sheffield, UK: Sheffield Academic Press, 1996.

Falkenstein, A. "Ein sumerisches Kultlied auf Samsu'iluna." *Archív Orientální* 17.1 (1949) 212–26.

Fensham, F. C. "Common Trends in Curses of the Near Eastern Treaties and *Kudurru*-Inscriptions compared with the Maledictions of Amos and Isaiah." *Zeitschrift für die altestamentliche Wissenschaft* 75 (1963) 155–75.

———. "The Curse of the Dry Bones in Ezekiel 37:1–14 Changed to a Blessing of Resurrection." *Journal of Northwest Semitic Languages* 13 (1987) 59–60.

Fine, H. A. "Studies in Middle-Assyrian Chronology and Religion." *Hebrew Union College Annual* 25 (1954) 116–30.

Fishbane, Michael. *Biblical Interpretation in Ancient Israel*. Oxford: Clarendon, 1985.

Fisher, David H. *Historians' Fallacies: Toward a Logic of Historical Thought*. New York: Harper & Row, 1970.

Fohrer, Georg. *Ezechiel*. Handbuch zum Alten Testamentum 13. Tübingen: Mohr, 1955.

Bibliography

———. "Die Glossen im Buche Ezechiel." In *Studien zur alttestamentlichen Prophetie (1949-1965)*, 204-21. Beihefte zur Zeitschrift für die alttestamentliche Wissenschaft 99. Berlin: Töpelmann, 1967.

———. *Die Hauptprobleme des Buches Ezechiel*. Beihefte zur Zeitschrift für die alttestamentliche Wissenschaft 72. Berlin: Töpelmann, 1952.

Foster, Benjamin R. *Before the Muses: An Anthology of Akkadian Literature*. 3rd ed. Bethesda, MD: CDL, 2005.

———. *From Distant Days: Myths, Tales, and Poetry of Ancient Mesopotamia*. Bethesda, MD: CDL, 1995.

Fox, Michael V. "The Rhetoric of Ezekiel's Vision of the Valley of the Bones." *Hebrew Union College Annual* 51 (1980) 1-15.

Fox, S. J. *Hell in Jewish Literature*. Northbrook, IL: Whitehall, 1972.

Frankfort, H. *Ancient Egyptian Religion: An Interpretation*. New York: Cornell University Press, 1948.

Freedy, Kenneth S. "The Glosses in Ezekiel i-xxiv." *Vetus Testamentum* 20 (1970) 129-52.

Friebel, Kelvin J. "The Decrees of Yahweh That Are 'Not Good': Ezekiel 20:25-26." In *Seeking Out the Wisdom of the Ancients: Essays Offered to Honor Michael V. Fox on the Occasion of His Sixty-fifth Birthday*, edited by R. L. Troxel, K. G. Friebel, and D. R. Magary, 21-36. Winona Lake, IN: Eisenbrauns, 2005.

Frymer-Kensky, T. "The Tribulations of Marduk: The So-Called 'Marduk Ordeal Text.'" *Journal of the American Oriental Society* 103 (1983) 131-41.

Fuhs, Hans F. "Ez 24: Überlegungen zu Tradition und Redaktion des Ezechielbuches." *Ezekiel and His Book*, edited by J. Lust, 266-82. Bibliotheca ephemeridum theologicarum lovaniensium 24. Leuven: Leuven University Press, 1986.

Fulco, W. J. *The Canaanite God Rešep*. American Oriental Series 8. New Haven: American Oriental Society, 1976.

Gadd, Cyril J. "The Harran Inscriptions of Nabonidus." *Anatolian Studies* 8 (1958) 35-92.

Galling, K. "Erwägungen zum Stelenheiligtum von Hazor." *Zeitschrift des deutschen Palästina-Vereins* 75 (1959) 1-13.

———. "Die Nekropole von Jerusalem." *Palästina-Jahrbuch* 32 (1936) 73-101.

Ganzel, Tova. "The Description of the Restoration of Israel in Ezekiel." *Vetus Testamentum* 60 (2010) 197-211.

Garber, David G. Jr. "'I Went in Bitterness': Theological Implications of a Trauma Theory Reading of Ezekiel." Paper presented at the annual meeting of the Society of Biblical Literature. Washington, DC, 2006.

———. "Trauma, History, and Survival in Ezekiel 1-24." PhD diss., Emory University, 2005.

Garscha, J. *Studien zum Ezechielbuch: Eine redaktionskritische Untersuchung von 1-39*. Europäische Hochschulschriften 23. Frankfurt: Lang, 1974.

Gaster, T. H. "Demon, Demonology." In *The Interpreter's Dictionary of the Bible*, edited by G. A. Buttrick, 1:818-22. Nashville: Abingdon, 1962.

Gerlemann, G. "חָיָה *ḥjh*," In *Theologisches Handwörterbuch zum Alten Testament*, edited by E. Jenni and C. Westerman, 1:549-57. Munich: Kaiser, 1971.

———. "מות *mût* sterben." In *Theologisches Handwörterbuch zum Alten Testament*, edited by E. Jenni and C. Westerman, 1:893-97. Munich: Kaiser, 1971.

———. "שְׁאוֹל šěôl Totenreich." In *Theologisches Handwörterbuch zum Alten Testament*, edited by E. Jenni and C. Westerman, 2:837–41. Munich: Kaiser, 1976.

Gibson, John C. L. *Hebrew and Moabite Inscriptions. Syrian Semitic Inscriptions I*. Oxford: Clarendon, 1971.

Gile, Jason. "Ezekiel 20: Israel's History." Unpublished essay.

———. Review of *Sexual and Marital Metaphors in Hosea, Jeremiah, Isaiah, and Ezekiel*, by Sharon Moughtin-Mumby. *Journal of Hebrew Scriptures* 9 (2009). No pages. Online: http://www.arts.ualberta.ca/JHS/reviews/reviews_new/review391.htm.

Goetze, A. "An Inscription of Simbar-Sihu." *Journal of Cuneiform Studies* 19 (1965) 121–22.

Grabbe, L. L. "The Seasonal Pattern and the Baal Cycle." *Ugarit Forschungen* 8 (1976) 57–63.

Graffy, Adrian. *A Prophet Confronts His People: The Disputation Speech in the Prophets*. Analecta Biblica 104. Rome: Biblical Institute Press, 1984.

Gray, G. B. *A Critical and Exegetical Commentary on the Book of Isaiah I–XXVII*. International Critical Commentary. Edinburgh: T. & T. Clark, 1912.

Grayson, A. K. *Assyrian and Babylonian Chronicles*. Texts from Cuneiform Sources 5. Locust Valley, NY: Augustin, 1975.

———. *Assyrian Royal Inscriptions*. Records of the Ancient Near East. Wiesbaden: Harrassowitz, 1972.

———. *Babylonian Historical-Literary Texts*. Toronto: University of Toronto Press, 1975.

Green, Margaret W. "The Eridu Lament." *Journal of Cuneiform Studies* 30 (1978) 127–67.

———. "The Uruk Lament." *Journal of the American Oriental Society* 104 (1984) 253–79.

Greenberg, Moshe. "Anthropopathism in Ezekiel." In *Perspectives in Jewish Learning*, edited by Monford Harris, 1–10. Chicago: College of Jewish Studies Press, 1965.

———. "Ezekiel." *Encyclopedia Judaica*, 6:1078–95. Jerusalem: Keter, 1971.

———. *Ezekiel 1–20: A New Translation with Introduction and Commentary*. Anchor Bible 22. Garden City, NY: Doubleday, 1983.

———. *Ezekiel 21–37: A New Translation with Introduction and Commentary*. Anchor Bible 22A. Garden City, NY: Doubleday, 1997.

———. "What Are Valid Criteria for Determining Inauthentic Matter in Ezekiel?" In *Ezekiel and His Book*, edited by J. Lust, 123–35. Bibliotheca ephemeridum theologicarum lovaniensium 74. Leuven: Leuven University Press, 1986.

Greenhill, William. *An Exposition of the Five First Chapters of the Prophet Ezekiel with Useful Observations Thereupon*. 2nd ed. London: M.S., 1650.

Greenspoon, L. J. "The Origin of the Idea of Resurrection." In *Traditions in Transformation: Turning Points in Biblical Faith*, edited by B. Halpern and J. D. Levenson, 247–321. Winona Lake, IN: Eisenbrauns, 1981.

Gruber, M. I. *Aspects of Nonverbal Communication in the Ancient Near East*. Rome: Biblical Institute, 1980.

Haag, E. "Ez 37 und der Glaube an die Auferstehung der Toten." *Trierer theologische Zeitschrift* 82 (1973) 78–92

Habel, Norman C. "The Form and Significance of the Call Narratives." *Zeitschrift für die alttestamentliche Wissenschaft* 77 (1965) 297–323.

Bibliography

Hackett, J. A. *The Balaam Text from Deir 'Allā.* Harvard Semitic Monographs 31. Chico, CA: Scholars, 1980.

Hallo, William W. *Origins: The Ancient Near Eastern Background of Some Modern Western Institutions.* Studies in the History and Culture of the Ancient Near East 6. Leiden: Brill, 1996.

Halperin, David J. "The Exegetical Character of Ezek. X 9–17." *Vetus Testamentum* 26 (1976) 129–41.

———. "Merkabah Midrash in the Septuagint." *Journal of Biblical Literature* 101 (1982) 351–63.

———. *Seeking Ezekiel: Text and Psychology.* University Park, PA: Pennsylvania State University Press, 1993.

Hals, R. M. *Ezekiel.* Forms of Old Testament Literature 19. Grand Rapids: Eerdmans, 1989.

Hanson, R. *The Method and Message of Jewish Apocalyptic.* Old Testament Library. Philadelphia: Fortress, 1964.

———. "Rebellion in Heaven, Azazel, and the Euhemeristic Heroes in 1 Enoch 6–11." *Journal of Biblical Literature* 96 (1977) 195–233.

Hartman L. F., and A. A. di Lella. *The Book of Daniel: A New Translation with Introduction and Commentary.* Anchor Bible 23. Garden City, NY: Doubleday, 1978.

Hasel, Gerhard. F. "Resurrection in the Theology of Old Testament Apocalyptic." *Zeitschrift für die altestamentliche Wissenschaft* 92 (1980) 267–84.

Hatch, E., and H. A. Redpath. *A Concordance to the Septuagint.* 1897. Reprint. Grand Rapids: Baker, 1983.

Hayes, John H., and Paul K. Hooker. *A New Chronology for the Kings of Israel and Judah and Its Implications for Biblical History and Literature.* Atlanta: John Knox, 1988.

Healey, J. F. "*MLKM/ RP UM* and the *Kispum.*" *Ugarit Forschungen* 10 (1978) 89–91.

———. "The Underworld Character of the God Dagan." *Journal of Northwest Semitic Languages* 5 (1977) 43–51.

Heider, G. C. *The Cult of Molek: A Reassessment.* Journal for the Study of the Old Testament Supplement Series 43. Sheffield, UK: JSOT, 1985.

Heintz, J.-G. "בְּאֵר *be'ēr.*" In *Theological Dictionary of the Old Testament*, edited by G. J. Botterweck and H. Ringgren, and translated by G. W. Bromiley, 1:463–66. Grand Rapids: Eerdmans, 1974.

Held, Moshe. "Pits and Pitfalls in Akkadian and Biblical Hebrew." *Journal of the Ancient Near Eastern Society of Columbia University* 5 (1973) 173–90.

Herodotous, *The Histories.* Translated by A. de Sealincourt. Penguin Classics. Baltimore: Penguin, 1954.

Heschel, A. J. *The Prophets.* New York: Jewish Publication Society, 1962.

Hill, D. *Greek Words with Hebrew Meanings Studies in the Semantics of Soteriological Terms.* Cambridge: Cambridge University Press, 1967.

Hiller, N., revision editor. *Illustrated Bible Dictionary.* 3 vols. Leicester, UK: Inter-Varsity, 1980.

Hillers, D. R. *Treaty-Curses and the Old Testament Prophets.* Biblica et orientalia 16. Rome: Pontifical Biblical Institute, 1964.

Hodge, C. *Systematic Theology.* 3 vols. Grand Rapids: Eerdmans, 1965.

Höffken, P. "Beobachtungen zu Ezechiel XXXVII 1–10." *Vetus Testamentum* 31 (1981) 305–17.

Hoekema, Anthony. "Amillenialism." In *The Meaning of the Millennium: Four Views*, edited by R. Clouse, 155-88. Downers Grove, IL: InterVarsity, 1977.
Hoffner, Harry A. "אוֹב *'ôbh*." In *Theological Dictionary of the Old Testament*, edited by G. J. Botterweck and H. Ringgren, and translated by G. W. Bromiley, 1:30-34. Grand Rapids: Eerdmans, 1964.
Höfner, Maria. "Die Stammesgruppen Nord- und Zentralarabiens in vorislamischer Zeit." In *Wörterbuch der Mythologie*. Vol. 1, *Götter und Mythen im Vonderen Orient*, 2nd ed., edited by H. W. Haussig, 407-82. Stuttgart: Klett-Cotta, 1983.
Hoftijzer, J., and G. van der Kooij. *Aramaic Texts from Deir 'Alla*. Documenta et Monumenta Orientis Antiqui. Leiden: Brill, 1976.
Hölscher, G. *Hesekiel: Der Dichter und das Buch*. Beihefte zur Zeitschrift für die alttestamentliche Wissenschaft 39. Giessen: Töpelmann, 1924.
Houk, C. B. "The Final Redaction of Ezekiel 10." *Journal of Biblical Literature* 90 (1971) 42-54.
Huffmon, Herbert B. "Prophecy in the Ancient Near East." In *The Interpreter's Dictionary of the Bible: Supplementary Volume*, edited by K. Crim, 697-700. Nashville: Abingdon, 1976.

———. "Prophecy in the Mari Letters." In *Biblical Archaeology Review* 3, edited by E. F. Campbell and D. N. Freedman, 199-224. Garden City, NY: Doubleday, 1970.
Irwin, W. A. *The Problem of Ezekiel: An Inductive Study*. Chicago: University of Chicago, 1943.
Irwin, W. H. *Isaiah 28-33: Translation with Philological Notes*. Rome: Pontificio Istituto Biblico, 1977.
Jacob, E. *Theology of the Old Testament*. New York: Harper, 1958.
Jacobsen, Thorkild. "The Graven Image." In *Ancient Israelite Religion: Essays in Honor of Frank Moore Cross*, edited by Patrick D. Miller, et al., 15-32. Philadelphia: Westminster, 1987.

———. *Treasures of Darkness: A History of Mesopotamian Religion*. New Haven: Yale University Press, 1976.
Jastrow, M. *A Dictionary of the Targumim, the Talmud Babli and Yerushalmi, and the Midrashic Literature*. 1971. Reprint. New York: Judaica Press, 1985.
Jean, C.-F., and J. Hoftijzer. *Dictionnaire des inscriptions sémitique de l'ouest*. Leiden: Brill, 1965.
Jenni, E. "Das Wort עוֹלָם in Alten Testament." *Zeitschrift für die altestamentliche Wissenschaft* 64.65 (1952/1953) 197-221/1-34.

———. "עוֹלָם *'ōlām* Ewigkeit." In *Theologisches Handwörterbuch zum Alten Testament*, edited by E. Jenni and C. Westerman, 2.228-43. Munich: Kaiser, 1976.
Jeremias, J. "ᾅδης." In *Theological Dictionary of the New Testament*, edited by G. Kittel and G. Friedrich, and translated by G. W. Bromiley, 1.146-49. Grand Rapids: Eerdmans, 1964.
Jerome, "Epistula LIII." In *Epistulae. Pars I: Epistulae I-LXX*, 460-61. Corpus scriptorium ecclesiasticorum latinorum 54. Vienna: Tempsky, 1910.

———. *Opera. Pars I. Opera Exegetica 4. Commentariorum in Hiezechielem Libri XIV*. Continental Commentaries series latina 75. Turnhout: Brepols, 1964.
Johnson, A. R. *The One and the Many in the Israelite Conception of God*. 2nd ed. Cardiff, UK: University of Wales, 1961.

———. *The Vitality of the Individual in the Thought of Ancient Israel*. Cardiff, UK: University of Wales, 1964.

Bibliography

Josephus, Flavius. *Against Apion.* Loeb Classical Library. Cambridge: Harvard University Press, 1976.

———. *Jewish Antiquities.* Loeb Classical Library. Cambridge: Harvard University Press, 1978.

———. *The Jewish War.* Loeb Classical Library. Cambridge: Harvard University Press, 1976.

Joüon, Paul. *Grammaire de l'Hébreu biblique.* Rome: Pontifical Biblical Institute, 1923.

Joyce, Paul M. *Ezekiel: A Commentary.* Library of Hebrew Bible/Old Testament Studies 482. London: T. & T. Clark, 2007.

———. "Ezekiel and Moral Transformation." In *Transforming Visions: Transformations of Text, Tradition, and Theology in Ezekiel,* edited by William A. Tooman and Michael A. Lyons, 139–58. Princeton Theological Monograph Series 127. Eugene, OR: Pickwick, 2010.

Kaiser, Otto. *A Commentary.* Old Testament Library. Philadelphia: Westminster, 1974. Translation of *Der Prophet Jesaja Kapitel 13–39.* Göttingen: Vandenhoeck & Ruprecht, 1973.

Kammenhuber, A. "Marduk: Philologisch II." In *Reallexikon der Assyriologie,* edited by Erich Ebeling, et al., 7:370–72. Berlin: DeGruyter, 1989.

Kaufmann, Y. *The Religion of Israel.* New York: Schocken, 1960.

Kees, H. *Totenglauben und Jenseitsvorstellungen der alten Ägypter.* Berlin: Akademie-Verlag, 1980.

Kelso, James L. *The Ceramic Vocabulary of the Old Testament.* Bulletin of the American Schools of Oriental Research: Supplementary Series 5-6. New Haven: American Schools of Oriental Research, 1948.

———. "Ezekiel's Parable of the Corroded Copper Caldron." *Journal of Biblical Literature* 64 (1945) 391–93.

Kent, R. G. *Old Persian.* 2nd ed. New Haven: American Oriental Society, 1953.

Kim, Brittany. "Yhwh as Jealous Husband: Abusive Authoritarian or Passionate Protector? A Reexamination of a Prophetic Image." In *Daughter Zion: Her Portrait, Her Response,* edited by Mark Boda, Carol Dempsey, and LeAnn Snow Flesher, 127–47. Society of Biblical Literature Hebrew Bible/Old Testament. Atlanta: Society of Biblical Literature, 2012.

King, L. W. *Babylonian Boundary Stones and Memorial-Tablets in the British Museum.* London: British Museum, 1912.

———. *The Letters and Inscriptions of Hammurabi.* London: Luzac, 1898–1900.

Klein, Jacob. "Lamentation over the Destruction of Sumer and Ur." In *The Context of Scripture,* vol. 1: *Canonical Compositions from the Biblical World,* edited by William H. Hallo and Lawson K. Younger Jr., 535–39. Leiden: Brill, 1997.

Klein, W. W., C. L. Blomberg, and R. L. Hubbard. *Introduction to Biblical Interpretation.* Nashville: Thomas Nelson, 1993.

Koehler, Ludwig, and Walter Baumgartner. *Lexicon in Veteris Testamenti Libros.* Leiden: Brill, 1953.

König, F. *Zarathustras Jenseitsvorstellungen und das Alte Testament.* Vienna: Herder, 1964.

Kraeling, C. H., et al. *The Excavations at Dura-Europos. Final report VIII,* Part I, *The Synagogue.* New Haven: Yale University Press, 1956.

Kraetzschmar, R. *Das Buch Ezechiel.* Göttingen: Vandenhoeck & Ruprecht, 1900.

Bibliography

Kramer, Samuel Noah, translator. "The Curse of Agade." In *Ancient Near Eastern Texts Relating to the Old Testament*, 3rd ed., edited by J. B. Pritchard, 646–51. Princeton, Princeton University Press, 1969.

———, translator. "Lamentation over the Destruction of Sumer and Ur." In *Ancient Near Eastern Texts Relating to the Old Testament*, 3rd ed., edited by J. B. Pritchard, 611–19. Princeton, Princeton University Press, 1969.

———. "The Lamentation over the Destruction of Nippur." *Acta Sumerologica (Japan)* 13 (1991) 1–26.

———. *Lamentation over the Destruction of Ur*. Assyriological Studies 12. Chicago: University of Chicago Press, 1940.

———. "Lamentations over the Destruction of Nippur: A Preliminary Report." *Eretz Israel* 9 (1969) 89–93.

Kreuzer, S. "Zur Bedeutung und Etymologie von *hištaḥawâ/yštḥwy*." *Vetus Testamentum* 35 (1985) 39–54.

Kuhl, C. "Die 'Wiederaufname'—ein literarisches Prinzip." *Zeitschrift für die altestamentliche Wissenschaft* 64 (1952) 1–11.

Kutler, L. "A 'Strong' Case for Hebrew *mar*." *Ugarit Forschungen* 16 (1984) 111–18.

Kutsch, Ernst. *Die chronologischen Daten des Ezechielbuches*. Orbus biblicus et orientalis 62. Göttingen: Vandenhoeck & Ruprecht, 1985.

Kutscher, E. Y. *The Language and Linguistic Background of the Isaiah Scroll (1QIsaa)*. Judean Desert Studies 6. Leiden: Brill, 1974.

Kutsko, John F. *Between Heaven and Earth: Divine Presence and Absence in Ezekiel*. Biblical and Judaic Studies from the University of California, San Diego 7. Winona Lake, IN: Eisenbrauns, 2000.

———. "Turning Swords into Plowshares: Ezekiel's Response to Imperial Rhetoric." Paper presented at the annual meeting of the Society of Biblical Literature. San Francisco, 1997.

Lambert, Wilfred G. "Ancient Mesopotamian Gods. Superstition, Philosophy, Theology." *Revue de l'histoire des religions* 207 (1990) 115–30.

———. *Babylonian Wisdom Literature*. Oxford: Clarendon, 1960.

———. "Enmeduranki and Related Matters." *Journal of Cuneiform Studies* 21 (1967) 128–31.

———. "The Historical Development of the Mesopotamian Pantheon: A Study in Sophisticated Polytheism." In *Unity and Diversity: Essays in the History, Literature, and Religion of the Ancient Near East*, edited by H. Goedicke and J. J. M. Roberts, 191–200. Baltimore: Johns Hopkins University Press, 1975.

———. "The Reign of Nebuchadnezzar I: A Turning Point in the History of Ancient Mesopotamian Religion." In *The Seed of Wisdom: Essays in Honour of T. J. Meek*, edited by W. S. McCullough, 3–11. Toronto: University of Toronto Press, 1964.

———. Review of *Das Era Epos*, by F. Gössman. In *Archiv für Orientforschung* 18 (1957–58) 395–401.

———. "Studies in Marduk." *Bulletin of the School of Oriental and African Studies* 47 (1984) 1–9.

———. "Studies in Nergal." *Biblica et orientalia* 30 (1973) 355–63.

Landsberger, Benno. "Akkadisch-Hebräische Wortgleichungen." In *Hebräische Wortforschung: Festschrift zum 80 Geburtstag von Walter Baumgartner*, edited by B. Hartmann, et al., 176–99. Vetus Testamentum Supplement Series 16. Leiden: Brill, 1967.

Bibliography

———. *Breif eines Bischofs von Esagila an König Asarhaddon.* Mededelingen der Koninklijke Nederlandse Akademie van Wetenschappen, Afd. Letterkunde 28.6. Amsterdam: Noordan-Hollandse Uitgeversmaatschappij, 1965.

Lang, Bernhard. "Afterlife: Ancient Israel's Changing Vision of the World Beyond." *Biblical Review* 4 (1988) 12–23.

———. *Ezechiel Der Prophet und das Buch.* Erträge der Forschung 153. Darmstadt: Wissenschaftliche Buchgesellschaft, 1981.

———. "Life after Death in the Prophetic Promise." *Congress Volume: Jerusalem 1986*, edited by J. A. Emerton, 144–56. Vetus Testamentum Supplement Series 40. Leiden: Brill, 1988.

———. *Monotheism and the Prophetic Minority: An Essay in Biblical History and Sociology.* The Social World of Biblical Antiquity. Sheffield, UK: Almond, 1983.

———. "A Neglected Method in Ezekiel Research." *Vetus Testamentum* 29 (1979) 39–44.

———. "No God but Yahweh! The Origin and Character of Biblical Monotheism." In *Monotheism*, 41–49. Concilium 177. Edinburgh: T. & T. Clarke, 1985.

———. "Street Theater, Raising the Dead, and the Zoroastrian Connection in Ezekiel's Prophecy." In *Ezekiel and His Book: Textual and Literary Criticism and Their Interrelation*, edited by J. Lust, 307–16. Bibliotheca ephemeridum theologicarum lovaniensium 74. Leuven: Leuven University, 1986.

———. "Zur Entstehung des biblischen Monotheismus." *Theologische Quartalschrift* 166 (1986) 135–42.

———. "זָבַח zābach." In *Theological Dictionary of the Old Testament*, edited by G. J. Botterweck and H. Ringgren, and translated D. E. Green, 4:17–29. Grand Rapids: Eerdmans, 1980.

Langdon, S. H. *Die neubabylonische Königsinschriften.* Vorderasiatische Bibliothek 4. Leipzig: Hinrichs, 1912.

Lapsley, Jacqueline E. *Can These Bones Live? The Problem of the Moral Self in the Book of Ezekiel.* Beihefte zur Zeitschrift für die alttestamentliche Wissenschaft, 301. Berlin: de Gruyter, 2000.

———. "Shame and Self-Knowledge: The Positive Role of Shame in Ezekiel's View of the Moral Self." In *The Book of Ezekiel: Theological and Anthropological Perspectives*, edited by J. Strong and M. Odell, 143–73. Atlanta: Society of Biblical Literature, 2000.

Laroche, E. *Catalogue des texts Hittites.* 2nd ed. Paris: Klinksieck, 1972.

Lemke, Werner E. "Life in the Present and Hope for the Future." *Interpretation* 38 (1984) 165–80.

Levenson, Jon D. "Ezekiel in the Perspective of Two Commentators," *Interpretation* 38/2 (1984): 210–17.

Levine, B. and J.-M. Tarragon, "Dead Kings and Rephaim: The Patrons of the Ugaritic Dynasty." *Journal of the American Oriental Society* 104 (1984) 649–59.

Lewis, T. J., and C. E. Armerding. "Circumcision." In *International Standard Bible Encyclopedia*, rev. ed., edited by G. W. Bromiley, 1:700–702. Grand Rapids: Eerdmans, 1988.

Lewis, T. J. *Cults of the Dead in Ancient Israel and Ugarit.* Harvard Semitic Monographs 5.39. Atlanta: Scholars, 1989.

Lewy, J. "The Late Assyro-Babylonian Cult of the Moon and its Culmination at the Time of Nabonidus." *Hebrew Union College Annual* 19 (1945–46) 434–49.

Bibliography

Lind, W. A. "A Text-Critical Note to Ezekiel 1: Are Shorter Readings Really Preferable to Longer?" *Journal of the Evangelical Theological Society* 27 (1984) 135–40.

Lods, A. "La 'mort des incirconcis.'" *Comptes rendus des seances de l'Académie des inscriptions et belles-lettres*, 87.2 (1943) 271–83.

Longman, Tremper III. *Fictional Akkadian Autobiography: A Generic and Comparative Study*. Winona Lake, IN: Eisenbrauns, 1991.

―――. "The Marduk Prophecy." In *The Context of Scripture*, vol. 1, *Canonical Compositions from the Biblical World*, edited by William W. Hallo and K. Lawson Younger, 480–82. Leiden: Brill, 1997.

Luckenbill, Daniel David. *Ancient Records of Assyria and Babylonia*. 2 vols. 1927. Reprint. New York: Greenwood, 1968.

Lust, J. "Exegesis and Theology in the Septuagint of Ezekiel: The Longer 'Pluses' and Ezek 43:1–9." In *VI Congress of the International Organization for Septuagint and Cognate Studies*, edited by C. E. Cox, 201–32. Atlanta: Scholars, 1987.

Maas, F. "חָתַת *ḥātat*." In *Theological Dictionary of the Old Testament*, edited by G. J. Botterweck and H. Ringgren, and translated by G. W. Bromiley, 5:277–83. Grand Rapids: Eerdmans, 1986.

Machinist, Peter B. "The Epic of Tukulti-Ninurta I: A Study in Middle Assyrian Literature." PhD diss., Yale University, 1978.

―――. "Literature as Politics: The Tukulti-Ninurta Epic and the Bible." *Catholic Biblical Quarterly* 38 (1976) 455–82.

Macintosh, A. A. *Isaiah xxi: A Palimpsest*. Cambridge: Cambridge University Press, 1980.

Malamat, Abraham. "The Last Kings of Judah and the Fall of Jerusalem An Historical-Chronological Study." *Israel Exploration Journal* 18 (1968) 137–55.

―――. "'Love Your Neighbor as Yourself': What it Really Means." *Biblical Archaeology Review* 16.4 (July/August 1990) 50–51.

―――. "A Mari Prophecy and Nathan's Dynastic Oracle." In *Prophecy: Essays Presented to Georg Fohrer*, edited by J. A. Emerton, 68–82. Beihefte zur Zeitschrift für die alttestamentliche Wissenschaft 150. Berlin: de Gruyter, 1980.

―――. "Prophetic Revelations in New Documents from Mari and the Bible." In *Volume du Congrès, Genève 1965*, 207–27. Vetus Testamentum Supplement Series 15. Leiden: Brill, 1966.

―――. "The Twilight of Judah in the Egyptian-Babylonian Maelstrom." In *Congress Volume, Edinburgh, 1974*, 123–45. Vetus Testamentum Supplements 28. Leiden: Brill, 1975.

―――. "'You Shall Love Your Neighbor as Yourself': A Case of Misinterpretation?" In *Die Hebräische Bibel und ihre zweifache Nachgeschichte: Festschrift für Rolf Rendtorff zum 65. Geburtstag*, edited by E. Blum, et al., 111–15. Neukirchen-Vluyn: Neukirchener, 1990.

Mandolfo, Carleen R. *Daughter Zion Talks Back to the Prophets: A Dialogic Theology of the Book of Lamentations*. Semeia Studies 58. Atlanta: Society of Biblical Literature, 2007.

Marcus, D. Review of *New Year with Canaanites and Israelites*, by J. C. de Moor. *Journal of the American Oriental Society* 93 (1973) 589–91.

Margulis, B. "The Psalm of Habakkuk: A Reconstruction and Interpretation." *Zeitschrift für die altestamentliche Wissenschaft* 81 (1970) 409–42.

Bibliography

Martin-Achard, R. *From Death to Life: A Study of the Development of the Doctrine of the Resurrection in the Old Testament.* Edinburgh: Oliver and Boyd, 1960.

Martinez, R. M. "Epidemic Disease, Ecology, and Culture in the Ancient Near East." In *The Bible in the Light of Cuneiform Literature: Scripture in Context III*, edited by W. W. Hallo, et al., 413–58. Ancient Near Eastern Texts and Studies 8. Lewiston, ME: Mellen, 1990.

McCarthy, D. J. "An Installation Genre?" *Journal of Biblical Literature* 90 (1971) 31–41.

McConville, J. G. *Grace in the End: A Study in Deuteronomic Theology.* Grand Rapids: Zondervan, 1993.

McDannell, C., and B. Lang. *Heaven: A History.* New Haven, CT: Yale University Press, 1988.

McEwan, G. J. P. *Priest and Temple in Hellenistic Babylonia.* Freiburger altorientalische Studien 4. Wiesbaden: Steiner, 1981.

Mein, Andrew. "Ezekiel as a Priest in Exile." In *The Elusive Prophet: The Prophet as a Historical Person, Literary Character and Anonymous Artist*, edited by J. C. De Moor, 199–213. Oudtestamentische Studiën, 45. Leiden: Brill, 2001.

Michalowski, Piotr. *The Lamentation over the Destruction of Sumer and Ur.* Mesopotamian Civilizations 1. Winona Lake, IN: Eisenbrauns, 1989.

Milgrom, Jacob, in conversation with Daniel I. Block. *Ezekiel's Hope: A Commentary on Ezekiel 38–48.* Eugene, OR: Cascade, 2012.

Milgrom, Jacob. "The Desecration of YHWH's Name: Its Parameters and Significance." In *Birkat Shalom: Studies in the Bible, Ancient Near Eastern Literature, and Postbiblical Judaism Presented to Shalom M. Paul on the Occasion of His Seventieth Birthday*, edited by Chaim Cohen, et al., 69–81. Winona Lake, IN: Eisenbrauns, 2008.

———. *Numbers.* Jewish Publication Society Torah Commentary. Philadelphia: Jewish Publication Society, 1990.

Millard, Alan R. "Another Babylonian Chronicle Text." *Iraq* 26 (1964) 19–23.

———. "In Praise of Ancient Scribes." *Biblical Archaeologist* 45 (1982) 143–53.

———. "Text and Comment." In *Biblical and Near Eastern Studies: Essays in Honor of W. S. LaSor*, edited by G. A. Tuttle, 245–52. Grand Rapids: Eerdmans, 1978.

Miller, Patrick D., Jr. "Animal Names as Designations in Ugaritic and Hebrew." *Ugarit Forschungen* 2 (1970) 177–86.

Miller, Patrick D., Jr., and J. J. M. Roberts. *The Hand of the Lord: A Reassessment of the "Ark Narratives" of 1 Samuel.* Johns Hopkins Near Eastern Studies. Baltimore: Johns Hopkins University Press, 1977.

Moenikes, A. "Messianismus im Alten Testament (vorapokalyptische Zeit)." *Zeitschrift für Religions- und Gesitesgeschichte* 40 (1988) 289–306.

Montet, P. *Eternal Egypt.* New York: New American Library, 1964.

Moran, William L., translator. "Divine Revelations." In *Ancient Near Eastern Texts Relating to the Old Testament*, 3rd ed., edited by J. B. Pritchard, 629–32. Princeton: Princeton University Press, 1954.

———. "New Evidence from Mari on the History of Prophecy." *Biblica* 50 (1969) 15–56.

Morenz, S. *Egyptian Religion.* Ithaca, NY: Cornell University Press, 1973.

Mowinckel, S. "Zum Psalm des Habakkuk." *Theologische Zeitschrift* 9 (1953) 1–23.

Muller, R. A. "Resurrection." In *International Standard Bible Encyclopedia*, rev. ed., edited by G. Bromiley, 4:145–50. Grand Rapids: Eerdmans, 1988.

Bibliography

Murray, D. F. "The Rhetoric of Disputation: Re-examination of a Prophetic Genre." *Journal for the Study of the Old Testament* 38 (1987) 95–121.

Musti, D. "Syria and the East." In *The Cambridge Ancient History*. Vol. II.1, *The Hellenistic World*, 2nd ed., 175–220. Cambridge: Cambridge University Press, 1984.

Neiman, David. "*PGR*: A Canaanite Cult-object in the Old Testament." *Journal of Biblical Literature* 67 (1948) 55–60.

Neujahr, Matthew. *Predicting the Past in the Ancient Near East: Mantic Historiography in Ancient Mesopotamia, Judah, and the Mediterranean World*. Brown Judaic Studies 354. Atlanta: Society of Biblical Literature, 2012.

Neuss, W. "Das Buch Ezechiel." In *Theologie und Kunst bis zum Ende des XII. Jahrhundert*. Beiträge zur Geschichte des alten Mönchtums und des Benediktinerordens 1–2. Münster: Aschendorffsche Verlagsbuchhandlung, 1912.

Neyrey, J. H. "Eternal Life." In *Harper's Bible Dictionary*, edited by P. J. Achtemeier, 282–83. San Francisco: Harper & Row, 1985.

Nobile, M. "Influssi Iranici nel Libro di Ezechiele?" *Antonianum* 63 (1988) 449–57.

Nougayrol, Jean. "Textes hépatoscopiques d'époque ancienne conservée au Musée du Louvre II." *Revue d'assyriologie et d'archéologie orientale* 40 (1946) 67–87.

———. "Textes Sumero-Accadiens das archives et bibliotheques privees d'Ugarit." *Ugaritica V.* Mission de Ras Shamra 16. Paris: Imprimerie Nationale, 1968.

Odell, Margaret S., and John T. Strong, editors. *Perspectives on Ezekiel: Theology and Anthropology*. Society of Biblical Literature Symposium Series 9. Atlanta: Scholars, 2000.

Odell, Margaret S. "An Exploratory Study of Shame and Dependence in the Bible and Selected Near Eastern Parallels." In *The Biblical Canon in Comparative Perspective*, edited by W. W. Hallo, K. L. Younger, Jr., and B. Batto, 217–33. Scripture in Context 4. Ancient Near Eastern Texts and Studies 11. Lewiston, NY: Mellen, 1991.

———. "The Inversion of Shame and Forgiveness in Ezekiel 16.59–63." *Journal for the Study of the Old Testament* 56 (1992) 101–12.

———. "You are What You Eat: Ezekiel and the Scroll." *Journal of Biblical Literature* 117 (1998) 229–48.

Oppenheim, A. L., translator. "Babylonian and Assyrian Historical Texts." In *Ancient Near Eastern Texts Relating to the Old Testament*, 3rd ed., edited by J. B. Pritchard, 265–317; 556–67. Princeton: Princeton University Press, 1969.

Orr, Avigdor. "The Seventy Years of Babylon." *Vetus Testamentum* 6 (1956) 304–6.

Oswalt, John N. *The Book of Isaiah Chapters 1–39*. New International Commentary on the Old Testament. Grand Rapids: Eerdmans, 1986.

———. "Recent Studies in the OT Eschatology and Apocalyptic." *Journal of the Evangelical Theological Society* 24 (1981) 289–302.

Pardee, D. "The Semitic Root *mrr* and the Etymology of Ugaritic *mt(r) // brk*." *Ugarit Forschungen* 10 (1978) 259–60.

Parker, R. A., and W. H. Dubberstein. *Babylonian Chronology 626 BC–AD 75*. Brown University Studies 19. Providence: Brown University Press, 1956.

Parunak, H. van Dyke. *Structural Studies in Ezekiel*. Ann Arbor, MI: Ann Arbor University Microfilms, 1978.

Patton, Corinne. "'Should Our Sister Be Treated Like a Whore?' A Response to Feminist Critiques of Ezekiel 23." In *The Book of Ezekiel: Theological and Anthropological Perspectives*, edited by J. Strong and M. Odell, 221–38. Atlanta: Society of Biblical Literature, 2000.

Bibliography

Pedersen, J. *Israel: Its Life and Culture*. London: Oxford University Press, 1926.
Petter, Donna L. *The Book of Ezekiel and Mesopotamian City Laments*. Orbis biblicus et orientalis 246. Göttingen: Vandenhoeck & Ruprecht, 2011.
Pettinato, G. *The Archives of Ebla: An Empire Inscribed in Clay*. Garden City, NY: Doubleday, 1981.
Pitard, W. T. "Post-Funeral Offerings to the Dead in Canaan and Israel." Paper presented at the annual meeting of the Society of Biblical Literature. Kansas City, November 24, 1991.
Polybius, *The Histories*. Translated by W. R. Paton. Loeb Classical Library. 6 vols. New York: Putnam's Sons, 1922.
Pope, M. H., and W. Röllig. "Die Mythologie der Ugariter und Phönizier." In *Wörterbuch der Mythologie*. Vol. 1, *Götter und Mythen im Vonderen Orient*, 2nd ed. edited by H. W. Haussig, 217–312. Stuttgart: Klett-Cotta, 1983.
Pope, M. H. "A Little Soul-Searching." *Maarav* 1 (1978) 25–31.
———. "Mot." In *The Interpreter's Dictionary of the Bible Supplementary Volume*, edited by K. Crim, 607–8. Nashville: Abingdon, 1976.
———. "Notes on the Rephaim Texts from Ugarit." In *Essays on the Ancient Near East in Memory of Jacob Joel Finkelstein*, edited by M. de jong Ellis, 163–82. Hamden, CT: Archon, 1977.
———. Review of *Beatific Afterlife in Ancient Israel and in the Ancient Near East*, by K. Spronk. *Ugarit Forschungen* 19 (1987) 452–63.
———. "The Word שׁחת in Job 9:31." *Journal of Biblical Literature* 5 (1964) 269–78.
Porten, B. *Archives from Elephantine: The Life of an Ancient Jewish Military Colony*. Berkeley: University of California Press, 1968.
Pritchard, J. B., editor. *The Ancient Near East in Pictures Relating to the Old Testament*. 3rd ed. Princeton: Princeton University Press, 1954.
Puech, Emil. "Milkom, le dieu Ammonite, en Amos 1:15." *Vetus Testamentum* 27 (1977) 177–25.
Rad, G. von. *Old Testament Theology*. 2 vols. New York: Harper & Row, 1962/65.
Reschid, F., and C. Wilcke. "Ein Grenzstein aus dem ersten(?) Regierungsjahr des Königs Marduk-šāpuk-zēri." *Zeitschrift für Assyriologie* 65 (1875) 34–62.
Reventlow, H. G. *Wächter über Israel: Ezekiel und seine Tradition*. Beihefte zur Zeitschrift für die alttestamentliche Wissenschaft 82. Berlin: Töpelmann, 1962.
Ribichini, F. S., and P. Xella. "'La valle dei passanti' (Ezechiele 39:11)." *Ugarit Forschungen* 12 (1980) 434–47.
Richter, Wolfgang. *Die sogenannten vorprophetischen Berufungsberichte: Eine literaturwissenschaftliche Studie zu 1 Sam 9,1–10, 16, Ex 3f. und Ri 6, 11b–17*. Forschungen zur Religion und Literatur des Alten und Neuen Testaments 101. Göttingen: Vandenhoeck & Ruprecht, 1970.
Riesenfeld, H. *The Resurrection in Ezekiel XXXVII and in the Dura-Europas Paintings*. Uppsala Universitets Arsskrift 11. Uppsala: Lundeqistska, 1948.
Ringgren, Helmer. *Israelite Religion*. Philadelphia: Fortress, 1966.
———. "Prophecy in the Ancient Near East." In *Israel's Prophetic Tradition: Essays in Honour of Peter R. Ackroyd*, edited by R. Coggins, A. Phillips, and M. Knibb, 1–11. Cambridge: Cambridge University Press, 1982.
Roberts, J. J. M. "The Hand of YHWH." *Vetus Testamentum* 21 (1971) 244–51.
———. "Mount Zaphon." In *Interpreter's Dictionary of the Bible: Supplementary Volume*, edited by K. Crim, 977. Nashville: Abingdon, 1962.

Bibliography

Robinson, H. W. "Hebrew Psychology." In *The People and the Book*, edited by A. S. Peake, 353–82. Oxford: Clarendon, 1925.

Rogers, R. W. *Cuneiform Parallels to the Old Testament*. 2nd ed. New York: Abingdon, 1926.

Römer, W. H. Ph. "Religion of Ancient Mesopotamia." In *Historia Religionum: Handbook for the History of Religions*. Vol. 1, *Religions of the Past*, edited by C. J. Bleeker and G. Widengren, 115–94. Leiden: Brill, 1988.

Rom-Shiloni, Dalit. "Ezekiel as the Voice of the Exiles and Constructor of Exilic Ideology." *Hebrew Union College Annual* 76 (2005) 1–45.

Rost, L. "Alttestamentliche Wurzeln der Ersten Auferstehung." In *In Memoriam Ernst Lohmeyer*, edited by W. Schmauch, 66–72. Stuttgart: Evangelisches Verlagswerk, 1951.

Rüssel, J. R. "Burial iii. In Zoroastrianism." *Encyclopaedia Iranica*, edited by E. Yarshater, 4.561–63. London: Routledge & Kegan Paul, 1982.

Sasson, Jack M. "Circumcision in the Ancient Near East." *Journal of Biblical Literature* 85 (1966) 473–76.

Savignac, J. de. "Le sense du terme Saphon." *Ugarit Forschungen* 16 (1984) 273–78.

Scharbert, Josef. *Der Schmerz im Alten Testament*. Bonner Biblische Beiträge. Bonn: Hanstein, 1955.

Schmökel, Hartmut, translator. "Mesopotamian Texts." In *Near Eastern Religious Texts Relating to the Old Testament*, edited by Walter Beyerlin, translated by J. Bowden, 68–145. Philadelphia: Westminster, 1978.

Schulz, H. *Das Todesrecht im Alten Testament: Studien zur Rechtsform der Mot-Jumat-Sätze*. Beihefte zur Zeitschrift für die alttestamentliche Wissenschaft 114. Berlin: Töpelmann, 162–92.

Schwartz, Baruch. "Ezekiel's Dim View of Israel's Restoration." In *The Book of Ezekiel: Theological and Anthropological Perspectives*, edited by J. Strong and M. Odell, 43–67. Atlanta: Society of Biblical Literature, 2000.

———. "The Ultimate Aim of Israel's Restoration in Ezekiel." In *Birkat Shalom: Studies in the Bible, Ancient Near Eastern Literature, and Postbiblical Judaism Presented to Shalom M. Paul on the Occasion of His Seventieth Birthday*, edited by Chaim Cohen, et al., 305–19. Winona Lake, IN: Eisenbrauns, 2008.

Segal, J. B. *Aramaic Texts from North Saqqara*. London: Egyptian Exploration Society, 1983.

Seybold, K. "חלה *chālāh*." In *Theological Dictionary of the Old Testament*, edited by G. J. Botterweck and H. Ringgren, and translated by G. W. Bromiley, 4:399–409. Grand Rapids: Eerdmans, 1964.

Sheppard, G. T., M. W. Anderson, J. A. Nicholas, W. S. Cranfield, editors. *English Protestant Biblical Commentary, 1601–1645*. Boston: Pilgrim, forthcoming.

Shield, Mary E. "An Abusive God? Identity and Power/Gender and Violence in Ezekiel 23." In *Postmodern Interpretations of the Bible: A Reader*, edited by A. K. M. Adam, 129–51. St. Louis: Chalice, 2001.

———. "Multiple Exposures: Body Rhetoric and Gender Characterization in Ezekiel 16." *Journal of Feminist Studies in Religion* 14 (1998) 5–18.

Simons, J. J. *Jerusalem in the Old Testament: Researches and Theories*. Leiden: Brill, 1952.

Sjöberg, A. W. "Ein Selbstpreis des Königs Hammurabi von Babylon." *Zeitschrift für Assyriologie* 20 (1961) 51–70.

———. "Prayers for King Hammurabi of Babylon." In *Ex Orbe Religionum: Studia Geo Widengren*, 58–71. Leiden: Brill, 1972.

Bibliography

Smilgis, Martha. "Hollywood Goes to Heaven." *Time*, 3 June 1991, 70–71.
Smith, Gary V. "Prophecy, False." In *International Standard Bible Encyclopedia*, rev. ed., edited by G. W. Bromiley, 3.984–86. Grand Rapids: Eerdmans, 1986.
Smith, Mark S., and Elizabeth Bloch-Smith. "Death and Afterlife in Ugarit and Israel." *Journal of the American Oriental Society* 108 (1988) 277–84.
Smith, Mark S. *The Early History of God: Yahweh and the Other Deities in Ancient Israel*. San Francisco: Harper & Row, 1990.
Smith, S. *Babylon Historical Texts Relating to the Capture and Downfall of Babylon*. London: Methuen, 1924.
Smith-Christopher, Daniel L. "Listening to Cries from Babylon: On the Exegesis of Suffering in Ezekiel and Lamentations." In *A Biblical Theology of Exile*, 75–104. Overtures to Biblical Theology. Minneapolis: Fortress, 2002.
Soden Wolfram von. "Entemenanki vor Asarhaddon nach der Erzählung vom Turmbau zu Babel und dem Erra-Mythos." *Ugarit Forschungen* 3 (1977) 253–63.
———. "Gibt es ein Zeugnis dafür, dass die Babylonier an die Wiederauferstehung Marduks geglaubt haben?" *Zeitschrift für Assyriologie* 51 (1955) 130–66.
———. "Der hymnische Dialekt des Akkadischen." *Zeitschrift für Assyriologie* 41 (1933) 125–30.
Sollberger, E., and J. R. Kupper. *Inscriptions royales sumériennes et akkadiennes*. Littératures anciennes du Proche Orient. Paris: Cerf, 1971.
Sommerfeld, W. *Der Aufstieg Marduks: Die Stellung Marduks in der babylonischen Religion des zweiten Jahrtausends v. Chr.* Alter Orient und Altes Testament 213. Neukirchen-Vluyn: Neukirchener, 1992.
———. "Marduk: Philologisch I." In *Reallexikon der Assyriologie*, edited by Erich Ebeling et al., 7:360–70. Berlin: DeGruyter, 1997–99.
Speiser, E. A., translator. "Akkadian Myths and Epics." In *Ancient Near Eastern Texts Relating to the Old Testament*, 3rd ed., edited by J. B. Pritchard, 60–119. Princeton, Princeton University Press, 1969.
Spek, R. J. van der. "The Babylonian Temple during the Macedonian and Parthian Domination." *Biblica et orientalia* 42 (1985) 547–54.
Spiegel, S. "Ezekiel or Pseudo-Ezekiel?" *Harvard Theological Review* 24 (1931) 256–57. Reprinted in *Pseudo-Ezekiel and the Original Prophecy: Critical Articles by Shalom Spiegel and Charles Cutler Torrey*, edited by M. Greenberg, 123–24. Yale Oriental Series 18. New York: Ktav, 1970.
Sprank, S. *Studien zu Ezechiel*. Beiträge zur Wissenschaft vom Alten und Neuen Testament 3.4. Stuttgart: Kohlhammer, 1926.
Spronk, K. *Beatific Afterlife in Ancient Israel and in the Ancient Near East*. Alter Orient und Altes Testament 219. Neukirchen-Vluyn: Neukirchener, 1986.
Stadelmann, L. J. *The Hebrew Conception of the World: A Philological and Literary Study*. Analecta Biblia 39. Rome: Pontifical Biblical Institute, 1970.
Stamm, J. J. *Die Akkadische Namengebung*. Darmstadt: Wissenschaftliche Buchgesellschaft, 1968.
Strabo. *Geography, Books 15–16*. Translated by H. L. Jones. Loeb Classical Library 241. Cambridge: Harvard University Press, 1930.
Streck, M. *Assurbanipal und die letzten assyrischen Könige bis zum Untergang Ninevehs*. 3 vols. Vorderasiatische Bibliothek 7. Leipzig: Hinrichs, 1916.
Strong, John T. "The God that Ezekiel Inherited." Paper delivered at the annual meeting of the Society of Biblical Literature. Atlanta, November 2010.

Strong, S. A. "On Some Oracles to Esarhaddon and Ashurbanipal." *Beiträge zur Assyriologie* 2 (1891–94) 625–45.
Stuart, Douglas K. *Hosea-Jonah*. Word Biblical Commentary 31. Waco, TX: Word, 1987.
Stulman, Louis, and Paul Kim. *You Are My People: An Introduction to Prophetic Literature*. Nashville: Abingdon, 2010.
Stulman, Louis. "Speaking on Behalf of the Losers: Reading Ezekiel as Disaster/Survival Literature." Paper presented at the annual meeting of the Society of Biblical Literature. New Orleans, November 2009.
Tadmor, Hayim. "Autobiographical Apology in the Royal Assyrian Literature." In *History, Historiography, and Interpretation*, edited by Hayim Tadmor and Moshe Weinfeld, 36–57. Jerusalem: Magnes, 1984.
———. "Historical Implications of the Correct Rendering of Akkadian *dâku*." *Journal of Near Eastern Studies* 17 (1958) 129–41.
———. "The Inscriptions of Nabunaid: Historical Arrangement." In *Studies in Honor of Benno Landsberger*, edited by H. Gütterbock and T. Jacobsen, 351–64. Chicago: University of Chicago Press, 1965.
Tallqvist, K. *Sumerisch-akkadische Namen der Totenwelt*. Studia Orientalia 5.4. Helsingfors: Societas Orientalis Fennica, 1934.
Tawil, H. "A Note on the Ahiram Inscription." *Journal of the Ancient Near Eastern Society of Columbia University* 3 (1970) 36.
Taylor, John B. *Ezekiel: An Introduction and Commentary*. Tyndale Old Testament Commentaries. Downers Grove, IL: InterVarsity, 1969.
Teixidor, J. *The Pagan God: Popular Religion in the Greco-Roman Near East*. Princeton: Princeton University Press, 1977.
Thielicke, H. *The Evangelical Faith*. 3 vols. Grand Rapids: Eerdmans, 1982.
Tiemeyer, Lena-Sofia. "To Read—Or Not to Read—Ezekiel as Christian Scripture." *Expository Times* 121 (2010) 481–88.
Tooman, William A. *Gog of Magog: Reuse of Scripture and Compositional Techniques in Ezekiel 38–39*. Forschungen zum Alten Testament 2.52. Tübingen: Mohr Siebeck, 2011.
Tromp, N. J. *Primitive Conceptions of Death and the Netherworld in the Old Testament*. Biblica et orientalia 21. Rome: Pontifical Biblical Institute, 1969.
Unger, E. *Babylon: Die heilige Stadt nach der Beschreibung der Babylonier*. 2nd ed. Berlin: de Gruyter, 1970.
Ungnad, A. "Datenlisten." In *Reallexikon der Assyriologie*, edited by Erich Ebeling, et al., 2:131–94. Berlin: deGruyter, 1938.
———. "Schenkungsurkunde des Kurigalzu mār Kadašman-Harbe." *Archiv für Keilschriftforschung* 1 (1923) 29–36.
Vanhoye, A. "L'utilisation du livre d'Ezéchiel dans l'Apocalypse." *Biblica* 43 (1962) 436–76.
Vaux, Roland de. *Ancient Israel*. New York: McGraw-Hill, 1967.
Vogt, E. *Untersuchungen zum Buche Ezechiel*. Analecta Biblia 95. Rome: Biblical Institute, 1981.
Wächter, L. *Der Tod im Alten Testament*. Arbeiten zur Theologie 2.8. Stuttgart: Calwer, 1967.

Bibliography

Wagner, M. *Die lexikalishen und grammatikalischen Aramäismen im Alttestamentlichen Hebräisch.* Beihefte zur Zeitschrift für die alttestamentliche Wissenschaft 96. Berlin: Töpelmann, 1966.

Waldman, N. M. "A Note on Ezekiel 1:18." *Journal of Biblical Literature* 103 (1984) 614–18.

Walker, C. B. F. "Babylonian Chronicle 25: A Chronicle of the Kassite and Isin II Dynasties." In *Zikir sumim: Assyriological Studies Presented to F. R. Kraus on the Occasion of his Seventieth Birthday,* edited by G. van Driel, et al., 398–417. Leiden: Brill, 1982.

Walvoord, J. F. *The Holy Spirit.* Grand Rapids: Zondervan, 1965.

Ward, W. A. "Egypto-Semitic *MR,* 'Be Bitter, Strong.'" *Ugarit Forschungen* 12 (1980) 357–60.

Watts, John D. W. *Isaiah 1–33.* Word Biblical Commentary 24. Waco, TX: Word, 1985.

Weems, Renita. *Battered Love: Marriage, Sex, and Violence in the Hebrew Prophets.* Overtures to Biblical Theology. Minneapolis: Fortress, 1995.

Weidner, E. *Die Inschriften Tukulti-Ninurtas I. und seiner Nachfolger.* Archiv für Orientforschung Beiheft 12. Graz, Austria: Weidner, 1959.

Weiherr, E. von. *Der babylonische Gott Nergal.* Alter Orient und Altes Testament 11. Neukirchen-Vluyn: Neukirchener, 1971.

Weinfeld, Moshe. *Deuteronomy and the Deuteronomic School.* Winona Lake, IN: Eisenbrauns, 1992.

———. "Divine Intervention in War in Ancient Israel and in the Ancient Near East." In *History, Historiography and Interpretation: Studies in Biblical and Cuneiform Literature,* edited by H. Tadmor and M. Weinfeld, 121–47. Jerusalem: Magnes, 1983.

Weisberg, D. B. "Royal Women of the Neo-Babylonian Period." In *Le Puluis et la royauté,* edited by P. Garelli, 447–54. Rencontre Assyriologique Internationale 19. Paris: Geuthner, 1974.

Weissbach, Franz H., and F. Wetzel. *Das Hauptheiligtum in Babylon, Esagila und Etemenanki.* Wissenschaftliche Veröffentlichungen der Deutschen Orient-Gesellschaft 59. Osnabrück: Zeller, 1967.

Weissbach, Franz H. *Die Keilinschriften der Achämeniden.* Vorderasiastische Bibliothek III. Leipzig: Hinrichs, 1911.

Westermann, Claus. *Basic Forms of Prophetic Speech.* Translation of *Grundformen prophetischer Rede* by H. C. White. Louisville: Westminster John Knox, 1991.

———. "Sprache und Struktur der Prophetie Deuterojesajas." In *Forschung am Alten Testament: Gesammelte* Studien, 124–34. Theologische Bücherei 24. München: Kaiser, 1964.

Wevers, John W. *Ezekiel.* New Century Bible. Grand Rapids: Eerdmans, 1969.

Whitley, Charles F. "The Term Seventy Years Captivity." *Vetus Testamentum* 4 (1954) 60–72.

Widengren, G. "Israelite-Jewish Religion." In *Historia Religionum: Handbook for the History of Religions.* Vol. 1, *Religions of the Past,* edited by C. J. Bleeker and G. Widengren, 225–317. Leiden: Brill, 1969.

Wildberger, Hans. *Jesaja.* Neukirchen-Vluyn: Neukirchener, 1965–82.

Williams, R. J. *Hebrew Syntax: An Outline.* Toronto: University of Toronto Press, 1967.

Williamson, H. G. M. *1 and 2 Chronicles.* New Century Bible. Grand Rapids: Eerdmans, 1982.

Bibliography

Willis, R. S. *Foundation Deposits in Ancient Mesopotamia.* Yale Near Eastern Researches 2. New Haven, CT: Yale University Press, 1968.
Wilson, R. R. "Prophecy in Crisis: The Call of Ezekiel." *Interpretation* 38 (1984) 117–30.
Wiseman, Donald J. "Babylon." In *The Illustrated Bible Dictionary of the Bible*, edited by N. Hillyer, 1:157–62. Leicester, UK: InterVarsity, 1980.
———. "The Laws of Hammurabi Again." *Journal of Semitic Studies* 7 (1962) 161–71.
———. *Nebuchadnezzar and Babylon.* Oxford: Oxford University Press, 1983.
———. "A New Test of the Babylonian Poem of the Righteous Sufferer." *Anatolian Studies* 30 (1980) 101–7.
Wolff, H. W. *Anthropology of the Old Testament.* Philadelphia: Fortress, 1974.
———. *Hosea.* Hermeneia. Philadelphia: Fortress, 1974.
———. *Joel and Amos.* Hermeneia. Philadelphia: Fortress, 1977.
Wright, G. E. "Deuteronomy." In *Interpreter's Bible*, edited by G. A. Buttrick et al, 2:307–537. Nashville: Abingdon, 1953.
Wu, D. Y. "Honour, Shame and Guilt in the Book of Ezekiel." PhD diss., Sydney University and Moore Theological College, 2013.
Xella, P. "Aspekte religiöser Vorstellungen in Syrien nach den Ebla- und Ugarit-Texten." *Ugarit Forschungen* 15 (1983) 288.
Yadin, Y. "New Gleanings on Resheph from Ugarit." *Biblical and Related Studies Presented to Samuel Iwry*, edited by A. Kort and S. Morschauser, 259–73. Winona Lake, IN: Eisenbrauns, 1985.
Yee, Gale A. "The Two Sisters in Ezekiel: They Played the Whore in Egypt." In *Poor Banished Children of Eve: Woman as Evil in the Hebrew Bible*, 111–34. Minneapolis: Augsburg Fortress, 2003.
Zimmerli, Walther. *A Commentary on the Book of the Prophet Ezekiel, Chapters 1–24.* Translated by R. E. Clements. Hermeneia. Philadelphia: Fortress, 1979.
———. *A Commentary on the Book of the Prophet Ezekiel: Chapters 25–48.* Translated by J. D. Martin. Hermeneia. Philadelphia: Fortress, 1983.
———. *Erkenntnis Gottes nach dem Buche Ezechiel: Eine theologische Studie.* Abhandlungen zur Theologie des Alten und Neuen Testaments 27. Zürich: Zwingli, 1954.
———. *Ezechiel.* Neukirchen-Vluyn: Neukirchener, 1969.
———. *I am Yahweh.* Edited by W. Brueggemann. Translated by D. W. Scott. Atlanta: John Knox, 1982.
———. "Ich bin Jahwe." In *Geschichte und Altes Testament*, 179–209. Tübingen: Mohr, 1953.
———. "The Message of the Prophet Ezekiel." *Interpretation* 23 (1969) 131–57.
———. "Das Wort des göttlichen Selbsterweises (Erweiswort), eine prophetische Gattung." In *Mélanges Bibliques rédigés en l'honneur de André Robert*, 154–64. Travaux de l'institut catholique de Paris 4. Paris: Bloud et Gay, 1957. An English translation is found in *I am Yahweh*.

Index of Modern Authors

Abusch, T., 124, 259
Ackerman, J. S., 228, 259
Ackerman, Susan, 53, 259
Ackroyd, Peter R., 86, 93, 276
Albertz, Rainer, 142, 148, 161, 259
Albright, William F., 187, 219, 259
Aldred, C., 180, 259
Allen, Leslie, xiv, 181–83, 187, 231, 234, 240, 242, 244, 246, 248, 256, 259
Alter, Robert, 155, 259
Andersen, F. I., 196, 259
Armerding, C. E., 181, 272
Aune, D. E., 174, 259

Balentine, Samuel E., 75, 259
Barkay G., 180, 259
Barrick, W. Boyd, 202, 259
Bartelmus, R., 189, 259
Barth, C., 176, 179, 196, 260
Barth, Karl, 170, 260
Bauckham, Richard, 193, 260
Baumann, E., 209, 260
Baumgärtel, F., 142, 260
Baumgartner, W., 190, 260
Bayliss, M., 186, 260
Ben-Ze'ev, Aaron, 63, 260
Berger, P. R., 88, 128, 130, 131, 133, 260
Berkhof, L., 170, 260
Berry, G. R., 204, 260
Bertram, G., 161, 260
Betts, T. J., 58, 260

Bevan, E. R., 136, 260
Birkeland, H., 193, 194, 264
Black, J. A., 125, 260
Bloch-Smith, Elizabeth, 180, 182, 185, 186, 187, 194, 260
Block, Daniel I., xiv, 2, 3, 13, 22, 25, 33, 35, 40, 42, 49, 60, 61, 69, 94, 100, 108, 116–18, 126, 140, 152, 164, 169, 190, 194, 199, 227, 257, 258, 260, 261, 274
Blomberg, Craig, 39, 270
Blumenthal, David R., 44, 261
Bodi, Daniel, 76, 78, 82, 83, 261
Böhl, F. M. Th., 115, 120, 261
Borger, Riekele/Rykle, 80, 84, 86, 100, 111, 117, 126, 127, 261, 262
Bromiley, G., 193, 262
Born, A. van den, 234, 262
Boyce, Mary, 194, 262
Brinkman, John A., 84, 114, 115, 119, 120, 124–26, 262
Brownlee, William H., 242, 245, 247, 262
Bruno, A., 218, 262
Burstein, S. M., 137, 262
Buswell. J. O., Jr., 170, 262
Butterworth, Brian, 49, 262

Cagni, Luigi, 82, 83, 124, 125, 173, 262
Caquot, A., 173, 262

283

Index of Modern Authors

Carroll, Robert, 44, 256, 262
Chiera, E., 110, 263
Clay, A. T., 114, 263
Clines, D. J. A., 166, 263
Cody, A., 187, 207, 209, 263
Cogan, Mordechai, 84, 92, 263
Coggins, R. J., 197, 263
Cooke, G. A., 152, 160, 202, 242, 263
Cooley, Robert E., 186, 263
Cooper, A., 183, 263
Cooper, Jerrold S., 77, 263
Cooper, Lamar E., 39, 263
Cornill, C. H., 182, 263
Cuddon, 15, 263

Dahood, Mitchell, 162, 173, 183, 196, 263
Dalley, Stephanie, 82, 83, 84, 263
Darr, Katheryn Pfisterer, xiv, 47, 256, 257, 263
Davidson, A. B., 159, 242, 263
Day, John, 173, 263
Day, Linda, 44, 264
Day, Peggy, 44, 264
Dempsey, Carol J., 44, 264
Demson, D. E., 190, 264
Di Lella, A. A., 195, 196, 268
Dietrich, M., 188, 264
Dijk-Hemmes, Fokkelien van, 44, 264
Dillard, R. B., 186, 264
Dommershausen, W., 180, 244, 264
Doran, R., 136, 264
Dossin, Georges, 78, 120, 264
Drijvers, H. J. W., 138, 264
Driver, G. R., 135, 137, 222, 240, 242, 243, 246, 264
Dubberstein, W. H., 238, 275
Duguid, Iain M., xiv, 43, 256, 264
Dussaud, R., 137, 264

Eaton, J. H., 219, 265
Ebach, J. H., 187, 265

Ebeling, Erich, 123, 173, 265, 270, 278, 279
Edzard, D. O., 110, 112, 265
Eichrodt, Walther, 174, 181, 185, 195, 196, 208, 209, 238, 265
Eilers, W., 135, 265
Eissfeldt, Otto, 180, 265
Ellermeier, F., 78, 265
Erickson, Millard J., 170, 265
Erlandsson, S., 191, 218, 265
Evans, John, 46, 50, 51, 69, 265
Ewert, David, 157, 265
Exum, J. Cheryl, 44, 265

Falkenstein, A., 113, 265
Fensham, F. C., 175, 190, 265
Fine, H. A., 115, 265
Fishbane, Michael, 176, 189, 265
Fisher, David H., 49, 265
Fohrer, Georg, 159, 208, 232, 233, 241, 265, 265, 273
Foster, Benjamin B., 79, 80, 81, 82, 100, 117, 266
Fox, Michael V., 154, 189, 197, 266
Fox, S. J., 193, 266
Frankfort, H., 193, 266
Freedman, D. N., 196, 259
Freedy, Kenneth S., 208, 230, 246, 266
Frymer-Kensky, Tikva, 127, 264, 266
Fuhs, Hans F., 230, 231, 232, 240, 241, 266
Fulco, W. J., 173, 266

Gadd, Cyril. J., 87, 131, 132, 160, 266
Galling, K., 187, 266
Ganzel, Tova, 48, 62, 63, 266
Garber, David G., Jr., 46, 266
Garscha, J., 170, 266
Gaster, T. H., 174, 266
Gerleman, G., 153, 171, 172, 179, 266

Index of Modern Authors

Gibson, John C. L., 77, 267
Gile, Jason, 44, 56, 267
Gössmann, 124, 125
Goetze, A., 124, 267
Grabbe, L. L., 193, 267
Graffy, Adrian, 227, 228, 233–35, 267
Gray, G. B., 217, 267
Grayson, A. K., 115, 116, 119, 120, 125, 132, 133, 136, 267
Green, Margaret W., 77, 267
Greenberg, Moshe, v, xiv, 6, 45, 49, 63, 70, 72, 150, 152, 170, 200, 202, 205, 209, 211, 212, 214, 215, 220, 253–58, 267, 278
Greenhill, William, 199, 267
Greenspoon, L. J., 196, 267
Gruber, M. I., 153, 267

Haag, E., 197, 267
Habel, Norman C., 216, 267
Hackett, J. A., 183, 268
Hallo, William H., 77, 100, 263, 268, 270, 273, 274, 275
Halperin, David, 44, 45, 63, 205, 209, 210, 214, 215, 268
Hals, R. M., 177, 268
Hanson, R., 182, 197, 268
Harrison, R. K., ix
Hartman, L. F., 195, 268
Hasel, Gerhard F., 197, 268
Hatch, E., 142, 268
Hayes, John H., 238, 268
Healey, J. F., 184, 187, 188, 268
Heschel, A. J., 149, 268
Heider, G. C., 186–88, 268
Heintz, J.-G., 178, 268
Held, Moshe, 179, 268
Heschel, A. J., 149, 162, 212, 268
Hill, D., 151, 161, 268
Hillers, D. R., 175, 268
Hodge, C., 170, 268
Höffken, P., 189, 268

Hoekema, Anthony, 39, 269
Hoffner, Harry A., 141, 269
Höfner, Maria, 138, 269
Hoftijzer, J., 183, 203, 269
Hölscher, G., 214, 234, 269
Hooker, Paul K., 238, 268
Houk, C. B., 208, 209, 214, 215, 269
Hubbard, Robert I., 39, 270
Huffmon, Herbert B., 219, 221, 269

Irwin, W. A., 216, 269
Irwin, W. H., 233, 269

Jacob, E., 161, 269
Jacobsen, Thorkild, 92, 113, 120, 269, 279
Jastrow, M. A., 183, 243, 269
Jean, C.-F., 203, 269
Jeremias, J., 192, 269
Johnson, A. R., 167, 269
Joyce, Paul, xiv, 47, 71, 256, 270

Kaiser, Otto, 197, 218, 233, 270
Kammenhuber, A., 115, 270
Kees, H., 193, 270
Kelso, James L., 240, 241, 243, 262, 270
Kent, G. J. R., xvii, 1, 261, 270
Kent, R. G., 135, 270
Kim, Brittany, 45, 46, 56, 63, 270
Kim, Paul, 279
King, L. W., 111, 119, 270
Kissling, P. J., xvii, 1, 261
Klein, Jacob, 77, 270
Klein, W. W., 39, 270
Kloner, A., 180, 259
König, F., 195, 270
Kooij, G. van der, 183, 269
Kraeling, C. H., 188, 270
Kraetzschmar, R., 246, 270
Kramer, Samuel Noah, 57, 77, 97, 270
Kreuzer, S., 153, 271
Kuhl, C., 176, 271

Index of Modern Authors

Kupper, J. R., 111, 278
Kutler, L., 162, 271
Kutsch, Ernst, 238, 271
Kutscher, E. Y., 203, 271
Kutsko, John F., 92, 93, 96, 271

Lambert, Wilfred G., 81, 82, 109, 114–16, 119, 120, 123–25, 173, 271
Landsberger, Benno, 83, 127, 262, 271, 279
Lang, Bernhard, 92, 176, 188, 194, 195, 197, 198, 232, 238, 241, 272, 274
Langdon, S. H., 129, 130, 133, 272
Lapsley, Jacqueline E., 47, 48, 65, 272
Laroche, E., 115, 272
Lemke, Werner E., 66, 272
Levenson, Jon D., 257, 267, 272
Levine, B., 184, 272
Lewis, T. J., 181, 186, 187, 272
Lewy, J., 132, 272
Lind, W. A., 205, 272
Lloyd, Delyth, 49, 262
Lods, A., 181, 272
Longman, Tremper III, 80, 87, 100, 117, 273
Loretz, O., 188, 264
Luckenbill, Daniel David, 84, 126, 273
Lust, Johan, 187, 257, 266, 267, 272, 273

Maas, F., 181, 273
Machinist, Peter B., 79, 80, 273
Macintosh, A. A., 218, 273
Malamat, Abraham, 53, 219, 238, 273
Mandolfo, Carleen R., 44, 273
Margulis, B., 219, 273
Martens, Elmer A., 44
Martin-Achard, R., 194, 196, 197, 273

Martinez, R. M., 173, 273
McCannell, C., 176, 194, 274
McCarthy, D. J., 228, 274
McConville, Gordon, 38, 274
McEwan, G. J. P., 137, 274
Michalowski, Piotr, 77, 274
Milgrom, Jacob, xiv, 49, 63, 65, 66, 258, 260, 274
Millard, Alan R., 124, 127, 139, 210, 274
Miller, Patrick D., 76, 181, 269, 274
Moenikes, A., 41, 274
Montet, P., 180, 274
Moran, William L., 78, 219, 274
Morenz, S., 188, 193, 274
Mowinckel, S., 219, 274
Muller, R. A., 197, 274
Murray, D. F., 228, 274
Musti, D., 137, 274

Neiman, David, 187, 275
Neujahr, Matthew, 80, 100, 117, 275
Neuss, W., 199, 275
Neyrey, J. H., 197, 275
Nobile, M., 193, 275
Nougayrol, Jean, 86, 110, 203, 275

Odell, Margaret S., xiv, xvii, 58, 65, 73, 256, 272, 275, 277
Oppenheim, A. L., 132, 275
Orr, Avigdor, 86, 275
Oswalt, John N., 30, 197, 275

Pardee, D., 162, 275
Parker, R. A., 238, 275
Parunak, H. van Dyke, 160, 275
Paton, Corinne, 45, 56, 275
Pedersen, J., 179, 275
Petter, Donna, 56, 275
Pettinato, G., 109, 173, 276
Pitard, W. T., 186, 276
Pope, M. H., 173, 179, 183, 184, 186, 263, 276

Index of Modern Authors

Porten, B., 135, 276
Premstaller, Volkmar, 256
Puech, Emil, 74, 276

Rad, G. von, 192, 217, 276
Redpath, H. A., 142, 268
Reeve, Robert, 49, 262
Reschid, F., 120, 276
Reventlow, H. G., 51, 175, 276
Reynolds, Fiona, 49, 262
Ribichini, F. S., 184, 276
Richter, Wolfgang, 175, 228, 276
Riesenfeld, H., 193, 276
Ringgren, Helmer, 174, 219, 220, 276
Roberts, J. J. M., 76, 147, 149, 212, 271, 274, 276
Robinson, H. W., 161, 276
Rogers, R. W., 123, 277
Röllig, W., 173, 276
Römer, W. H., 173, 277
Rom-Shiloni, Dalit, 66, 277

Sasson, Jack M., 181, 277
Scharbert, Josef, 46, 277
Schmökel, Hartmut, 78, 277
Schulz, H., 175, 277
Schwartz, Baruch, 45, 48, 49, 65, 66, 67, 70, 71, 277
Segal, J. B., 135, 277
Seybold, K., 242, 277
Shield, Mary E., 44, 277
Simons, J. J., 187, 277
Sjöberg, A. W., 109, 111, 112, 277
Smilgis, Martha, 169, 277
Smith, Gary V., 158, 227, 278
Smith, Mark, 173, 186, 194, 278
Smith, S., 132, 278
Smith-Christopher, Daniel L., 46, 278
Soden, Wolfram von, 82, 120, 127, 278
Sollberger, E., 111, 278
Sommerfeld, W., 109, 110, 112, 113, 115, 120, 278

Speiser, E. A. 120, 121, 278
Spek, R. J. van der, 137, 278
Spiegel, S., 199, 278
Spronk, K., 176, 179, 183, 184, 186, 187, 193–97, 276, 278
Stadelmann, L. J., 178, 179, 278
Stamm, J. J., 113, 278
Streck, M., 221, 278
Strong, John T., xvii, 50, 73, 221, 272, 275, 277, 278
Strong, S. A., 251, 279
Stuart, Douglas K., 196, 279
Stulman, Louis, 46, 47, 279
Sweeney, Marvin A., 227, 237

Tadmor, Hayim, 84, 116, 132, 279, 280
Tallqvist, K., 179, 279
Tarragon, J.-M., 184, 272
Tawil, H., 183, 279
Taylor, John B., 187, 234, 279
Teixidor, J., 137, 138, 279
Thielicke, H., 170, 279
Tiemeyer, Lena-Sofia, 45, 46, 57, 279
Tooman, William A., 49, 261, 270, 279
Tromp, N. J., 173, 176, 179, 279
Tuell, Steven Shawn, xiv, 256

Unger, E., 114, 129, 130, 279
Ungnad, A., 110, 112, 114, 279

Vaux, Roland de, 92, 186, 279
Vogt, E., 162, 279

Wagner, M., 243, 280
Waldman, N. M., 206, 280
Walvoord, John F., 156, 280
Ward, W. A., 162, 280
Watts, John D. W., 197, 233, 280
Weems, Renita, 44, 280
Weidner, E., 115, 280
Weiherr, E. von, 173, 280
Weinfeld, Moshe, 54, 279, 280

Index of Modern Authors

Weisberg, D. B., 131, 132, 280
Weissbach, Franz H., 88, 128–30, 280
Westermann, Claus, 142, 148, 161, 227, 259, 280
Wevers, John W., 187, 230, 238, 246, 280
Whitley, Charles F., 86, 280
Widengren, G., 193, 194, 277, 280
Wilcke, C., 120, 276
Wildberger, Hans, 233, 280
Williams, R. J., 160, 280
Williamson, H. G. M., 186, 280
Willis, R. S., 115, 281
Wilson, R. R., 200, 206, 209, 281
Wiseman, Donald J., 112, 114, 128, 130, 136, 281
Wolff, H. W., 165, 195, 196, 281
Wright, Christopher J. H., xiv, 256
Wright, G. E., 186, 281
Wu, D. Y., 65, 281

Xella, P., 184, 276, 281

Yadin, Y., 173, 281
Yee, Gail A., 44, 281

Zimmerli, Walther, 49, 50, 150, 152, 160, 170, 175, 183, 184, 187, 189, 193, 194, 202, 203, 205, 206, 209, 211, 213, 214, 216, 217, 230, 238, 242, 244, 246, 257, 281

Index of Ancient Authors

Arrian

Anabasis	135, 136, 259
3.16.3	136
3.16.5	136
7.16.5–7	136
7.17.2–3	136
7.17.2	134

Ben Sirach

Ecclesiasticus

12:10	243
44:1–15	253–54

Herodotus

Histories	1, 129, 134, 135, 181
1.140	194
2.104	181

Jerome 1

"Epistula III"	199, 269
Opera, Pars. I, 3–4	199

Josephus

Against Apion	269
1	136, 192

Jewish Antiquities	270
18.14	192
8.10.3	181

Jewish Wars	270
2.163	192

Polybius

Histories	276
5.79.8	137

"Pseudo-Hecataeus"	264
2.917–19	136

Strabo	278
16.1.5	130, 134, 136
16.1.15	136

Index of Selected Subjects

Abandonment, divine, 27, 31, 32, 34, 35, 37, 40, 57, 73–99, 116–18, 125, 127
Abraham, 5, 13, 15, 34, 39, 46, 69
Adad-guppi, 87–88, 91, 131, 160
Akitu. *See* New Year's Festival
Amos, 1, 46, 49
Ancestor worship. *See* Cult of the dead
Andrew of St. Victor, 2
Aqhat, 164
Ashurbanipal, 107, 127, 128, 220, 221, 279
Adad-guppi, autobiography of, 87–88, 91, 131, 160

Baal, 147, 173, 193, 194, 196, 267
Bel. *See* Marduk/Bel
Ben Sirach, 253
Blessing/s
   covenant, 5, 15, 24, 36, 37, 39, 68, 71, 72
   Marduk's, 102, 107, 115, 118, 134

Call narrative, 216–17, 228, 267
Call of Ezekiel, x–xi, 3, 4, 6, 8, 17, 18, 27, 58, 69, 73, 206, 208–10, 216–19, 222, 281
Calvin, 2, 262
Chemosh, 74, 77
Covenant, 5, 7, 11, 13–15, 20, 21, 23, 24, 29, 31, 32, 34, 35–38, 43, 45, 50–56, 63, 65, 69–72, 75, 76, 92, 95, 96, 97, 99, 155, 165, 166, 167, 172, 175, 181, 190, 195, 198, 233, 254
   Abrahamic, 12
   Davidic, 12, 27
   Israelite, 12, 23, 27, 29, 31, 35
   Nebuchadnezzar's with Zedekiah, 31
   new, 156
   old, 156
   renewal, 165
Covenant Blessing/s. *See* Blessing/s, covenant
Covenant curse/s. *See* Curse/s
Cult of the dead, 184, 186–88, 260

Curse/s
   of Agade, 77, 79, 90, 96, 263, 270
   covenant, 13–15, 32, 33, 36–38, 57, 75, 76, 79, 97, 127, 175, 190, 195, 197, 265, 268
Cyrus Cylinder, 88–89, 91, 133
Cyrus, 9, 11, 26, 88–89, 91, 133, 134, 136

Daniel, x, 8, 10, 26, 69, 142, 218
David, 5, 13, 14, 26, 27, 38, 40–42, 50, 62, 69, 71, 97, 157, 165, 187
Deified/beneficent spirits, 186, 188, 193–94

Index of Selected Subjects

Demon, malevolent spirits, 82, 117, 173, 174, 262
Disputation speech, 15, 29, 59, 91, 227–51, 274
Dura-Europos, 138, 188, 270, 276

Egypt, Egyptians, x, 3, 6, 9, 10, 15, 24–26, 28, 32, 34, 35, 51, 52, 54, 55, 59, 60, 62, 67–69, 71, 135, 138, 147, 148, 151, 162, 176, 177, 180, 183, 184, 188, 189, 191, 193, 194, 198, 266, 273
Enuma Elish, 120–22
Esagila, 80, 83, 84–88, 110, 112, 115, 122, 125, 127, 129–34, 136, 137, 262, 271, 280
Esarhaddon, 84, 86, 87, 90, 97, 126–28, 220, 221
Exile, exiles, x, 3–5, 8–11, 16, 21, 25–27, 31, 33, 37, 38, 45–47, 51, 52, 54, 57–62, 65–67, 74, 76, 81, 86, 91, 96, 99, 118, 127, 149, 155, 166, 189, 191, 192, 239, 251
Ezekiel
the person, ix–xi, 2–4, 10
prophetic priest, ix–xi, 3, 18, 21, 58, 260, 274

Formula
covenant, 31, 50, 54, 165
divine self-introductory, 32, 50–52, 64, 229
hostile orientation, 4, 97
messenger, 230, 231, 236, 242, 248
oath, 110
recognition, 32, 46, 52, 69, 229, 265
signatory, 229, 250
word event, 6, 7, 10, 229, 230, 238

Fury, wrath, anger [divine], 22, 33, 35, 46, 48–51, 54, 55, 59, 62–64, 66, 67, 69, 70, 72, 77, 79–85, 87, 89, 95–98, 147, 161, 172, 175, 231, 232, 242, 245, 247–50

Gilgamesh Epic, 182, 185, 263
Gog (and Magog), 2, 6, 13, 29, 30, 32, 40, 49, 51, 69, 164, 166, 174, 183, 261, 279
Grace, divine, xvi, 2, 19, 21–24, 32, 34, 35, 44–72, 165
Gregory the Great, 1

Hades. *See also* Sheol, 170, 192, 195
Hammurabi Laws, 111, 112, 281
Holistic interpretation, xiv, 210, 255, 257
Hosea, 1, 17, 49, 196

Inspiration, 33, 143, 144, 146, 152, 158–61, 163, 175
Isaac, 34
Isaiah, x, 1, 12, 17, 30, 49, 74, 138, 142, 160, 176, 191, 196, 217, 220, 233, 237, 248

Jacob, 34, 50, 74, 165, 166
Jealousy/passion (divine), 12, 15, 23, 24, 30–32, 45, 48, 56, 63, 64, 67, 94, 96, 260, 270
Jehoiachin, ix, x, 8, 25, 26, 59, 60–62, 221, 261
Jehoiakim, x, 8, 60
Jeremiah, xi, 10, 17, 25, 49, 54, 59, 61, 72, 99, 130, 156, 159, 164, 171, 216, 221, 233, 256
Jerome, 1, 199
Josiah, x, 8, 60, 69, 187

kābôd ("glory") of YHWH, 13, 21, 30, 32, 73, 74, 92, 153, 213–15, 217

Index of Selected Subjects

Lament
  lamentation, 55–57, 94, 119, 162, 170
  Sumerian, 57, 77, 79–81, 89, 90–91, 95
Love
  divine, 22, 32, 45, 46, 49, 53, 64, 70, 79, 113, 114, 134, 237
  human, xvi, 20, 53, 156, 237

Malachi, 21, 49, 235
Marduk Prophecy (Prophetic Speech of Marduk), v, 80–81, 82, 84, 89, 90, 95, 100–107, 117, 119, 273
Marduk/Bel, 27, 74, 79, 80–90, 95, 97, 100–107, 108–39, 259–62, 266, 270–73, 276, 278
Merciful, mercy (divine), 44, 62, 71, 89, 113, 127
Messiah, 29, 39–43
Micah, 59
Moses, 19, 39, 46, 54, 66, 67, 69, 159, 216, 261
Mot, 172–74, 193, 198, 276

Nabonidus, 87, 88, 93, 128, 131–32, 134, 160, 266, 272
Nabopolassar, 8, 87, 128, 129, 131
Nabu/Nebo, 74, 100, 104, 114, 123, 126, 128, 132, 134, 136–38
Nebuchadnezzar I, 80, 81, 138, 271
Nebuchadnezzar II, x, 3, 5, 8, 9, 13, 15, 27, 30, 31, 37, 51, 59, 61, 62, 72, 95, 99, 119, 120, 124, 128–31, 138, 172, 174, 190, 238, 250, 251, 281
New Year's Festival, 9, 125, 126, 127, 132, 193, 194, 260, 261, 273
Nippur, 56, 57, 77, 90, 97, 101, 112, 117, 124, 135, 263, 271

Oracles
  against foreign nations, vii, 4, 6–7, 13, 16, 28, 30, 32, 142, 176, 184, 185, 191, 192, 198, 221
  judgment, 6, 7, 10, 15, 28, 32, 38, 50, 91, 186, 188, 191, 251
  salvation, vii, 6, 7, 11, 12, 42, 165, 189
Origen, 1

Pillars of security (Israel's), 5, 11, 12, 14, 19, 27, 38, 237
Poem of Erra and Ishum (Erra Epic), 76, 78, 82–84, 89, 90, 91, 95, 96, 124–26, 173, 261–63, 278
Prophetic Letter from Mari (*ARM* X No. 50), 78

Renewal, Israelite, 29, 38, 52, 71, 156, 157, 158, 164, 165, 167, 250
Rephaim, shades, 180–86, 193–95, 272, 276
Resurrection, revitalization, 31, 38–39, 153, 155, 190, 193–97, 260, 265, 267, 268, 273, 274, 276
Return
  of deity, 72, 74, 76–78, 80, 82, 84, 86, 87, 90–93, 96–98, 101, 102, 116, 118, 127, 134
  of people from exile, 8, 9, 11, 26, 39, 40, 48, 76, 77, 96, 166, 190, 194

Seed of Kingship, 81–82, 89, 90
Shades. *See* rephaim
Shame and honor, 45, 47, 48, 58, 64–65, 130, 165, 182, 247
Sheol, 169–98, 233
Siege (of Jerusalem), x, 9, 174, 238–39, 250–51

Index of Selected Subjects

Sinai, 5, 23, 27, 55, 67
Spirit, Holy, v, xi, xvii, 13, 31, 33,
    38, 39, 49, 140–68, 189, 190,
    198, 260, 261
Spirit, pouring out of, 164–66
Sumerian Laments, 56, 57, 76, 77,
    79–81, 89–91, 95, 97

Tel Abib, 10, 26, 149
Triangle, covenant, vii, 14, 63
Tukulti Ninurta Epic, 78–80, 89

Zechariah, 9, 10, 49
Zedekiah, x, 8, 26, 31, 61, 79
Zion/Zion theology, 5, 11, 41, 42,
    50, 69, 75, 99, 270, 273
Zoroaster, Zoroastrian, 194, 195,
    262, 272, 277

Index of Scripture

Old Testament

Genesis

2:7	141, 150, 154, 195
2:17	196
3:19	196
4:10	245
6–9	37
6:4	181, 182
6:5	182
6:11–12	182
6:22–26	182
7:11	211
7:22	151
10:15–16	53
15:7	54
15:20–21	53
17	181
17:8	60
18:23–33	46
26:14	63
28:15	74
34:7	160
41–47	59
45:25	60

Exodus

1–15	32
3:1–4:17	216
3:8	53, 55, 71
3:17	55
5:23	71
6:2–8	54
6:3	54
6:4	60
6:6	71
6:8	54
6:9	54
6:10	54
6:14	54
6:22	54
7:5	68
12:1	10
13:5	55
14:4	68
14:8	68
16:35	60
18:8	71
18:9	71
18:10	71
20:5	64
20:7	69
23:19	240
32:10–14	46
32:12	67, 69, 250
32:14	250
33:3	55
34:6–7	70
34:7	70
34:14	64
34:26	240

Leviticus

10:11	xi
14:34	60
16:7–10	244
16:8	174
16:10	174
16:26	174
17:7	174
17:10–16	244
17:13	244
18:3	60
19:31	141
20:6	141
20:24	55
20:27	141
21:11	195
21:4–5	xi
25:38	60
26	13, 15, 75, 175, 32
26:14–39	14, 69
26:17	75
26:24	75
26:25	175
26:30	75, 187
26:30	75
26:40–41	71
26:40–45	70
26:40–46	14
26:40–46	38
26:4–13	15
26:43	75

Numbers

4:30	x
5:12–31	63
6:6	195
12:6	161
13:2	60
13:17	60
13:19	60
13:27	55
13:28	60
13:29	53
14:8	55
14:13–16	68, 69
14:18	70
14:30	54
16:13	55
16:28	159
21:17–18	234
25:2	186
26:55–56	244
27:12	183
27:21	xi
32:32	60
33:51	60
34:2	60

Deuteronomy

1:22	60
1:37	66
3:26	66
4:6–8	55
4:21	66
4:24	64
4:25–28	14
4:29–31	71
4:30–31	14, 70
4:34	148
5:9	64
5:11	69
5:15	148
6:3	55
6:10	60
6:15	64
6:19	55
6:21–25	55
6:21	148
6:24	55
6:25	55
7:1	53
10:16	156
11:9	55
14:1	186
14:21	240
17:14–20	41
18:11	141

Index of Scripture

Deuteronomy (cont.)

20:16	60, 141
22:21	160
26:9	55
26:14	186
26:15	55
26:18–19	68
27:3	55
28	13, 15, 32, 75, 175
28:8–12	68
28:8–11	68
28:10	69
28:15–68	14, 69
28:20	175
28:25–26	180, 190
28:64–68	57
29:14–29	14
29:21[22]	243
30:1–20	38
30:1–10	70
30:1–5	71
30:6	156
31:6	75
31:17–18	75
31:17	75
31:20	55
32:17	174
32:20	75
32:22	178
32:24	161, 175
32:33	161
32:39	197
32:40	54
32:49	60
33:10	xi

Joshua

1:5	75
4:21–24	68
5:6	55
5:12	60
7:9	68
7:15	160
10:40	141
11:11	141
13:6	244
18:6–10	244
19:51	244
22:11	60
22:32	60
24:3	60
24:19	64

Judges

6:1–24	216
6:9	71
6:15	75
9:23	174
9:27	234
11	121
20:6	160
21:21	234

1 Samuel

2:12–28	237
3:15	161
9:9	161
9:11	161
9:18	161
9:19	161
10:18	71
12:22	75
15:1	175
16:1	175
16:14	174
17:35	71
17:46	68
22:2	162
25:25	160
28:3	141
28:7–8	141
28:9	141
28:13	185

2 Samuel

7	41, 97
8:18	187

2 Samuel (cont.)

12:1	175
22:5–6	174
22:10	211
22:16	141, 151

1 Kings

6:13	75
8:57	75
8:60	68
9:20	53
10:15	60
12:33	159
13:22	180
14:10–11	180
15:23	243
15:29	141
17:17–24	196
17:17	141
18:46	148, 211
22	158
22:19–23	158
23:29–30	8
24:1–17	59

2 Kings

2:2	175
2:4	175
2:6	175
3:27	245
4:18–37	196
4:38–41	240
4:38	239
13:2	160
13:20–21	196
18:4	250
18:22	250
19:14–19	68
20:16–18	x
21:6	141
21:14	75
21:18	187
21:26	187
22–23	250
22:1	8
22:3	3
22:14–17	69
22:19–20	216
23:1–25	x
23:3	160
23:24	141
23:29–30	8
23:30	187
23:31–34	60
24:8–17	25
24:8–16	60
24:9	61
24:10–17	8
24:14–16	ix
24:14–15	59
24:15–16	3
24:15	61
25:1	238
25:25–26	25
25:27–30	26, 61

1 Chronicles

9:22	161
9:24	148
12:34[33]	163
12:39[38]	163
16:18	60
24–26	244
26:28	161
29:29	161

2 Chronicles

7:22	54
11:15	174
16:7	161
16:10	161
16:12	186, 243
21:19	243
24:20	75
31	250
33:6	141

Index of Scripture

2 Chronicles (*cont.*)

33:20	187
36:9	61

Ezra

1:1–4	9
2	26
9:9	75

Nehemiah

1	26
3:31	60
3:32	60
9:15	54
9:17	70
9:28	75
13:20	60

Job

2:10	160
3:13	185
3:18	185
4:9	141, 151
6:4	161
7:9	185
7:11	162
10:1	162
12:23	240
12:31	240
13:13–22	192
13:24	74
14:13–22	192
16:18	245
18:14	174
26:5	184
26:7	147
27:3	141, 151
27:5–6	151
30:8	160
30:27	240
31:7	160
32:8	141, 151
32:19	141
33:4	141, 151
33:18	153
33:20	153
33:22	153
33:28	153
34:14–15	151, 196
34:14	141, 151
34:29	74
38:1	147
38:17	179
40:6	147

Psalms

9:14[13]	179
10:1	75
10:11	74
12:3[2]	163
13:2[1]	74
14:1	160
16:3–4	186
16:11–12	196
18:5–6[4–5]	174
18:16[15]	141, 151
22:25[24]	74
22:30[20]	178
26:2	163
27:9	74
30:8[7]	74
42:4[3]	74
42:11[10]	74
44:25[24]	75
48:3[2]	147
49:15–16[14–15]	196
51	157
51:11[9]	75
51:12[10]	164
51:12–13[10–11]	157
51:13[11]	140
53:3[3]	160
58:5[4]	161
63:10[9]	178
69:18[17]	74
74:19	153

Index of Scripture

Psalms (cont.)

74:22	160
78:50	153
79:10	74
86:5	70
86:11	163
86:15	70
88:7[6]	178
88:10[10]	184
88:15[14]	74
89:13[12]	147
94:14	75
102:3[2]	74, 243
103:5[4]	70
103:8[7]	70
104:29–30	151
104:29	75, 196
104:30	167
105:11	60
105:37	54
105:43	54
106:28	186
106:37	174
107:18	179
115:2	74
136:11	54
136:12	148
139:1–6	163
139:7[6]	167
139:15	178
139:23	163
140:4[3]	161
143:3	153, 183
143:7	74
145:8	70
150:6	141

Proverbs

1:32	72
2:18	184
4:3–4	60
6:18	249
6:32–35	63
16:33	244
17:7	160
30:32	160
31:24	60

Ecclesiastes/Qoheleth

3:18–21	196
12:5	183
12:7	196

Song of Songs

3:6	60
8:6–7	64

Isaiah

1:4	30
2:6	75
2:22	141
5:19	30
6	10
6:1–8	216
6:1–5	213
6:8	175
8:1	220
8:11	211
8:16–18	220
8:17	75
8:19	141
8:23—9:6[9:1–7]	41
9:2	234
9:5–6[6–7]	41
11:1–5	41
11:2–5	41
11:6–9	41
14	176, 191
14:9–20	184
14:9	184, 192
14:13–14	147
16:10	234
21:1–10	218
21:3–4	218
23:8	60
24:14–19	233

Index of Scripture

Isaiah (cont.)

24:21	188
25:8	174
26:7–19	176
26:14	184
26:19	178, 184, 196
28:7	161
28:9	159
28:14	236
28:15	174
28:18	174
29:4	141
30:8	221
30:10	161
30:33	141, 248
32:5–6	160
32:15	165
34:14	174
38:10	179
38:15	162
41:17	74
42:5	141, 151
42:6	36
42:14	141
44:1–4	165
44:23	178
46:1–2	74, 138
49:6	36
49:14–25	235
49:14	75
51:4	36
53:10–12	197
54:7	75
54:8	75
56:2–4	26
57:16	141, 151
58:13	26
59:2	75
59:7	249
60:1	36
60:3	36
63	167
63:10	140, 157
63:11	140, 157
63:19	211
64:6[7]	75
65:2	160
65:3–5	186

Jeremiah

1:4–10	216
1:4	10
1:7	175
1:11	10
1:13	10, 59, 239
2:1	10
2:19	72
2:23	184
3:6	72
3:8	72
3:11	72
3:12	72
3:22	72
4:4	156
4:14	249
4:23	207
5:6	72
7:22	54
7:29	75
8:5	72
9:20[21]	174
11:4	54
11:5	55
11:20	163
12:3	163
12:7	75
14:7	72
14:9	75
14:18	243
15:17	211
16:4	180, 243
16:5	186
17:10	163
18:8	250
18:18	159
22:20	183
22:24–30	61
22:30	221

Jeremiah (cont.)

23:1–8	241
23:5–6	41
23:6	41
23:9–40	159
23:13–40	158
23:16	159
23:23	75, 159
23:33	75
23:39	75
25:13	221
25:34–38	241
27:1–3	8
28:1–4	8, 9
29	26
29:5–7	26
29:23	160
30:2	221
31:29	233
31:32	54
31:33	156
32:21	54
32:22	55
32:39	163
33:5	75
34:13	54
34:17–20	190
36	221
41:1–2	25
42:18	249
44:6	249
45:1	221
48:7	74
49:3	74
49:36	148
50:2–3	130
51:39	197
51:44	130
51:47	130
51:52–53	130
51:57	197
51:59	8
52:16	25

Lamentations

3:6	183
3:55	178
3:56	75
5:20	75

Ezekiel

1–24	5, 31, 142, 186
1:1—23:27	27
1–3	3, 6, 15
1:1—3:27	27
1:1—3:21	8
1:1—3:15	189
1	xi, 72, 200, 201, 208, 209, 214, 215, 218
1:1–28	xi, 12, 18, 30, 73, 208
1:1–13	27
1:1–12	209
1:1–3	25, 208
1:1–2	74, 215
1:1	x, 3, 8–10, 150, 161, 178
1:2–3	9, 10
1:2	26
1:3	3, 61, 148, 211
1:4–28	xvii, 95, 191, 199–226, 200, 208
1:4–5	201, 208
1:4	147, 152, 201, 202, 204, 206, 207, 209, 212
1:5–15	201
1:5–14	151, 206
1:5	201, 204, 206, 207, 209, 212
1:6–9	207
1:6–7	208
1:6	201, 206, 209, 223, 224, 225, 226
1:7	9, 201, 202, 212
1:8–10	223–26
1:8–9	205, 226
1:8	201, 204
1:9	201, 202
1:10–12	207

Index of Scripture

Ezekiel (*cont.*)

Reference	Pages
1:10	201, 208, 212, 214, 224
1:11	171, 201, 202, 204, 208
1:12–17	184
1:12	152, 201–4, 209
1:13–14	207
1:13	201, 202, 205, 206, 208, 209, 212, 214, 232
1:14–28	27
1:14	203, 205–7, 212
1:15–21	206, 207, 209, 223–26
1:15–18	201, 223
1:15–16	208
1:15	9, 206, 208, 209
1:16	201, 202, 204, 212
1:17	201, 202, 214
1:18	201, 202, 206, 213
1:19–26	201
1:19–21	152
1:19	33, 201, 202, 224
1:20–22	202
1:20–21	153, 225
1:20	201–4
1:21	33, 201, 202
1:22–27	207
1:22–26	31
1:22–25	207
1:22–23	208
1:22	184, 201–3, 206, 208, 209, 212, 213
1:23	171, 201, 202, 204, 205
1:24–25	201, 205
1:24	201, 204, 205
1:25–26	204
1:25	201, 203, 206
1:26–28	209
1:26	201, 203, 207, 208, 212
1:27–28	208
1:27	205, 212
1:28—3:15	18
1:28—3:9	208
1:28—2:2	33, 213
1:28	153, 202, 207, 212, 213
2:1	153
2:2	33, 153, 154, 158
2:3–4	99
2:3	34–36, 70, 175, 232
2:4–7	222
2:4	175
2:5–8	5
2:5	x, 10, 239
2:6	232, 239
2:8—3:3	69, 72
2:8	xi, 232, 239
2:9	207
2:10	9, 55, 170
2:20	9
3:1–20	171
3:5–11	5
3:6–11	222
3:6	175
3:7–8	99
3:7	5
3:8	5
3:9	5, 239
3:11	27
3:12–15	27, 208
3:12	33, 149
3:14–15	161
3:14	33, 148, 149
3:15	xi, 10, 26, 213
3:16–21	xi, 12, 18, 27, 155, 175
3:16	9
3:22–27	xi, 4, 8, 18, 27
3:22	148, 149, 211
3:23–24	33, 153
3:24	x, 33, 154, 158
3:26–27	5
3:32	185
4–24	91
4–23	232
4–11	6
4:1—11:25	28
4:1—5:17	18, 28
4:1–17	97
4:1–3	12
4:3	4, 154
4:4–6	xi, 70

Index of Scripture

Ezekiel (*cont.*)

4:6	242
4:9–17	12
4:12–15	4
4:14	x, 10
5:2	147
5:4	12
5:5–15	12
5:5–7	32
5:5	36
5:6–7	36
5:6	36
5:7–17	97
5:8	97
5:10	175
5:11	31, 49, 155, 250
5:12	171, 172
5:13	46, 48, 50, 64, 67, 70, 172, 250
5:14	64
5:15	48, 49, 64, 70, 175
5:16–17	12
5:16	172, 175
5:17	33, 70, 174
5:21	70
6	15
6:1–14	18, 28, 36
6:1–7	12
6:2	4
6:3	175
6:4	171, 175
6:5	171, 187, 246
6:7	171
6:8–10	19, 38, 58, 62
6:9	62, 64, 65
6:10	51
6:11–14	12
6:11	33, 174
6:12	48, 171, 172
6:14	51
7:1–27	12, 18, 28
7:1	9
7:3	49, 57, 70, 231
7:4	49, 51, 250
7:8	48, 57, 70, 172, 231
7:9	49, 51, 57, 250
7:13	153
7:15	33, 171, 174
7:20–24	12
7:23	242
7:26	172
7:27	51, 175
8–11	xi, 3, 12, 13, 30, 72, 93, 97
8:1—11:25	8, 28, 74, 93, 189, 215,
8:1—10:22	12, 18
8:1	x, 4, 8, 9, 26, 33, 74, 148, 149, 158, 211, 215
8:2	207, 212
8:3–16	94
8:3	33, 64, 94, 149, 150, 161, 178, 211
8:5–18	31, 91, 155
8:5–17	36
8:5	64, 94, 149
8:6	94, 149
8:7–18	xi
8:7	149, 207
8:9	94
8:10	94, 207
8:12	75, 91
8:13	94
8:14	149
8:15	94
8:16	149
8:17—9:10	91
8:17	94
8:18	32, 48, 49, 95, 232, 250
9	93
9:1	172
9:3	95
9:4	94
9:5–8	91
9:5	49, 250
9:6	171, 172
9:8	10, 48
9:9	75, 91, 94, 242

Index of Scripture

Ezekiel (*cont.*)

9:10	32, 49, 95, 232, 250
9:11	214
10	152, 202, 209, 214, 215
10:1–13	95
10:1	207, 214
10:2	214, 232
10:4	95
10:7	214
10:8–17	214
10:9–22	215, 223–26
10:9–12	223
10:9	207
10:11	214
10:13–16	224
10:13	214
10:14	214
10:15	95, 215
10:17–21	225
10:17	33, 152, 153
10:18	95, 214
10:19	95
10:20–22	214
10:20	95, 215
10:22	215, 226
11	60, 239, 241
11:1–21	12
11:1–13	18
11:1–12	236, 237
11:1	149
11:2–12	235, 241
11:2	249
11:3	233, 236
11:5–6	163
11:5	150, 158
11:6	183
11:7–11	95
11:7	236
11:9	175
11:10	51, 175, 231, 236
11:11	175, 231, 236
11:13	10, 15, 171, 172, 174, 175
11:14–21	13, 18, 19, 48, 58, 96
11:14–17	235
11:14–16	26
11:15	58, 59, 96, 236, 251
11:16–21	58, 91
11:16–20	38
11:16–17	38
11:16	96, 236
11:17–21	58
11:17	236
11:18–11	96
11:19–20	38
11:19	163
11:20	31, 50
11:22–25	12, 18
11:24	33, 61, 149, 150
11:25	15, 96
12–24	6
12:1—24:27	28
12:1–20	28
12:1–16	12
12:1	10
12:2–4	5
12:6	4
12:9	5
12:11	4, 165
12:13	61, 171
12:14	147
12:15	51
12:16	33, 51, 174
12:17–28	99
12:17–20	12, 19
12:20	51
12:21—14:11	28
12:21–28	18
12:21–25	18
12:22	172, 233, 236
12:23	236
12:25	5, 10, 250
12:26–28	10, 18
12:27	236
12:28	10, 236
13	33, 158
13:1–23	18
13:1–16	18, 159

Index of Scripture

Ezekiel (*cont.*)

13:1	165
13:2	165
13:3	159, 160, 161
13:4	165
13:6	175
13:9	50, 51, 165
13:10	50
13:11–13	147
13:13	48, 49, 70, 172
13:14	51, 172
13:15	48, 172
13:17–23	18
13:18	50
13:19	50, 171
13:21	50, 51
13:23	50, 51
14:1–23	12
14:1–11	5, 18, 37, 99
14:1	4
14:3	163
14:4	163
14:7	163
14:8	50, 51, 75, 172, 175
14:9–11	191
14:9	50, 172, 175
14:10	70
14:11	31, 50, 70
14:12—15:8	18, 28
14:12–23	12
14:13	172, 175
14:15–20	191
14:17	172, 175
14:19	48, 175
14:21	33, 174, 175
14:22	46
15:1–8	12
15:3	57
15:7	51
16	2, 13–15, 24, 32, 34, 52, 54, 56
16:1–63	12, 18, 28
16:1–60	12
16:1–14	20, 21, 23, 32
16:1–3	22
16:1–2	52
16:3–34	22
16:3–5	22
16:3	15, 52
16:4–14	53
16:4–6	53
16:4	172
16:5	53, 250
16:6–14	22
16:6	33
16:7–8	53
16:8	53
16:9–14	53
16:15–43	32
16:15–34	22, 23
16:15–22	22, 36
16:20–21	245
16:21	172, 174
16:23–34	22
16:23–29	36
16:26–27	155
16:27–43	56
16:27	64, 232, 247, 250
16:29	60
16:33	49
16:35–43	22, 23
16:35–36	22
16:36	49
16:37–42	22
16:37	49
16:38	48, 64, 174, 231
16:41	175
16:42	48, 64, 250
16:43	22, 232
16:44–63	23
16:44–59	182
16:44–53	32
16:44–52	22, 36
16:44	22
16:45–46	22
16:47–52	22
16:47	172
16:52–63	42

Index of Scripture

Ezekiel (*cont.*)

Reference	Pages
16:52	64
16:53–63	22
16:53–58	22
16:54	64
16:57	64
16:58	232
16:59–63	22, 48
16:59–62	70
16:60–63	19, 23, 38
16:60	32
16:61–63	45, 46
16:61	64
16:62	38, 52
16:63	64
17:1—22:31	28
17	31, 60, 62
17:1–24	12, 18, 28
17:1–9	234
17:2	232, 233
17:3–4	13, 60, 61
17:4	62
17:5–6	61
17:7–21	61
17:7–8	62
17:10	146
17:12	60
17:13	31, 181
17:14	31
17:15	31
17:16	31, 171
17:17	172, 174
17:18	31
17:19	31
17:21	51, 147
17:22–24	13, 61, 62
17:22–23	61, 62, 97
17:22	40, 60, 62
17:24	10, 32, 51, 70, 250
18	15, 26
18:1–32	12, 14, 18, 28, 37, 155, 171, 175
18:1–2	36
18:2	34, 233, 236
18:3–20	235
18:8	70
18:9	70
18:10	174
18:22	70
18:23	175
18:28	70
18:30–32	33
18:30	57, 70, 175
18:31	70
18:32	172, 175
19:4	172, 178
19:5	172
19:8	172, 178
19:1–14	12, 18, 28
19:10–13	61
19:12	48, 146
19:13	62
20	2, 14, 38, 52, 54, 55, 69
20:1–44	12, 18, 28, 99
20:1–4	54
20:1–3	4
20:1	9, 10, 26
20:2–4	52
20:4	239
20:5–9	35, 54
20:6	55
20:7	31, 54
20:8	48, 70, 172
20:9	31, 69
20:10–17	35, 54
20:10–11	55
20:12	54
20:13	31, 48, 172, 175
20:14	31, 69
20:15	54, 55
20:16	160
20:17	49, 172, 175, 250
20:18–26	35, 54
20:19	54, 55
20:20	54
20:21	31, 48, 70, 172
20:22	31, 69
20:23	54

Index of Scripture

Ezekiel (*cont.*)

Reference	Pages
20:24	31
20:25	55, 15, 182
20:26	54, 245
20:27–29	35, 54
20:27	34
20:28	54
20:30–31	36, 38, 54
20:31	31, 245
20:32–38	38, 54
20:32	163, 236
20:33–34	48
20:33	48
20:34–44	235
20:34	48
20:38	70
20:39–44	54
20:39	31
20:41	38, 241
20:42–43	45
20:42	52, 54
20:43	31, 64, 65
20:44	31, 52, 66, 172
21:1–37[20:45—21:32]	28
21:1–22[20:45—21:17]	18
21:1–4[20:45–48]	4
21:5–37[1–32]	13, 30
21:5[20:49]	10, 15
21:6–22[1–17]	12
21:8–10[3–5]	175
21:8[3]	172, 175
21:9[4]	172, 175
21:12[7]	164
21:14[9]	239
21:15[10]	172
21:16[11]	171
21:17[12]	50
21:20[15]	172
21:22[17]	48, 250
21:23–32[18–27]	12, 18
21:27[22]	171, 174
21:29[24]	70
21:30–32[25–27]	12
21:30[25]	171
21:33[28]	64, 172
21:34[29]	171
21:35[30]	175
21:36[31]	48, 172
22:1–31	28
22:1–16	18
22:1–12	242
22:1–3	12
22:2	232, 239
22:3	174, 232
22:4	64, 174
22:6	174
22:9	174, 232
22:11	232
22:12	174
22:14	10, 32, 70, 250
22:15	232, 249
22:17–22	18
22:20	48, 49, 70
22:21	232
22:22	50
22:23–31	18
22:24	48, 232
22:27	172, 174, 232
22:30	172
22:31	48, 172, 175
23	2, 14, 15, 52, 56, 242
23:1–49	12, 18, 28
23:4	56
23:5–21	36
23:5	49
23:9–10	56
23:9	49
23:10	171, 174
23:11	172
23:13	232
23:14	61
23:15	61
23:16	61
23:21	232
23:22–35	56
23:22	49
23:24	231
23:25	48, 64, 161

Index of Scripture

Ezekiel (cont.)

23:27	232
23:29	232
23:34	70
23:35	232
23:36	52
23:38–39	31
23:39	172, 174
23:44	232
23:45	174, 231
23:47	171
23:48	232
23:49	51, 70, 232
24	xi
24:1–27	229
24:1–15	12
24:1–14	xvii, 18, 28, 227–52, 229, 236
24:1–3	235
24:1–2	237, 238
24:1	9, 10, 229, 230
24:2	238, 251
24:3–14	229, 232
24:3–11	246
24:3–6	59
24:3–5	229, 230, 234, 235, 239
24:3–4	238
24:3	5, 231–34, 236, 237, 245
24:4–5	236, 246
24:4	239, 240, 246, 248
24:5	248
24:6–13	235
24:6–8	230, 235, 237, 242
24:6	230–32, 234, 235, 241–44
24:7–8	231, 232, 244
24:7	242
24:8	48, 232, 242, 245
24:9–14	237
24:9–13	232, 235
24:9–12	248
24:9–10	229, 232, 248
24:9	231, 232, 235, 245
24:10–14	231
24:10–12	246
24:10	230, 239, 248, 249
24:11–14	230
24:11–13	232
24:11–12	248
24:11	232, 240, 241, 243, 246, 249
24:12–14	247
24:12	249
24:13–14	248, 249
24:13	48, 232, 250
24:14	32, 49, 57, 70, 229, 230, 232, 235, 236, 250
24:15–27	xi, 18, 28, 229
24:15	229
24:16–27	12
24:16–24	174
24:16	xvi, 53
24:17	171, 187
24:18–19	15
24:18	x, 171, 236
24:20	10
24:21	53
24:22	187
24:24	4, 51
24:27	4, 51, 229
25–48	5
25:1—48:35	28
25–32	6, 13, 15, 30, 142
25:1—32:32	28
25–28	12
25:1—28:23	7, 28
25:1–17	18, 28
25:1–7	6, 19
25:1–5	6
25:1–2	7
25:1	6, 172
25:2	4
25:5	69
25:6–7	6, 7
25:7	51, 69, 172, 172, 175
25:8–11	6, 7
25:8–9	19

Index of Scripture

Ezekiel (*cont.*)

25:9–12	248
25:11	51, 69, 175
25:12–24	7
25:12–14	6, 19
25:13	172, 175
25:14	48–51, 70
25:15–17	6, 7, 19
25:15	172, 174
25:16	172, 175
25:17	48, 51, 69
26:1—28:19	6, 7, 28
26:1–21	18
26:1	6, 9
26:4	172
26:5	70
26:6	51, 69, 171
26:8	171
26:11	171
26:14	51, 70
26:15	171
26:16	171
26:17	172
26:18	171
26:19–21	176
26:20	171, 175, 178, 179, 183
26:21	185
26:33–39	57
27	60
27:1–36	18
27:3	60
27:11	171
27:13	60
27:15	60
27:17	60
27:20	60
27:22	60
27:23	60
27:24	60
27:26	142
27:27	171
27:29	171
27:36	185
28	10
28:1–10	18, 19, 191
28:8–10	171
28:8	171, 172, 178, 180
28:9	171
28:10	70, 180
28:11–19	18
28:16	175
28:17	172
28:19	185
28:20–32	6
28:20–26	28
28:20–23	7, 18, 19
28:21	4
28:22	31, 51, 69, 175
28:23	6, 33, 51, 69, 171, 174, 175
28:24–26	6, 7, 13, 19, 30
28:25	31, 34, 50
28:26	51, 52, 175
29:1—32:32	6, 7, 10, 28
29:1–21	18
29:1–16	7, 18
29:1	6, 9, 10
29:2	4
29:3–5	191
29:5	51, 74
29:6	69
29:8	172, 175
29:9	51, 69
29:16	51, 69
29:17–21	7, 18
29:17	3, 6, 9, 10
29:20–26	19
29:21	40, 52
30:1–19	7, 18
30:4	171
30:6	171
30:7	172
30:8	51, 69
30:11	172
30:12	70
30:13	175, 181
30:14	175
30:15	48, 50, 172, 175

Index of Scripture

Ezekiel (*cont.*)

30:19	51, 69, 175
30:20–26	7, 18
30:20	6, 9, 10
30:24	171, 175
30:25	51, 69, 175
30:26	51, 69
31:1–18	7, 18
31:1	6, 9, 10
31:9	63, 64
31:10–20	18
31:11	181
31:12	171, 172
31:14–18	176
31:14	171, 176, 178, 181
31:15	171, 176, 178, 179
31:16	171, 175, 176, 178–80
31:17	171, 176, 178
31:18	171, 176, 178, 180
31:23–33	18
31:25	34
32–34	172
32	180
32:1–16	7, 18
32:1	6, 9, 10
32:2–8	91
32:4	74
32:10	171, 175
32:12	172, 175
32:13	175
32:15	51
32:17–32	7, 18, 176, 177, 180, 181, 184, 185, 188, 191
32:17–18	177
32:17	6, 9, 10, 181
32:18	171, 176, 178
32:19–21	177
32:19	171, 176, 178
32:20	171, 176, 192
32:21	171, 176, 178, 179, 181, 182, 185
32:22–32	179
32:22–30	177
32:22–26	179, 189
32:22–24	171
32:22	171
32:23	171, 178, 179, 181
32:24	171, 176, 178, 185
32:25	171, 176, 178, 185
32:26	171, 176, 178
32:27	171, 176, 178, 179, 182, 185, 246
32:28	171, 176, 185
32:29	171, 176, 178, 185
32:30	64, 171, 176, 178, 185
32:31	171, 176, 177, 185
32:32	171, 176, 177, 178
33–48	142
33–39	6
33:1–20	12, 28, 155, 171, 175
33:1–9	18
33:2	242
33:10–20	18
33:10	70, 236
33:11	175
33:12	70
33:20	57, 175
33:21–22	5, 18, 28, 97
33:21	9, 10, 26
33:22	148, 149, 211
33:23–29	12, 18, 29, 235
33:24	34, 233
33:25	174, 236
33:29	51
33:30–33	x, 4, 15, 18, 29
33:31	50, 160
33:33	x, 10
34–48	38, 39
34:1—48:35	29
34–39	158
34:1—39:29	29
34	15, 40, 41, 42, 62, 71, 241
34:1–31	12, 18, 19, 29
34:1–10	18
34:2	159
34:4	172
34:6	50, 71

310

Ezekiel (cont.)

34:8	50, 71
34:10	50, 71
34:11–13	38
34:11–12	71
34:11	50, 71
34:12	50, 71
34:13	71
34:15	50, 71
34:16	38, 71, 172, 175
34:17–19	71
34:17	50, 71
34:19	50, 71
34:20–22	71
34:22–23	40
34:22	50, 71
34:23–24	12, 14, 39, 42, 62, 91, 97
34:23	50
34:24	31, 50, 70, 71
34:25–32	91
34:25–31	32, 97
34:25–30	15
34:25–29	12, 39
34:25	71, 172
34:26–27	71
34:27	52
34:28	71
34:29–30	52
34:29	71
34:30–31	31, 38, 71
34:30	50, 71
34:31	50, 71
35:1—36:26	12
35:1—36:15	19, 29, 96
35:1–15	18
35:2	4
35:4	51, 69
35:7	175
35:8	171
35:9	51, 69
35:10	96
35:11	49, 50, 64, 70, 175
35:12	69
35:15	51, 69
36–48	172
36	15, 46
36:1–15	19, 97
36:5	64, 70, 96
36:6	48, 64
36:7	54
36:9	97
36:11	52
36:12	50
36:15	64
36:16–38	18, 19, 29, 40, 97
36:16–32	12, 31, 33, 96
36:16–21	69
36:16–18	31
36:17–19	66
36:18	48, 174
36:19–23	97
36:19	231
36:20–32	31
36:21	49, 66
36:22–32	14, 15, 66, 157
36:22	66
36:23	66, 69
36:24	38, 72
36:25–29	157, 158
36:25–28	38
36:26–32	47
36:26–27	33, 155, 164, 189
36:27–28	156
36:28–38	97
36:28	31, 50
36:29–30	39
36:29	72
36:30	64
36:31–32	45
36:31	64, 65
36:32	64
36:33–36	12
36:36	10, 32, 52, 69, 70, 250
36:37–38	12
36:37–32	97
36:38	52

Index of Scripture

Ezekiel (*cont.*)

37	15, 23, 184, 188, 193, 194, 196, 197
37:1–14	12, 13, 15, 18, 19, 29, 33, 40, 153, 155, 170, 188, 189, 239
37:1–10	189
37:1	33, 148, 149, 150, 211, 246
37:2	38
37:3–5	246
37:3	10, 189
37:4	159
37:6	52
37:7	15, 246
37:9	147, 171, 195, 239
37:10	15, 196
37:11–14	189, 195
37:11	172, 233, 236, 246
37:12–13	189
37:12	50, 236
37:13	50, 52
37:14	10, 32, 52, 70, 155, 250
37:15–28	18, 29, 40, 42
37:15–21	12
37:16–23	15
37:16–20	222
37:21–28	62
37:21–25	42, 91
37:22–25	12, 39, 40
37:22–24	97
37:23–24	38
37:23	31, 50, 70
37:24–28	14
37:24	50
37:25–28	12, 97
37:25	34, 50
37:26–28	39, 155
37:26–27	12, 42
37:26	32, 39, 172
37:27	50
37:28	52, 69
38–39	13, 30, 40
38:1—39:29	19, 29, 39
38:1—39:20	12
38:1–23	6
38:1	29, 163
38:2–4	6
38:2	4
38:5	163
38:10	163
38:12	36
38:14	50
38:16	31, 50, 69
38:17	50
38:18–19	50
38:18	48, 49, 70
38:19	64
38:23	13, 29, 30, 31, 33, 69
39:1–29	6, 29
39:1–2	6
39:5	70
39:6	174, 33, 51, 69, 175
39:7	31, 50, 69
39:8	70
39:11	183
39:14	183
39:18	181
39:21–29	12, 29
39:21–23	33
39:21–22	51
39:21	13, 30
39:23	69, 75
39:24	70, 75
39:25–29	91
39:25	34, 49, 62, 64, 66, 70
39:27	31
39:28	51, 52
39:29	33, 75, 165
40–48	6, 12, 30, 40, 41, 155
40:1—48:35	18, 19, 29, 39
40–46	3, 13
40–43	xi, 12, 30, 31
40:1—46:24	12
40:1—43:11	29
40:1—43:5	97
40:1–4	29

Ezekiel (cont.)

40:1	9, 10, 26, 33, 74, 148, 149, 211
40:2	161, 211
40:5—42:20	290
40:39	172
40:42	172
41–43	72
41	200
42:9	204
42:16–20	148
43:1–14	18
43:1–9	29
43:1–5	91
43:3	161, 172
43:5	33, 149
43:7–9	98, 186, 187
43:7	66, 171
43:8	49, 66, 70, 172, 175
43:9	171
43:10—46:24	98
43:10–13	222
43:10–11	29
43:10	64
43:11	64
43:12—46:24	29
43:25–27	241
44–46	26
44:1–14	xi
44:3	41
44:4	207
44:10	70
44:11	172
44:12	54, 70
44:23	50
44:25	171
45:7–8	41
45:8	50
45:9	50
45:21—46:12	41
46:18	42, 50
47:1—48:35	91
47:1—48:29	29
47:1—48:7	12
47:1–12	98
47:1	171
47:8	171
47:13—48:29	98
47:14	54
47:21–23	13, 30
47:23–29	12
48:8–22	12
48:21	41
48:30–35	12, 29
48:35	13, 30, 41

Daniel

1:1	8
7:2	148
8:8	148
8:27	218
9:4–19	69
9:15	54
10:5	207
10:7–9	218
10:16	161
10:17	141
11:4	148
12:2	185, 193

Hosea

3	10
3:5	41
6:1–3	196
7:5	159, 161
11:7	72
12:8	60
13:4	197
13:14	174, 190
14:5	72

Joel

2:13	70, 250
2:17	74
2:18—3:2[2:29]	165
4:13[3:13]	240

Index of Scripture

Amos

1:15	74
3:12	71
6:7	186
7:1–9	46
7:1–8	10
8:1–12	10
9:1–4	10
9:11	41

Jonah

2:7[6]	178
3:10	250
4:2	70, 250

Micah

3:2–3	241
3:4	75
5:1–4[2–5]	41
5:5	41
7:10	74
7:18–20	70

Nahum

1:1	221
1:2	64
3:16	60

Habakkuk

2:2	221
2:5	174
3	218
3:16	219

Zephaniah

1:11	60

Haggai

1:2–11	235
1:12	175

Zechariah

1:8	207
2:1[1:18]	207
2:5[1]	207
2:10[6]	148
2:12–13[8–9]	175
2:15[11]	175
4:8	10
4:9	175
5:9	204, 207
6:5	148
6:9	10
6:15	175
9:9–10	41
12:10	165
14:21	60

~

New Testament

Matthew

3:16	211
6:19–20	243
9:24	185
24:31	148

Luke

3:21	211
16:19–31	191
16:23	192
23:23	192

John

1:16–17	xvi
1:51	211
3:1–8	33
3:5–8	157
4:23–24	37
11:11	185

Index of Scripture

Acts

2:4	166
2:5	165
2:22	165
2:27	192
2:33	166
2:36	165
2:38	166
7:56	211
8:14–17	166
9:1–9	217
10	165
10:11	211
10:44–48	166
11:16	166
19:6	166
22	217
22:4–8	217
23:6–9	197
26	217
26:12–18	217

Romans

3:23	23

1 Corinthians

11:30	185
15:51	185

2 Corinthians

1:22	166
5:8	192

Ephesians

1:13	166
1:14	24
2:1–3	23
4:30	166

Philippians

1:23	192

1 Thessalonians

4:14	185
4:17	193
5:10	185

Hebrews

1:1–2	xvi
12:22	192

James

5:2–3	243

1 Peter

2:9–10	24
3:19	192

2 Peter

1:21	33, 158

Revelation

	217, 220, 221
1:9	221
1:17	217
4:1–11	211
7:1	148
14:8	138
16:19	138
17:5	138
18:2	138
18:10	138
18:21	138
19:11	211

www.ingramcontent.com/pod-product-compliance
Lightning Source LLC
Chambersburg PA
CBHW030433300426
44112CB00009B/984